DBKDA 2017

The Ninth International Conference on Advances in Databases, Knowledge, and Data Applications

GraphSM 2017

The Fourth International Workshop on Large-scale Graph Storage and Management

May 21 - 25, 2017

Barcelona, Spain

DBKDA 2017 Editors

Andreas Schmidt, Karlsruhe Institute of Technology / University of Applied Sciences

Fritz Laux, Reutlingen University, Germany

Dimitar Hristovski, Faculty of Medicine, Ljubljana, Slovenia

Shin-ichi Ohnishi, Hokkai-Gakuen University, Japan

Printed from e-media with permission by:

Curran Associates, Inc.
57 Morehouse Lane
Red Hook, NY 12571

Some format issues inherent in the e-media version may also appear in this print version.

Printed by Curran Associates, Inc. (2017)

International Academy, Research, and Industry Association (IARIA)
412 Derby Way
Wilmington, DE 19810

Phone: (408) 893-6407
Fax: (408) 527-6351

petre@iaria.org

Additional copies of this publication are available from:

Curran Associates, Inc.
57 Morehouse Lane
Red Hook, NY 12571 USA
Phone: 845-758-0400
Fax: 845-758-2633
Email: curran@proceedings.com
Web: www.proceedings.com

TABLE OF CONTENTS

DBKDA 1: DATA AND PROCESS PROVENANCE

A Privacy Focused Formal Model of Authorization for Data Modeled using Semantic Web Technologies 1
J. Reuben

A Novel Approach to User Involved Big Data Provenance Visualization 10
I. Yazici, M. Aktas, M. Gokturk

A Large Scale Synthetic Social Provenance Database 16
M. Baeth, M. Aktas

On a Weight for Partial Inner Dependence AHP Using Sensitivity Analyses 23
S. Ohnishi, T. Yamanoi

DBKDA 2: DATA QUERY, ACCESS, MINING, AND CORRELATION

Customer Churn Prediction in Telecommunication with Rotation Forest Method 26
M. Yildiz, S. Albayrak

Data Validation for Big Live Data 30
M. Crowe, C. Begg, F. Laux, M. Laiho

A Pseudometric for Gaussian Mixture Models 37
L. Zhou, W. Ye, B. Wackersreuther, C. Plant, C. Bohm

A Data Mining Framework for Product Bundle Design and Pricing 43
Y. Li, H. Wang, Q. Gao

DBKDA 3: DATABASES CONTENT PROCESSING

Preference Miner: A Database Tool for Mining User Preferences 52
M. Endres

A Column-Oriented Text Database API Implemented on Top of Wavelet Tries 54
S. Bottcher, R. Hartel, J. Manuel

CitySense: Retrieving, Visualizing and Combining Datasets on Urban Areas 61
D. Karidi, H. Nakos, A. Efentakis, Y. Stavrakas

Statistical Implicative Analysis Approximation to KDD and Data Mining: A Systematic and Mapping Review in Knowledge Discovery Database Framework 70
R. Pazmino-Maji, F. Garcia-Penalvo, M. Conde-Gonzalez

DBKDA 4: KNOWLEDGE AND DECISION BASES

A Knowledge Graph for Travel Mode Recommendation and Critiquing 78
B. Karakostas, D. Kardaras

BayesNet and Artificial Neural Network for Nowcasting Rare Fog Events: Two Different Models for 1-Hour Fog Prediction at Linate Airport 84
G. Zazzaro, G. Romano, P. Mercogliano

OntoEDIFACT: An Ontology for the UN/EDIFACT Standard 91
B. Ouchenne, M. Itmi

A Causality-Based Feature Selection Approach For Multivariate Time Series Forecasting 97
Y. Hmamouche, A. Casali, L. Lakhal

DBKDA 5 / GRAPHSM: GRAPH ANALYSIS, MANAGEMENT AND APPLICATIONS

The Absolute Consistency Problem of Graph Schema Mappings with Uniqueness Constraints 103
T. Hayata, Y. Ishihara, T. Fujiwara

A Network-based Approach to Evolution of MEDLINE 111
A. Kastrin, T. Rindflesch, D. Hristovski

Author Index

DBKDA 2017

Foreword

The Ninth International Conference on Advances in Databases, Knowledge, and Data Applications (DBKDA 2017), held between May 21 - 25, 2017 - Barcelona, Spain, continued a series of international events covering a large spectrum of topics related to advances in fundamentals on databases, evolution of relation between databases and other domains, data base technologies and content processing, as well as specifics in applications domains databases.

Advances in different technologies and domains related to databases triggered substantial improvements for content processing, information indexing, and data, process and knowledge mining. The push came from Web services, artificial intelligence, and agent technologies, as well as from the generalization of the XML adoption.

High-speed communications and computations, large storage capacities, and load-balancing for distributed databases access allow new approaches for content processing with incomplete patterns, advanced ranking algorithms and advanced indexing methods.

Evolution on e-business, ehealth and telemedicine, bioinformatics, finance and marketing, geographical positioning systems put pressure on database communities to push the 'de facto' methods to support new requirements in terms of scalability, privacy, performance, indexing, and heterogeneity of both content and technology.

DBKDA 2017 also featured the following Workshop:

- GraphSM 2017: The Third International Workshop on Large-scale Graph Storage and Management

We take here the opportunity to warmly thank all the members of the DBKDA 2017 Technical Program Committee, as well as the numerous reviewers. The creation of such a high quality conference program would not have been possible without their involvement. We also kindly thank all the authors who dedicated much of their time and efforts to contribute to DBKDA 2017. We truly believe that, thanks to all these efforts, the final conference program consisted of top quality contributions.

Also, this event could not have been a reality without the support of many individuals, organizations, and sponsors. We are grateful to the members of the DBKDA 2017 organizing committee for their help in handling the logistics and for their work to make this professional meeting a success.

We hope that DBKDA 2017 was a successful international forum for the exchange of ideas and results between academia and industry and for the promotion of progress in the fields of databases, knowledge and data applications.

We are convinced that the participants found the event useful and communications very open. We also hope that Barcelona provided a pleasant environment during the conference and everyone saved some time for exploring this beautiful city.

DBKDA 2017 Chairs:

Fritz Laux, Reutlingen University, Germany
Andreas Schmidt, Karlsruhe Institute of Technology / University of Applied Sciences Florin Rusu, University of California Merced, USA

Sergio Ilarri, University of Zaragoza, Spain
Jerzy Grzymala-Busse, University of Kansas, USA
Filip Zavoral, Charles University Prague, Czech Republic
Konstantinos Kalpakis, University of Maryland Baltimore County, USA

DBKDA Industry/Research Advisory Committee
Peter Kieseberg, SBA Research, Austria
Mike Gowanlock, Massachusetts Institute of Technology | Haystack Observatory, USA
Shin-ichi Ohnishi, Hokkai-Gakuen University, Japan
Thomas Triplet, Ciena inc. / Polytechnique Montreal, Canada
Stephanie Teufel, iimt - international institute of management in technology | University of Fribourg, Switzerland
Rajasekar Karthik, Oak Ridge National Laboratory, USA
Erik Hoel, Esri, USA
Daniel Kimmig, solute GmbH, Germany

GraphSM Chairs
Dimitar Hristovski, Faculty of Medicine, Ljubljana, Slovenia
Andreas Schmidt, Karlsruhe Institute of Technology / University of Applied Sciences Karlsruhe, Germany

DBKDA 2017

Committee

DBKDA Steering Committee

Fritz Laux, Reutlingen University, Germany
Andreas Schmidt, Karlsruhe Institute of Technology / University of Applied Sciences Florin Rusu, University of California Merced, USA
Sergio Ilarri, University of Zaragoza, Spain
Jerzy Grzymala-Busse, University of Kansas, USA
Filip Zavoral, Charles University Prague, Czech Republic
Konstantinos Kalpakis, University of Maryland Baltimore County, USA

DBKDA Industry/Research Advisory Committee

Peter Kieseberg, SBA Research, Austria
Mike Gowanlock, Massachusetts Institute of Technology | Haystack Observatory, USA
Shin-ichi Ohnishi, Hokkai-Gakuen University, Japan
Thomas Triplet, Ciena inc. / Polytechnique Montreal, Canada
Stephanie Teufel, iimt - international institute of management in technology | University of Fribourg, Switzerland
Rajasekar Karthik, Oak Ridge National Laboratory, USA
Erik Hoel, Esri, USA
Daniel Kimmig, solute GmbH, Germany

DBKDA 2017 Technical Program Commiittee

Taher Omran Ahmed, Aljabal Algharby University, Azzentan, Libya / College of Applied Sciences, Ibri, Sultanate of Oman
Markus Aleksy, ABB AG, Germany
Jose L. Arciniegas H., Universidad del Cauca, Columbia
Zeyar Aung, Masdar Institute of Science and Technology, UAE
Gilbert Babin, HEC Montréal, Canada
Zouhaier Brahmia, University of Sfax, Tunisia
Martine Cadot, LORIA-Nancy, France
Ricardo Campos, Polytechnic Institute of Tomar, Portugal
Paola Carrara, CNR IREA, Italy
Chin-Chen Chang, Feng Chia University, Taiwan
Yung Chang Chi, National Cheng Kung University, Taiwan
Byron Choi, Hong Kong Baptist University, Hong Kong
Gabriel David, INESC TEC | University of Porto, Portugal
Maria del Pilar Angeles, UNAM, Mexico
Vincenzo Deufemia, University of Salerno, Italy
Juliette Dibie, AgroParisTech, France
Cedric du Mouza, CNAM, Paris
Gledson Elias, Federal University of Paraíba (UFPB), Brazil

Markus Endres, University of Augsburg, Germany
Manuel Filipe Santos, Universidade do Minho | Research Centre Algoritmi, Portugal
Ingrid Fischer, Universität Konstanz, Germany
Barbara Gallina, Mälardalen University, Sweden
Faïez Gargouri, University of Sfax, Tunisia
Pedro Gil Madrona, UCLM, Spain
Mike Gowanlock, Massachusetts Institute of Technology | Haystack Observatory, USA
Bernard Grabot, Ecole Nationale d'Ingénieurs de Tarbes, France
William Grosky, University of Michigan-Dearborn, USA
Jerzy Grzymala-Busse, University of Kansas, USA
Dirk Habich, Technische Universität Dresden, Germany
Erik Hoel, Esri, USA
Martin Hoppen, Institute for Man-Machine Interaction - RWTH Aachen University, Germany
Wen-Chi Hou, Southern Illinois University, USA
Hamidah Ibrahim, Universiti Putra Malaysia, Malaysia
Sergio Ilarri, University of Zaragoza, Spain
Abdessamad Imine, INRIA-LORIA Nancy Grand-Est, France
Vladimir Ivančević, University of Novi Sad, Serbia
Wassim Jaziri, Taibah University, KSA
Imed Kacem, Université de Lorraine, France
Konstantinos Kalpakis, University of Maryland Baltimore County, USA
Verena Kantere, University of Geneva, Switzerland
Benjamin Karsin, University of Hawaii, USA
Rajasekar Karthik, Oak Ridge National Laboratory, USA
Peter Kieseberg, SBA Research, Austria
Daniel Kimmig, solute GmbH, Germany
Petr Křemen, Czech Technical University in Prague, Czech Republic
Anne Laurent, University of Montpellier, France
Fritz Laux, Reutlingen University, Germany
Lenka Lhotska, Czech Institute of Informatics, Robotics and Cybernetics | Czech Technical University in Prague, Czech Republic
Jerry Chun-Wei Lin, Harbin Institute of Technology, China
Chunmei Liu, Howard University, USA
Yanjun Liu, Feng Chia University, Taiwan
Stephane Maag, Telecom SudParis, France
Tanu Malik, DePaul University, USA
Gerasimos Marketos, Hellenic Open University, Greece
Elio Masciari, ICAR-CNR, Italy
Michele Melchiori, Università degli Studi di Brescia, Italy
Fabio Mercorio, University of Milan - Bicocca, Italy
Antonio Messina, ICAR-CNR, Italy
Mario Mezzanzanica, University of Milan Bicocca, Italy
Cristian Mihaescu, University of Craiova, Romania
Mohamed Mkaouar, ISAAS, Tunisia
Francesc D. Muñoz-Escoí, Universitat Politècnica de València (UPV), Spain
Lammari Ilham Nadira, Conservatoire National des Arts et Métiers, France
Khaled M. Nagi, Alexandria University, Egypt
Shin-ichi Ohnishi, Hokkai-Gakuen University, Japan

Rasha Osman, University of Khartoum, Sudan
Benoît Otjacques, LIST - Luxembourg Institute of Science and Technology, Luxembourg
Francesco Parisi, University of Calabria, Italy
Bernhard Peischl, Institute for Software Technology | Graz University of Technology, Austria
Hai Phan, New Jersey Institute of Technology, USA
Gianvito Pio, University of Bari Aldo Moro, Italy
Elaheh Pourabbas, National Research Council | Institute of Systems Analysis and Computer Science "Antonio Ruberti", Italy
Praveen R. Rao, University of Missouri-Kansas City, USA
Manjeet Rege, University of St. Thomas, USA
Jan Richling, South Westphalia University of Applied Sciences, Germany
Miguel Romero, Simons Institute | UC Berkeley, USA
Florin Rusu, University of California Merced, USA
M. Saravanan, Ericsson Research, India
Idrissa Sarr, Université Cheikh Anta Diop, Dakar, Sénégal
Andreas Schmidt, Karlsruhe Institute of Technology / University of Applied Sciences Karlsruhe, Germany
Sebastian Schrittwieser, TARGET Research Center, Austria
Erich Schweighofer, University of Vienna, Austria
Nematollaah Shiri, Concordia University, Canada
Patrick Siarry, Université Paris-Est Créteil, France
Sergio Tessaris, Free University of Bozen-Bolzano, Italy
Olivier Teste, University of Toulouse 2 Jean Jaurès - IRIT
Stephanie Teufel, iimt - international institute of management in technology | University of Fribourg, Switzerland
Nicolas Travers, CNAM-Paris, France
Thomas Triplet, Ciena inc. / Polytechnique Montreal, Canada
Robert Ulbricht, Robotron Datenbank-Software GmbH, Dresden, Germany
Lucia Vaira, University of Salento, Italy
Maurice van Keulen, University of Twente, Netherlands
Genoveva Vargas-Solar, French Council of Scientific Research, LIG-LAFMIA, France
Ismini Vasileiou, Plymouth University, UK
Damires Yluska de Souza Fernandes, Federal Institute of Education, Science and Technology of Paraíba, Brazil
Feng George Yu, Youngstown State University, USA
Filip Zavoral, Charles University Prague, Czech Republic
Qiang Zhu, University of Michigan, USA

GraphSM Chairs

Dimitar Hristovski, Faculty of Medicine, Ljubljana, Slovenia
Andreas Schmidt, Karlsruhe Institute of Technology / University of Applied Sciences Karlsruhe, Germany

Technical Program Committee

Zeina Abu-Aisheh, University François Rabelais de Tours, France
Patrick Appiah-Kubi, University of Maryland University College, USA
Dimitar Hristovski, Faculty of Medicine, Ljubljana, Slovenia
Erik Hoel, Esri, USA

Martin Hoppen, Institute for Man-Machine Interaction | RWTH Aachen University, Germany
Verena Kantere, University of Geneva, Switzerland
Christian Krause, SAP SE, Potsdam, Germany
Jean-Yves Ramel, University François Rabelais de Tours, France
Andreas Schmidt, Karlsruhe Institute of Technology / University of Applied Sciences Karlsruhe, Germany
Herna L. Viktor, University of Ottawa, Canada
Gottfried Vossen, University of Münster, Germany
Jim Webber, Neo Technology, USA
KwangSoo Yang, Florida Atlantic University, USA
Albert Zündorf, Kassel University, Germany

Copyright Information

A Privacy Focused Formal Model of Authorization for Data Modeled using Semantic Web Technologies

Jenni Reuben
and Simone Fischer-Hübner

Karlstad University
651 88 Karlstad, Sweden
Email: [firstname.lastname]@kau.se

***Abstract*—Origin of digital artifacts is asserted by digital provenance information. Provenance information is queried for proof statement validations, failure analysis, as well as replication and attribution validations. The history of a data instance that specifies dependency among different data items that produce the data instance is better captured using semantic web technologies. However, such provenance information contains sensitive information such as personally identifiable information. Further, in the context of Semantic Web knowledge representation, the interrelationships among different provenance elements imply additional knowledge. In this paper, we propose an authorization model that enforces the purpose limitation principle (an essential data protection principle) for such semantically related information. We present the formalization of the security policy, however the policy does not directly conforms to the desired authorization outcome. Therefore, security properties for important relationships such as subset, set union and set intersection are defined in order to ensure the consistency of the security policy. Finally, a use case scenario demonstrating the defined security policy and the properties is presented to indicate the applicability of the proposed model.**

***Index Terms*—Semantic Web; Access control; Security; Privacy; Purpose binding; OWL; RDF.**

I. Introduction

Provenance is a well known concept in the art world, it refers to the documented history of an art object, which is used to evaluate the significance of the art object in relation to other similar objects [1]. Similarly, digital provenance describes how a digital object has been brought to its current state. Such provenance information accounts for proof statement validations, failure analysis, as well as replication and attribution validations. In support of various provenance related queries, access to the provenance traces is desirable. We consider that this functionality of an application is facilitated by a repository (or several repositories in the case of distributed environment) that stores provenance traces. Subsequently, regulated access to these stores has become a crucial requirement to prevent provenance data misuse.

Nevertheless, controls to enforce legitimate access to provenance information should account for two important factors of digital provenance. First, emerging applications of provenance such as semantic web, e-science and cyberinfrastructure [2] demands provenance information to be available on the web, interpretable by machines, effectively discovered and interoperable. This is evident from an array of PROV specifications - a recent standardization efforts from W3C Provenance Working Group, which are based on semantic web principles. Second, provenance information often contains sensitive information such as *i*)personally identifiable information [3]–[6] and *ii*) semantically revealing relationships of different provenance elements, which would enable inference of additional personal data [7]. Therefore, a comprehensive approach to the enforcement of access restrictions is required in which, both the privacy requirements of the stored data and the semantic richness of the involved data model are taken into account.

Most often than not, research in provenance access control tends to focus on identity-based authorization [8]–[10]. Little attention has been paid to rule-based authorization models, i.e., the models that take into account certain attributes of the data, which may be denoted in terms of security labels, usage purposes, etc. Furthermore, few research [11]–[14] have investigated solutions to the access regulation problem when the data is enriched with formal semantics.

The aim of the paper is to provide an authorization model that takes into account both the data privacy attributes and the semantic richness of the data model. The present work extends the previous formal privacy model by Fischer-Hübner [15] that enforces data protection principles such as *purpose binding* and *necessity of data processing*. In particular, in the current model, the degree of access restriction granularity is enhanced by introducing purpose hierarchy and additional security properties are defined for the semantically enriched data.

Specific contributions of the paper are as follows:

- We identify additional necessary components for enforcing authorization that is based on the purpose limitation principle. Further, we formalized the security policy that constrain the data access based on the purposes for which the authorization objects are collected (Section III). In particular, the consistency of the security policy in the presence of web ontology's class interrelationships are ensured by the security properties defined for subclass, class union and class intersection relationships (Section III-B).

- A use case is presented that demonstrates the applicability of the defined security policies and properties of the proposed model (Section IV).

This paper is organized as follows. In Section II, we describe the background knowledge of a Semantic Web information system and a brief introduction to the Task-Based Privacy model. Definitions of the required components for formalizing the authorization model, and for the formalization of the model's security properties are presented in Section III. Section IV demonstrates the applicability of the model by means of a use case scenario. The current state-of-the-art is analyzed in Section V followed by the conclusions of the paper, which is presented in Section VI.

II. Preliminaries

In this section, we present the background knowledge on the Semantic Web query answering. Semantic web is a web that is targeted for automated reasoning, integration and interoperability. This is realized by enabling the machines to understand the information content. Nevertheless, the technologies that support Semantic web vision need to be weaved into the well-established web standards such as Universal Resource Identifier (URI) and eXtensible Markup Language (XML).

The starting point for making the machines understand the web contents is to give the contents a well-defined meaning [16]. Intuitively, knowledge representation technology from artificial-intelligence research provides an excellent way to define and to reason about things that exists in a domain of interest. Accordingly, the information in the web documents can be described, thereby providing a meaningful structure to the web contents. Given the meanings and the sets of inference rules, the machines can conduct automated reasoning. On a related note, this notion of adding structured and semantical annotations to actual data lends itself to the concept of provenance, which is a metadata describing data.

A. Semantic Annotations

The Resource Description Framework (RDF) specifies that the descriptions that annotate the web information take the form of a triple. The RDF triple form is similar to the subject, verb, object structure of an elementary English sentence [17]. Intuitively, this makes the descriptions to be readily encoded using XML tags [16]. Formally, the description asserts that a particular thing (some entities in the domain of interest) has a property (relation) with certain values (again referring to the entities in the domain of interest). A set of RDF triples is known as RDF graph and a collection of organized RDF graphs is called a RDF dataset. The RDF triple for the statement "John is a person" is shown in Figure 1. Correspondingly, Figure 2 shows the RDF graph, which represents the entities in the RDF triple as nodes and the relations as directed edges.

B. Defining the Semantics

As mentioned earlier in this section, meanings of the terms used in the semantic annotations are provided by another Semantic Web component called ontologies. Different from the ontologies in the metaphysical context, an ontology in the Semantic Web context refers to a computational artifact that formally defines and categorizes entities that exist in a domain of interest as well as explicate the relations between the entities. As a result, intelligent agents in the Semantic Web context can unambiguously deduce the meaning of the things in the world (domain of interest). The World Wide Web Consortium (W3C) Web Ontology Working Group standardizes the Web Ontology Language (OWL) as a formal language for representing ontologies in the Semantic Web. An example of parts of PROV ontology (PROV O) [18], which is encoded using RDF/XML syntax specifications is shown in figure 3.

```
<rdf:RDF
  xmlns:rdf="http://www.w3.org/1999/02/22-rdf
      -syntax-ns#">
  <rdf:Description rdf:about="http://example.
      com/~jwille#john">
  <rdf:type
    rdf:resource="http://example.com/person-
        voc#Person"/>
</rdf:Description>
</rdf:RDF>
```

Figure 1. RDF triple

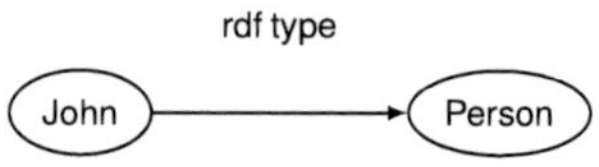

Figure 2. RDF graph

Furthermore, as OWL ontologies are grounded on the formal logic using OWL 2 $DirectSemantics$ [19], additional inferences can be derived from the explicit declarations. For example, an ontology that includes the information that Mary is a mother and every mother is a women, implicitly specifies that Mary is a women.

Ontologies and ontology-based semantic annotations are used in many application scenarios such as Semantic Web search engines, provenance, etc. Access to the triples subsequently to the RDF graphs is facilitated by The Simple Protocol and RDF Query Language (SPARQL). SPARQL 1.1 [20] includes an extension point, which specifies OWL-based semantics for query evaluation.

However, this notion of semantic interpretations and derivation of implicit information introduce novel access control challenges. Access control mechanisms developed for XML do not readily lend themselves to the notion of automated reasoning of the RDF graphs. In the Semantic Web context, the authorization objects encompass relationships among entities and the additional RDF graphs that follow from such relationships rather than the structure of a web document. The model we propose is a mandatory access control whereby the active agents of the system must comply to certain rules for a successful access. The access policy of our model is based on the purpose of the access. It is evolved from the Task-Based Privacy model [15], which technically enforces essential data protection principles such as "purpose binding" and "necessity

```
<!DOCTYPE rdf:RDF[
  <!Entity owl "http://www.w3c.org/2002/07/owl#
      ">]>
<rdf:RDF xmlns:owl ="http://www.w3.org
    /2002/07/owl#"
  xmlns:rdf ="http://www.w3.org/1999/02/22-rdf-
      syntax-ns#"
  xmlns:rdfs="http://www.w3.org/2000/01/rdf-
      schema#">
<owl:Ontology rdf:about="">
  <rdfs:label>Example Ontology</rdfs:label>
  <rdfs:comment>An example ontology</
      rdfs:comment>
</owl:Ontology>
<owl:Class rdf:ID="Entity" />
<owl:Class rdf:ID="Agent" />
<owl:ObjectProperty rdf:ID="wasAttributedTo" /
    >
<owl:DatatypeProperty rdf:ID="value" />
<owl:Class rdf:ID="Person">
  <rdfs:subClassOf rdf:resource="#Agent">
</owl:Class>
</rdf:RDF>
<owl:Class rdf:ID="plan">
  <rdfs:subClassOf rdf:resource="#Entity">
  <rdfs:subClassOf>
    <owl:Restriction>
      <owl:onProperty rdf:resource="#
          wasAttributedTo"/>
      <owl:someValuesFrom rdf:resource="&Pers;
          person"/>
    </owl:Restriction>
  </rdfs:subClassOf>
</owl:Class>
```

Figure 3. An example of an OWL ontology encoding parts of the PROV data model

of data processing" .

C. Task-Based Privacy Model

The key idea of the Task-Based Privacy model is to place technical controls for enforcing data protection principles such as purpose binding and necessity of data processing.

The authorization policy is expressed in terms of the purposes that are assigned to the active agents and to the passive objects of a system. Data objects are categorized into object-classes, which are assigned a set of specified purposes representing the usage purposes of the data objects in those classes. The tasks that operate on those objects are also assigned appropriate purposes. Tasks are specific to an application, hence depending on the applications a task could comprises of several functionalities. Each task or simply a functionality serves exactly one purpose. The active agents are authorized to perform a set of tasks, which is further restricted by the kind of data transformations that are allowed for each task. Given these components, the central security property of the model is defined as:

Purpose binding property: An active agent is permitted to access a data object, only if the purpose of the task that the agent currently performs is contained in the set of purposes specified for the object-class that encloses the data object(s).

III. Privacy Preserving Authorization Model for Semantic Annotations

We consider, in this work that the data usage is constrained by the purpose limitation principle. This is required for complying with the European Union (EU) General Data Protection Regulation (GDPR) and other privacy laws. EU GDPR (Art.5 1(b)) mandates that the processing of personal data should only be permitted if it is necessary to serve the purposes for which the data is collected [21].

A. Model Components

Definition 1: **(Subjects S)** *A subject is an active agent of a system, which is properly identified and authenticated. S is set of active subjects.*

$$S = \{s_1, s_2, ...s_n\}$$

OWL ontology is a formal specification that includes categories of entities (referred to as classes in OWL terminology), and structured vocabularies that explicate the relationships among the classes. Relationships include both the taxonomy of classes and other relationships among the classes. A relationship other than the class taxonomy is the relation between the instance of two class, which are the domain and the range of the relationship.

Definition 2: **(OWL Ontology)** *An OWL ontology O is defined as a tuple,*

$$O = (C, T_c, R)$$

Where, C is a set of OWL classes $\{c_1, c_2, ..., c_i\}$, T_c is the set of terms that explicate the taxonomy of classes and R refers to the set of other types of relations among the instances I of the classes in C. $R = \{r_1, r_2 ..., r_n\}$, where r_i is a relation from c_i to c_j $(i \neq j)$, given that $Dom(r_i) = \{I_{c_i} \in c_i \mid \exists I_{c_j} \in c_j, (I_{c_i}, I_{c_j}) \in r_i\}$ and $Ran(r_i) = \{I_{c_j} \in c_j \mid \exists I_{c_i} \in c_i, (I_{c_i}, I_{c_j}) \in r_i\}$.

Definition 3: **(RDF triple)** *A RDF triple, which is of the form (statement-subject ($\mathcal{S}_{rdf}$), predicate ($\mathcal{P}_{rdf}$), statement-object ($\mathcal{O}_{rdf}$)) is an element of the* Cartesian product *of* $((C \cup B) \times (T_c \cup R) \times (C \cup L))$. Where,

- $\mathcal{S}_{rdf} \in (C \cup B)$, such that $\exists c_i \in C : \mathcal{S}_{rdf} \in c_i$ and B is a set of blank nodes.
- $\mathcal{P}_{rdf} \in (T_c \cup R)$.
- $\mathcal{O}_{rdf} \in (C \cup L)$, such that $\exists c_i \in C : \mathcal{O}_{rdf} \in c_i$ and L is a set of literals.

A RDF graph G is a finite set of RDF triples. However, in addition to the direct mappings of RDF instances to OWL classes and respective relationships, additional RDF triples and graphs are entailed. This is due to the interpretation of how the OWL classes and terms are connected in the direct-semantics-based OWL ontology. We refer to these additional RDF instances as entailments. Accordingly, the authorization objects is defined as follow;

Definition 4: (**Authorization objects**) *An authorization object is a subgraph of G that explicitly and implicitly conforms to the OWL ontology O under the OWL 2 direct semantics. A set of authorization objects is denoted as $\mathcal{O}_A$.*

An application is made up of several tasks. Examples tasks of a hospital information system are admission, diagnosing, surgery, care transfer, discharge, and billing. Definitions 5-10 are derived from the Task-Based Privacy model [15].

Definition: 5: (**Tasks**) *Tasks are operations through which the subjects access the authorization objects. T is a set of all tasks that are defined for a system.*

$$T = \{t_1, t_2, ...t_n\}$$

Each subject will be authorized for a subset of tasks either depending on their roles in an organization or on other contextual attributes.

Definition 6: (**Authorized tasks**) *A set of tasks that a subject is authorized to perform is provided by a task assigning function.*

$$AT : S \rightarrow 2^T \setminus \emptyset$$

where, $AT(s_i)$ is the set of authorized tasks of s_i.

We further distinguish the current task that the subject is performing from its authorized set of tasks. If there is no current task for a subject, then a standard value "Nil" is assigned as its current task.

Definition: 7: (**Current task**) *Current task is the task that a subject is currently performing,*

$$CT : S \rightarrow T \cup \{Nil\}$$

Information, specifically personally identifiable information, is collected and stored for certain usage purposes. As pointed out earlier, it is required by data protection laws (e.g., the EU GDPR) that the processing of such information should be permitted where it is necessary to serve those purposes. Accordingly, the tasks that access the information for processing must be assigned a specific purpose that they are designed to serve. As an example, in a hospital information system, an admission task, which is designed to serve the admission purpose is only allowed to operate on information that is collected for the administrative purpose.

Definition: 8: (**Purposes**) *The set of all purposes for which data is collected and processed in an application is denoted by P*

$$P = \{p_1, p_2, ..., p_n\}$$

Relationship between the purposes play a crucial role. Hierarchically structured purposes can, *i)* improve the granularity of the access control rules by constraining the access to specific sub purposes and *ii)* lend itself well to specify interconnected purposes to related OWL classes. Set P is defined to have an order relation $\leq$ and forms a partially ordered set (P,$\leq$). The hierarchical structure we propose for the purposes is exemplified and illustrated in figure 4. The top level nodes are "super" purposes that dominates their children. As a consequence, tasks and authorization objects are identified both from the purposes directly assigned to them and from the purpose subsumption relation. Correspondingly, in order to be aligned with the hierarchically structured purposes, the tasks, which are designed to serve the purposes need to be hierarchically structured as well. Figure 5 shows an example of a task hierarchy with diagnosing as the super task, which is assigned the super purpose MT. Further, its two sub tasks General Check and Kidney Check are assigned sub purposes GT and KT respectively.

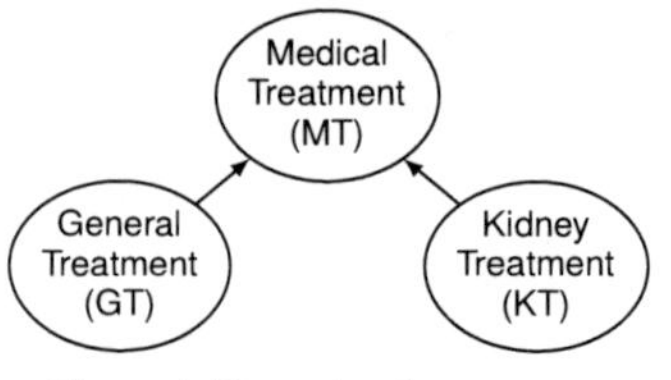

Figure 4. Example of a purpose hierarchy

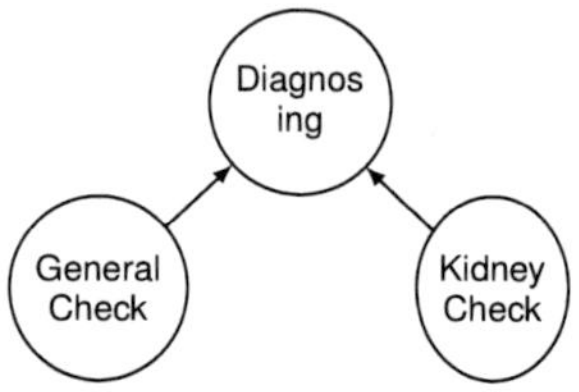

Figure 5. Example of a task hierarchy

Definition 9: (**Purpose of a task**) *For each task in an application, there exists a purpose in set P that is served by the task.*

$$\phi_T : T \rightarrow P$$

Where ϕ_T is a purpose assigning function for tasks and $\phi_T(t_i)$ is the purpose of the task t_i

Further, the authorization objects $\mathcal{O}_A$ of a system need to have specified purposes for which they are collected and stored. However, determining purposes for every RDF instances is time-consuming and error-prone. Hence, in this paper we consider that every OWL class in a domain of interest is assigned a set of usage purposes. The relationships R that are specific to the instances of a class and the instances themselves inherit the purposes of that class.

Definition 10: (**Purposes of OWL classes**) *Each OWL class in a domain of interest are assigned a non-empty set of purposes.*

$$\phi_C : C \rightarrow 2^P \setminus \emptyset$$

Where ϕ_C is a purpose assigning function for OWL classes and $\phi_C(c_i)$ are the purposes of the elements and the relationships R of the class c_i.

In the original Task-Based Privacy model a set of data transformation procedures are defined for each tasks. In order for a subject to perform its tasks it needs to be authorized to execute certain transformation procedure on the authorization objects. In the Semantic Web context however, query answering is the major essential operation [22]. Hence, we consider query answering as the only action by the subjects S on the authorization objects $\mathcal{O}_A$, in access control terms this represents the $READ$ action and denoted as $READ(\mathcal{O}_A)_S$.

B. Model Constraint and Properties

In this subsection, we formally define the security policy that constraints the behavior of a Semantic Web query answering system such that subjects only receive the information that they allowed to receive. Further, we define security properties that need to fulfilled by the system in order to control the inference of specific information from a general set of information.

*Security Policy-1: (**S1**): A subject is granted read access to $\mathcal{O}_A$, only if the purpose of a subject's current task is contained in the set of purposes of the OWL classes that enclose the $\mathcal{O}_A$ or is a super purpose of a purpose in that set.*

$$\forall s_i \in S, \mathcal{O}_A \in G : READ(\mathcal{O}_A)_{s_i} \\ \Rightarrow \phi_T(CT(s_i)) \in \phi_C(C(\mathcal{O}_A)) \vee \\ \phi_T(CT(s_i)) \geq p_j, for\ p_j \in \phi_C(C(\mathcal{O}_A))$$

*Security Policy-2: (**S2**): The subject must be authorized to execute its current task.*

$$\forall s_i \in S : CT(s_i) \in AT(s_i)$$

The current task $CT(s_i)$ of s_i must be an element of its authorized tasks.

Security Properties: However, the soundness of the security policy (S1) is challenged by the interrelationships among the classes of O. In this sub section, we define security properties for OWL class taxonomies to ensure $S1$ is consistent. Properties for subclass, class union, and class intersection are defined.

Sublcass: Subclass axioms represent the taxonomy of OWL classes that describe the domain of interest K. Semantically, lower level nodes are more specific than the generic higher level nodes in a OWL class hierarchy [23]. In this context, to restrict access to specific subclasses, specific purposes need to be assigned to the subclasses. However, subclass axioms also imply membership of parent classes and this is an allowed inference. Hence, for the reasoning engine to include this inference, the purposes of the subclasses need to be included in the purpose assignment of their parent classes.

C1 (Subclass): Given the classes B, D and if $B \subseteq D$, then the purpose assigned to the subclass B must be included in the purposes assigned to its parent class D. If $B \subseteq D \Rightarrow \phi_C(B) \subseteq \phi_C(D)$.

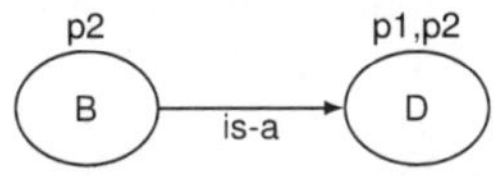

Figure 6. Example purpose assignments for subclass relationships

Figure 6 shows an illustrative example, where the subclass B is assigned the purpose p2 and that the purpose is included in the purposes for D. $S1$ implies that the task that is assigned the purpose p2 is allowed to view the instances of B and the semantic relation (implicit knowledge) that B is a subclass of D. Whereas, the task that is assigned the purpose p1 is allowed to view only instances of the more general class D.

Class Union: The union of two or more classes consist of instances that are member of at least one of those classes. Semantically, the union encompasses of instances of one or more specific subclasses. In this context, the purpose assignments of the specific subclasses that comprise an union class are included in the purpose assignments of that union class.

C2 (Class Union): Given the classes A, B, D and if A is a result of set $union$ of its subclasses B and D, then the purposes assigned to A must include the purposes assigned to its subclasses. If $A = B \cup D \Rightarrow \phi_C(A) \supseteq \phi_C(B) \cup \phi_C(D)$.

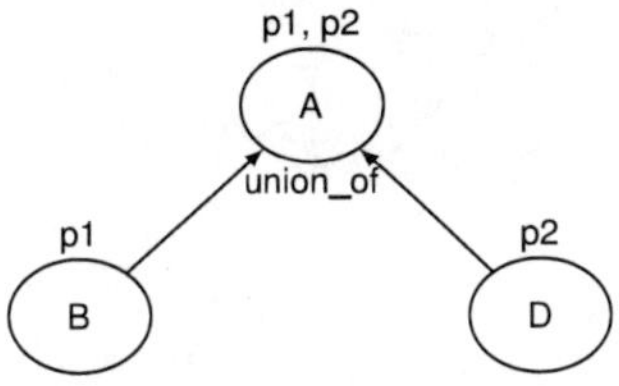

Figure 7. Example purpose assignments for class union relation

Figure 7 shows an illustrative example, where the union class A includes the purpose assignments p1, p2 of B and C respectively. According to $S1$ the tasks that are assigned either p1 or p2 are allowed to view the individuals of respective subclasses including the knowledge about the union.

Class Intersection: The intersection of two or more classes contains exactly every individual, which is a member of those concerned classes. Semantically, *i)* the overlapped class is more specific than the generic overlapping classes and *ii)* the overlapped class combines individuals belonging to two or more distinct classes which may have been collected for different purposes. Hence, access to the overlapped class must be constrained, so that unauthorized inference of the respective overlapping class is prevented as well as the illegal inference of overlapped class from the overlapping class. As consequence of the purpose hierarchy introduced in III-A, the purpose assignment of the overlapped class needs to dominate the purpose assignments of its overlapping classes.

C3 (Class Intersection): Given the classes B, D, E and if E is a result of set $intersection$ of B, D then the purpose assignment of E must dominate the purpose assignments of its overlapping classes. If $E = B \cap D$ then $\phi_C(E) \geq \phi_C(B) \wedge \phi_C(E) \geq \phi_C(D))$ and $\phi_C(E)$ is the lowest super purpose of B and D in the purpose hierarchy (i.e any other super purpose of B and D is dominating $\phi_C(E)$).

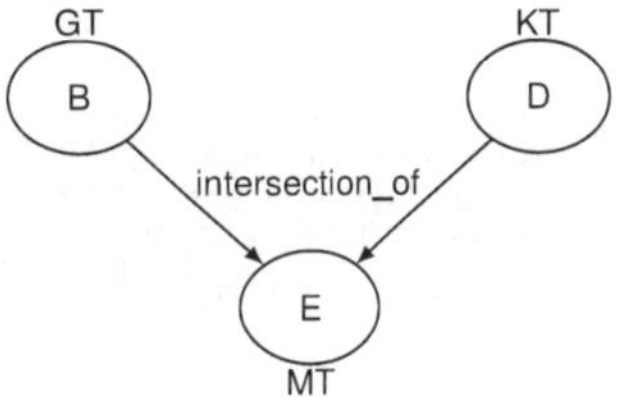

Figure 8. Example purpose assignments for class intersection relation

Figure 8 shows an illustrative example. The overlapping classes B and D are respectively assigned sub-purposes GT and KT from the example purpose hierarchy presented in Figure 4. In the Figure 4, it shows that MT is the super-purpose in the hierarchy that subsumes GT and KT. According to $S1$, the task

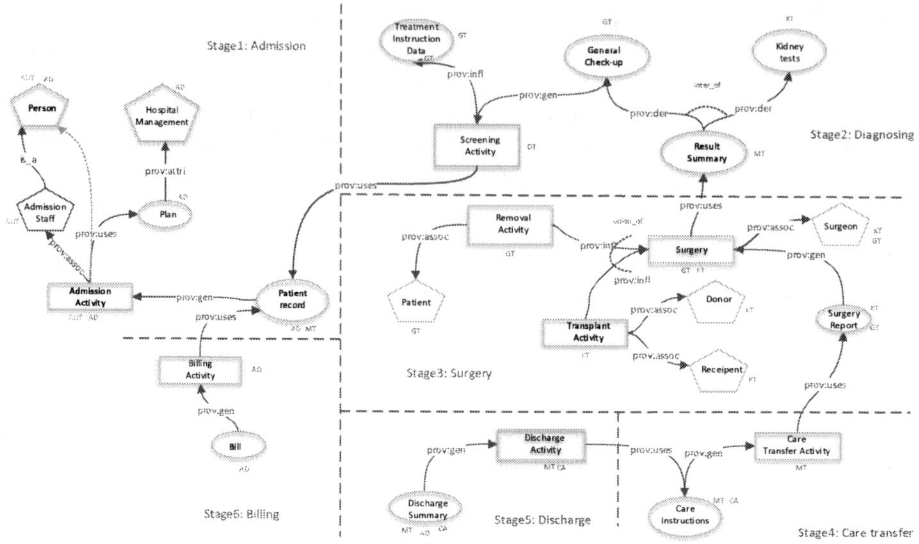

Figure 9. An example of a provenance OWL ontology for an imaginary surgical scenario

that is assigned MT which inherently subsumes the subtasks with purposes GT and KT is allowed to view the individuals of B, D and E. Whereas the subtasks with purpose assignments GT or KT is allowed to view the instances of the respective overlapping classes.

IV. Use Case: Access to Provenance Information in a Hospital Information System

An imaginary hospital called St.Mark hospital tracks provenance for the web documents to serve various provenance related automated queries. RDF is used to describe the provenance of web information using the ontology PROV-O. Access to such information needs to be managed for security, and especially for privacy reasons. The authorization policy of St.Mark hospital information is based on the purpose limitation principle. We consider the surgical part of the hospital service in this example. A patient needs to be admitted and diagnosed for a surgery procedure, hence the data usage purposes listed in Table I are identified for this scenario;

Table I. Purposes for data processing in a surgical care scenario

Purposes
Administration (AD)
Audit (AUT)
General Treatment (GT)
Kidney Treatment (KT)
Medical Treatment (MT)
Care Transfer (CA)

Graphical representation of the provenance ontology encompasses of OWL classes, taxonomy and relationships in a imaginary surgical scenario is shown in Figure 9

According to the PROV-Data Model (PROV-DM) [24], the ellipses represent the data items, the rectangles represent the processes or the activities that act on the data items and the hexagons represent the respective agents. Each of these PROV elements are modeled as OWL classes in Figure 9 including the respective relationships, which are also modeled in accordance with the PROV-DM. Each OWL class is assigned a set of purposes for which the data is collected and stored. In the following subsections we present a set of examples of, how the purpose limitation principle is enforced using the model described in Section III. In particular, we illustrated using an imaginary scenario, the security properties of the proposed model and the details of directly assigned and indirectly derived sub purposes.

A. Security Properties: Subclass and Union of Subclasses

In the OWL semantics, being member of a subclass implicitly means being member of a respective superclass. Hence, a query to an instance of a subclass includes the information that the instance is also a member of a superclass. Since super classes are more generic than the specific subclasses, the query to the superclass instances however, should not include the knowledge of the corresponding subclasses. Thereby, unauthorized inference of specific information from general information is prevented.

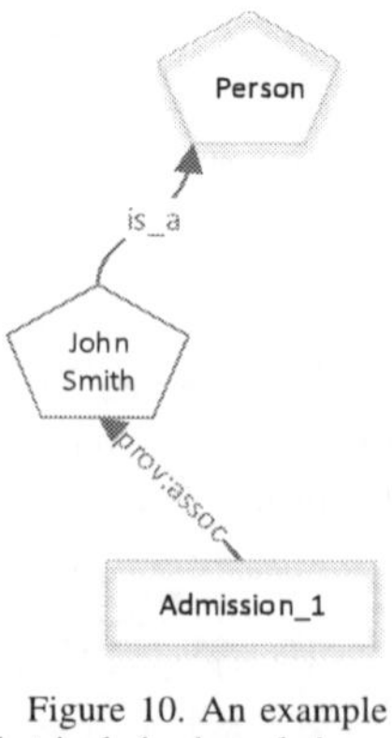

Figure 10. An example of a RDF subgraph that includes knowledge of respective super class

In Figure 9, "admission staff" class is more specific than the generic "person" class. According to $S1$, an auditor who is performing audit provenance query as part of an audit task to fulfill the audit purpose is authorized to read the RDF subgraph that is stored for audit purpose.

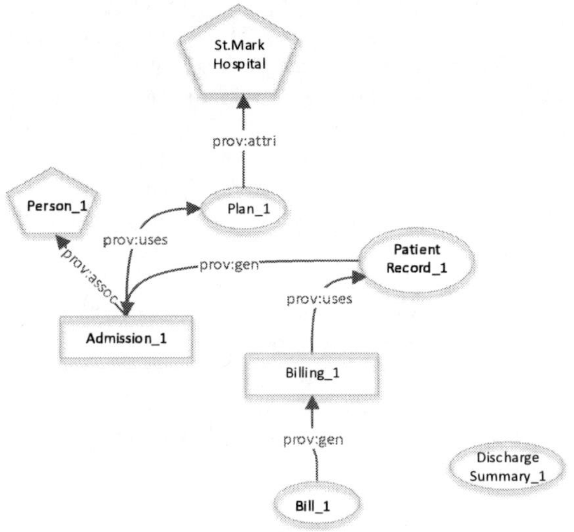

Figure 11. An example of a RDF subgraph pertaining to administration purpose

The resulting RDF subgraph is shown in Figure 10, which includes the implicit knowledge that "John Smith" who is an admission staff is also a member of a "person" class. Whereas, an administrator, who is executing a query that is related to the admission task for performing the administrative purpose, will receive the RDF subgraph depicted in Figure 11. This subgraph does not include the knowledge about a specific admission staff but the knowledge that the associated PROV agent, is a member of a "person" class.

The same principle is applied to the union of two or more subclasses. The classes that add up to a union are more specific than the generic union class. Querying for instances of subclasses that comprise the union includes the knowledge that the subclasses are part of an union class. Likewise, querying the instances of the union class includes the knowledge of the subclasses that comprise the union. This is because, unlike the generic super class that is an abstraction of infinite number of specific classes, the union class consist of exactly a finite number of subclasses.

In Figure 9, "Surgery" is a union of "Removal activity" and "Transplant activity" with purposes "GT" and "KT" respectively. Figure 12 shows an example of a returned RDF sub graph for a provenance query related to a general-check task that fulfills the general treatment purpose. The subgraph includes the knowledge that "Polyp removal" is part of an union class "Surgery".

B. Security Property: Class Intersection

In OWL class intersection, the overlapped class is more specific than the overlapping classes. Hence, it must be ensured that unauthorized inference of overlapped class from the generic overlapping class is prevented. Similarly, the inference from the overlapped class to the overlapping class need to be permitted because if a subject get hold of the all the overlapping classes then the subject can easily infer the overlapped class. This achieved in our model by means of the super-purposes and sub-purposes hierarchy. As result of the semantics behind the super-purpose, the overlapped classes need to be assigned super-purposes. Thereby, authorization on the overlapped class subsumes the purposes of the overlapping classes.

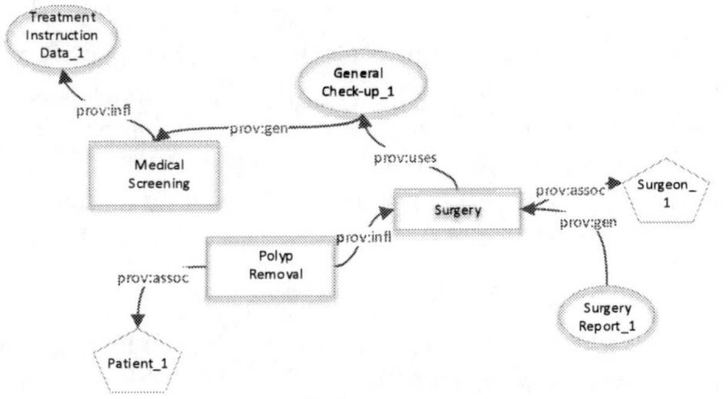

Figure 12. An example RDF subgraph for class union

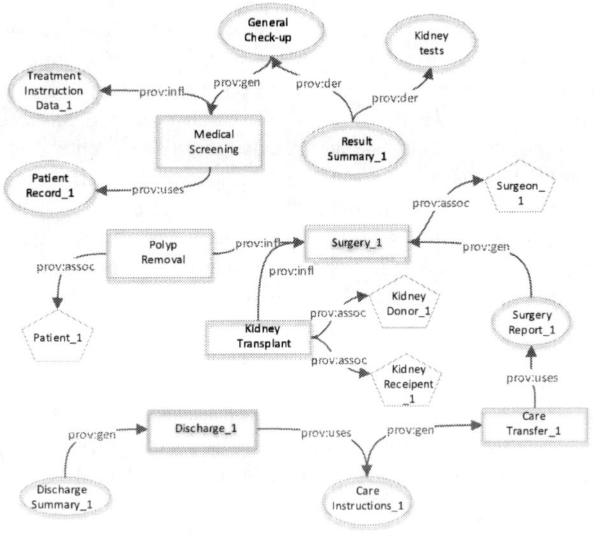

Figure 13. An example RDF subgraph that includes instances that are due to the indirectly derived purposes

In Figure 9, "Result Summary" is more specific than the generic overlapping classes "General Checkup" and "Kidney tests". A specialist executing a provenance query as part of the diagnosing task for the fulfillment of the medical treatment (MT) purpose, will receives the RDF subgraph shown in Figure 13. The subgraph does not only include the instance of the overlapping class "Result Summary" but also the knowledge that it is an intersection of classes "General Checkup" and "Kidney tests". This is due to the fact that the purposes of both the "General Checkup" and "Kidney tests" classes are the sub purpose of MT. According to $S1$, a task, which is assigned a super purpose can access the information pertaining to its corresponding sub purposes. However, the RDF subgraph returned for the task that is assigned a sub-purpose GT does not include the knowledge of the overlapped class (see Figure 12).

V. RELATED WORK

Much research on access control for provenance information does not acknowledge the emerging Semantic Web principles that underly the web provenance architecture. One exception is the work by Cadenhead et al. [25], they extend the access control language for generalized provenance model [26] with regular expressions. Regular expressions are used to identify relevant parts of the RDF graphs that represent provenance. Although, the policy specification of their model includes access purposes, they did not consider the entailments provided by OWL or RDF semantics.

Further, considerable amount of research has been devoted to investigate the access control models for RDF data stores. Jain et al. [13] propose a mandatory access control model for the RDF data stores that include derived RDF statements that follow from a RDF schema. However, OWL semantics that we have considered in our model are formally grounded and hence are more precise than the RDF schema. Furthermore, their model is based on a linear hierarchy of security classification labels assigned to the data objects, which is not pragmatic to define in the context of emerging applications except for the military domain. There are lot of research efforts on access control policy languages that specify access restrictions for semantically enriched information. Amongst which, the most relevant one is the work done by Kaushik et al. [12]. They propose a constraint logic based policy language to represent disclosure constraints for exposing parts of the ontology, and removing or desensitizing sensitive ontological concepts. However, in their model the disclosure constraints are not based on the access restriction attributes of the access objects, which is the primary focus of our model. On the similar basis, the work by Qin et al. [14] is an identity-based access control model rather than a mandatory access control model. Although, similar to our model their model is based on the relations between the OWL classes and how those relations can reveal information about one class from that of the other. We ascertain that both the work can be extended using our model.

Finally, significant amount of research effort has been put on automatic processing of privacy policies that enforce purpose limitation over the personal data access. Two main policy languages that formally represent enterprise data processing requirements are EPAL [27] and PPL [28]. Data usage restriction of these languages, however, are centered around data objects that does not represent semantic relationships. Similarly, Task-Based Privacy model [15] places technical controls for the implementation of legal privacy requirements such as purpose limitations but again the focuses is on the data objects that are not semantically enriched.

VI. CONCLUSIONS AND FUTURE DIRECTION

The major strength of our model is that it recognizes the characteristics of the protection objects rather than the characteristics of the subjects. We ascertain however, that our model can be integrated into the role-based access control by authorizing the tasks to the roles instead of the subjects. In our model, we consider that the restriction attributes are for each OWL class including its relationships. However, the relationships that connect individuals of different classes might involve different type of semantics than class taxonomy hence may require a discrete access restriction attributes on its own. Furthermore, the abstraction on the OWL relationships due to our model introduces violation of integrity with respect to the OWL relationships. Figure 11 shows such a violation, where the instance "Discharge Summary_1" is unrelated to any class. Hence, in our future work we consider to study unauthorized inferences result from the OWL class relationships besides the OWL class taxonomy and consider to devise an abstraction mechanism for mitigating unauthorized inferences, which respect the OWL relationship constraints.

ACKNOWLEDGMENTS

The authors are thankful to the SMARTSOCIETY, a project of the 7th Framework Programme for Research of the European Community under grant agreement no. 600854, for funding the research that resulted in this publication. We extend our thanks to Rose-Mharie Åhlfeldt and anonymous reviewers for their invaluable feedbacks.

REFERENCES

[1] L. Moreau, P. Groth, S. Miles, J. Vazquez-Salceda, J. Ibbotson, S. Jiang, S. Munroe, O. Rana, A. Schreiber, V. Tan, and L. Varga, "The Provenance of Electronic Data," Commun. ACM, vol. 51, no. 4, Apr 2008, pp. 52–58. [Online]. Available: http://doi.acm.org/10.1145/1330311.1330323

[2] T. Hey and A. E. Trefethen, "Cyberinfrastructure for e-Science," Science, vol. 308, no. 5723, 2005, pp. 817–821.

[3] J. Cheney and R. Perera, "An Analytical Survey of Provenance Sanitization," CoRR, vol. abs/1405.5777, 2014. [Online]. Available: http://arxiv.org/abs/1405.5777

[4] S. B. Davidson, S. Khanna, S. Roy, J. Stoyanovich, V. Tannen, and Y. Chen, "On provenance and privacy," in ICDT'11. ACM, 2011, pp. 3–10.

[5] U. Braun, S. Garfinkel, D. A. Holland, K.-K. Muniswamy-Reddy, and M. I. Seltzer, Provenance and Annotation of Data: International Provenance and Annotation Workshop, IPAW 2006, Chicago, IL, USA, May 3-5, 2006, Revised Selected Papers. Berlin, Heidelberg: Springer Berlin Heidelberg, 2006, ch. Issues in Automatic Provenance Collection, pp. 171–183. [Online]. Available: http://dx.doi.org/10.1007/11890850_18

[6] U. Braun, A. Shinnar, and M. I. Seltzer, "Securing Provenance," in Proc. of the 3rd Conf. on Hot Topics in Security, ser. HOTSEC'08, 2008, pp. 4:1–4:5.

[7] J. Reuben, L. A. Martucci, S. Fischer-Hübner, H. Packer, H. Hedbom, and L. Moreau, "Privacy Impact Assessment Template for Provenance," in Proc. of the Workshop on Challenges in Information Security and Privacy Management at the 11th International Conference on Availability, Reliability and Security, August 2016.

[8] A. Syalim, Y. Hori, and K. Sakurai, "Grouping provenance information to improve efficiency of access control," in Advances in Information Security and Assurance, ser. LNCS. Springer Berlin Heidelberg, 2009, vol. 5576, pp. 51–59.

[9] A. Rosenthal, L. Seligman, A. Chapman, and B. T. Blaustein, "Scalable Access Controls for Lineage," in 1st Workshop on the Theory and Practice of Provenance, ser. TAPP. USENIX, 2009.

[10] A. Chebotko, S. Chang, S. Lu, F. Fotouhi, and P. Yang, "Secure scientific workflow provenance querying with security views," in 9th Int. Conf. on Web-Age Information Management, ser. WAIM, Jul 2008, pp. 349–356.

[11] T. Cadenhead, V. Khadilkar, M. Kantarcioglu, and B. Thuraisingham, "Transforming Provenance Using Redaction," in Proc. of the 16th ACM Symp. on Access Control Models and Technologies, ser. SACMAT '11. ACM, 2011, pp. 93–102.

[12] S. Kaushik, D. Wijesekera, and P. Ammann, "Policy-based Dissemination of Partial Web-ontologies," in Proceedings of the 2005 Workshop on Secure Web Services, ser. SWS '05. ACM, 2005, pp. 43–52, ISBN: 1-59593-234-8, URL: http://doi.acm.org/10.1145/1103022.1103030 [accessed: 2018-04-08].

[13] A. Jain and C. Farkas, "Secure Resource Description Framework: An Access Control Model," in Proceedings of the Eleventh ACM Symposium on Access Control Models and Technologies, ser. SACMAT '06. ACM, 2006, pp. 121–129, ISBN: 1-59593-353-0, URL: http://doi.acm.org/10.1145/1133058.1133076 [accessed: 2017-04-08].

[14] L. Qin and V. Atluri, "Concept-level Access Control for the Semantic Web," in Proceedings of the 2003 ACM Workshop on XML Security, ser. XMLSEC '03, 2003, pp. 94–103, ISBN: 1-58113-777-X, URL: http://doi.acm.org/10.1145/968559.968575 [accessed: 2017-04-08].

[15] S. Fischer-Hübner, IT-security and Privacy: Design and Use of Privacy-enhancing Security Mechanisms. Berlin, Heidelberg: Springer-Verlag, 2001.

[16] T. Berners-Lee, J. Hendler, and O. Lassila, "The Semantic Web," Scientific American, vol. 284, no. 5, 2001, pp. 28–37.

[17] M. Lanthaler, D. Wood, and R. Cyganiak, "RDF 1.1 Concepts and Abstract Syntax," W3C, W3C Recommendation, Feb. 2014, URL: http://www.w3.org/TR/2014/REC-rdf11-concepts-20140225/ [accessed: 2017-04-08].

[18] T. Lebo, D. McGuinness, and S. Sahoo, "PROV-o: The PROV ontology," W3C, W3C Recommendation, Apr 2013, URL: http://www.w3.org/TR/2013/REC-prov-o-20130430/ [accessed: 2017-04-08].

[19] B. C. Grau, P. Patel-Schneider, and B. Motik, "OWL 2 web ontology language direct semantics (second edition)," W3C, W3C Recommendation, Dec. 2012, URL: http://www.w3.org/TR/2012/REC-owl2-direct-semantics-20121211/ [accessed: 2017-04-08].

[20] B. Glimm and C. Ogbuji, "SPARQL 1.1 entailment regimes," W3C, W3C Recommendation, mar 2013, URL: http://www.w3.org/TR/2013/REC-sparql11-entailment-20130321/ [accessed: 2017-04-08].

[21] European Commission, "Regulation (EU) 2016/679 of the European Parliament and of the Council of 27 April 2016 on the protection of natural persons with regard to the processing of personal data and on the free movement of such data, and repealing Directive 95/46/EC (General Data Protection Regulation)," 2016.

[22] I. Kollia, B. Glimm, and I. Horrocks, "SPARQL Query Answering over OWL Ontologies". Springer Berlin Heidelberg, pp. 382–396, ISBN: 978-3-642-21034-1, URL: http://dx.doi.org/10.1007/978-3-642-21034-1_26 [accessed: 2017-04-08].

[23] P. Hitzler, M. Krötzsch, B. Parsia, P. F. Patel-Schneider, and S. Rudolph, "OWL 2 Web Ontology Language Primer (Second Edition)," Dec 2012, URL: https://www.w3.org/TR/owl2-primer/ [accessed: 2017-04-08].

[24] L. Moreau and P. Missier, "PROV-DM: The PROV Data Model," W3C, W3C Recommendation, Apr. 2013, URL: http://www.w3.org/TR/2013/REC-prov-dm-20130430/ [accessed: 2017-04-08].

[25] T. Cadenhead, V. Khadilkar, M. Kantarcioglu, and B. Thuraisingham, "A Language for Provenance Access Control," in Proc. of the 1st ACM Conf. on Data and Application Security and Privacy, ser. CODASPY '11. ACM, 2011, pp. 133–144.

[26] Q. Ni, S. Xu, E. Bertino, R. Sandhu, and W. Han, An Access Control Language for a General Provenance Model. Berlin, Heidelberg: Springer Berlin Heidelberg, 2009, pp. 68–88, ISBN: 978-3-642-04219-5, URL: http://dx.doi.org/10.1007/978-3-642-04219-5_5 [accessed: 2017-04-08].

[27] P. Ashley, S. Hada, G. Karjoth, C. Powers, and M. Schunter, "Enterprise privacy authorization language (EPAL 1.2)," Submission to W3C, vol. 156, 2003.

[28] PrimeLife, "PrimeLife – Privacy and Identity Management in Europe for Life: Policy Languages," Available at http://primelife.ercim.eu/images/stories/primer/policylanguage-plb.pdf, 2011.

A Novel Approach to User Involved Big Data Provenance Visualization

Ilkay Melek Yazici, Mehmet S. Aktas
Computer Engineering Department
Yildiz Technical University
Istanbul, Turkey
email:ilkay.yazici@std.yildiz.edu.tr,
mehmet@ce.yildiz.edu.tr

Mehmet Gokturk
Computer Engineering Department
Gebze Technical University
Koceli, Turkey
email: gokturk@bilmuh.gyte.edu.tr

Abstract—We are living in the "big data" age. In many ways, big data is equivalent to complexity or mess. Extracting relevant information from any complex environment is a challenging but necessary task required in every scientific field. An assortment of graphs, figures, and charts have been developed to visualize *n*-dimensional data since the early ages of science. In the recent past, the number of dimensions in a visualization were limited by computational factors. Visualizing *n*-dimension is difficult but achievable by using data projection and reduction methods. Unfortunately, these methods often introduce ambiguities and inaccuracies, which can subtly corrupt results. Data provenance chronicles the core life cycle of a data set, which includes data source and creation processes, accounts for many of the processing techniques that a data set is subject to, like debugging, auditing and quality control. Additionally, data protection mechanisms such as data access control and authenticity valuation methods are also tracked by provenance. In this paper, we introduce an effective method to visualize and analyze semantic provenance data by adhering to the Human Computer Interaction principles. Our proposed data provenance visualization system involves the user in the visualization process. By capturing and analyzing a user's attentiveness and perception level, we develop a provenance visualization system with specific visualization types and methodologies.

Keywords-big data; provenance; visualization; open provenance model (OPM); human machine interface(HMI).

I. INTRODUCTION

Data provenance records the journey of data from its creation to its application [1]. Data provenance is produced with complex transformations and processes like workflows [2]. Data provenance collection systems capture provenance on the fly. However, their collection mechanisms may be faulty and have dropped provenance notifications. Hence, provenance records may be partial, partitioned, or simply inaccurate [3]. Incompleteness and inconsistency of provenance records, if they exist, are a challenge for analyzing provenance datasets.

As more information technology (IT) systems are developed and implemented, the interpretation requirements for big provenance data also increase [4]. Data visualization is an important field, which offers many techniques to develop an intuitive interpretation of data, often by way of efficient visualization capabilities [5]. Therefore, data visualization is an important step in the process of maximizing perception efficiency [6].

Data visualization is considered visual communication by many experts. Many visual communication techniques create processes that improve visual data representation via diagrammatic displays that use data properties, variables, and information units. Effective visualization can assist users with analyzing and evaluating data by making complex data more accessible, clear and usable [7].

In this paper, our goal is to help users by generating an effective provenance visualization process that complies with Human Computer Interaction (HCI) principles and user navigation models. A mind map for an experimental protocol will be used to jointly explore provenance and user interaction. To achieve these goals, this study states the following objectives, which are briefly described below:

Objective 1: Achieve user-assisted visualization of Big Provenance. We will develop real-time and offline visualization techniques by capitalizing on existing visualization techniques from relevant fields. In our case, we concern ourselves with the social media domain. We will research existing provenance visualization methods for temporal provenance data and analyze the various visualization techniques and methodologies. A user's preference for customized visualizations, and their perception of these preferred methods, will be analyzed using HCI evaluation methods. The results will be used to improve the visualization system.

Objective 2: Design and create Big Provenance visualization methods, such as visualization layouts, and templates. Few research studies on provenance visualization exist in the literature. We will study and extend the existing methodologies and introduce novel visualization layouts that deal with temporal provenance data. We argue that new customized layouts and visualization methodologies can be developed. The techniques need to be based on both the provenance data domain and user requirements.

Objective 3: Develop domain-independent Big Provenance visualization. We will study existing domain-independent provenance specifications for data representation. Particularly, we will consider Open

Provenance Model (OPM) and Provenance Ontology (PROV-O) specifications.

The remainder of this paper is organized as follows: Section II provides the relevant literature review. Section III discusses various application scenarios to describe the scope of this research. Section IV reviews our proposed methodology and Section V describes the aspects of Human Machine Interface (HMI) that are important to this study. Finally, Section VI presents the conclusion and future work of our paper.

II. LITERATURE SUMMARY

Kunde's seminal work [12] on Provenance Visualization Components provides us with an important set of requirements, summarized below:

a) Process: a summary of the process as a sequence of data inspection steps;
b) Results: user-centric and includes the intermediate- and end-results of interactions;
c) Relationship: the relationship between actors or interactions;
d) Timeline: observations of time;
e) Participation: the accuracy of the participants
f) Compare: describes the distinction between two subjects
g) Interpretation: the individual visualization related to the end user's special questions

In his considerable research, Chen's visualization goal is to satisfy the audience or reader. He addresses Kunde's requirements as follows: a-c) Chen's visualization tool is based on a known provenance model called Open Provenance Model (OPM) for provenance representation. This model represents entities and relationships as nodes and edges on a graph [9]. OPM models can represent a full graph with process steps and process results, an abstract graph with any of them; d) OPM represents time information as edges and nodes; e) OPM represents participation by agents. Chen's tool enable users to evaluate the accuracy of the participations visually; f) a tool is used for comparing attributes of nodes. Chen extended the DePiero graph-matching algorithm to compare provenance graphs; g) Chen developed a customized layout algorithm and a visual style to interpret specific use cases.

In Chen's research, network application provenance is studied from large-scale distributed apps that run on large testbeds like the Planet Lab or in network simulations like the provenance data from NASA satellite imaginary.

Provenance visualization research is often restricted to small graphs, graph matching techniques and graph layouts. Taverna is a scientific workflow management system (SWMS) that benefits from Chen's visualization method. Taverna helps answer questions based on experimental results. VisTrails is another SWMS that can navigate workflows by using the users intuition to compare workflows, intermediate- or end- results, or to evaluate the results. Probe-It is a popular SWMS that allows scientists to focus on intermediate or final visualization results for back and forth provenance [8].

The Prototype Lineage Server (PLS) enables users to get lineage information by searching metadata groups that can provide helpful details about the workflow transformations and data products. Pedigree Graph is a tool in Multiscale Chemical Science (CMCS) and Multi-Scale Chemistry (MSC); it uses a portal to view multi-dimensional provenance. The My Grid tool displays graphs based representations of RDF-coded provenance by using Haystack. Provenance Explorer, reliable provenance visualization tool that creates customized dynamic views of scientific provenance data depending on the user requirements and access privileges.

In another study [8], Chen collected e-science provenance data, which yielded an OPM visualization Direct Acyclic Graph (DAG). The temporal representation of provenance graphs has generated partitions that maintain temporal order between node subsets by using the Logical-P algorithm [8]. Graph annotations and fully labeled graphs are visualization tools for representation. Temporal representation failures can be detected in workflow executions or the provenance capture.

III. APPLICATION FEATURES

Features of study like ontology model, layout components, use cases and visualization tool are presented in this section.

A. *Ontology*

Ontologies are at the heart of any semantic technology. An ontology is formally defined as a set of specifications associated with a concept. Many researchers use ontologies as mechanisms for sharing and reusing information. Ontologies can easily express relationships between identifiers. They share many qualities with knowledge representation systems.

PROV-O: The PROV ontology (PROV-O) is an OWL-based ontology that allows PROV-data models to use RDF mapping developed by W3C. The PROV-O terms are defined as classes and properties, and they are grouped into three categories: starting point terms, expansion terms and qualifying relationship terms to provide an incremental input to the ontology [11].

Starting point term classes and properties are used to creating simple provenance descriptions that can be detailed using the terms of other categories. Ultimately, starting point term classes are a small set of classes and properties that create simple, initial provenance descriptions. PROV-O categories are listed and defined below:

- **Entity**: An entity is a conceptual, digital, physical or virtual object with specific aspects. It can be real or imaginary.
- **Activity**: An activity is an action that repeats over a period-of-time and is acted upon by entities; actions may include processing, consuming, modifying, transforming, using, relocating or generating entities.

- **Agent**: An agent is an operation (or operator) that is responsible for activities, for the existence of an entity, and for the activities of other agents.

The three main classes are correlated and use the properties that are illustrated in Figure 1.

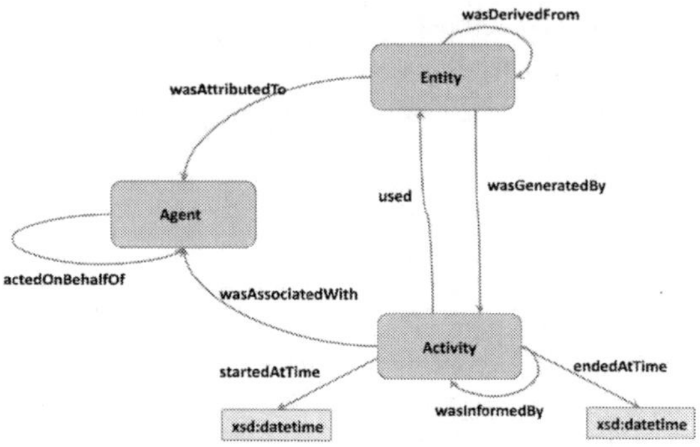

Figure 1. Starting Point classes and their properties. This figure is obtained from the PROV-O Ontology document in [11].

Extended classes and properties provide additional actions that may be used to relate classes in the Starting Point category. Qualified classes and properties provide elaborate information about relations using Starting Point and Expanded features.

B. *Layouts*

A layout is a main component in data provenance visualization; it improves the comprehension of a user. A layout depends on user requirements and the origin of provenance data [9]. A researcher often needs to see multiple layouts and determine the layout , which is the most meaningful and relevant. As an example, the hierarchical provenance visualization layout is a provenance graph that is separated into layers according to relationships; the most important relationships appear at the top layer and the final results appear at the bottom of visualization.

Figures 2, 3 and 4 shows customized layout examples. As mentioned earlier, in provenance visualization a circle denotes a process while a square denotes an artifact [15].

C. *Use Cases*

Provenance visualization concepts are difficult to develop. To have a general visualization technique, care must be taken to prevent the loss of connection between an application domain's specific requirements and data provenance interpretation.

The main purpose of this study is to develop several visualization concepts and evaluate them based on concrete requirements. The provenance community supports the development of different visualization techniques and evaluates them for possible application domains.

In the proposed research, to define scope, we outline potential application areas and their associated Interactive Provenance Visualization solution requirements.

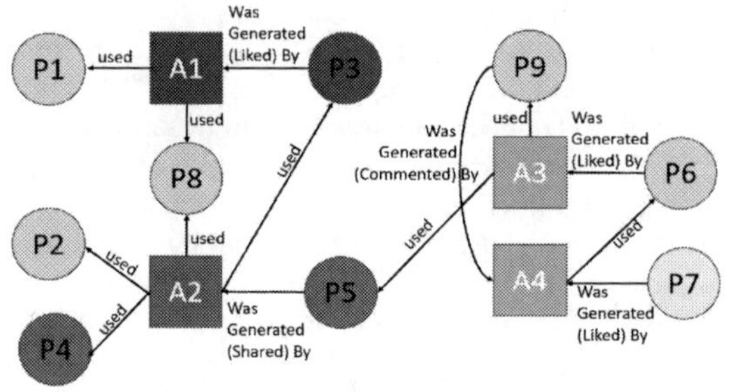

Figure 2. The time-to-complete process and artifacts

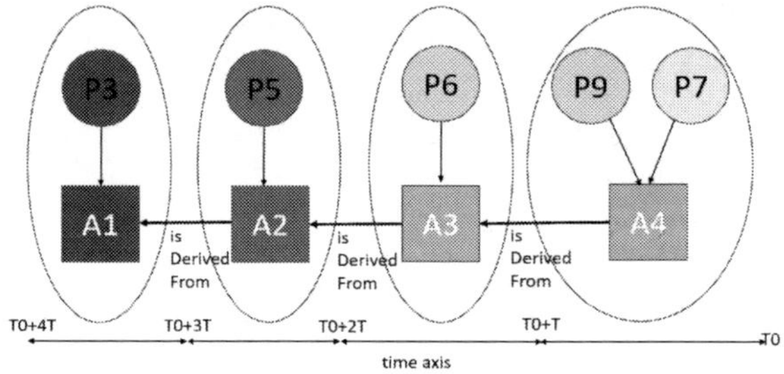

Figure 3. The time-to-complete individual processes and artifact relationships

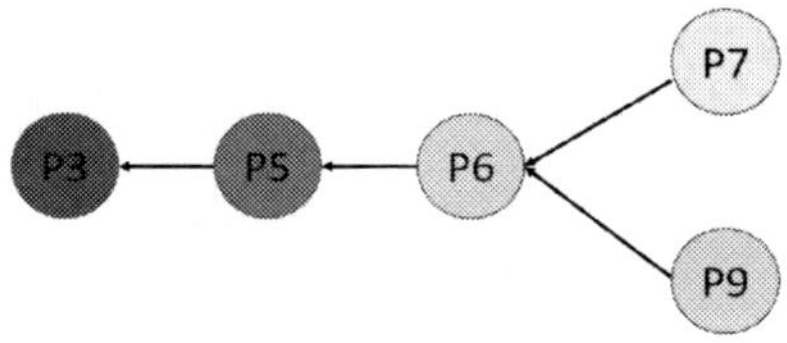

Figure 4. Lineage or process order

1) *Social Media Provenance Visualization:*

We have witnessed social media growing at an unprecedented rate in the last decade. Social media has inherent characteristics and pathways that enable nefarious activities, which could hinder its growth. Social media provide users with a platform to communicate with a large audience in a simple way. The unprecedented scale by, which users can communicate and the rate of information transfer is virtually unseen in conventional media like newspaper, radio, T.V. Social media data is user-generated, massive, distributed, noisy, dynamic, and unstructured-in-nature.

Social media data is primarily available in the form of an individual users' attributes, user-user connections (links), or user-generated content such as text, photos, and videos. The visualization requirements of age-based social life data from creation to archiving is one of the motivations of this work [10].

2) E-Science Provenance Visualization:

e-Science is computational, science-intensive data found in highly distributed network environments. Research into e-Science provenance focuses on the capturing, modeling, and storage of provenance data. In e-Science, considerably larger volumes of data with higher complexity exists because their systems are continuously running for extended periods to support scientific experimentation [8]. One of the motivations of this research is to find methods to improve visualization data provenance in the e-Science domain.

D. CYTOSCAPE

Cytoscape is an open source software platform that provides visualization tools using the interaction between networks and biologic pathways to integrate multiple networks that have expression profiles, annotations, and state data. Cytoscape was developed and designed for molecular biological research, but later became a general platform for complex visualization and analysis. Cytoscape's basic set of features include analysis, integration and visualization; they are provided by the core distribution of Cytoscape.

One of the strongest features of Cytoscape is that it allows the use of plugins to develop new visualization techniques. By supporting detailed and overlaying visualization with supplementary tools, Cytoscape is a suitable development environment for general provenance visualization. Provenance graph visualization that can interact with a Karma provenance server to extract provenance in XML form, can be created via a Cytoscape plugin [9].

IV. METHODOLOGY

In this study, temporal representation and stream data provenance visualization will be analyzed. We will research how to achieve provenance visualization of temporal provenance data by developing a set of visualization techniques and methodologies. Real-time visualization and offline visualization will be implemented. We apply developed methods on test case scenarios in social media domains.

Chen's provenance visualization steps will be used as a base for our test case scenarios [9].

A. Incremental Loading

Provenance data can be very large and dense. The lineage records or PROV-O annotations alone provide an opportunity to capture additional information about data execution or creation. To support visualization over large graphs, a system must be able to read XML-formatted provenance graphs with and without annotations. A KOMADU system will be the basis of this research. A KOMADU system is a data capture and visualization system. It was developed for scientific data provenance in the Data to Insight Center at Indiana University. KOMADU generates PROV-O compliant XML files that doesn't have annotations for Processes or Artifacts.

For scalability purposes, we will first investigate how to manage scalability in our developed solution. Provenance data features, i.e., lifecycle metadata on activities, will be reduced to create a reduced-dimension visualization. We will eliminate redundant data and generate provenance data partitions to group different visualization items to increase user's perception [9]. Data scalability for the proposed temporal representation process can be improved by using MapReduce programming paradigm [16].

B. Customized Layouts

Customized layouts developed in Chen's study include extending the hierarchical layout algorithm that sorts sibling nodes, grouping layout algorithms, creating concatenated string-embedded layout algorithms for provenance data like a history chain [9], which will be referenced in our study. Research on the improvement of existing layouts and the development of new customized layouts will be realized by considering user navigation models, HCI principles and provenance data nature.

The Bilkent University data visualization research group [13] has several projects on compound graph visualization based on several different customized layout displays. Their layout model handles the followings:

- levels of nesting
- inter-graph edges span multiple levels of nesting
- non-leaf nodes links in the nesting hierarchy

C. Visual Style

In data provenance visualization, Chen has created a default visual style for provenance graphs, using magenta for artifacts, different predefined colors for a different type of edges [9].

New visualization styles, according to HCI studies on related attributes like size, color, etc., and Gestalt rules parameters, are subject to the study. We will research how to achieve provenance visualization of temporal provenance data that is associated with different existing visualization techniques and methodologies. User attraction and perception towards the customized visualizations will be handled by user HCI evaluations and will be used to improve the visualization system. Gestalt rules will be examined to find adaptation-related principles to increase usability of the system [9].

D. Abstract View

Provenance relationships are complex graphs that overwhelm researchers. To eliminate and summarize provenance visualization, Chen's two approaches are:

- Clustering neighbor nodes
- Eliminating process/artifact

The process of clustering neighboring nodes into a single node was introduced using a plug-in in Cystoscape. This approach is helpful while exploring a provenance graph and dealing with graphs that have many nodes [8].

In the second-phase, a process of elimination removes process nodes that connect two artifact nodes with a "was generated by" incoming edge and "used" outgoing edge. The process node is changed by a new "was derived from" edge. This process of graph abstraction and pruning removes any unnecessary info and limits the graph size

In this section, we will study new approaches for summarization and elimination processes of provenance data. Using MapReduce programming paradigm, data abstraction on the proposed temporal representation process can be enhanced.

E. Graph Comparison

To satisfy provenance analysis, graph comparison is a key process. In Chen's study, Direct Clustering Algorithm (DCA) is used to compare two provenance graphs by finding the best matched and unmatched nodes [9]. The DCA algorithm basically depends on the order of inputs. For example, B to A is not same as A to B. In this research, an improved DCA algorithm will be developed and implemented to compare graphs. The comparison of more than two graphs is also an important task, for reasons below.

- Provenance data can exist in a high-dimensional space. This causes graphs to have thousands of nodes and attributes, which makes clustering of such data tremendously difficult
- Difficult to locate both structural and nonstructural information and combine it into a single uniform attribute space

V. HUMAN MACHINE INTERACTION ASPECTS

In this study, we propose an improved data provenance visualization system that involve user in the visualization process by capturing and analyzing user's attention and perception level towards specific visualization types and methodologies.

A. User Involved Visualization

The proposed system involves the user; the user can improve usability and increase the system's effectiveness. The system will support user-based navigation by capturing a user's attraction to and perception of a specific set of layouts/methodologies. At first, the distinct existing layouts will be studied to visualize big provenance data. If necessary, depending on the characterization of the provenance data and user requirements, new customized layouts will be introduced.

B. HCI Model Construction

We will measure the user's perception and analyze the level of provenance visualization for a set of abstract layouts by capturing and analyzing a user's attention, attraction and perception level. After that, the correlation between the attraction/perception level and type of provenance data visualization will be determined to find suitable layouts/visual styles for specific kind of requirements or specific data domains. A layout/visual style HCI model will be constructed to verify this process. In the user perception level, the following 2 methods are proposed:

1. Questionnaire: a set of questions based on experimental protocols will be asked to analyze attraction/perception level
2. Eye Tracking: gaze parameters are used to extract perception information based on literature parameters.

VI. CONCLUSION AND FUTURE WORK

We have discussed provenance and techniques for provenance visualization. We are interested in providing an effective solution to visualize and analyze semantic provenance data by adhering to HCI principles. Efficient visualization helps users to analyze and understand data using valid evidence. Visualization makes complex data more accessible, understandable and usable.

According to provenance data interpretation requirements, the development of provenance visualization is difficult to create. One of the most enduring challenges is to maintain the relationship between the data and its application.

Our improved data provenance visualization system that places the user in the loop, captures and analyzes the user's attention and perception level while he/she reviews specific visualization types and methodologies suggested by the system. The system then analyzes this information to determine the best type of visualization. In this way, the user determines the visualization process autonomously.

The goal of the system is to help the user navigate exploration provenance visualization. A user's mind map typically determines what is going on in an experiment. A mind map model will be used to interact with the user and explore visualization activities.

The major contributions of this research include the following:

- We develop an effective user-navigated provenance visualization system. We will introduce a temporal provenance data visualization solution with aspects of HCI research. Our approach will be based on user preferences and perception levels after reviewing several visualization layouts and types of provenance visualization. To increase the effectiveness of visualization, a user's attraction/perception level will be captured and analyzed.
- Domain independent visualization: We will abide by the recommendations of W3C's PROV-O specifications for provenance representation. Since

PROV-O specifications are domain-independent, the representation does not provide domain-specific vocabulary for our case study domains (e.g. social media data). Ontologies that define related domains will be introduced for specific domain representations.

- Customized Visualization Layouts and methodologies: In this paper, to understand large-scale data provenance, new abstract layouts, based on various studies, will be developed to provide customized layouts to the user.
- A highly scalable and high-performance visualization system will be used in our test case scenarios. We will deal with critically large scale provenance data. To make our system scalable, we will use techniques like incremental loading and compression. The effectiveness of visualization, graph matching, and partitioning will be improved to provide faster query times in provenance graph data.
- Real-time support for the continuous and real-time analysis of Big Provenance data and stream data visualization will be provided via a series of stream processing techniques. User-assisted real-time visualization, anomaly detection, and root cause tracing will be analyzed in terms of provenance graphs.
- A platform-independent PROV-O Cystoscope plug-in will be developed to visualize provenance based on different layouts and visual style elements.

Our future work will be focusing on the details of the methodology that we briefly outlined in this discussion paper. Our work remains in applying our research to the use cases and conducting experiments based on our research methodology.

ACKNOWLEDGMENT

This study is being supported by the TUBITAK-3501-Career Development Program (CAREER) with the Project ID: 114E781. We would like to thank Yildiz Technical University Software Quality Laboratory for supporting this research and allowing us to use their computer facilities for this study. As always, we are grateful for the help of the extended team of our department.

REFERENCES

[1] B. Glavic, "Big Data Provenance: Challenges and Implications for Benchmarking", WBDB 2012 - 2nd Workshop on Big Data Benchmarking, pp. 72–80.

[2] Y. L. Simmhan, B. Plale, and D. Gannon, "A Survey of Data Provenance Techniques", Technical Report IUB-CS-TR618

[3] Oxford English Dictionary (OED), "The fact of coming from some particular source or quarter, source, derivation", (2017, April 20) Retrieved from http://en.wikipedia.org/wiki/ Provenance.

[4] R. Hasan, R. Sion, and M. Winslett, M., "Preventing History Forgery with Secure Provenance", ACM Transactions on Storage, 5(12), May 2009.

[5] E. Olshannikova, A. Ometov, Y. Koucheryavy, and T. Olsson, "Visualizing Big Data with Augmented and Virtual Reality: Challenges and Research Agenda", Journal of Big Data, 2015.

[6] R. Tard'io, A. Mat'e, and J., Trujillo, "An Iterative Methodology for Big Data Management",2015 IEEE International Conference on Big Data (Big Data), 2015, pp 545-550.

[7] J. Steele, and N. Illinsky, "Beautiful Visualization, Looking at data Through the Eyes of Experts", O'Reilly Media, 2010.

[8] P. Chen, and B. A. Plale, "Big Data Provenance Analysis and Visualization", IEEE/ACM International Symposium on Cluster, Cloud and Grid Computing, 15th, 2015.

[9] P. Chen, B. Plale, Y. W. Cheah, D. Ghoskal, S. Jensen, and Y. Luo, "Visualization of Network Data Provenance", 978-1-4673-2371-0/12/$31.00, IEEE, 2012.

[10] G. Barbier, Z. Feng, P. Gundecha, and H. Liu, "Provenance Data in Social Media" , Synthesis Lectures on Data Mining and Knowledge Discovery, 2013.

[11] T. Lebo, S. Sahoo, and D. McGuinness, "W3C PROV-O: The PROV Ontology Proposed Recommendation 12.03.2013", Technical report, W3C, March 2013.

[12] M. Kunde, H. Bergmeyer and A. Schreiber, "Requirements for a Provenance Visualization Component", IPAW, 2008.

[13] U. Dogruoz, E. Giral, A. Cetintas, A. Civril, and E. Demir, "A Layout Algorithm for Undirected Compound Graphs", Information Sciences, 2009, pp 980-994.

[14] P. Chen, and B. Plale, "Visualizing Large Scale Scientific Data Provenance", 2012 Super Computing Conference, High Performance Computing, Networking, Storage and Analysis (SCC) Workshop, USA, 2012.

[15] P. Chen, B. Plale, and M. S. Aktas, "Temporal Representation for Scientific Data Provenance", 978-1-4673-4466-1/12/$31.00, IEEE, 2012, pp 1-8.

[16] J. Dean, and S. Ghemawat, "MapReduce: A Flexible Data Processing Tool." Commun. ACM 53(1), (2010), pp 72-77.

A Large Scale Synthetic Social Provenance Database

Mohamed Jehad Baeth, Mehmet S. Aktas
Computer Engineering,
Yıldız Technical University
Istanbul / Turkey
Email: mohamed.jehad.baeth@std.yildiz.edu.tr , mehmet@ce.yildiz.edu.tr

***Abstract*—Provenance about data derivations in social networks is commonly referred as social provenance, which helps in estimating data quality, tracking of resources, and understanding the ways of information diffusion in social networks. We observed several challenges related to provenance in the social network domain. First, provenance collection systems capture provenance on the fly; however, their collection mechanism may be faulty and have dropped provenance notifications. Hence, social provenance records may be partial, partitioned, or simply inaccurate. Although current provenance systems deliver a source of real provenance data, these systems do not provide a controlled provenance generation environment; and there are few that contain provenance with failures. Synthetic provenance databases are available in other domains, such as e-Science; but there is also a need for such a database in the social networking domain. To address these challenges, this study introduces a large-scale noisy synthetic social provenance database, which includes a high volume of large-size social provenance graphs. It also introduces metrics that can be used to capture such vital information as provenance for calculating data quality and user credibility.**

***Index Terms*— data quality, large-scale database, provenance, social networks, synthetic workflow simulation.**

I. INTRODUCTION

Social networks are described as online communities and groups of individuals communicating in a Web-based environment, in which their users can interact with each other by posting, commenting, or showing sentiment actions provided by the social network. In addition, social media have been used for gathering information about large-scale events, such as fires, earthquakes, and other disasters, all of which impact government and nongovernment organizations at the local, national, or even international level. Individuals also use social media to find reliable information about what is going on around them and thus are able to leverage new information as quickly as possible [1].

Social media deliver users a large-scale and easy-to-use platform that cannot be achieved using traditional media. Understanding information propagation in social media provides additional context, such as knowing the information originator and its transition modifications until the end of its life cycle. The normal social media user applies such knowledge to evaluate the trustworthiness and correctness of this information [2]. As in real life, the quality of information or objects created in social networks value is affected by its provenance.

We observed several challenges related to provenance in the social network domain. First, existing social networks do not provide any programming interface for accessing the provenance information of the data published therein; and there are no existing mechanisms for identifying and tracing data objects. Provenance collection systems capture provenance on the fly. However, their collection mechanisms may be faulty and have dropped provenance notifications. Hence, social provenance records may be partial, partitioned, or simply inaccurate. Incompleteness and inconsistency of provenance records, if they exist, are a challenge for analyzing provenance datasets [3], [4]. There is a need for a synthetically created social provenance database that is modeled on real social interactions and populated with failure patterns. Although synthetic provenance databases are available in other domains, such as e-Science, there is a need for such a database in the social networking domain as well. Second, social provenance records can grow large quickly because of the high number of participating actors. Although the number of services involved in e-Science workflows is in the order of hundreds, this number can grow to a scale in the order of thousands or millions of social interactions that take place on social media.

To address the abovementioned challenges, this study introduces a large-scale noisy synthetic social provenance database, which includes a high volume of large social provenance graphs. The study also introduces metrics that can be used to capture such vital information as provenance for calculating data quality and user credibility.

The remainder of this paper is organized as follows: Section 2 reviews related work. Section 3 discusses the social provenance metrics that are proposed to be included in social provenance datasets. Section 4 examines our methodological way of creating a synthetic social provenance dataset. Analysis of the generated provenance dataset is addressed in Section 5.

II. RELATED WORK

Several provenance systems currently exist that function as a source of provenance data. However, these systems do not deliver a controlled provenance generation environment; and there are few examples of such systems that can generate provenance with failures [5]. On the other hand, there are several synthetic workloads that have been developed for many different purposes. Some were used in the area of distributed systems [6]–[8]; some were generated for use in the networking research area [9], [10]; and each was used to evaluate performance, as well as for benchmarking purposes, in their respective areas. Lately, there has been increasing interest in generating synthetic social workloads in the social network domain. Although social networks have high availability, sometimes the collection of social network data may not be feasible due to privacy concerns, where access to such data is restricted to analysts. Some of the introduced synthetic social network generators rely on samples of similar datasets, such as in [11], where a social media dataset can be cloned from an existing set of statistics. Another interesting example of a recent synthetic social network generator [12] simulates the LinkedIn social network. Here, the generation process had two stages. The first stage was the construction of the base network. The second was the addition of LinkedIn endorsements where users can publicly verify that people they know are qualified in the skill that they claim for themselves. However, neither of these simulated network data attempt to model failures. The unreliability of the protocol between the provenance tool and the application are discussed in [5], where a 10 GB database with several scientific workflows was generated using WORKEM, a workflow emulator tool [13]. The database was generated based on real-life e-Science workflows. This study used the Karma provenance capture and management system to manage the scientific provenance datasets, which were compatible with the Open Provenance Model (OPM). The use of such a simulated database in unmanaged workflows is discussed in [14].

To the best of our knowledge, there are no generated workloads and synthetic provenance datasets that have been developed specifically for social provenance research. This study introduces a large-scale noisy synthetic social provenance database, including a high volume of large-size social provenance graphs. It also introduces metrics that can be used to capture such vital information as provenance, which can be used for calculating data quality and user credibility in social networks.

III. SOCIAL PROVENANCE DATABASE REQUIREMENTS

Cheah *et al.* identified several requirements that must be met for a provenance database [5]: large scale, diversity, and realism. A provenance database should consist of a significant number of provenance records to support research at scale and should be drawn from varied workflows that have different characteristics in terms of size, breadth, and length. Also, the composition of workflows used to generate the provenance should have failure characteristics. In addition to abovementioned requirements, we added another requirement: usability. We argue that a provenance database should address not only the generic requirements, but also its domain-dependent requirements.

In this study, we generated a social provenance database that meets the abovementioned requirements as follows: We met the diversity requirement by generating three different types of social provenance, each representing a different scale of social interactions. The categories of social interactions that we used are 100, 1K, and 5K. For each type of social interaction, we created a hundred social-workflow execution traces. We met the realism requirement by producing the same dataset with a 10 percent rate of notification failure and a 10 percent execution failure rate. (Cheah *et al.* generated a noisy 10 GB provenance database with failure characteristics [5] for scientific datasets. Their study included failure characteristics for both provenance-notification failures and workflow-execution failures. Note that we do not consider the latter, since a social workflow is not dependent on a specific workflow. Finally, we met the usability requirement by taking into account the major research problems in the social network domain. Here, we are particularly motivated by research problems that have been investigated by the PRONALIZ project, a Turkish National Science Foundation–funded research project [15]. PRONALIZ investigates the use of provenance in social media to develop methodologies for detection of information pollution and violation of copyrights. We created a publicly accessible Web page for this database and made it available for download at [16]. Throughout the experience of using social media, it can be inferred that its users face two major problems. One is the determination of data authenticity and quality. It is challenging to rate the reliability of a source in a user-generated content platform, where sources might propagate false information, causing the spread of a polluted material. Thus, it would be difficult to determine the actual quality of data and how much weight the data should be given. The second problem is the uncertainty of data visibility due to the dynamic nature of content shared on social media, in which changes can occur on the platform's privacy settings or at the user level by applying more restrictive privacy measures. These policies determine copyrights on a user's shared data. User data, which are intended to be disseminated in a friend circle, may be spread via resharing within the social network. Users are not aware of who can see their data or apply a process to the data. Thus, problems like violation of copyrights can arise. To create a social provenance database that can be used by researchers to address these problems, we identified a number of metrics.

To obtain a better understanding of metrics and an improved definition of the credibility or trustworthiness of an information source, we first need to present our social network provenance model, which we believe can be used as a generic model for provenance representation on all existing social networks.

Users in social networks tend to provide numerous pieces of information about themselves, which varies from one social network to another. For example, a Twitter user has a dedicated area for only his or her bio, location, personal website URL, and date of birth, whereas a Facebook user can provide much more information, such as personal interests, political affiliation, books read, movies watched, educational background, and schools attended. Table 1 shows some of these attributes or types of information and the percentage of users who have added this information to their Facebook profiles and left it public for everyone to see, according to [17].

TABLE I. LIST OF ATTRIBUTES AND PERCENTAGE OF USERS WHO REVEAL THEM ON FACEBOOK.

Attribute	Percentage
Current City	30.17
Gender	81.77
Relationship Status	26.24
Education and Word	25.13
Email	1.32
Interested in	18.66
Music	45.77
Movies	27.92
Activities	18.74
Television	33.30

The availability of such information plays an important role in the creation of social network provenance metrics. The metrics used in generated social workflows are as follows:

A. *User Information Provenance Availability Measure*

The availability of a user's personal information indicates trustworthiness of this user as for Social network user getting information from another well-known user lends credibility to this information. The availability function, as defined by [17], objectively quantifies progress in obtaining a user's personal attribute values. The availability function describes how much user provenance metadata are available for the statement of interest, in that it allows a user to perform a simple comparison of search strategies employed to obtain provenance attributes. It also allows prioritizing attributes by giving each a specific weight, where the sum of the weights of all attributes is 1; and an attribute with a weight of 0 will have no effect on the outcome of the measure.

B. *User Information Provenance Legitimacy Measure*

Finding a user provenance attribute might provide some insight; however, a certainty measure of those attributes is needed to indicate validity of found attributes. This can be made by matching found attribute values with attributes found in other sources. The legitimacy function is computed by averaging the number of independent social media sites used to verify the attribute and is proposed to quantify whether or not the provenance attribute values found are valid [17].

C. *User Information Provenance Social Popularity Measure (Prestige Centrality)*

Typically, a high-profile social network user, who might represent a celebrity or an important individual, has a large number of followers. In other words, a famous user enjoys high popularity, indicated by having many ties with others. In the case of an undirected graph, which is the situation in some social networks, such as Facebook, this metric can instead be represented by centrality, where an actor with a high degree of importance maintains numerous contacts with other network users. A central user occupies a structural position (network location) that serves as a source or conduit for larger volumes of information exchange and other resource transactions with other actors. This can be measured by simply calculating the summation of each actor's number of degrees in a nondirected graph and then normalizing it by dividing it by the maximum number of degrees allowed by the social network.

D. *Information Provenance Social Impact Measure*

The importance of a piece of information may be inferred by the number of social activities associated with it. For example, a tweet with a high number of Favor, Retweet, and Reply operations may reflect the controversial nature of that information.

Thus, we calculate data proximity in the context of a user's relationships by measuring the social interactions of users who are not directly connected to the subject, divided by the total number of interactions on a piece of information, and dividing the set of all directly not connected users who have performed a social action on a piece of information posted by a user to the set of all unique users who have performed a social action

E. *Information Prominence or Proximity Prestige*

Thus, we calculate data proximity in the context of a user's relations by measuring the social interactions of users who are not directly connected to the subject, divided by the total number of interactions on a piece of information, and dividing the set of all directly not connected users who have performed a social action on a piece of information posted by a user by the set of all unique users who have performed a social action.

F. *The Impact of a Post on a User's Prestige*

An increase in the number of followers in response to a post on a social network might provide an indication of the importance of these data. For example, on Twitter a nonprestigious user may gain a very large number of followers by posting valuable information or introducing a piece of information. This should show the impact of the information published on the prestige of its publisher. Table 2, below, shows different categorizations of the presented metrics.

TABLE II. LIST OF SOCIAL PROVENANCE ATTRIBUTES CAPTURED IN THE SOCIAL PROVENANCE DATABASE

Metric	Graph Type		Perspective		Time Dependent
	Directed	Non-Directed	Data in the Center	User in the Center	
Verifiability	X	X		X	
Popularity	Prestige	Centrality		X	
Availability	X	X		X	
Social Impact	X	X	X		
Prestige	X		X		X
Artifact Impact	X		X	X	X

IV. GENERATION OF THE SYNTHETIC DATASET

Normally, a scientific workflow describes the accomplishment of a scientific objective process, which is expressed by the task being done and its dependencies. Typically, scientific workflow tasks are computational steps for scientific simulations or data analysis steps [18]. On the other hand, a social workflow is always bound to run on a social network. Its operations and data are defined by the social network itself. In turn, each social network names the social operations and data formats differently. To obtain a dataset with controllable characteristics that capture the nature of information propagation on social media, we created a fully synthetic dataset imitating Twitter. This synthetic dataset was designed to meet criteria that may not be achievable when collecting data from a Twitter live feed due to users' privacy settings and availability of different types of personal information, which can impose real issues when evaluating to-be-developed misinformation-detection algorithms. We choose to use W3C's PROV for provenance and metadata modeling rather than its predecessor Open Provenance Model OPM. In this study, we introduce a set of properties that can be used to map the social operations to PROV-O entities. Table 3 lists these properties along with their explanations. Fig. 1 shows how we mapped Social Provenance attributes to each PROV-O entity.

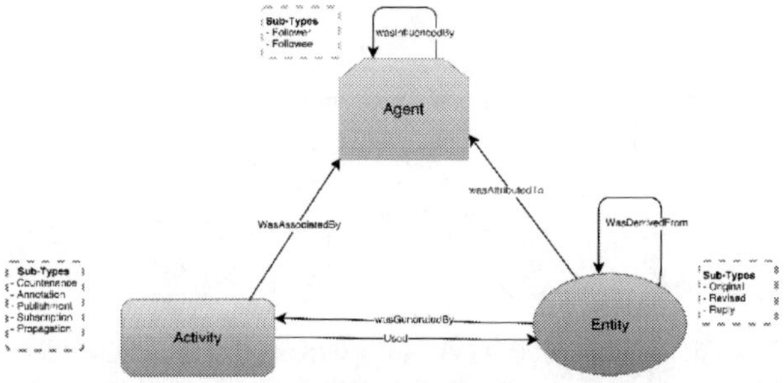

Figure 1. PROV-O Specification based Provenance Nodes and social provenance sub-types.

TABLE III. TERMINOLOGY IN THE PROPOSED SOCIAL NETWORK PROVENANCE MODEL

Sub-Type (Properties)	Explanation	Equivalence in Social Networks
Countenance	To support or approve a statement or an entity or its content	Like(v), Favor(v)
Annotation	to remark, make an observation or make criticism	Reply, Comment
Publishment	To issue textual or graphical materials for public distribution	Post(v), tweet(v)
Subscription	To follow or watch the movement or course/progress of something or someone	Follow, get notified
Propagation	To reproduce transmit, spread or disseminate.	Share, Retweet
Follower	A person who follows another and becomes a subscriber to his/her feed of tweets.	Follower, Liker
Followee	A person who is being tracked on a social media website or application.	User
Original	The blog or post in its state at time of creation by its original creator	Tweet(n), Post(n)
Revised	Reconsider and alter (something) in the light of further evidence.	Retweet, Shared post

Twitter is described to be the largest data source openly accessible to everyone through its stream and search API. Thus, it is the source of much recent research. Currently, many tools have been developed based on mining the large amount of data for information such as tracking earthquakes, world health and the spread of communicable diseases, or even providing real-time information during crises by extracting information from users' Twitter feeds. In short, Twitter is currently used to mobilize emotionally and physically. Social workflows represent an abstract view of the various social patterns observed on Twitter. It can be understood, visualized, and represented in different formats; thus, analysis of it may also be conducted.

A simple workflow normally represents tweets of users who have no intention of engaging or creating a general topic by not using a hashtag. Such tweets usually tend to generate minimal engagement limited to the user's followers. However, high-prestige users with very large numbers of followers can stimulate many interactions and create a widespread impression. On the other hand, we define a composite social workflow as a group of separate workflows, where all users are using a unified topic. Generally, in such events, the majority of the participating users employ a global hashtag or the directed mention of a celebrity's official Twitter account. An example of such social interactions is solidarity and debate where normally an opinion-based community is polarized [19]. Users' interaction dynamics and patterns were observed and analyzed in different social events than belongs to different topic [20]. The study shows different characteristics of the collected social workflows observed from real Twitter data. The possible numbers of user engagements and social interactions in our generated social workflows were derived from these observations, as shown in Table 4. We generated workflows for each of the described categories, in which each workflow is executed four times with different failure-generation modules.

TABLE IV. GENERATED SOCIAL WORKFLOWS USERS' POOL AND NUMBER OF SOCIAL INTERACTIONS

Users Pool	Number of Social Interactions	Number of generated workflows
10	10	100
10	100	100
100	100	400
1000	1000	500
5000	5000	500
5000	10000	100

A. Database Generation Framework

The four components used in the creation of the provenance database were WorkflowGen, WorkflowSim, ProvToolbox, and the Komadu provenance repository. Fig. 2 shows an overview of the framework.

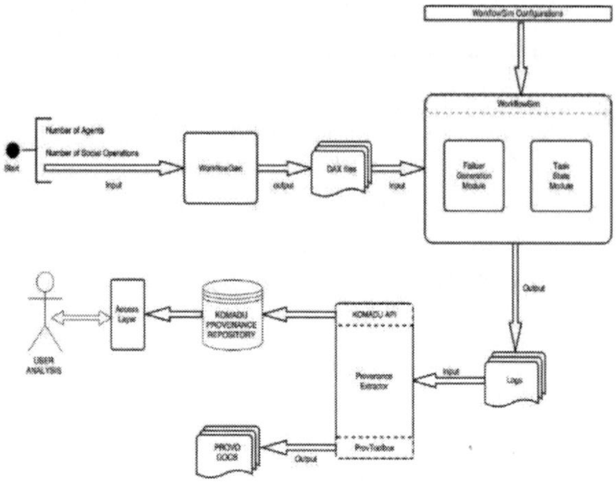

Figure 2. Social Provenance Dataset Generation Framework

Komadu [21] is a standalone provenance capture and visualization system for capturing, representing, and manipulating provenance. It uses the W3C PROV standard [22] considered to be the successor to the Karma [23] provenance capture system.

WorkflowSim is an open-source workflow simulator. It models workflows using a DAG model and supports implementations of some popular dynamic and static workflow schedulers and task-clustering algorithms [24]. WorkflowSim also has failure modeling that supports two failure types on both the job and task levels. Failure rates generated by WorkflowSim are modifiable according to user preference [24]. WorkflowGen, on the other hand, is a tool developed by the same team for the purpose of creating custom DAX workflows to facilitate evaluation of workflow algorithms and systems on a range of workflow sizes, thus creating realistic synthetic workflows resembling those used in the real world similar to the ones gathered from Twitter [25]. We used WorkflowSim as a simulation environment to execute the DAX files generated by WorkflowGen. DAX files represents the abstract description of a single workflow in XML format. The provenance recorded from the logs of the simulation were generated using ProvToolBox and put into Komadu [26].

B. Generated Workflows

The client responsible of the generation of random tweet data consider that any social scenario, no matter how many users are engaged in it or how many social activities has been made upon it, if visualized will be shaped as a multiforked sequential graph. First, the client keeps track of entities linked to the main workflow created either by retweeting or replying. In addition, the client considers only social activities that may be executed on a tweet in that context: Tweet, Like, Retweet, and Reply. The client also creates a pool of agents, where each agent has its own set of popularity, availability, and verifiability values. Finally, the client considers that every social operation is affected by the last social operation made on the same entity. Clients start by creating an initial activity representing a tweet operation, which leads to the creation of the original tweet entity. From that point, the client randomly invokes social operations until the wanted number of operations is reached. The following table shows the Prov-O representation of relationships between entities, agents, and activities created at every iteration, depending on the social operation type.

TABLE V. PROV-O REPRESENTATION OF SOCIAL OPERATIONS AND ENTITIES

Social Operation	Prov-O representation
Post	Generation(tweet_activity, main_tweet) Attribution(main_tweet, agent1) Association(tweet_activity, main_tweet)
Like	Association(new_agent, like_activity) Usage(like_activity, tweet_x)
Retweet	Association(new_agent, retweet_activity) Generation(retweet_activity, new_tweet) Usage(retweet_activity, tweet_x) Attribution(new_tweet, new_agent) Derivation (new_tweet, tweet_x)
Reply	Association(new_agent, reply_activity) Generation(reply_activity, new_tweet) Usage(reply_activity, tweet_x) Attribution(new_tweet, new_agent)

We generated 1600 workflows with 100, 1000, 5000, and 10000 social operations and 500 workflows for every category except for the 10K we generated 100 workflows. The workflows were generated with different sizes of agent pools, ranging from 10 to 5000 agents, and then executed in the following forms:

- Social workflows with complete successful runs.
- Social workflows with simulation execution faults generated using WorkflowSim's fault-generation module, which represents missing notifications coming from the social network to specific actions.
- Social workflows with provenance collection faults, in which some of the provenance data extracted are dropped. This type of fault represents errors that might happen during provenance ingestion into the data repository. The dropped provenance data are selected randomly during workflow simulation at a 10 percent rate.
- Social workflows with faults on both execution and provenance collection levels.

We observed 6400 workflow executions. Fig. 3 shows the distribution of workflows by execution case. In total, we had 1936 successfully executed workflow provenances, 1246 workflows with execution failures, 1917 workflow execution provenances with 10 percent notification drops, and 1283 workflow execution provenances with both failure types. The final size of the dataset is around 10 GB of *.provn* provenance files.

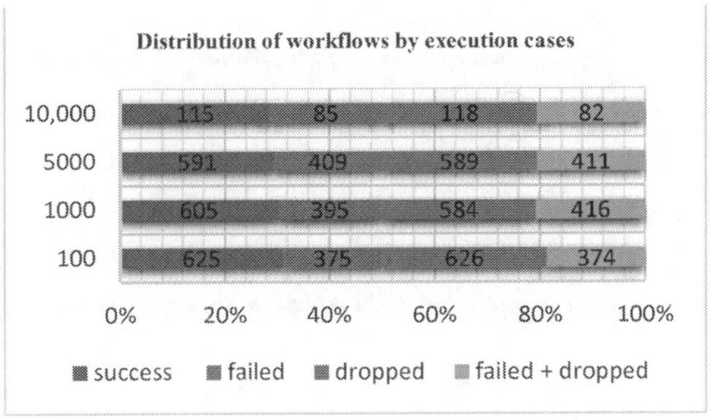

Figure 3. Distribution of Workflows by execution cases

Our observations of individual faulty runs also show that the larger a workflow, the higher the failure rate and the dropped notification rate. The following figures below provide samples from all kinds of generated provenance data of all types of social workflows. Fig. 4 shows the visualization of 10 successful social operations workflow runs.

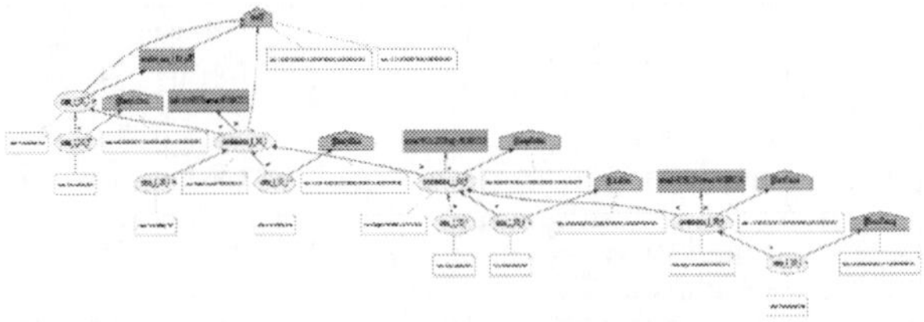

Figure 4. provenance visualization of a successful workflow run

Fig. 5 shows the provenance visualization of 10 social operations workflows with provenance collection failures. It may be observed that some of the relations are missing within the provenance visualization presented in Fig. 2.

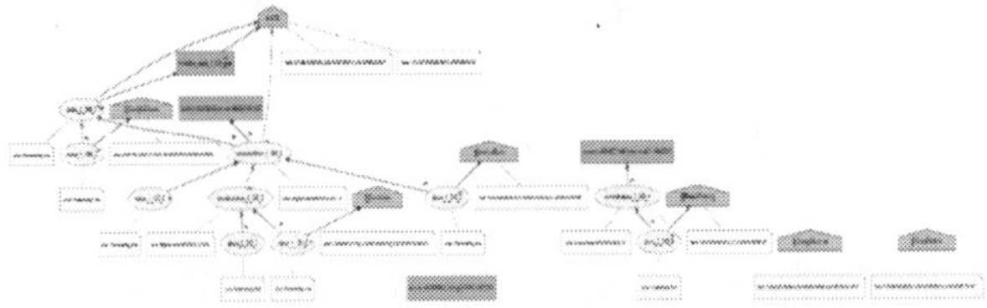

Figure 5. provenance visualization of a workflow execution with provenance collection 10% error rate

Fig. 6 shows the provenance visualization of the same 10 social operations workflow executions with errors on both the notification collection level and provenance ingestion level. Missing activities and missing dangling entities are both observed in the visualization below.

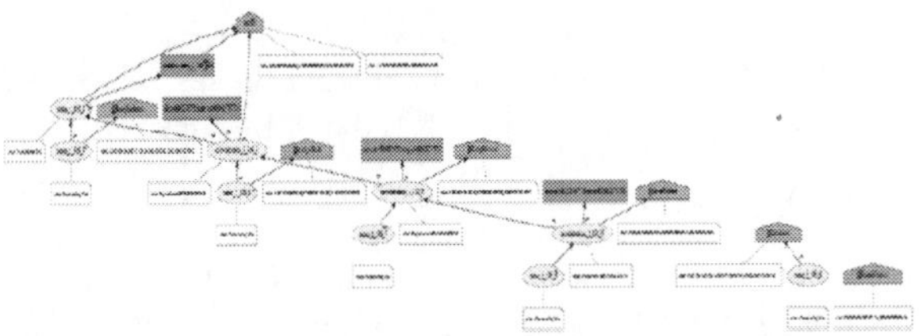

Figure 6. provenance visualization of a workflow execution with both provenance collection error and notification failure error

The social provenance database was developed to serve as a test platform for development of failure-resilient misinformation-detection algorithms.

V. Conclusion

In this paper, we have shown the need for a large-scale simulated social provenance database. Taking Twitter as an example, we introduced a large-scale noisy synthetic social provenance database, in which we used various social provenance metrics and attributes to capture vital information for calculating data quality and user credibility. The introduced provenance database consists of social workflows of different-size and different-breadth workflows, each created with randomly generated social interaction scenarios utilizing WorkflowSim and WorkflowGen tools. It also has failure characteristics that represent both notification drop failures and provenance collection failures to simulate real-life provenance capture. We created a publicly accessible website at [15] to make the dataset available for research that deals with large-size and high-volume provenance graphs that are downloadable directly as XML files and are accessible through a Komadu repository query interface. We are now using the provenance database to study social provenance quality and to develop misinformation and copyright violation detection algorithms.

Acknowledgment

This study is part of the PRONALIZ project supported by TUBITAK's (3501) National Young Researchers Career Development Program (Project No: 114E781, Project Title: Provenance Use in Social Media Software to Develop Methodologies for Detection of Information Pollution and Violation of Copyrights).

Refrences

[1] S. Ranganath, P. Gundecha, and H. Liu, "A tool for assisting provenance search in social media," *Proc. 22nd ACM Int. Conf. Conf. Inf. Knowl. Manag. - CIKM '13*, pp. 2517–2520, 2013.

[2] I. Taxidou, T. De Nies, and R. Verborgh, "Modeling Information Diffusion in Social Media as Provenance with W3C PROV," In Proceedings of the 24th International Conference on World Wide Web (WWW '15 Companion), pp. 819–824, 2015.

[3] P. Chen, B. Plale, and M. S. Aktas, "Temporal representation for scientific data provenance," in *2012 IEEE 8th International Conference on E-Science, e-Science 2012*, 2012.

[4] P. Chen, B. Plale, and M. S. Aktas, "Temporal representation for mining scientific data provenance,"

Futur. Gener. Comput. Syst., vol. 36, pp. 363–378, 2014.

[5] Y. W. Cheah, B. Plale, J. Kendall-Morwick, D. Leake, and L. Ramakrishnan, "A noisy 10GB provenance database," *Lect. Notes Bus. Inf. Process.*, vol. 100 LNBIP, no. PART 2, pp. 370–381, 2012.

[6] K. Sreenivasan and A. J. Kleinman, "On the construction of a representative synthetic workload," *Commun. ACM*, vol. 17, no. 3, pp. 127–133, 1974.

[7] P. Mehra and B. Wah, "Synthetic workload generation for load-balancing experiments," *IEEE Parallel Distrib. Technol.*, vol. 3, no. 3, pp. 4–19, 1995.

[8] R. Bodnarchuk and R. Bunt, "A synthetic workload model for a distributed system file server," *Proc. 1991 ACM SIGMETRICS Conf. Meas. Model. Comput. Syst. - SIGMETRICS '91*, pp. 50–59, 1991.

[9] S. Antonatos, K. G. Anagnostakis, and E. P. Markatos, "Generating realistic workloads for network intrusion detection systems," *ACM SIGSOFT Softw. Eng. Notes*, vol. 29, no. 1, p. 207, 2004.

[10] B. D. Noble, M. Satyanarayanan, G. T. Nguyen, and R. H. Katz, "Trace-based mobile network emulation," *Proc. ACM SIGCOMM '97 Conf. Appl. Technol. Archit. Protoc. Comput. Commun. - SIGCOMM '97*, pp. 51–61, 1997.

[11] A. M. Ali, H. Alvari, A. Hajibagheri, K. Lakkaraju, and G. Sukthankar, "Synthetic Generators for Cloning Social Network Data," *BioMedCom*, pp. 1–9, 2014.

[12] H. Pérez-Rosés and F. Sebé, "Synthetic generation of social network data with endorsements," *J. Simul.*, vol. 9, no. 4, pp. 279–286, 2014.

[13] L. Ramakrishnan, D. Gannon, and B. Plale, "WORKEM: Representing and emulating distributed scientific workflow execution state," *CCGrid 2010 - 10th IEEE/ACM Int. Conf. Clust. Cloud, Grid Comput.*, pp. 283–292, 2010.

[14] M. S. Aktas, B. Plale, D. Leake, and N. K. Mukhi, "Unmanaged workflows: Their provenance and use," *Stud. Comput. Intell.*, vol. 426, pp. 59–81, 2013.

[15] "Pronaliz Project." [Online]. Available: https://sites.google.com/view/pronaliz/home, retrieved: 15/02/2017.

[16] "synthetic social provenance database." [Online]. Available: https://sites.google.com/view/pronaliz/datasets, retrieved: 28/03/2017.

[17] G. Barbier, Z. Feng, P. Gundecha, and H. Liu, *Provenance Data in Social Media*, vol. 4, no. 1, pp. 1–84, 2013.

[18] I. Wassink et al. "Analysing scientific workflows: Why workflows not only connect web services," in *SERVICES 2009 - 5th 2009 World Congress on Services*, 2009, no. PART 1, pp. 314–321.

[19] M. Transfeld and I. Werenfels, "#Hashtagsolidarities: Twitter debates and networks in the MENA region," no. March, pp. 1–62, 2016.

[20] E. Del Val, M. Rebollo, and V. Botti, "Does the type of event influence how user interactions evolve on twitter?," *PLoS One*, vol. 10, no. 5, pp. 1–32, 2015.

[21] I. Suriarachchi, Q. Zhou, and B. Plale, "Komadu: A Capture and Visualization System for Scientific Data Provenance," *J. Open Res. Softw.*, vol. 3, no. 1, p. e4, 2014.

[22] W3C, "The PROV Data Model.," 2016. [Online]. Available: https://www.w3.org/TR/prov-dm/, retrieved: 15/02/2017.

[23] B. Cao, B. Plale, G. Subramanian, E. Robertson, and Y. Simmhan, "Provenance information model of Karma version 3," in *SERVICES 2009 - 5th 2009 World Congress on Services*, 2009, no. PART 1, pp. 348–351.

[24] W. Chen, M. Rey, and M. Rey, "WorkflowSim : A Toolkit for Simulating Scientific Workflows in Distributed Environments," *8th IEEE Int. Conf. eScience 2012 (eScience 2012)*, pp. 1–8, 2012.

[25] R. Ferreira, W. Chen, R. Ferreira, W. Chen, G. Juve, K. Vahi, and E. Deelman, "Community Resources for Enabling Research in Distributed Scientific Workflows Community Resources for Enabling Research in Distributed Scientific Workflows," no. October, 2014.

[26] L. Moreau, "ProvToolbox: Java library to create and convert W3C PROV data model representations." [Online]. Available: http://lucmoreau.github.io/ProvToolbox/ , retrieved: 15/02/2017.

On a Weight for Partial Inner Dependence AHP Using Sensitivity Analyses

Shin-ichi Ohnishi, Takahiro Yamanoi
Faculty of Engineering
Hokkai-Gakuen University
Sapporo, Japan
email: {ohnishi, yamanoi}@hgu.jp

***Abstract* - The Analytic Hierarchy Process (AHP) is widely employed in a field of decision making, and its inner dependence version is useful for cases in which criteria are not enough independent. In this research, we investigate "partial inner dependence" structure, i.e., only some elements (subset) of the criteria are independent. For the partial inner dependence AHP, we propose a new kind of fuzzy weight representation that is valid even if a data matrix is not consistent or reliable enough. The representation can be defined by using the results of two kinds of the sensitivity analyses and fuzzy set.**

Keywords - AHP; fuzzy set; sensitivity analysis.

I. INTRODUCTION

The Analytic Hierarchy Process (AHP) proposed by T.L. Saaty in 1977 [1] is widely used in decision making, because it reflects humans feelings naturally. The normal AHP assumes independence among all criteria, although it is difficult to choose enough independent elements. The inner dependence AHP [2] is used to solve this kind of problem when criteria have dependency. However, inner dependence method requires dependency matrix for all elements even if some criteria are independent. In this research, we employ "partial inner dependence" structure. Our method divides a set of criteria to two subsets such as a dependent part and an independent part, then we can easily understand a relation among elements.

On the other hand, the comparison data matrix may not have enough consistency when AHP is applied, because, for instance, a problem may contain too many criteria to make decision. It means that answers from decision-makers, i.e., components of the matrix, do not have enough reliability. They may be too ambiguous or too fuzzy [3][5]. To avoid this issue, we usually have to revise again, but it takes a lot of time and costs. Then, we consider that weights should also have ambiguity or fuzziness. Therefore, it is necessary to represent these weights using fuzzy set.

In our research, we first apply sensitivity analysis to normal AHP to analyze how much the components of a pairwise comparison matrix influence the weight and/or consistency indices of the matrix. Next, we define new fuzzy weight representation of criteria for partial inner dependence AHP using L-R fuzzy numbers [4][6][7][8]. At last, we then propose overall fuzzy weight of alternatives when a comparison matrix among elements does not have enough consistency.

In Sections 2 and 3, we introduce the partial inner dependence AHP, consistency index and sensitivity analyses for AHP. Then, in Section 4, we define fuzzy weight for partial inner dependence structure, and Section 5 is a summary.

II. CONSISTENCY AND INNER DEPENDENCE

In this section, we introduce the processes of the normal AHP, its consistency and inner dependence extension.

A. Normal AHP

Usually, the AHP consists of following 4 processes.

(Process 1) Representation of structure by a hierarchy. The problem under consideration can be represented in a hierarchical structure. At the middle levels, there are multiple criteria. Alternative elements are put at the lowest level of the hierarchy.

(Process 2) Paired comparison between elements at each level. A pairwise comparison matrix A is created from a decision maker's answers. Let n be the number of elements at a certain level, the upper triangular components of the matrix a_{ij} ($i< j = 1,\ldots,n$) are 9, 8, .. , 2, 1, 1/2, …, or 1/9. These denote intensities of importance from element i to j. The lower triangular components a_{ji} are described with reciprocal numbers, for diagonal elements, let $a_{ii} = 1$.

(Process 3) Calculations of weight at each level. The weights of the elements, which represent grades of importance among each element, are calculated from the pairwise comparison matrix. The eigenvector that corresponds to a positive normalized (so as sum of components is 1) eigenvalue of the matrix is used in calculations throughout in the paper.

(Process 4) Priority of an alternative by a composition of weights. With repetition of composition of weights, the overall weights of the alternative, which are the priorities of the alternatives with respect to the overall objective, are finally found.

B. Consistency

Since components of the comparison matrix are obtained by comparisons between two elements, coherent consistency is not guaranteed. In AHP, the consistency of the comparison matrix A is measured by the following consistency index (C.I.)

$$\text{C.I.} = \frac{\lambda_A - n}{n-1}, \quad (1)$$

where n is the order of comparison matrix A, and λ_A is its maximum eigenvalue (Frobenius root).

If the value of C.I. becomes smaller, then the degree of consistency becomes higher, and vice versa. It is said that the comparison matrix is consistent if $\text{C.I.} \leq 0.1$.

C. Partial Inner Dependence Method

The normal AHP ordinarily assumes independency among criteria, although it is difficult to choose enough independent elements in practice. The dependency means some kind of interaction among the elements. Inner dependence AHP [2] is used to solve this type of problem even for the case that criteria have dependency.

In the inner dependence method, using a dependency matrix $F=\{ f_{ij} \}$, we can calculate modified weights $\boldsymbol{w}^{(n)}$ as follows,

$$\boldsymbol{w}^{(n)}=F\boldsymbol{w} \quad (2)$$

where $\boldsymbol{w}$ represents weights from independent criteria, i.e., normalized weight of normal AHP and dependency matrix F consists of eigenvectors of influence matrices that represent dependency among criteria. However, inner dependence method requires dependency matrix for all elements even if some criteria are independent. In this research, we employ "partial inner dependence" structure, and then we can easily understand a relation among elements.

In a partial inner dependence AHP, we can divide a criteria set $C = \{X_1, X_2, \ldots, X_n\}$ to two subsets, dependent part $C_a = \{X_1^{(a)}, X_2^{(a)}, \ldots, X_{n1}^{(a)}\}$ and independent part $C_b = \{X_1^{(b)}, X_2^{(b)}, \ldots, X_{n2}^{(b)}\}$, $n_1 + n_2 = n$, they are determined whether the element is independent criterion or not. Let weights of C_a be $\boldsymbol{w}^{(a)} = (w_{i_1}^{(a)}),\ i_1 = 1, \ldots, n_1$, and weight of C_b be $\boldsymbol{w}^{(b)} = (w_{i_2}^{(b)}),\ i_2 = 1, \ldots, n_2$.

First, we calculate modified weight of dependent criteria subset $\boldsymbol{w}^{(an)} = (w_{i_1}^{(an)})$, using dependency matrix F as follows:

$$\boldsymbol{w}^{(an)} = F\boldsymbol{w}^{(a)}. \quad (3)$$

Then, the partial crisp (i.e. not fuzzy yet) weight $\boldsymbol{w}^{(pn)} = (w_i^{(pn)}),\ i = 1, \ldots, n$ is made by the following connection.

$$\boldsymbol{w}^{(pn)} = (w_1^{(an)}, \ldots, w_{n_1}^{(an)}, w_1^{(b)}, \ldots, w_{n_2}^{(b)}) \quad (4)$$

Using this modified criterion weight, we can easily calculate the priority of alternatives, i.e., overall weight of alternatives with respect to overall objective.

III. SENSITIVITY ANALYSES

When we use AHP in some applications, it often occurs that a comparison matrix is not consistent or that there is not great difference among the overall weights of the alternatives. In these cases, it is very important to investigate how components of the pairwise comparison matrix influence its consistency or the weights. In this study, we use a method that some of the present authors have proposed before. It evaluates a fluctuation of the consistency index and the weights when the comparison matrix is perturbed. It is useful because it does not change the structure of the data.

Since the pairwise comparison matrix is a positive square matrix, Perron-Frobenius theorem holds. From Perron-Frobenius theorem, the following theorem about a perturbed comparison matrix holds.

Theorem 1 *Let $A = (a_{ij})$, $(i, j = 1, \ldots, n)$ denote a comparison matrix and let $A(\varepsilon) = A + \varepsilon D_A$, $D_A = (a_{ij} d_{ij})$ denote a matrix that has been perturbed. Let λ_A be the Frobenius root of A, $\boldsymbol{w}$ be the eigenvector corresponding to λ_A, and $\boldsymbol{v}$ be the eigenvector corresponding to the Frobenius root of transposed A'. Then, a Frobenius root $\lambda(\varepsilon)$ of $A(\varepsilon)$ and a corresponding eigenvector $\boldsymbol{w}(\varepsilon)$ can be expressed as follows*

$$\lambda(\varepsilon) = \lambda_A + \varepsilon\lambda^{(1)} + o(\varepsilon), \quad (5)$$

$$\boldsymbol{w}(\varepsilon) = \boldsymbol{w} + \varepsilon\boldsymbol{w}^{(1)} + \boldsymbol{o}(\varepsilon), \quad (6)$$

where

$$\lambda^{(1)} = \frac{\boldsymbol{v}' D_A \boldsymbol{w}}{\boldsymbol{v}' \boldsymbol{w}}, \quad (7)$$

$\boldsymbol{w}^{(1)}$ is an n-dimension vector that satisfies

$$(A - \lambda_A I)\boldsymbol{w}^{(1)} = -(D_A - \lambda^{(1)} I)\boldsymbol{w}, \quad (8)$$

where $\boldsymbol{o}(\varepsilon)$ denotes an n-dimension vector in which all components are $o(\varepsilon)$.

About a fluctuation of the consistency index, the following corollaries hold.

Corollary 1 *Using appropriate* g_{ij}, *we can represent the consistency index* C.I.(ε) *of the perturbed comparison matrix* $A(\varepsilon)$ *as follows*

$$\mathrm{C.I.}(\varepsilon) = \mathrm{C.I.} + \varepsilon \sum_i^n \sum_j^n g_{ij} d_{ij} + o(\varepsilon). \qquad (9)$$

To see g_{ij} in (9) in Corollary 1, we can determine how the components of a comparison matrix impart influence on its consistency.

Corollary 2 *Using appropriate* $h_{ij}^{(k)}$, *we can represent the fluctuation* $w^{(1)}=(w_k^{(1)})$ *of the weight (i.e., the eigenvector corresponding to the Frobenius root) as follows*

$$w_k^{(1)} = \sum_i^n \sum_j^n h_{ij}^{(k)} d_{ij}. \qquad (10)$$

Then, we can evaluate how the components of a comparison matrix impart influence on the weights, to see $h_{ij}^{(k)}$ in (10).

Proofs of these corollaries are shown in [4].

IV. Fuzzy Weights Representations

When a comparison matrix has poor consistency (i.e., 0.1<C.I.<0.2), components of the comparison matrix are considered to be fuzzy because they are results from human fuzzy judgment. Therefore weight should be treated as fuzzy numbers [4][6].

Definition 1 (fuzzy weight) Let $w_k^{(pn)}$, $k = 1,\ldots,n$, be a crisp weight of criterion k of partial inner dependence model, and g_{ij} | $h_{ij}^{(k)}$| denote the coefficients found in Corollary 1 and 2. If 0.1<C.I.<0.2, then a fuzzy weight of partial inner dependence criteria $\tilde{w}^{(pn)} = (\tilde{w}_k^{(pn)}), k = 1,\ldots,n$ can be defined by

$$\tilde{w}_k^{(pn)} = (w_k^{(pn)}, \alpha_k, \beta_k)_{LR} \qquad (11)$$

where

$$\alpha_k = \mathrm{C.I.} \sum_i^n \sum_j^n s(-, h_{ij}^{(k)}) g_{ij} \mid h_{ij}^{(k)} \mid, \qquad (12)$$

$$\beta_k = \mathrm{C.I.} \sum_i^n \sum_j^n s(+, h_{ij}^{(k)}) g_{ij} \mid h_{ij}^{(k)} \mid, \qquad (13)$$

Using the above definition, the overall fuzzy weight of alternative l ($l = 1,\ldots,m$) can be calculated as follows:

$$\tilde{v}_l = \sum_k^n \tilde{w}_k^{(pn)} u_{kl} \qquad (14)$$

where u_{kl}, $k = 1,\ldots,n,\ l = 1,\ldots,m$ is weight of the l-th alternatives with only respect to the criterion k.

V. Conclusion and Future Work

There are many cases in which data of AHP does not have enough consistency or reliability and structure of a problem does not contain complete independent criteria. For these cases, we propose a fuzzy weight representation and compositions for incomplete inner dependence structure using results of sensitivity analyses and fuzzy set. Our approach can not only show how to represent weight of criteria and alternatives, but also makes it possible to investigate how the result of AHP has fuzziness even if data are not enough consistent or reliable.

In the next step, we will compare the partial inner dependence AHP and the normal AHP with real data.

References

[1] T. L. Saaty, The Analytic Hierarchy Process. McGraw-Hill, New York, 1980.

[2] T. L. Saaty, Inner and Outer Dependence in AHP, University of Pittsburgh, 1991

[3] D. Dubois and H. Prade, Possibility Theory An Approach to Computerized Processing of Uncertainty, Plenum Press, New York (1988)

[4] S. Ohnishi, H. Imai, and M. Kawaguchi, "Evaluation of a Stability on Weights of Fuzzy Analytic Hierarchy Process using a sensitivity analysis," J. Japan Soc. for Fuzzy Theory and Sys., 9(1), Jan. 1997, pp.140-147.

[5] S. Ohnishi, D. Dubois, H. Prade, and T. Yamanoi, "A Fuzzy Constraint-based Approach to the Analytic Hierarchy Process," Uncertainty and Intelligent Information Systems, June 2008, pp.217-228.

[6] S. Ohnishi, T. Yamanoi, and H. Imai, "A Fuzzy Weight Representation for Inner Dependence AHP," Journal of Advanced Computational Intelligence and Intelligent Informatics, Vol.15, No.3, June 2011, pp. 329-335.

[7] S. Ohnishi and T. Yamanoi, " Applying Fuzzy weights to Triple Inner Dependence AHP," DBKDA2015, June 2015.

[8] S. Ohnishi and T. Yamanoi, " Fuzzy Weight Representation for Double Inner Dependence Structure in 4 Levels AHP," MODOPT2016, May 2016.

Customer Churn Prediction in Telecommunication with Rotation Forest Method

Mümin Yıldız
Computer Engineering Department
Yıldız Technical University
Istanbul, Turkey
Email: muminyildiz@outlook.com

Songül Albayrak
Computer Engineering Department
Yıldız Technical University
Istanbul, Turkey
Email: songul@ce.yildiz.edu.tr

***Abstract*—The main task of customer churn prediction is to estimate subscribers who may want to leave from a company and provide solutions to prevent possible churnes. In recent years, estimating churners before they leave has became valuable in the environment of increased competition among companies. The research in this paper was done to estimate churners for companies in the telecommunication industry showing how prediction efficacy is increased by balancing the data with down sampling and classifying by the rotation forest method. The performance level of these techniques are compared with Antminer and C4.5 decision tree. The comparisons are done by using the dataset taken from American Telecommunication Company and accuracy, sensitivity and specificity are used for the performance criteria.**

***Keywords*–Customer Churn Prediction; Data Mining; Telecommunication; Rotation Forest; Antminer.**

I. Introduction

Customer churn has became highly important for companies because of increasing competition among companies, increased importance of marketing strategies and conscious behavior of costumers in the recent years. Customers can easily trend toward alternative services. Companies must develop various strategies to prevent these possible trends, depending on the services they provide.

During the estimation of possible churns, data from the previous churns might be used. An efficient churn predictive model benefits companies in many ways. Early identification of customers likely to leave may help to build cost effective ways in marketing strategies. Customer retention campaigns might be limited to selected customers but it should cover most of the customer. Incorrect predictions could result in a company losing profits because of the discounts offered to continuous subscribers. Therefore, the right predictions of the churn customers has became highly important for the companies.

The prominent role that the telecommunication sector has come to occupy worldwide makes it all the more important to develop prediction mechanisms along the lines of churn prediction. Few statistics show the importance of the customer retains in this sector. One of the remarkable studies shows that 1% increase in the customer retain campaigns may result in the 5% increase in the overall values of the companies [1]. In wireless network telecommunication industry, the monthly rate of customer churn is 2.2% and the annual rate of customer churn is 27% [2]. The yearly cost of customer churn is 4 billion dollars in Europe and America, and it is 10 billion dollars in the entire world [2]. We may suppose that 1.5 million customers would stay in the same company by increasing the correct prediction at the rate of 1%. This may yield to 54 million dollars benefit for the companies annually [3].

In the literature, many researches have been conducted to increase the prediction rates of costumer churns in the telecommunication industry. The scope of this researches covers creating new models, developing existing models, combining of existing models, attribute derivation and outlier analysis techniques.

Tsai and Lu [5] used two different hybrid models to develop a customer churn prediction model. The developed hybrid model is a combination of two artificial neural networks and the second hybrid model is a combination of self organizing maps and artificial neural networks. First models are used for data reduction and second models are used for actual classifier. Kechadi and Buckley [2] used attribute derivation process to increase the correct prediction rate. Bayesian Belief Network method is tried in a study which is conducted by Kisioglu and Topcu [1]. Verbeke et al. [6] increased the accuracy by using two different rules extraction method. This methods were AntMiner+ and ALBA. Bock and Poel [7] used two different rotation based ensemble classifiers. These are Rotation Forest and Adaboosts. Yeshwanth et al. [8] suggested a new hybrid model that combines C4.5 decision tree and genetic programming. Zhao et al. [3] used one class support vector machine to increase the performance. Ghorbani et al. [9]created a new hybrid model by combining neural network, tree models and fuzzy modeling.

Ant-Miner+ algorithm is working by using the 'divide and conquer' technique. Firstly, it starts with all of the training data. Then it creates the best rule, which includes a subset of training data and then the best rule is added to the list of previously discovered rules. After that the samples, which are covered by this rules are removed from the training data and everything starts again with the reduced training data-set. This iteration continues until when there is only a few remaining samples in training data. At this stage, a default rule is created which covers the remaining samples.

Rotation forest method is a new generation ensemble learning algorithm. It is based on creating subsets by using principal component analysis method as a feature extraction technique [4]. In this research, it has been observed that rotation forest method gives better results than antminer+ method, which is used by Verbeke. To make comparison, the same data-set is used with Verbeke's research and same evaluation criteria, such as accuracy, sensitivity and specificity ratios are examined. It is accepted that supposing a customer that will leave as would not leave and losing him is much more important than giving unnecessary promotions to customers who will not leave as would leave. For these reason sensitivity is seems to be more important than specificity.

The rest of the paper is organized in this following manner: Section 2 explains the rotation forest. Section 3 presents the data, data processing and evaluation criteria. In Section 4, results of rotation forest, Ant-Miner+ and C4.5 methods are compared. Finally, our conclusion is offered.

II. Rotation Forest

Rotation forest algorithm, which started to be used in literature in recent years and was put forth as the new generation on learning algorithm is based on forming a classifier ensemble by using principal component analysis, which is a feature extraction technique [4]. The basic working principle of rotation forest algorithm is similar to random forest and more than one trees are used. However, dataset that is used in the training of every decision tree in forest is determined by principal component analysis. At the phase of training of decision trees in the forest, the training dataset is divided into random subsets and features are extracted from each subset by using principal component analysis. The features that have the highest distinctiveness are determined after feature extraction. All components are considered to keep the variance of dataset same. For every classifier, the diversity is protected in classifiers ensemble by feature extraction. Basic steps of rotation forest algorithm are shown below [4].

Let X denotes training dataset, Y denotes class labels in dataset and F donates number of feature. If we suppose that training dataset includes n number of features and N number of customers, x training dataset is in from of a N by n matrix. Let Y be a vector and it shows the class label in the form of $[y_1, \ldots, y_N]$. Suppose these datasets is separated to K subsets times that is about same number with F and there are L classifiers (decision trees), which denoted by $[D_1, \ldots, D_L]$ in rotation forest according to operating principle of rotation forest algorithm. In this case, the training dataset is determined by processing steps below for every $D_{(i)}$ decision tree in rotation forest.

Step 1. F is split into K independent subsets randomly. Every independent subset should have M=n/ K features.

Step 2: Suppose that F_{ij} is the subset that consist of j feature, which was used in training of classifiers D_i and X_{ij} are the subsets that consists of features of F_{ij} in X dataset. In this case a new training dataset is determined as 75% train and 25% test of dataset by bootstrap method. After that covariance matrix C_{ij} is calculated applying principal component analysis to the newly created dataset.

Step 3: R_i transformation matrix is generated by equation (3) by using calculated covariance values.

$$R_i = \begin{bmatrix} a_{i,1}^{(1)}, a_{i,1}^{(2)}, ..., a_{i,1}^{(M_1)} & [0], & \cdots & [0] \\ [0] & a_{i,2}^{(1)}, a_{i,2}^{(2)}, ..., a_{i,2}^{(M_2)}, & \cdots & [0] \\ \vdots & \vdots & \ddots & \vdots \\ [0] & [0] & \cdots & a_{i,2}^{(1)}, a_{i,K}^{(2)}, ..., a_{i,2}^{(M_K)} \end{bmatrix}$$

Every column of R_i matrix is rearranged according to original feature and rotation matrix R_i^a is obtained. Consequently, XR_i^a dataset, which will be used in the training of D_i classifiers is obtained. This process steps are applied for every classifier in rotation forest. Classification results, which belongs to every decision tree in the forest by using transformed dataset takes a vote.

III. Methodology

This section describes the properties of datasets, preprocessing steps and evaluation criteria.

A. Dataset

Larose's dataset is obtained from wireless network telecommunication company, the dataset consists of 5000 customers information. Every customer has 21 feature and there is no missing data. The amount of churn customers is 14.3% of total customer for the coming tree months. More information about Larose dataset can be found on Larose (2005) [10]. The best 10 features of the Larose dataset that was selected by the information gain technique and their explanations are shown at Table 1.

TABLE I. BEST 10 FEATURES.

Feature Name	Feature Description	Value
international_plan	International call usage	Yes/No
total_day_minutes	Daily total talk time	Minutes
number_customer_service_calls	Number of call to customer service	
voice_mail_plan	Voice mail usage	Yes/No
total_eve_minutes	Total talk time in evening	Minutes
state	Living place	
total_day_charge	Daily Total spent credits	
number_vmail_messages	Number of voice messages	
total_intl_calls	Total number of international call	
total_intl_charge	Total spent credits of international calls	

B. Data Preprocessing

Classification tends to be in favor of majority classes when there exists unbalance in the dataset. Distribution of the used dataset has 14.3% churn customers and 85.7% non churn customers. For this reason, down sampling process is applied to dataset. In the down sampling process subsets are generated that will have x times churn customer and 2x times non churn customer. To generate subsets, firstly 20 empty sets are created and all churn customers are added to these sets. Non churn customers are selected as randomly. The important point in here is one non churn customer can be chosen more than one time for a subset. By these methods all subsets are created and they have 2121 customers. 707 of them are churn (33.3%) and 1414 of them are non churn (66,7%) customers. This process increased the sensitivity rate significantly. Comparisons are made with the average ratios of these 20 subset.

C. Evaluation Criteria

Classification results of the used techniques were compared by using class confusion matrix that is shown at Table 3.

The cost per customer is decreasing while the total number of the customer is increasing for serving companies in the telecommunications sector. So, instead of supposing a customer that will leave as would not leave and losing him(FN), unnecessary promotions might be given to a customer by supposing the customer that will not leave as would leave (FP) (Keeping FN low is more important than keeping FP low. That mean sensitivity is more important than specificity.)

TABLE II. CLASSIFICATIN RESULTS.

	Technique	Accuracy (%)	Sensitivity (%)	Specificty (%)
Original Dataset	Rotation Forest	**95.68**	**73.4**	99.49
	AntMiner+ [6]	90.85	37.09	**99.71**
	C4.5 [6]	93.59	64.93	98.34
Down Sampling	Rotation Forest(Subsets Average)	92.49	**84.57**	96.46
Oversampling	AntMiner+ [6]	**93.15**	65.76	**97.72**
	C4.5 [6]	91.66	80.82	93.45

TABLE III. CLASS CONFUSION MATRIX.

		PREDICTED		TOTAL
		Churn Customer	Non Churn Customer	
ACTUAL	Churn Customer	TP True Positive	FN False Negative	Actual Positive Number
	Non Churn Customer	FP False Positive	TN True Negative	Actual Negative Number
TOTAL		Predicted Positive Number	Predicted Negative Number	Total Customer Number

Sensitivity and specificity rates are observed because of primary focus is to find churn customers. Accuracy rates do not show the truth when there is unbalance between classes but this is also shown in the table. Sensitivity shows the rate of correctly estimated churn customers and specificity shows the rate of correctly estimated non churn customers. Accuracy sensitivity and specificity ratios are shown in equation (1) - (3).

$$Accuracy = \frac{TP+TN}{TP+TN+FP+FN} \tag{1}$$

$$Sensitiviy = \frac{TP}{TP+FN} \tag{2}$$

$$Specificity = \frac{TN}{TN+FP} \tag{3}$$

Sensitivity is more important than specificity because finding churn customer more important. The best classification results are shown in bold.

IV. RESULTS

Rotation forest method is compared with antminer+, which is defended by Verbeke to evaluate the results. Principal component analysis is used for feature extraction, and the C4.5 decision tree is used as classifier in rotation forest technique. Additionally, to compare with classical methods, results of C4.5 decision tree, which was used by Verbeke is shown in Table 2 with their own findings. Antminer+ and C4.5 methods were calculated in the original dataset and in the oversampled dataset by Verbeke [6].

The classification results by using rotation forest method in entire dataset and average of classification results by using rotation forest method in twenty subsets, which were created by down sampling method are shown in Table 2. The best results are shown in bold. This results are compared with antminer+ and C4.5 decision tree algorithms.

According to original dataset rotation forest gave the best result with 73% of success considering sensitivity rate. This method is 8.47% more successful than C4.5 decision tree method and 36.31% than antminer+. Rotation forest algorithm is 0.22% lower than antminer+ in specificity rate. The difference is negligible. Rotation forest is better by 1.15% than C4.5 in specificity rate. Rotation forest has achieved 95.68%, C4.5 has achieved 93.59% and antminer+ has achieved 90.85% success in accuracy rate. According to this results rotation forest is the best technique.

For the down sampled data, average of classification results of 20 subsets that were classified by rotation forest and were balanced by down sampling has achieved 84.57% sensitivity rate in balanced dataset. Classification result of antminer+ algorithm has calculated 65.76% and classification result of C4.5 algorithm has calculated 80.82% in sensitivity rate with oversampled data. Antminer+ has achieved best result with 97.72% in specificity rate. The result of rotation forest algorithm is 96.46% and it is worse than antminer+ algorithm. However, the sensitivity rate is more important than the specificity rate for customer churn prediction. So success achieved with rotation forest is better than antminer+ and C4.5 decision tree. Antminer+ has achieved 92.49% in accuracy rate. Rotation forest has achieved 92.49%. Antminer+ is better by a small difference of 0.66 than rotation forest in accuracy rate.

Rotation forest algorithm is the best method for this dataset because of accuracy does not reflect the truth as explained in Section 3.C and sensitivity rate is more important than specificity rate. Moreover, balancing data process is a very important factor to find correct churn customer. Sensitivity is increased 11% by using rotation forest method after data balancing. The data balancing process is giving realistic and reliable results although the accuracy rate decreases.

Lets compare rotation forest and antminer+ methods financially. Suppose that a company has one million customer and 15% of them will leave. Rotation forest method will find churn customers 20% more correct according to the antminer+ algorithm. That mean is to keep more 30,000 customer in the company. Lets assume that the average bill in America is $ 100, the telecommunication company will win three million dollars yearly by the rotation forest method by this way.

V. CONCLUSION

According to the results, rotation forest is better than C4.5 decision tree and antminer+ because increasing of true prediction of churn customer rate is more important. The difference of between rotation forest and antminer+ algorithms is 36.31% in original dataset for sensitivity rate. Balancing data is increased all sensitivity rates. According to this results rotation forest method is the best algorithm and 18.81% more successful than antminer+ in terms of sensitivity.

REFERENCES

[1] P. Kisioglu and I. Y. Topcu, "Applying Bayesian belief network approach to customer churn analysis: a case study on the telecom industry of Turkey." Expert Systems with Applications 38, 2010, pp. 7151-7157.

[2] B. Huang, M. T. Kechadi, and B. Buckley, "Customer churn prediction in telecommunications." Expert Systems with Applications, 39(1), 2012, pp. 1414-1425

[3] Y. Zhao, B. Li, and X. Li, "Customer churn prediction using improved one-class support vector machine." Lecture Notes in Artificial Intelligence, 3584, 2005, pp. 300—306

[4] J. J. Rodrigez, L. l. Kuncheva, and J. A. Carlos, "Rotation Forest; A New Classifier Ensemble Method." IEEE Transactions on Pattern Analysis and Machine Intelligence, 28(10), 2006, pp. 1619–1630.

[5] C. F. Tsai and Y. H. Lu, "Customer churn prediction by hybrid neural networks." Expert Systems Application, 36(10), 2009, pp. 12547—12553, doi:

[6] W. Verbeke, D. Martens, C. Mues, and B. Baesens, "Building comprehensible customer churn prediction models with advanced rule induction techniques." Expert Systems with Applications, 38, 2011, pp. 2354—2364.

[7] K. W. Bock and D. V. Poel, "An empirical evaluation of rotation-based ensemble classifiers for customer churn prediction." Expert Systems with Applications, 38(10), 2011 pp. 12293--12301.

[8] V. Yeshwanth, V. V. Raj, and M. Saravanam, "Evolutionary churn prediction in mobile networks using hybrid learning", Proc. of XXIV Florida Artificial Intelligence Research Society Conference, 2011, pp. 471– 476.

[9] A. Ghorbani, F. Taghiyareh, and C. Lucas, "The application of the locally linear model tree on customer churn prediction." Proceedings of the International Conference of Soft Computing and Pattern Recognition (SOCPAR'09), Malaysia, 2009, pp. 472—477.

[10] D. Larose,(2005). Discovering knowledge in data:An introduction to data mining. New Jersey, USA: Wiley

Data Validation for Big Live Data

Malcolm Crowe, Carolyn Begg
School of Computing
University of the West of Scotland
Paisley PA1 2BE, UK
email: {malcolm.crowe|carolyn.begg}@uws.ac.uk

Fritz Laux
Fakultät Informatik
Reutlingen University
D-72762 Reutlingen, Germany
email: fritz.laux@fh-reutlingen.de

Martti Laiho
DBTechNet
www.dbtechnet.org
email: martti.laiho@gmail.com

***Abstract*—Data Integration of heterogeneous data sources relies either on periodically transferring large amounts of data to a physical Data Warehouse or retrieving data from the sources on request only. The latter results in the creation of what is referred to as a virtual Data Warehouse, which is preferable when the use of the latest data is paramount. However, the downside is that it adds network traffic and suffers from performance degradation when the amount of data is high. In this paper, we propose the use of a readCheck validator to ensure the timeliness of the queried data and reduced data traffic. It is further shown that the readCheck allows transactions to update data in the data sources obeying full Atomicity, Consistency, Isolation, and Durability (ACID) properties.**

Keywords–data validation; virtual data integration; ETags; row-version validation.

I. INTRODUCTION

For the Data Integration scenario (see Figure 1), we assume a set of heterogeneous data sources $\{D_{ij}\}$ belonging to and managed by a (disparate) set of contracting parties $\{C_i\}$, which provide Views V_i for a Requester R (e.g., a regulatory body, enterprise, or government). The databases that store the data in a variety of formats adopted by the different contractors, remain under the control of their respective owners. We also note that in our example the regulatory body R is normally concerned with aggregated data rather than with individual records and the contractors are generally also responsible for the privacy and security of the data they hold. But, importantly, in all our examples R is concerned with the current situation and up-to-date aggregations are required and queried from a Global View V of the *live* data set $\{D_{ij}\}$. These requirements make it undesirable to create and store a single big data set at R.

To illustrate the situation let's take the Ebola outbreak in West Africa in 2014. The World Health Organization (WHO) takes the role of R in our model and C_1 is given by the Choithram Memorial Hospital in Freetown. The demographic information about Sierra Leone shall be provided by Statistics Sierra Leone, C_2 in our model. There are more hospitals C_i in Sierra Leone, Guinea, and Liberia as well as official statistics offices. We leave them out to not overload our example. C_1 records all patient data, diagnosis and treatment but provides only non-sensitive data as an aggregated view V_1 to the WHO. C_2 also provide a view V_2 of a portion of the statistical data collected. To not complicate the integration we assume that both views provide the residence of the patient and the location (city/quarter or village) in the same coding.

With V_1 and V_2 provided, R can build an integrated view V providing data that allow the analysis of the distribution and spreading of the disease. It is evident that the data must be up-to-date (live data) in order to monitor the spreading and allow decisions for improving quarantine and treatment. We continue this example in more detail and implement it in Section IV-B.

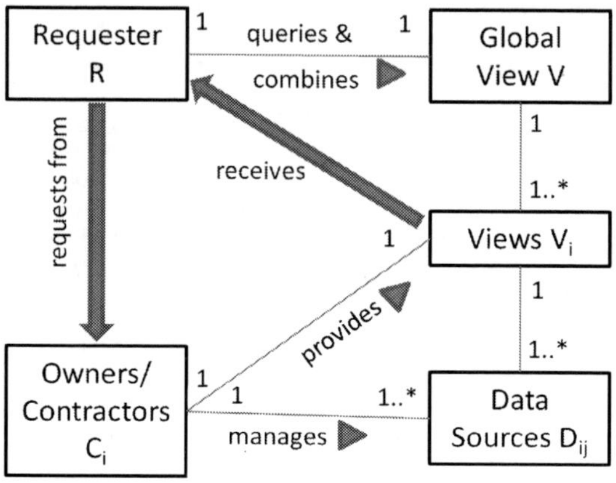

Figure 1: Schema and relationships of the virtual data integration scenario

Big Live Data as discussed here consists of data sets that are subject to real-time updates (*live* data) and *big* not just in terms of size in bytes but also in the sense that they span multiple areas of responsibility and ownership. The scenarios we have in mind include international and other regulatory bodies, where data belong to and is managed by separate entities (including governments), and in business examples such as supply chain, manufacturing, project management and construction, where each contractor or company produces their data but an overseeing body must have access to a global view of this data to support decision-making at the highest level to enable the management and coordination of the data contributors.

The term "Big Data" is usually applied to scenarios characterised by the "4 Vs". We consider that all of these apply to the scenarios presented here:

- **Velocity** refers to the significant volumes of new data that can be created and/or updates made at speed in the individual D_{ij}. Because of velocity, it is not feasible to keep making fresh collections of all data at R.
- **Volume** refers to the significant volumes of data held across many separate data sources D_{ij}, which are required wholly or in part to provide the *live* data for R.

- **Variety** refers to the range of possible data models (e.g., relational, NoSQL, XML) and data types used by the D_{ij}. A *live* (on-line access to D_{ij}) implementation of V will need to resolve transformation and semantic issues associated with a variety of data types. It is the responsibility of C_i to provide a consistent View V_i and it is R's task to transform these views into a Global View V.
- **Veracity** refers to the range in the data quality (from high to lower levels) of the data held in the separate D_{ij}. The C_i have a responsibility to ensure the reliability and veracity of their data. A *live* implementation of V should aim for maximum coherency and consistency of the overall data collected, but as a minimum, any data at R should be on consistent results from the D_{ij} (resp. V_i) as at a particular time.

In this paper, we refer to the veracity property as correctness, and apply this concept both for current results, which should be consistent and up to date, and for stored results, which should be a correct snapshot of the state of affairs at the time they were computed. We note that most Big Data implementations have difficulty with correctness if the data is subject to change.

A. Contribution

In our scenario, R should also be able to check that the most recent results obtained from the C_i are still correct, and perform other checks for validation, maybe including supplementary data gathered from other sources. Greater care over data curation, ownership and provenance in such complex scenarios can help to achieve a higher fidelity of data. The present paper proposes the use of a readCheck validator in order to check the timeliness of a query result and reduce the data traffic between the sources and the requester. The same mechanism can be used to implement an optimistic concurrency control mechanism for heterogeneous and geographically distributed data sources. This enables distributed *live* updates to the underlying data sources obeying full Atomicity, Consistency, Isolation, and Durability (ACID) properties.

B. Structure of the Paper

With the following overview of Related Work on data integration the context for our validation concept will be settled. Section III introduces the concepts of Row Version Validation (RVV) and ETags for Web data caching, which are the basis for a generalised data validation. Then, these concepts are combined and applied to query processing for joined and aggregated data over a virtual Data Warehouse (DWH). The technical realisation of the validation mechanism via Representational State Transfer (REST) services is explained in Section IV and applied to general query processing over a virtual DWH. The extended syntax for the global schema design is presented in Subsection IV-B and illustrated with an example. The paper ends with a summary of our findings from the pilot implementation and gives an outlook on ideas for future work.

II. Related Work

Since the beginning of 1980 many papers on data integration have been published. The research of Inmon [1] and Jarke [2] concentrated on the DWH approach using Extract-Transform-Load (ETL) techniques [3]–[6], schema matching [7] and integration [8], [9]. Kimbal et al. [10] present methods on how to support the whole DWH live-cycle including schema design, ETL methods, and how to implement and deploy such a system. Later, the focus changed to real-time ETL or virtual DWH [11], [12]. Myronovych and Boreisha [13] discuss how XML Web Services can be used for the ETL process in the context of Enterprise Information Integration.

Since for legal and practical reasons, the use of ETL techniques are not available in our case, the focus will be on how R can manage to collect correct information using the REST architectural style proposed by Fielding [14]. This will lead us to consider the use of HyperText Transfer Protocol (HTTP) [15] techniques such as ETags [16], and how these can relate to database transaction concepts.

In this paper, we turn to the question of data validation. If R has collected the result of a query from the set of contractors, and wishes to publish a report, or take action as a result, how can R check that the data obtained from the contractors are still current?

For performance reasons data is often cached. Usually cached data is only valid during a time defined by a Time-To-Live (TTL) indicator. After that it is considered stale and will be evicted from the cache. Many works on cache management has been published over the years (DBLP reports 477 matches to "cache management"), but most of the propositions are specific to certain architectures (e.g. OLAP [17], J2EE [18]), require support from the network nodes [19] or are optimised for special use cases [20]. Some require column stores [21], a middle tier [22], [23] or database support [24] [25]. As we do not expect any specific architecture or technology from the data sources, most of these sophisticated caching is not usable for us.

Caching of query results is however desirable to avoid unnecessary network and processing load. This is dealt with today on the Internet by considering validators for cached data. This departure from stateless HTTP is extremely useful in our context because it enables us to set up mechanisms similar to ACID transactions for the extreme cases of distributed data considered here. HTTP offers ETags [16] in response to allow caching of results, and ETags can be used for validating a step in a transaction. ETags are very similar to the RVV concept [26] or Multi-Version Concurrency Control (MVCC), successfully used in PostgreSQL [27], SQL server [28], Oracle etc. to provide optimistic execution. In fact the ETag can coincide with the RVV validator for requests that return only one row of a base table.

Xiong Fengguang and his colleagues [29] present a framework for virtual data integration of heterogeneous data sources using XML as interface. Jinqun Wu [30] implements the approach using Web services as data adapters. The adapter also provides access to metadata which is helpful for data discovery and query optimization. The implementation uses two caches, one for the metadata and the other for query parsing and result caching. However, it is not explained, how the freshness of data is ensured. As XML tends to be very verbose the performance of the conversion to and from XML is unclear. Naoki Take et al. [31] also propose virtual integration for operation support systems. The authors argue to use a mediated relational schema as integration basis. A wrapper maps event data to a virtual table which can be accessed if the necessary parameter is provided in the WHERE-clause. This is similar to our approach, but we prefer the REST style for accessing non-relational resources. The performance results confirm that queries to a virtual integration database are one magnitude slower than to a materialized one. This clearly calls for some caching when using a virtual mediated schema.

III. Concepts for Data Validation

First, we present the ideas of RVV and ETags as basis for our general validation mechanism, called *readCheck*. Second, the readCheck is used to validate the freshness and consistency of queried data and build an optimistic concurrency control protocol on it.

A. Row-version validation

The RVV protocol is a type of version control mechanism, which can be used for a form of optimistic concurrency control, alongside or in preference to other versioning measures such as MVCC. The model implementations of RVV in the Laiho/Laux paper [26] envisage a sequence generator to ensure uniqueness of RVV values, so that new values of this sequence are added as a special row-version column in base tables on each INSERT or UPDATE. Some Database Management Systems (DBMSs) include row versioning mechanisms that can be used for this. Otherwise the code for doing this is implemented as database triggers on these tables.

Our scenario is a bit different as such a guarantee is hard to provide by the contractors (not all data sources D_{ij} need to be databases). On the other hand as we will see, if ETags are part of the service offered to R by the C_i they can provide a suitable version stamp instead. In an *RVV transaction*, a read-write transaction or "long transaction" consisting of a sequence of read actions followed by some write actions, we should have the following steps:

1) The first read action (selection query) also reads and records the version stamp(s). Note: With MVCC or reading from a cache this may already be stale data.
2) The version stamp obtained can be optionally used as a validation predicate in later SQL-operations, or included in a precondition. The precondition would only need to compare the old version stamp with the new one to ensure that the data has not been changed in the meantime. If the version stamp is no longer valid, it is best to start again from the beginning as some of the data being used is already out of date.
3) In the same way the RVV predicate is then included in the search condition of the write actions (UPDATE or DELETE) to the database (bypassing the cache if any).
4) If no rows are affected in step 3) the transaction failed. This may be because a) the version stamp obtained in step 1 was already outdated (possible with optimistic concurrency control), b) there have been intervening update(s) by concurrent transaction(s), or c) the row has been deleted by a concurrent transaction.

Case 4c) can be detected by a new read action without the RVV predicate in the same transaction. If the result is NOT FOUND then case 4c) is true, otherwise 4a) or 4b) apply. In these cases, it may be worth starting the RVV transaction again from the beginning with new search values depending on the application.

B. RVV and complex selections

RVV is just for one row, and in the Laiho/Laux model is an integer value associated with a base table row that is changed if any change is made to a value in the row. If we were to define a view using a join, or embedded arrays, then we could extend the idea of RVV for such a complex row so that it comprises all base table rows selected for that row of the view, and would change if any of these where changed. For example in whatever join of two base tables, $J = A \bowtie B$ say, the RVV of each resultant row j of J will include the RVVs from the contributing rows of the base tables. We could therefore implement RVVs to allow compound values, so that the RVV for a join could be a comma-separated list of values or a vector of integers.

If the RVV model of Laiho/Laux [26] is extended in this way it can be used to validate the results of join queries, or more complex selections where a row in the selection embeds values from rows of other tables.

If the business application wishes to make a change to a derived table (update or delete) such RVVs can then be used to validate and carry out the operation on the relevant base table rows. The semantics of updating a value in a row of a derived table will often be reasonable, and it could be meaningful to support a delete operation on a derived table. A use case for updating or deleting data could arise from new or changed/corrected information that arise from sources external (e.g., a regulatory body or multinational organisation) to the owner of data source.

All of the above in our scenario remains within an individual V_i, and an RVV as seen from R could be extended to identify the contractor(s) involved, so that the results of R's queries could be updatable, depending on the permissions granted to R.

C. ETags as version stamps

As not all data sources are databases or have SQL interfaces, another mechanism is needed to avoid stale data. Fielding and Reschke propose in RFC 7232 [16] a header field in an HTTP request, called *ETag*. This ETag should serve as a validator for the freshness of data. An Etag should be returned for any GET request for a Web resource, possibly returning a lot of data. If we generalise its use to arbitrary queries, we would like the ETag validator to confirm that the results obtained for the query are still valid. In fact, ETags can be used in subsequent requests as preconditions; that is, if a requested ETag is no longer valid, the server should reply according to the HTTP protocol with "412 Precondition failed". Thus, the ETag protocol has useful similarities with the RVV protocol above. If the GET is a REST request in our scenario, in general the data returned will be related or linked in some way but will not in general come from a single row or base table, but the ETag will be effectively a version stamp for the returned data. Moreover, if the returned data is for a single row in a base table (or more complex selection as above), then the RVV if available can be used as ETag for the result.

In our scenario, we consider particular sorts of selection and aggregation queries that combine data gathered from the V_i, and if REST is used we can hope to have an ETag e_i from each one that contributes data. This will give R a version stamp $\vec{e}$ for the overall selection or aggregation, by combining the contributing ETags in some suitable way, from which we can extract any required e_i by string manipulation.

Where aggregation occurs it is not really practical or desirable for validators to identify all of the rows that contributed to the result. But we would like the ETag to let us discover whether the base tables involved have been modified since our results were computed, by extending it to indicate the extent of information read (e.g., tables, or specific rows if practicable) and for each table the most recent version stamp of the rows accessed.

For performance reasons the ETag could be applied to a hierarchical data structure, beginning on the detail level of a data element and propagating up to the top level of a database. So if a query request is executed and the result has been previously cached, it is sufficient to ask the underlying data source to test if the ETag of the requested aggregate has changed since the last time. If there was no change, the last result is still valid. If the query involves multiple sources and only some have changed, it is possible to build the new result by refreshing only the changed values in the cache.

With this framework, we can specify a Versioned REST protocol for our scenario analogous to the one described in III-A. In the four-step protocol it is only necessary to replace a query with a GET-request and the RVV with the ETag validator.

D. Management of distributed transactions using readCheck

It is possible to extend ETag and RVV concepts to implement "long transactions" for the virtual integration scenario and call it *readCheck*. The readCheck needs to include in addition to the ETag or RVV value a unique transaction identifier (server, database, timestamp, taNo). It is then possible to use the readCheck validator in a similar way as the RVV to provide an optimistic concurrency protocol. We only need to arrange that readChecks are remembered in intermediate results for any rows that have come from other servers and such validators can be accumulated for checking at commit time. For simple transactions, where all write actions are delayed to the commit stage of the transaction, the readCheck can be used to guarantee ACID behaviour. We note that some database management systems offer snapshot isolation for transactions, thus effectively delaying all changes to the database to follow the commit process.

The validation machinery requires the following steps:

1) readCheck information is accumulated by the contractor for all queries Q that are part of the transaction. With proxies (or caching) the values read may already be stale.
2) At any stage, the sequence of queries Q belonging to a transaction can be decomposed to Q_i and sent to the respective databases (bypassing proxies or caches) to check that $\vec{r}(Q)$ is still correct. If not, the data held by the contractor is stale and the transaction will not be able to commit.
3) The write action and implied commit needs to be sent to the database itself (bypassing proxies or caches) accompanied by the list of readCheck data. If all readCheck data is still valid the write action is performed. The database is only locked while the serialization condition is checked.

It is recommended that the contractor should receive updated readCheck data for the state after the transaction commits.

Assuming all the contractors have a way of rolling back aborted transactions (better than taking a backup beforehand), the readCheck mechanism would support the use of an optimistic two-phase commit (2PC) protocol suitable for distributed transactions. This can be realized as follows:

- Any serialization conflict will be detected if the readCheck has changed since the start of the transaction. As no changes to the database has be executed, the transaction can simply be aborted.
- If no conflict was detected the 2PC is executed. If all participating data sources agree, the write phase is entered otherwise the transaction is aborted (no writes will take place).

If during the write phase an error occurs, the affected data source must nevertheless guaranty that the write will be executed after the error is removed. This completes the 2PC protocol.

IV. Implementation of the readCheck Mechanism

As a slight generalisation of the Laiho/Laux concept of RVV, let us suppose that we have to hand a database implementation in which the transaction serialisation mechanism provides a monotonically increasing integer identifier $r(d)$ that it attaches as the RVV for any affected base table row d, and define $r(T)$ as the integer identifying the most recent change to table T.

Then, for any query Q on a single database, the readCheck $\vec{r}(Q)$ is a list or vector of integers defined recursively as follows:

1) if Q selects only a single row d from a base table by specifying a key value k, then $\vec{r}(Q) := (r(d))$. (Example: singleton query for Table T_1, see Figure 2)
2) if Q selects specific rows $d_1, .., d_n$ from a base table, by specifying key values $k_1, ..k_n$, then $\vec{r}(Q) = (r(d_1), .., r(d_n))$.
3) if Q selects a single row d from a join of base tables $T_1, .., T_n$ by specifying key values, where d is constructed from rows d_1 in T_1, d_2 in T_2 etc., then $\vec{r}(Q) = (r(d_1), .., r(d_n))$.
4) if Q selects some other set of rows, or all rows, from a base table T, then $\vec{r}(Q) := (r(T))$ i.e., a vector containing a single integer identifying the most recent change to table T. (Example: predicate query for Table T_2, see Figure 2)
5) if Q is a join, merge, union etc. of queries Q_1 and Q_2, then $\vec{r}(Q) := \vec{r}(Q_1) \times \vec{r}(Q_2)$ (Example: Q query decomposition by rewrite on Views V_i, see Figure 2)
6) if Q is the result of aggregation or other SQL operation on previous results from another query Q', then $\vec{r}(Q) =$

$\vec{r}(Q')$, since the data for Q is no fresher than the data in Q'.

The specific key values mentioned in 2) above must be explicit at the outermost level of Q, and not computed as part of the evaluation. This will allow efficient re-computation of Q as there is no need to perform a full evaluation of the query. Only those rows have to be retrieved that have changed its values since the last result caching. Then, a sufficient condition for the results of Q to be unchanged is that $\vec{r}(Q)$ is unchanged.

We note in passing that the calculation of $\vec{r}(Q)$ for a given query is very efficient. This is obvious because the readCheck vector has only a small dimension because of conditions 2) and 3). If a large set of rows or unknown data sets are selected, the readCheck value of the table is used.

This definition can be adapted for a multi-database query by creating a string representation combining the name of each contributing database with a string version $s(Q)$ of $\vec{r}(Q)$ (provided that the database agent is required to generate equal strings $s(Q)$ for equal $\vec{r}(Q)$). Such a combined string can then be used as an ETag validator for the associated HTTP request as described above.

This readCheck mechanism has been implemented as proof-of-concept using the Pyrrho [32] DBMS. This DBMS is built as a relational database on the .NET framework with pure optimistic concurrency control. It has been rigorously developed to deliver serializable transactions providing full ACID properties and support most of the SQL 2011 syntax. Its API allows application data models based on versioned objects. Each versioned value contains a readCheck string and updates to versioned objects use PUT, POST and DELETE operations similar to a REST service.

A. *Query Scenario with ReadCheck*

In order to illustrate the virtual integration and the use of the readCheck mechanism lets assume a distributed query Q issued by R against the Global View V.

As in Figure 2 the query Q is rewritten according to the Views V_i and each decomposed query Q_i is executed by the respective contractor C_i. It is the contractor's responsibility to provide the readCheck vector for the query result.

For example, C_1 executes Q_1 and computes $\vec{r}(Q_1) = (r(d), r(T))$ where $r(d)$ will be just the RVV value for the selected row d of table T_1 and $r(T_2)$ is the RVV value of the row that was last changed in T_2. The reason for using this value is that the select with predicate could comprise too many rows to include all its RVV efficiently in the readCheck vector.

The price for this implementation is that it might happen that the predicate query for table T_2 is unnecessarily re-executed when the original query Q is issued again. This happens if a row in table T_2 has been changed that is not included in the query predicate. This "false positive" could be avoided if the readCheck only considers rows meeting the predicate. The down side of such an approach would be that the RVV of all rows included in the query must be remembered along with the readCheck value. Nevertheless, it is the responsibility of the C_i to determine how to calculate the readCheck validator. In fact, the underlying data sources might

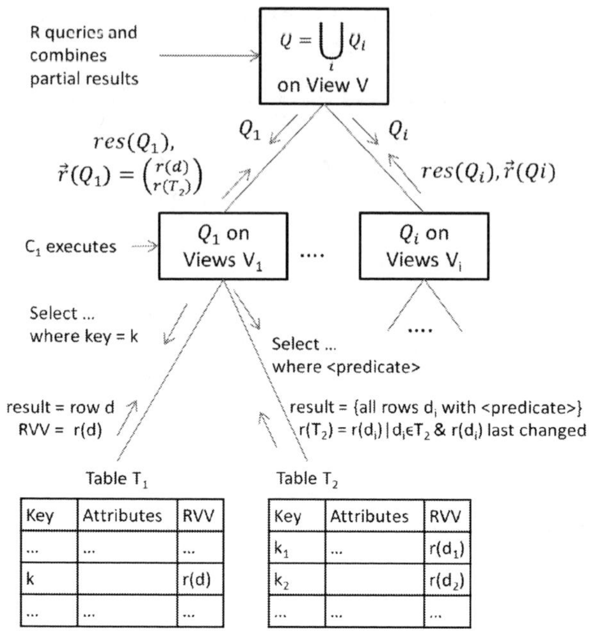

Figure 2: A general query scenario collecting data from multiple data providers

not be relational nor provide an RVV. So the contractor would need to establish its own readCheck mechanism in accordance with the definition above.

Depending on the API the results $res(Q_i)$ are delivered to R in a GET-response or as SQL result set. Finally R assembles (e.g., joins, union, etc.) the partial results according to the global view V.

B. *Global schema design*

Any data warehousing system needs a mechanism for creating a global schema. For our experiments we used a schema extension for integrating REST Views into a database schema. The BNF-schema definition has therefore been extended to include REST views into a database in the following way: (The ... represent the former DDL syntax of Pyrrho that is not shown for simplicity. The SQL syntax for Pyrrho can be found in Chapter 7 of [32])

ViewDefinition := ...| CREATE VIEW [ViewSpecification] id AS GET {Metadata} .

Metadata := ...| string .

ViewSpecification := ...| OF '(' TableClause [',' TableClause]')' [UriType] .

UriType := [Abbrev_id]'^^'([Namespace_id] ':' id | uri) . We pick up the example from the introduction to illustrate this syntax and implement it as follows:

/* C1: Hospital DB */

```
create table D (ID int(11) NOT NULL, name
varchar(45), rCode int, birthdate datetime,
admission datetime, diagnosis varchar(45), treatment
```

```
|-----------------|---------|-----------------|
|LOCATION         |DIAGNOSIS|PERCENTAGE       |
|-----------------|---------|-----------------|
|East End Freetown|Ebola    |0.00133333333333 |Statistics:578:474 ;;Hospital|1109|[76-0];Statistics:490:474;Statistics|831|[78-0]
|West End Freetown|Ebola    |0.0019999999999999|Statistics:667:474 ;;Hospital|1109|[76-0];Statistics:490:474;Statistics|831|[78-0]
|-----------------|---------|-----------------|
SQL>
```

Figure 3: Results from the queries of the example scenario

```
varchar(45), PRIMARY KEY (ID));

insert into D values
(1, 'Joe Soap', 2, date'2003-04-12',
date'2014-09-20', 'Ebola', 'IV fluid,
electrolytes'),
(2, 'Milly Soap', 2, date'2007-10-12',
date'2014-10-06', 'Ebola', 'IV fluid,
electrolytes'),
(3, 'Betty Boop', 1, date'1996-10-12',
date'2014-10-06', 'bacterial infection',
'antibiotics'),
(4, 'John Bell', 3, date'2009-11-14',
date'2014-09-10', 'Ebola', 'electrolytes'),
(5,'Benny Hall', 2, date'2007-10-10',
date'2014-10-06', 'Ebola', 'IV fluid,
electrolytes');

create view E as select rCode, extract(year from
(admission-birthdate)) as age, admission, diagnosis,
treatment, count(*) as patients from D group by
rCode, age, admission, diagnosis, treatment;
```

/* C2: Statistics DB */

```
create table H (rCode int NOT NULL, location
varchar(45), inhabitants int, under10 int, 10to20
int, 20to30 int, over30 int, lastUpdated datetime,
PRIMARY KEY (rCode));

insert into H values
(1,'Central Freetown',300000, 80000, 75000, 65000,
80000, date'2014-10-20'),
(2,'East End Freetown',500000, 150000, 120000,
100000, 130000, date'2014-10-20'),
(3,'West End Freetown',200000, 50000, 40000, 40000,
120000, date'2014-10-20');

create view K as select rCode, location,
inhabitants, under10, lastUpdated from H;
```

/* Requester Schema */

```
create view V1 of (rCode int, age int, admissionDate
date, diagnosis char, treatment char, patients int)
as get 'http://servD1:8180/Hospital/Hospital/E';

create view V2 of (rCode int, location char,
inhabitants int, under10 int, lastUpdated date)
as get 'http://servD2:8180/Statistics/Statistics/K';

create view V as select * from V1 natural join V2;
```

The view definitions of V1, V2 and V here do not copy data from database D_{11} or D_{21}; the REST Views V1 and V2 are defined using a URL metadata string for the servers hosting the databases. But R can obtain values from C1 and C2 using RESTful operations.

For instance a) the percentage of young Ebola patients under 10 years of age or b) the total number of treated patients by quarters (of Freetown) and diagnosis can be analysed.

```
select location, diagnosis, patients/under10)*100 as
percentage from V where age < 10;
```

The result of this query is given in Figure 3. The RVV and readCheck information for each row of the result table are provided by the Pyrrho database. Activating the -v flag prints these information on the right of the result table. So the first row of the join has an RVV of "Statistics:578:474". This is the concatenation of the RVV Statistics table H, log position 578 (location "East End Freetown") from transaction 474 and the Hospital contribution to this row (which is blank because of aggregation). The result of the above query is produced from the view V which results from two REST GET operations that produce two ETags and one RVV. ETag "Hospital|1109|[76-0]" says that the transaction log position was 1109 and any change to table 76 (table D) will invalidate the data. The second REST operation on view K produces RVV "Statistics:490:474" because it returns a single row from the same transaction 474 (location "East End Freetown") and the ETag "Statistics|831|[78-0]" with log position 831 and table 78 (table E).

Pyrrho's open-source implementation of the REST view automatically makes V2 an updatable view provided V2 has the necessary permissions on the Statistics DB (owner C2) and generates PUT, POST and DELETE operations on H that result from updates on the view K resp. V2. These operations can be used to curate the data, e.g. with:

```
update V set inhabitants = 199000, under10 = 49000
where rCode = 3;
```

and

```
delete from V2 where rCode = 5;
```

In real situations, things would not always be so simple, and column renaming and conversion between types and structures would result in a more complex definition of the view V. It seems to us that the REST View concept could be made interoperable, as B does not need to understand the structure or implementation of A's readCheck string, and only requires the property that $s(Q)$ is unchanged if the values read during evaluation of query Q are unchanged.

V. Conclusion and Future Work

This paper presents the beginnings of a formalism and practical strategy to manage Big Live Data. We show that such a virtual DWH can be based on the REST architecture using a mechanism similar to RFC7232 ETags or row version validators to ensure up-to-date and verifiable results. With the help of readCheck an optimistic concurrency mechanism can be implemented to support distributed transaction processing. Such a contract would be subject to alteration (e.g., a change in contractual responsibility) and readCheck would help to underpin a secure mechanism for managing such a change as described in III-D.

The readCheck mechanism can be implemented efficiently and be further used to optimise query processing so that only changed data sets need to be re-queried and combined with previous results. Our pilot implementation of these ideas using the Pyrrho database and complex views shows the applicability of the concept.

The data transformation from V_i to V assumes no data conflict and at present is manually defined but we plan to use metadata to support the data transformation and global schema design. Another point for future work is data curation and making data provenance transparent to the requester of a query.

REFERENCES

[1] W. H. Inmon, *Building the Data Warehouse*, 4th ed.,John Wiley & Sons, pp 49-50, 2005.

[2] M. Jarke, M. Lenzerini, Y. Vassiliou, and P. Vassiliadis, *Fundamentals of Data Warehouses*, 2nd ed., Springer, 2003.

[3] M. Bouzeghoub, F. Fabret, and M. Matulovic, "Modeling Data Warehouse Refreshment Process as a Workflow Application", In Proceedings of the International Workshop on Design and Management of Data Warehouses (DMDW99), Heidelberg, Germany, pp. 6/1 - 6/11, 1999.

[4] P. Vassiliadis, A. Simitsis, and S. Skiadopoulos, "Conceptual modeling for ETL processes", In Proceedings of the 5th ACM international workshop on Data Warehousing and OLAP (DOLAP 2002), pp. 14-21, 2002.

[5] A. Simitsis, "Mapping conceptual to logical models for ETL processes", In Proceedings of the 8th ACM international workshop on Data warehousing and OLAP (DOLAP 2005), pp. 67-76, 2005.

[6] A. Karakasidis, P. Vassiliadis, and E. Pitoura, "ETL queues for active data warehousing", In Proceedings of the 2nd international workshop on Information quality in information systems (IQIS 2005), pp. 28-39, 2005.

[7] M. V. Mannino and W. Effelsberg, "Matching Techniques in Global Schema Design", In Proceedings of the First International Conference on Data Engineering (ICDE 1984), Los Angeles, California, pp. 418-425, 1984.

[8] F. Put, "Schema Translation during Design and Integration of Databases", In Proceedings of the 9th International Conference on Entity-Relationship Approach (ER 1990), Lausanne, Switzerland, pp. 431-453, 1990.

[9] S. B. Navathe, T. Sashidhar, and R. Elmasri, "Relationship Merging in Schema Integration", VLDB 1984, pp. 78-90, 1984.

[10] R. Kimbal, L. Reeves, M. Ross, and W. Thornthwaite, *The Data Warehouse Lifecycle Toolkit: Expert Methods for Designing, Developing, and Deploying Data Warehouses*, John Wiley & Sons, February 1998.

[11] R. Srinivasan, C. Liang, and K. Ramamritham, "Maintaining Temporal Coherency of Virtual Data Warehouses", In Proceedings of the 19th IEEE Real-Time Systems Symposium (RTSS 1998), Madrid, Spain, pp. 60-70, 1998.

[12] M. Gorawski and R. Malczok, "Distributed Spatial Data Warehouse Indexed with Virtual Memory Aggregation Tree", 2nd International Workshop STDBM'04, Toronto, Canada, pp. 25-32, 2004.

[13] O. N. Myronovych and Y. E. Boreisha, "Web Services-Based Virtual Data Warehouse as an Integration and ETL Tool", In Proceedings of The 2005 International Symposium on Web Services and Applications (ISWS 2005), Las Vegas, Nevada, USA, pp. 52-58, 2005.

[14] R. T. Fielding, *Architectural Styles and the Design of Network-based Software Architectures* (Ph.D.). University of California, Irvine, 2000.

[15] R. T. Fielding et al., "Hypertext Transfer Protocol HTTP/1.1", RFC 2616, IETF, 1999, URL: https://datatracker.ietf.org/doc/rfc2616/ [last accessed: 2017-01-18].

[16] R. T. Fielding and J. Reschke (eds), "Hypertext Transfer protocol (HTTP/1.1): Conditional Requests", RFC 7232, IETF, 2014, URL: https://datatracker.ietf.org/doc/rfc7232/ [last accessed: 2017-01-18].

[17] P. Marques and O. Belo, "Adaptive OLAP Caching - Towards a better quality of service in analytical systems", The 2nd International Conference on Business Intelligence and Technology (BUSTECH 2012), Nice, France, pp. 42-47, 2012.

[18] F. Perez-Sorrosal, M. Patiño-Martinez, R. Jimenez-Peris, and B. Kemme, "Consistent and Scalable Cache Replication for Multi-Tier J2EE Applications", in Proceedings R. Cerqueira and R. H. Campbell (eds), Middleware 2007, ACM/IFIP/USENIX 8th International Middleware Conference, pp. 328-347, 2007, Lecture Notes in Computer Science, vol. 4834, Springer 2007, ISBN: 978-3-540-76777-0.

[19] M. Bilal and S.-G. Kang, "A Cache Management Scheme for Efficient Content Eviction and Replication in Cache Networks", IEEE Access, Vol. 5, pp. 1692-1701, 2017, DOI: 10.1109/ACCESS.2017.2669344.

[20] C. Viana-Ferreira, L. S. Ribeiro, S. Matos, and C. Costa, "Pattern recognition for cache management in distributed medical imaging environments", Int. J. Computer Assisted Radiology and Surgery 11(2): 327-336 (2016)

[21] S. Müller, R. Diestelkämper, and H. Plattner, "Cache Management for Aggregates in Columnar In-Memory Databases", The 6th International Conference on Advances in Databases, Knowledge, and Data Applications (DBKDA 2014), Chamonix, France, pp. 139-147, 2014.

[22] Q. Luo et al., "Middle-tier database caching for e-business", in M. J. Franklin, B. Moon, and A. Ailamaki (eds), Proceedings of the ACM SIGMOD International Conference on Management of Data, pp. 600-611, 2002.

[23] P. A. Bernstein, A. Fekete, H. Guo, R. Ramakrishnan, and P. Tamma, "Relaxed-currency serializability for middle-tier caching and replication", in S. Chaudhuri, V. Hristidis, and N. Polyzotis (eds), Proceedings of the ACM SIGMOD International Conference on Management of Data Conference, pp. 599-610, 2006.

[24] S. Ghandeharizadeh and J. Yap, "Cache augmented database management systems", Proceedings of the 3rd ACM SIGMOD Workshop on Databases and Social Networks, New York, USA, pp. 31-36, 2013, DOI: 10.1145/2484702.2484709.

[25] O. Asad, "AdaptCache: Adaptive Data Partitioning and Replication for Distributed Object Caches", in Proceedings of the Doctoral Symposium of the 17th International Middleware Conference, pp. 3:1-3:4, 2016, DOI: 10.1145/3009925.3009928.

[26] M. Laiho and F. Laux, "Implementing Optimistic Concurrency Control for Persistence Middleware Using Row Version Verification", The 2nd International Conference on Advances in Databases, Knowledge, and Data Applications (DBKDA 2010), Les Menuires, France, pp. 45-50, 2010.

[27] A. Kapila, "Well-known Databases Use Different Approaches for MVCC", EnterpriseDB, Bedford, MA, USA, 2015, URL: https://www.enterprisedb.com/well-known-databases-use-different-approaches-mvcc [last accessed: 2017-01-19].

[28] S. Howard, "SQL Server MVCC with read_committed_snapshot", 2012, URL: http://appcrawler.com/wordpress/2012/07/28/sql-server-mvcc-with-read_committed_snapshot/ [last accessed: 2017-01-19].

[29] X. Fengguang, H. Xie, and K. Liqun, "Research and implementation of heterogeneous data integration based on XML", The 9th International Conference on Electronic Measurement & Instruments (ICEMI2009), pp. 4:711-4:715, 2009

[30] Jinqun Wu, "Heterogeneous Data Integration Model Based on Virtual View", Proceedings of The 7th International Conference on Computer Science & Education (ICCSE 2012), Melbourne, Australia, pp. 815-817, 2012.

[31] N.Take, M. Nishio, and H. Seshake, "OSS Data Integration using Virtual Databases", 15th Asia-Pacific Network Operations and Management Symposium (APNOMS), pp. 1-6, 2013.

[32] M. K. Crowe, *The Pyrrho DBMS Version 5.6*, 2016, URL: http://pyrrhodb.com, [last accessed: 2017-01-18].

A Pseudometric for Gaussian Mixture Models

Linfei Zhou*, Wei Ye*, Bianca Wackersreuther*, Claudia Plant† and Christian Böhm*
* Institute for Computer Science, Ludwig-Maximilians-Universität München
† Department of Computer Science, University of Vienna
Email: *{zhou, ye, wackersb, boehm}@dbs.ifi.lmu.de, †claudia.plant@univie.ac.at

***Abstract*—Efficient similarity search for uncertain data is a challenging task in many modern data mining applications such as image retrieval, speaker recognition and stock market analysis. A common way to model the uncertainty of the objects is using probability density functions in the form of Gaussian Mixture Models (GMMs), which have the ability to approximate any arbitrary distribution. However, there is a lack of suitable similarity measures for GMMs. Hence, in this paper we propose a similarity measure, Pseudometric for GMMs (PmG). The advantage of PmG is that it is efficient in computation because of its closed-form expression for GMMs, and it fulfills the triangle inequality which is necessary for many techniques like clustering and embedding. Extensive experimental evaluations of the proposed similarity measure on various real-world and synthetic data sets demonstrate a considerably better performance than that of the existing similarity measures, in terms of run-time and result quality in classification and clustering.**

Keywords–Gaussian Mixture Models, Similarity Measures, Metric

I. Introduction

Information extraction systems capable of handling uncertain data objects is an actively investigated research field. Many modern applications like speaker recognition systems [1, 2], content-based image and video retrieval [3, 4], biometric identification and stock market analysis can be supported by uncertain data representation. As a general class of Probability Density Functions (PDF), Gaussian Mixture Model (GMM) consists of a weighted sum of univariate or multivariate Gaussian distributions, allowing a concise but exact representation of uncertain data objects [5]. A good example of using objects represented by GMMs is managing multimedia data [6]. A 90 minutes movie contains about 130,000 single images. It requires large storage capacities as well as enormous computational effort for content-based retrieval. Storing the movie as GMMs will dramatically reduce the resource consumption while guaranteeing a high accuracy of the search result.

Besides the modeling of uncertainty, the efficiency of similarity search on uncertain data is another important aspect. For data objects represented by GMMs, Rougui et al. [7] have built a bottom-up hierarchical tree based on the calculation of the complete similarity matrix for all GMMs. However, it is only usable for static data sets, since it has no convenient insertion and deletion strategy, which depends on a proper similarity measure and requires a corresponding custom-built structure. The suitable similarity measures of GMMs for the indexing trees are yet to be developed and tested. A competitive candidate for such a similarity measure has the competencies to guarantee high efficiency in its computation and to facilitate indexing and further analysis. As we will demonstrate, our technique proposed in this paper is highly efficient because it enables closed-form computation. Moreover, our technique has the property of being a pseudometric, thus indexing techniques like VP-tree [8] can be applied for efficient search and embedding techniques like multidimensional scaling facilitate the subsequent analysis of the data set. To our knowledge, several studies [9]–[14] have dealt with defining similarity measures for GMMs, but only a few of them have closed-form expressions and none of them is a metric or pseudometric.

The main contributions of this paper are:

- We propose a pseudometric for GMMs (PmG), which is a similarity measure for GMMs. We derive the closed-form expression and prove that it is a pseudometric. The closed-form expression has a great advantage in calculation, and the properties of pseudometric are required by many analysis techniques.
- We define Normalized Matching Probability (NMP), which can be constituted to form novel similarity measures that have closed-form expressions for GMMs.
- Experimental evaluation demonstrates both the effectiveness and efficiency of PmG.

The rest of this paper is organized as follows: Section II gives the basic definition of GMMs, metric and pseudometric. Section III defines NMP and PmG, and gives the proof of the pseudometric properties of PmG. Section IV shows the experimental studies for verifying the efficiency and effectiveness of the proposed similarity measure. In Section V, we survey the previous work. Finally, Section VI summarizes the paper and presents some ideas for further research.

II. Formal Definitions

In this section, we summarize the formal notations for GMM. GMM is a probabilistic model that represents the probability distribution of observations. The definition of GMM is shown as follow.

Definition 1: (Gaussian Mixture Model) Let $\mathbf{x} \in \mathbb{R}^D$ be a variable in a D-dimensional space, $\mathbf{x} = (x_1, x_2, ..., x_D)$. A Gaussian Mixture Model $\mathcal{G}$ is the weighted sum of m Gaussian functions, defined as:

$$\mathcal{G}(\mathbf{x}) = \sum_{1 \le i \le m} w_i \cdot \mathcal{N}_i(\mathbf{x}) \quad (1)$$

where $\sum_{1 \le i \le m} w_i = 1$, $\forall i \in [1, m], w_i \ge 0$, and Gaussian component $\mathcal{N}_i(\mathbf{x})$ is the density of a Gaussian distribution with a covariance matrix Σ_i:

$$\mathcal{N}_i(\mathbf{x}) = \frac{1}{\sqrt{(2\pi)^D|\Sigma_i|}}\exp\left(-\frac{1}{2}(\mathbf{x}-\mu_i)^T\Sigma_i^{-1}(\mathbf{x}-\mu_i)\right)$$

Specially, when Σ_i is a diagonal matrix, $\mathcal{N}_i(\mathbf{x})$ can be reformulated as:

$$\mathcal{N}_i(\mathbf{x}) = \prod_{1\leq l\leq D}\frac{1}{\sqrt{2\pi\sigma_{i,l}^2}}\exp\left(\frac{-(x_l-\mu_{i,l})^2}{2\sigma_{i,l}^2}\right)$$

where $\sigma_{i,l}$ is the l-th element on the diagonal of Σ_i.

Most of dissimilarities are distances, and they are also metrics if the following definition is matched.

Definition 2: (Metric)

Given an nonempty set of objects $\mathscr{P}(\mathbb{R}^D)$, a mapping $d: \mathscr{P}(\mathbb{R}^D)\times\mathscr{P}(\mathbb{R}^D)\longrightarrow\mathbb{R}^+$ is a metric when the following properties always hold for any object $\mathcal{X},\mathcal{Y},\mathcal{Z}\in\mathscr{P}(\mathbb{R}^D)$.

- **Non-negativity**: $d(\mathcal{X},\mathcal{Y})\geq 0$
- **Identity of indiscernibles**: $d(\mathcal{X},\mathcal{Y})=0\Leftrightarrow\mathcal{X}=\mathcal{Y}$
- **Symmetry**: $d(\mathcal{X},\mathcal{Y})=d(\mathcal{Y},\mathcal{X})$
- **Triangle inequality**: $d(\mathcal{X},\mathcal{Y})+d(\mathcal{Y},\mathcal{Z})\geq d(\mathcal{X},\mathcal{Z})$

A pseudometric is a mapping that satisfies the axioms for a metric, except that instead of the identity of indiscernbles, $d(\mathcal{X},\mathcal{X})=0$ but for some distinct objects $\mathcal{X}\neq\mathcal{Y}$, possibly $d(\mathcal{X},\mathcal{Y})=0$.

The properties of the metric, especially the triangle inequality, are essential to index structures such as M-tree and VP-tree for efficient queries, and they are fully required by some techniques like DBSCAN. For similarity measures without the metric properties, specialized index and analysis methods are needed to guarantee the efficiency and the applicability of certain techniques.

III. Pseudometric for Gaussian Mixture Models

In this section, we extend Matching Probability (MP) into NMP, and derive its closed-form expression for GMMs. NMP provides a fundamental closed-form calculation for GMMs, and it can be used to define other similarity measures for GMMs. Specifically, we define PmG, a pseudometric for GMMs.

A. Normalized Matching Probability

MP considers all the possible positions of true feature vectors, and sums up the joint probabilities of two PDFs. Here we define NMP for GMMs.

Definition 3: (Normalized Matching Probability) Given two GMMs $\mathcal{G}_1(\mathrm{x})$ and $\mathcal{G}_2(\mathrm{x})$ with diagonal covariance matrices in space $\mathbb{R}^D$, we define the NMP $\langle\mathcal{G}_1,\mathcal{G}_2\rangle$ as follows:

$$\langle\mathcal{G}_1,\mathcal{G}_2\rangle = \int_{\mathbb{R}^D}\mathcal{G}_1^{'}(\mathbf{x})\cdot\mathcal{G}_2^{'}(\mathbf{x})\mathrm{d}\mathbf{x} \quad (2)$$

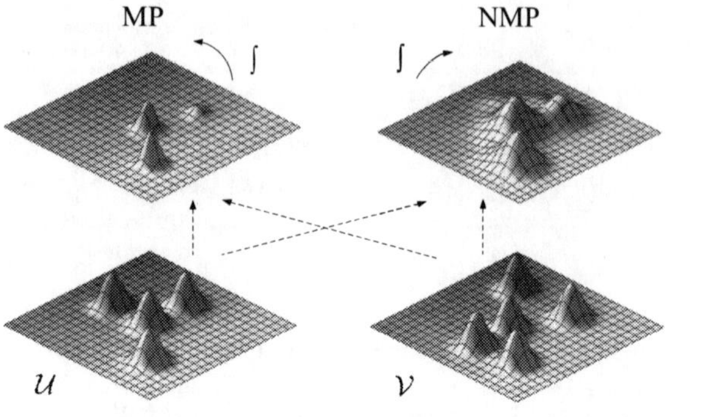

Figure 1: Demonstration of MP and NMP between GMM objects $\mathcal{U},\mathcal{V}$ in a two-dimensional space.

where $\mathcal{G}^{'}(\mathrm{x}) = \sum_{1\leq i\leq m}\prod_{1\leq l\leq D}\mathcal{N}(\mu_{i,l},\sigma_{i,l}^2/w_i)$. m,μ and σ are the parameters of GMM $\mathcal{G}$ (see Definition 1).

Figure 1 demonstrates MP and NMP between two GMM objects $\mathcal{U},\mathcal{V}$. As the measures of similarity, both MP and NMP integrate the similar parts of Gaussian components, as shown in the top of the figure. Because of the normalization operation, NMP gains a greater values than MP and emphasizes the shared parts.

For the closed-form expression of $\langle\mathcal{G}_1,\mathcal{G}_2\rangle$, we can derive it from the following equation.

$$\begin{aligned}
&\langle\mathcal{G}_1,\mathcal{G}_2\rangle\\
&=\sum_{i=1}^{m_1}\sum_{j=1}^{m_2}\prod_{l=1}^{D}\frac{\sqrt{w_{1,i}w_{2,j}}}{2\pi\sqrt{\sigma_{1,i,l}^2\sigma_{2,j,l}^2}}\int \mathrm{e}^{-\frac{(x-\mu_{1,i,l})^2}{2\sigma_{1,i}^2/w_{1,i}}-\frac{(x-\mu_{2,j,l})^2}{2\sigma_{2,j,l}^2}}\mathrm{d}x\\
&=\sum_{i=1}^{m_1}\sum_{j=1}^{m_2}\prod_{l=1}^{D}\frac{\mathrm{e}^{-\frac{(\mu_{1,i,l}-\mu_{2,j,l})^2}{2(\sigma_{1,i,l}^2/w_{1,i}+\sigma_{2,j,l}^2/w_{2,j})}}}{\sqrt{2\pi(\sigma_{1,i,l}^2/w_{1,i}+\sigma_{2,j,l}^2/w_{2,j})}}\\
&=\sum_{i=1}^{m_1}\sum_{j=1}^{m_2}\prod_{l=1}^{D}\mathcal{N}(\mu_{1,i,l},\mu_{2,j,l},\frac{\sigma_{1,i,l}^2}{w_{1,i}}+\frac{\sigma_{2,j,l}^2}{w_{2,j}})
\end{aligned}$$

If two GMMs are very disjoint, NMP between them is close to zero. To obtain a higher NMP, it is required that two GMMs have similar shapes, i.e. similar parameters.

A closed-form expression is intrinsically valuable for computation. It saves extra efforts to get a good approximation by avoiding simulation methods like Monte-Carlo, which may cause a significant increase in computation time and the loss of precision. Therefore, closed-form expressions are well received in many applications, especially in real-time applications.

Based on NMP, we can get a set of similarity measures with closed-form expressions for GMMs. For example, we can define a distance as follows.

$$d(\mathcal{G}_1,\mathcal{G}_2) = 1-\frac{\langle\mathcal{G}_1,\mathcal{G}_2\rangle}{\sqrt{\langle\mathcal{G}_1,\mathcal{G}_1\rangle\langle\mathcal{G}_2,\mathcal{G}_2\rangle}}$$

There are several similarity measures based on MP have been proposed [10, 12, 13], and we can easily extend NMP on them.

B. Pseudometric for GMMs

On the basis of NMP, we define a pseudometric for G-MMs, PmG. Likewise, PmG determines the square differences between normalized GMMs, sums them up by integration and returns the root of the integration. The definition of PmG is shown as follows.

Definition 4: (Pseudometric for GMMs) Given two GMMs $\mathcal{G}_1(\mathrm{x})$ and $\mathcal{G}_2(\mathrm{x})$ with diagonal covariance matrices in space $\mathbb{R}^D$, we define the PmG of them as follows:

$$d_{\text{PmG}}(\mathcal{G}_1, \mathcal{G}_2) = \sqrt{\langle \mathcal{G}_1, \mathcal{G}_1 \rangle + \langle \mathcal{G}_2, \mathcal{G}_2 \rangle - 2 \cdot \langle \mathcal{G}_1, \mathcal{G}_2 \rangle} \quad (3)$$

Obviously, PmG has a closed-form expression for GMMs with diagonal covariances. Then we give the proof that PmG fulfills three properties of a metric.

Lemma 3.1: PmG is a pseudometric.

Proof: **Non-negativity:**

According to the definition of NMP, for any $\mathcal{G}_1, \mathcal{G}_2$, $\langle \mathcal{G}_1, \mathcal{G}_1 \rangle + \langle \mathcal{G}_2, \mathcal{G}_2 \rangle - 2 \cdot \langle \mathcal{G}_1, \mathcal{G}_2 \rangle \geq 0$. Thus $d_{\text{PmG}}(\mathcal{G}_1, \mathcal{G}_2) \geq 0$. If $\mathcal{G}_1 = \mathcal{G}_2$, $d_{\text{PmG}}(\mathcal{G}_1, \mathcal{G}_2) = 0$.

Symmetry:

Obviously, $d_{\text{PmG}}(\mathcal{G}_1, \mathcal{G}_2) = d_{\text{PmG}}(\mathcal{G}_2, \mathcal{G}_1)$.

Triangle Inequality:

Since $d_{\text{PmG}}(\mathcal{G}_1, \mathcal{G}_2)$ can be reformed to the ℓ^2 norm of $\mathcal{G}_1^{'}$ and $\mathcal{G}_2^{'}$, its triangle inequality can be proved easily. ■

Having the property of triangle inequality, metric or pseudometric can employ various of metric trees to make accesses to the data objects more efficient. Otherwise, specialized index and analysis methods are needed to guarantee the efficiency and applicability of index, which means extra efforts.

IV. Experimental Evaluation

In this section, we provide experiments on both real-world and synthetic data sets to show the effectiveness and efficiency of the proposed pseudometric for GMMs. Classification and clustering, which are the major subdivisions of pattern recognition techniques, as well as the run-time of similarity calculation are used in the evaluation.

For Kullback-Leibler (KL) divergence [15] based similarity measures, only matching based approximation (KLm) [9] is included in this paper since it is one of the best-performing approximations [16].

All the experiments are implemented with Java 1.7, and executed on a regular workstation PC with 3.4 GHz dual core CPU equipped with 32 GB RAM. For all the experiments, we use the 10-fold cross validation and report the average results over 100 runs.

A. Data Sets

Synthetic data and four kinds of real-world data, including activity data, image data, audio data, and weather data, are used in the experiments. For the data objects, GMMs are estimated using Expectation-Maximization (EM) algorithm (implementation provided by WEKA).

Activity data [17] is collected from 15 participants performing seven activities. Assuming that participants complete a single activity in three seconds, we regard the 150 continuous measurements of acceleration on three axes as one data object. Thus 1083 objects are generated for participant 1.

Image data [18] is a collection of images taking under various viewpoints. In this paper, we use the gray images recording 100 objects from 72 viewpoints. Every image (192×144) is smoothed by a Gaussian filter with a standard deviation of five pixels.

Audio data [19] consists of speech from ten speakers, the names of who are shown as follows: Aaron, Abdul Moiz, Afshad, Afzal, Akahansson, Alexander Drachmann, Afred Strauss, Andy, Anna Karpelevich and Anniepoo. Every wav file is split into ten fragments, transformed into frequency domain by Fast Fourier Transform.

Weather data [20] is the historical weather data of 908 airports in Europe from 2005 to 2014. The features of Weather data are temperature and humidity, and only the average values of each day are used.

The synthetic data sets [21] are generated by randomly choosing mean values between 0 and 100 and standard deviations between 0 and 5 for each Gaussian component. The weights are randomly assigned, and they sum up to one within each GMM. Since there is no intuitive way to assign class labels for GMMs in advance, here we use the synthetic data sets only for the run-time evaluation.

B. Effectiveness Evaluation

In the evaluation of classification, we employ the simplest and widely used algorithm k-Nearest Neighbors (k-NN), rather than the other more complex techniques, to compare the effectiveness of the similarity measures, since we are not interested in tuning classification accuracy to its optimum.

Varying k in k-NN and the number of Gaussian components in each GMM, we start with experiments on Activity data. As shown in Figure 2, PmG has a better performance than the other similarity measures for different k. With the increase number of Gaussian components in each GMM, the classification accuracies of PmG sightly increase, and generally outperform the other measures. For all the four real-world data sets, we fix the numbers of Gaussian components and report the results of 1-NN classification accuracies in Table I, where the highest accuracies of each column are marked in bold and with •, while the second highest ones are just marked in bold. We can see that PmG achieves the highest or second highest accuracies among all the similarity measures.

To compare the usability of the proposed similarity measure for unsupervised data mining, we perform clustering experiments on all four real-world data sets. Instead of k-means algorithm, the k-medoids is used here since it works

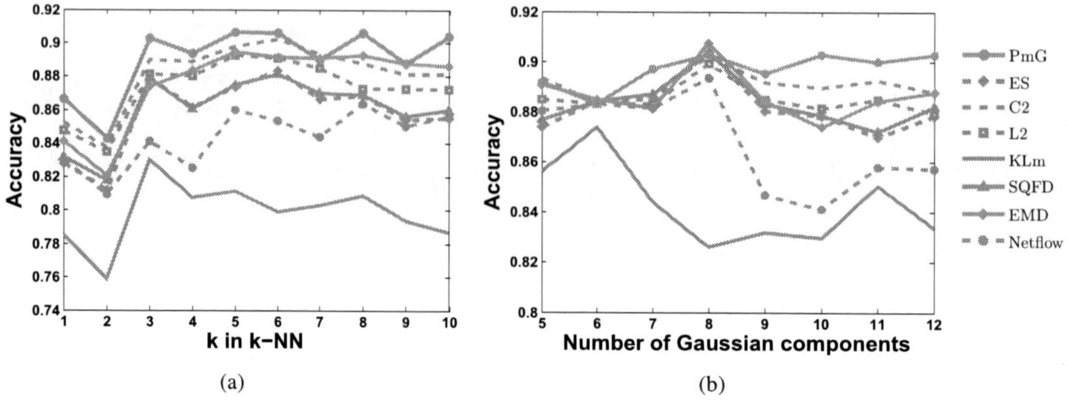

Figure 2: Classification results of Activity data. The numbers of Gaussian components in GMMs generated from data objects in (a) are fixed as ten. In (b), k in k-NN is fixed as three.

TABLE II. CLUSTERING RESULTS OF k-MEDOIDS.

	Activity (k=7)			**Image** (k=100)			**Audio** (k=10)			**Weather** (k=14)		
	Purity	NMI	FM	Purity	NMI	FM	Purity	NMI	FM	Purity	NMI	FM
PmG	**.82±.03**	**.49±.04**	**.56±.07**	**.43±.00**	**.69±.00**	**.30±.01**	**.56±.04**	**.45±.03**	**.40±.03**	**.58±.01**	**.23±.01**	.22±.03
ES	.73±.05	.37±.03	.39±.03	.40±.01	.67±.00	.28±.01	.49±.04	.37±.02	.33±.03	.55±.02	.18±.02	.21±.03
C2	.77±.06	.39±.07	.45±.07	.40±.00	.67±.00	.27±.00	.46±.05	.34±.03	.32±.03	.53±.02	.16±.02	.22±.04
L2	.77±.03	.37±.04	.44±.06	.40±.01	.66±.00	.27±.01	.48±.04	.36±.03	.33±.02	.54±.02	.17±.01	.20±.02
KLm	.74±.03	.41±.03	.50±.05	.40±.00	.66±.00	.27±.00	.46±.05	.38±.03	.33±.04	.47±.01	.15±.01	**.26±.03**
SQFD	.72±.04	.35±.03	.39±.04	.40±.01	.66±.00	.27±.00	.51±.04	.38±.03	.35±.03	.54±.01	.17±.01	.21±.02
EMD	.79±.04	.45±.05	.48±.07	.33±.01	.58±.00	.21±.01	.47±.03	.40±.03	.34±.03	.57±.01	.21±.01	.23±.03
Netflow	.74±.07	.36±.08	.44±.05	.39±.00	.66±.00	.27±.00	.49±.03	.45±.04	.38±.04	.56±.01	.20±.01	.19±.02

TABLE I. 1-NN CLASSIFICATION RESULTS OF REAL-WORLD DATA.

	Activity ($m = 10$)	**Image** ($m = 5$)	**Audio** ($m = 5$)	**Weather** ($m = 10$)
PmG	**.865±.030** •	**.852±.010** •	**.851±.044**	**.761±.032** •
ES	.834±.032	**.827±.010**	.804±.035	.740±.030
C2	**.859±.032**	.827±.010	.803±.039	.730±.033
L2	.853±.032	.826±.010	.802±.039	.737±.028
KLm	.793±.039	.823±.010	.825±.037	.717±.030
SQFD	.843±.030	.825±.014	.808±.028	.724±.035
EMD	.848±.033	.519±.014	.809±.032	**.758±.047**
Netflow	.838±.030	.813±.010	**.857±.032** •	.757±.051

with arbitrary similarity measure, making it more suitable in our situation. We evaluate the clustering results using three widely used criteria, Purity, Normalized Mutual Information (NMI) and F1 Measure (FM).

Table II illustrates the evaluation of clustering results when using different similarity measures on four real-world data sets. PmG achieves the best performance among all the measures on all three criteria, except for FM on Weather data.

C. Efficiency Evaluation

Every similarity measure evaluated in this paper has a time complexity of $O(m_1 \cdot m_2 \cdot D)$, where m_1 and m_2 are the numbers of Gaussian components in GMMs that are used for similarity calculating, and D is the dimensionality of data space. To support the theoretical time complexity, we provide comparisons by scaling m and D on synthetic data sets.

We calculate distance matrices for all the synthetic data sets, and as mentioned before, the average time cost of 100 runs are reported. Figure 3 shows the comparison of run-time between all the similarity measures on synthetic data sets with different numbers of Gaussian components in each GMM and different data dimensionality. The run-time of all similarity measures has a quadratic relation with the component number and a linear dependence with data dimensionality. PmG has a similar performance with ES, C2 and L2. With the increase of components number, EMD and Netflow gain more than PmG in time-cost. For varying dimensionality, the tendencies of all the similarity measures are very similar.

Comparing the query efficiency of linear scan and metric tree, we illustrate the time-cost of queries in Figure 4. Figure 4(a) demonstrates the linear relation between the query time and the number of data objects in linear scan queries. When

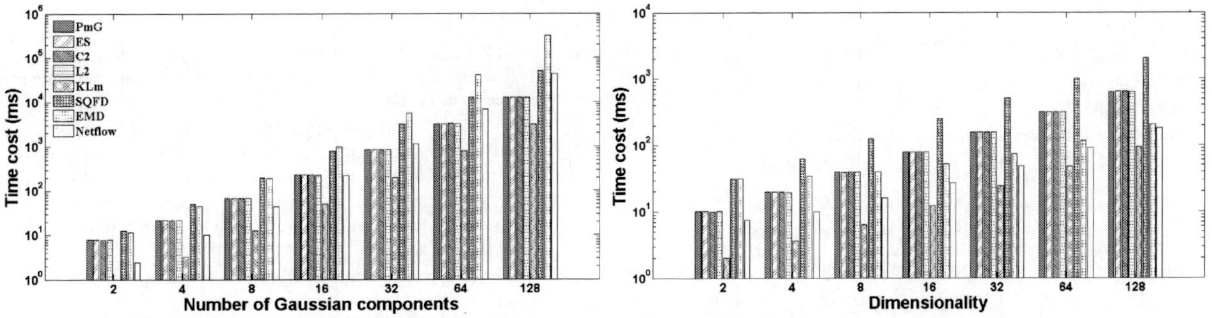

(a) Varying the number of Gaussian components.

(b) Varying data dimensionality.

Figure 3: Time cost of linear scan queries on synthetic data sets. In (a), the data dimensionality is fixed as two. The numbers of Gaussian components are set as ten in (b).

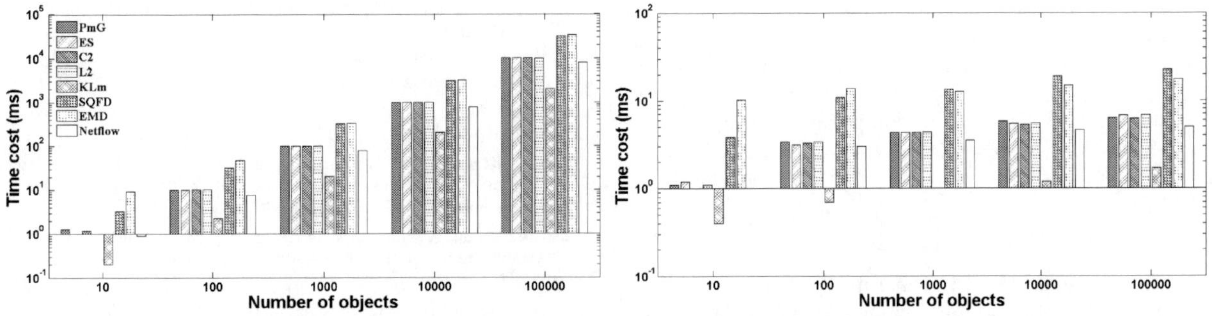

(a) Time cost of linear scan queries.

(b) Time cost of VP-tree queries.

Figure 4: Time cost of queries when varying the number of data objects. Each GMM used here has ten Gaussian components in a two-dimensional space. The capacity of nodes in the VP-tree is set to 32.

using VP-tree, as shown in Figure 4(b), there are great improvements in query efficiency for all the similarity measures. However, only PmG, EMD and Netflow can guarantee query accuracies among them.

V. Related Work

This section gives a survey and discussion of similarity measures for GMMs in previous work. Firstly we summarize approximation approaches for GMMs, then we discuss similarity measures that have closed-form expressions.

The Kullback-Leibler divergence [15] is a common way to measure the distance between two PDFs. It is given by $d_{\mathrm{KL}}(f_1\|f_2) = \int f_1(x)\log\frac{f_1(x)}{f_2(x)}\mathrm{d}x$. For the properties of metric, the KL divergence only satisfies the non-negativity property, although its symmetric version $(|\frac{1}{2}d_{\mathrm{KL}}(f_1\|f_2)+\frac{1}{2}d_{\mathrm{KL}}(f_2\|f_1)|)$ also satisfies the symmetry property. Moreover, it has a closed-form expression for Gaussian distributions, but no such expression for GMMs exists.

To compute the distance between GMMs by the KL divergence, several approximation methods have been proposed. A commonly used approximation to $d_{\mathrm{KL}}(f_1\|f_2)$, the Gaussian approximation, replaces f_1 and f_2 with two Gaussian distributions, whose means and covariance matrices depend on those of GMMs. Another popular way is to use the minimum KL divergence of Gaussian components that are included in two G-MMs. Moreover, Hershey et al. [11] have proposed the product of Gaussian approximation and the variation approximation, but the former tends to greatly underestimate $d_{\mathrm{KL}}(f_1\|f_2)$ while the latter does not satisfy the positivity property. Besides, Goldberger et al. [9] have proposed KLm and the unscented transformation based KL divergence(KLt). KLm works well when the Gaussian elements are far apart, but it cannot handle the overlapping situations, which are very common in real-world data sets. KLt solves the overlapping problem based on a non-linear transformation. Cui et al. [16] have compared the six approximation methods for KL divergence with Monte Carlo sampling, where the variation approximation achieves the best result quality, while KLm give a comparable result with a much faster speed.

Besides the approximation similarity methods for GMMs, several methods with closed-form expression have been proposed. Helén et al. [10] have described a squared Euclidean distance, which integrates the squared differences over the whole feature space. It has a closed-form expression for GMMs. Sfikas et al. [13] have presented a KL divergence based distance C2 and a Bhattacharyya-based distance for GMMs. Jensen et al. [12] used a normalized L2 distance to measure the similarity of GMMs in mel-frequency cepstral coefficients from songs. Beecks et al. [22] have proposed SQFD for GMMs to model the similarities between images. However, none of these similarity measures with closed-form expression for GMMs obeys the triangle inequality.

VI. Discussion and Conclusions

In this paper, we have proposed PmG for GMMs. As a metric, PmG enables storing GMMs in any metric tree and applying analysis techniques that require the properties of triangle inequality. In our experimental evaluations on real-world data sets, we have demonstrated the effectiveness of the proposed similarity measure. PmG outperform the other measures on different types of data sets in both classification and clustering.

Due to the potentially different number of Gaussian components in GMMs, there is still not much specialized indexing structure for GMMs exist. Using matching probability as the similarity measure, Böhm et al. [23] and Zhou et al. [24] have decomposed each GMM into its components to support the indexing of GMMs. A specialized dynamic index for GMMs using a metric or pseudometric is a promising perspective.

Acknowledgment

We thank Thomas Abeel for sharing the code implementations of k-medoids algorithm, Damien Di Fede for sharing his implementation of Fast Fourier Transform, Mzechner for his/her implementation of audio file processing.

References

[1] W. M. Campbell, D. E. Sturim, and D. A. Reynolds, "Support vector machines using GMM supervectors for speaker verification," IEEE Signal Process. Lett., vol. 13, no. 5, 2006, pp. 308–311.

[2] D. A. Reynolds, T. F. Quatieri, and R. B. Dunn, "Speaker verification using adapted gaussian mixture models," Digital Signal Processing, vol. 10, no. 1-3, 2000, pp. 19–41.

[3] P. KaewTraKulPong and R. Bowden, "An improved adaptive background mixture model for real-time tracking with shadow detection," in Video-based surveillance systems. Springer, 2002, pp. 135–144.

[4] Z. Zivkovic, "Improved Adaptive Gaussian Mixture Model for Background Subtraction," in ICPR, 2004, pp. 28–31.

[5] D. Reynolds, "Gaussian mixture models," Encyclopedia of Biometrics, 2015, pp. 827–832.

[6] S. Ou, C. Lee, V. S. Somayazulu, Y. Chen, and S. Chien, "Low complexity on-line video summarization with gaussian mixture model based clustering," in ICASSP, 2014, pp. 1260–1264.

[7] J. E. Rougui, M. Gelgon, D. Aboutajdine, N. Mouaddib, and M. Rziza, "Organizing Gaussian mixture models into a tree for scaling up speaker retrieval," Pattern Recognition Letters, vol. 28, no. 11, 2007, pp. 1314–1319.

[8] P. N. Yianilos, "Data structures and algorithms for nearest neighbor search in general metric spaces," in ACM/SIGACT-SIAM SODA, 1993, pp. 311–321.

[9] J. Goldberger, S. Gordon, and H. Greenspan, "An efficient image similarity measure based on approximations of kl-divergence between two gaussian mixtures," in ICCV, 2003, pp. 487–493.

[10] M. L. Helén and T. Virtanen, "Query by example of audio signals using euclidean distance between gaussian mixture models," in ICASSP (1), 2007, pp. 225–228.

[11] J. R. Hershey and P. A. Olsen, "Approximating the kullback leibler divergence between gaussian mixture models," in ICASSP, 2007, pp. 317–320.

[12] J. H. Jensen, D. P. W. Ellis, M. G. Christensen, and S. H. Jensen, "Evaluation of distance measures between gaussian mixture models of mfccs," in ISMIR, 2007, pp. 107–108.

[13] G. Sfikas, C. Constantinopoulos, A. Likas, and N. P. Galatsanos, "An analytic distance metric for gaussian mixture models with application in image retrieval," in ICANN (2), 2005, pp. 835–840.

[14] S. Zeng, R. Huang, H. Wang, and Z. Kang, "Image retrieval using spatiograms of colors quantized by gaussian mixture models," Neurocomputing, vol. 171, 2016, pp. 673–684.

[15] S. Kullback, Information theory and statistics. Courier Dover Publications, 2012.

[16] S. Cui and M. Datcu, "Comparison of kullback-leibler divergence approximation methods between gaussian mixture models for satellite image retrieval," in IGARSS, 2015, pp. 3719–3722.

[17] "Uci archive: Activity recognition data," http://archive.ics.uci.edu/ml/machine-learning-databases/00287/, accessed: 2017-03-27.

[18] "Aloi image data," http://aloi.science.uva.nl/, accessed: 2017-03-27.

[19] "Speaker recognition data," http://www.repository.voxforge1.org/downloads/SpeechCorpus/Trunk/Audio/Main/16kHz_16bit/, accessed: 2017-03-27.

[20] "Weather of airports data," https://drive.google.com/open?id=0B3LRCuPdnX1BZ0d4RXIxMDVzakE, accessed: 2017-03-27.

[21] "Synthetic data sets," https://drive.google.com/open?id=0B3LRCuPdnX1BMzlHaUJYSFlpU1U, accessed: 2017-03-27.

[22] C. Beecks, A. M. Ivanescu, S. Kirchhoff, and T. Seidl, "Modeling image similarity by gaussian mixture models and the signature quadratic form distance," in ICCV, 2011, pp. 1754–1761.

[23] C. Böhm, P. Kunath, A. Pryakhin, and M. Schubert, "Querying objects modeled by arbitrary probability distributions," in SSTD, 2007, pp. 294–311.

[24] L. Zhou, B. Wackersreuther, F. Fiedler, C. Plant, and C. Böhm, "Gaussian component based index for GMMs," in ICDM, 2016, pp. 1365–1370.

A Data Mining Framework for Product Bundle Design and Pricing

Yiming Li
Faculty of Computer Science
Dalhousie University
Halifax, Canada
email: ym510041@dal.ca

Hai Wang
Sobey School of Business
Saint Mary's University
Halifax, Canada
email: hwang@smu.ca

Qigang Gao
Faculty of Computer Science
Dalhousie University
Halifax, Canada
email: qggao@cs.dal.ca

Abstract— **Product bundling is a marketing strategy that has been widely studied in research literature and extensively used in practice. With the growing quantity of products and huge possible bundling combinations, it is necessary to develop algorithmic approaches to determine which products should be in a profitable bundle, and what the proper price is for a bundle. In this paper, we propose a new data mining framework for product bundle design and bundle pricing. This framework incorporates the time value of money in data mining tasks, and it is capable of determining the product combination and price of a bundle in order to maximize the profit. We also demonstrate the efficiency of this data mining framework through experiments and simulations.**

Keywords-data mining; bundling; bundle design; bundle pricing; marketing strategy

I. INTRODUCTION

To meet consumers' needs and expectations is the basic principle for sellers to survive in the current fierce competitive business environment. Sellers often adopt various promotion strategies to attract more consumers/buyersto increase their revenues. Bundling is a promotion strategy in which sellers provide multiple products or events as a single package with a discounted price [21]. Bundling has become prevalent as it can benefit bothbuyers and sellers.

From the consumer/buyer's perspective, bundling can provide benefits such as

- 8% monetary savings on average [8].
- Saving search cost, which will increase the willingness to purchase [17].

From the seller's perspective, selling bundles can benefit them from the following aspects:

- Increasing the number of buyers and thus increasing sales [8].
- Easier for newly released products to be noticed and accepted by consumers/buyers [17].
- Saving packaging and distribution cost [4].

In this paper, we propose a data mining framework for solving the bundle design problem. Our framework can help sellers obtain a good knowledge of their consumers by analyzing their purchase patterns and reservation price in different time periods, as well as design profitable bundles with proper price and strategies to increase sales. We demonstrate that the proposed framework is able to achieve significantly better performance on analyzing the *price elasticity of demand* (PED) and estimating the buyers' *reservation prices*. The PED measures the change of quantity demanded of a product with respect to the changes of the price, with other things being equal [20]. The *reservation price* of a buyer is the highest price that the buyer is willing to pay for a particular product [22]. The main contributions of this paper are summarized as follows:

- Many previous proposed methods on bundle pricing either make strong assumptions on the reservation prices (e.g., the reservation prices are known), or estimate the reservation prices based on consumers' survey data. Our proposed framework uses consumer/buyer's previous purchase behaviors rather than a marketing survey as the data source for estimating buyers' reservation prices. In contrast to the consumers' survey data, which are usually of small size and subjective, and may be inconsistent and incomplete, historical purchasing transaction data are of large size, accurate and objective.
- Our proposed framework also incorporates the time value of money in data mining tasks, and analyzes the PED in order to obtain accurate estimation of buyers' reservation prices. Considering time as a factor can help with understanding consumers' purchase behaviors in different time periods and designing proper bundles to meet consumers' varying requirements, which is missing in previous bundling studies. The estimated buyers' reservation prices serve as the basis for bundle design and bundle pricing.
- Our proposed framework is generic and does not limit to specific data mining algorithms. For example, new association rule mining algorithms can be integrated into our proposed framework to improve the efficiency and effectiveness for determining the possible product combinations within a bundle.

The remainder of this paper is organized as follows. Section II formulates the bundle design problem and the bundle pricing problem. Section III describes our data mining framework for bundle design and pricing. Section IV shows the performance of the proposed approach through experiments and simulations. Section V remarks the conclusions and the future work.

II. RELATED WORK AND PROBLEM FORMULATION

Bundling has been extensively studied and applied in retailing [2][13][15][16], entertainment [6][22], e-commerce [1][3][16][19], travel planning [9][10], telecommunication [23] as well as the service sector [12][18].

Two main problems associated with bundling in the previous research literature are the bundle design problem and the bundle pricing problem. Suppose that there are N distinct products available for bundling, the $2^N-(N+1)$ possible product combinations for bundling (excluding the bundles with a single product) make this problem extremely complex for sellers, especially when N is large [9]. Bundle design is a process of selecting product combinations to be promoted and sold as a bundle, which should be rational, practical, and in accordance with consumers' preferences. The main objective for providing bundles is to attract more buyers and hence increase the sales for sellers.

Moreover, a more remarkable principle that needs to be considered in bundle design is to know exactly what consumers/buyers want. It is more beneficial for sellers to provide flexible bundles that consumers can choose along with their preferences and needs.

Bundle pricing is about deciding the optimal price for a bundle. Objective of the term "optimal" here can vary based on their different business goals, such as maximization of profit, revenue, attendance, or market share [7].

The consumer's reservation price, defined as the highest price that a consumer is willing to pay for a product, is a key factor in bundle design [22]. The relationship between reservation price and the actual price of a product determines whether or not a consumer will make a purchase. Another factor in bundle design is bundling strategy. Three bundling strategies have been widely studied in previous research. *Pure component*, or unbundling, is the traditional way in which consumers/buyers can only purchase products or services separately with their original prices [20]. It allows consumers to see the sales process clearly and pick up exactly the product they want. On the contrary, in the *pure bundling* strategy, sellers provide several products together as a bundle, and buyers can purchase only the whole bundle rather than individual products [20]. Combining these two strategies, the *mixed bundling* strategy is a more flexible one that the seller offers both individual products and the whole bundle [20].

In this paper, we will focus on data mining techniques for solving (1) the bundle design problem, which is to determine what product combinations should be in a bundle, (2) the bundle pricing problem, which is to determine the "optimal" price for a bundle, given a specific bundling strategy (i.e., the pure component, pure bundling or mixed bundle strategy).

III. THE PROPOSED DATA MINING FRAMEWORK

We propose a data mining framework for bundle design and pricing, which is illustrated in Figure 1. One of the important features of the proposed framework is to incorporate the time value of money for estimating consumers' reservation prices. The notations used in our proposed framework are listed in Table I.

TABLE I. NOTATIONS

N	The number of items for sale $I = \{i_1, i_2, \dots, i_N\}$
M	The number of consumers $C = \{c_1, c_2, \dots, c_M\}$
T	The set of transaction data generated by consumers. Observations that belong to a specific consumer c with an item i can be represented as $\{T_{c,i}\}_{c\in C, i\in I}$
S	The number of years that covered by transaction dataset $Y = \{y_1, y_2, \dots, y_S\}$
p	Unit price of an item
v	The sales volume for an item
RI	An M×N matrix containing consumers' reservation price intervals for all products

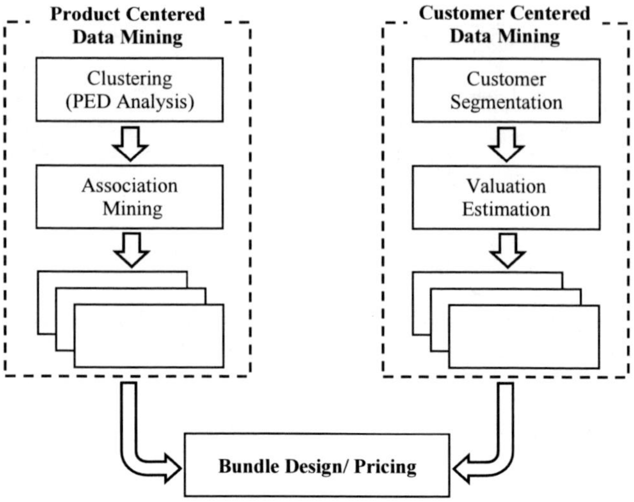

Figure 1. The data mining framework for products bundle design and pricing

Features of the Framework

1) The PED analysis

PED is used to measure the change of quantity demanded of a product or service in its price, with other things being equal. For elastic products, an increase in unit price will lead to fewer units sold, resulting in a downward-slopping curve in its graphic representation with quantity on the horizontal axis and price on the vertical axis.

The demand curve also expresses consumers' willingness and abilities to pay for a product in a given period of time. That is, with consumers' reservation prices and other determinants remaining the same, changes of unit price lead to movements along the same demand curve. However, a change in consumers' reservations will cause a positive or negative shift in demand curves. Based on these economic concepts, we adopt Principle Component Analysis (PCA) and K-means algorithm to analyze the fluctuations of the consumer's reservation price.

Given a set of transaction data, sales volume and price for an item in a month can be extracted easily. The average price is calculated if unit price changes within a month. As a result, we can get a list for each product, which contains the year, month, sales volume, and unit price. Next step is to calculate the average sales volume and price in the same month within S years (see (1)), assuming p_m and $v_m$are unit price and volume of an item in the month m. The objective to use the mean instead of individual ones is to avoid bias due to some random factors including weather, holidays, or unexpected events. For example, if the weather in a year gets warm much earlier than other years, the sales of short sleeve shirts will start increasing and reach the peak in advance.

$$\overline{p_m} = \frac{1}{S} * \sum_{m=1}^{S} p_m \qquad (1)$$

$$\overline{v_m} = \frac{1}{S} * \sum_{m=1}^{S} v_m$$

The $(\overline{v_m}, \overline{p_m})$ pairs for all 12 months may be distributed in more than one parallel demand curves in its graphic representation, if all other determinants stay equal. The following step is to find the months on the same or very close curves. PCA is a common-used method for dimensionality reduction, which is achieved by detecting the directions of the first several largest variances in the data, and transforming the original data into the data expressed in terms of new axes. We adopt PCA to find the principle component in downward-slopping direction, which represents the trend of demand curves for elastic goods, then build a new axis *x'* in this direction and another axis *y'* as orthogonal to the first one. By mapping data points to *y'* axis, points on the same curve are closer while points on different curves are far away from others.

Then, K-means is applied to discover month clusters using the transformed data points. Each one of them represents a month. The value of K depends on a heuristic learning method using Within Cluster Sum of Squared Error (WCSSE), defined as

$$E = \sum_{i=1}^{K} \sum_{p \in G_i} |p - m_i|^2 \qquad (2)$$

where p is an object in data collection, m_i is the mean value of all objects in cluster G_i[11]. With K increasing, the first one that makes WCSSE smaller than a threshold will be set as the number of month clusters $G = \{G_1, G_2, \dots, G_K\}$. Each cluster contains an uncertain number of months and the cluster, which includes the month m is denoted as G_m.

The process and result of PCA and K-means can be illustrated using Figure 2. Black points are original points representing the relationship between quantity and unit price in each month. Colored points are the mapping result using PCA. Points in an oval are the ones being grouped in a cluster using K-means algorithm.

2) Customer segmentation

Clustering techniques have been applied to solve customer segmentation problem due to its efficiency and ability to process large datasets. In our research, we adopt K-means algorithm to discover customer segments since it is efficient in modeling and capable of producing understandable results. Customers' information including gender, age and income provided while registration, along with transaction records, are transformed into features in the clustering process. Similar to PED analysis, a WCSSE threshold is set to determine the optimal number of customer segments.

3) Valuation estimation

A consumer's reservation price for the same product may be various in different periods depending on trackable factors

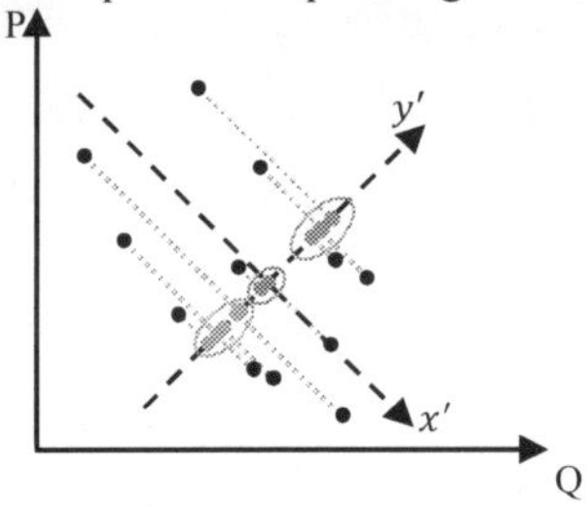

Figure 2. Process of PCA and K-means

like season and demand, and some unpredictable factors as well. Sales price is determined by market supply and demand, which will be affected by the cost of material, technology, and inflation. These two variables are uncertain, but the relationship between them can be represented by consumers' purchase records. It is assumed consumers are rational. In other words, a consumer's reservation price for an item is equal to or greater than the unit price if he made a purchase. Therefore, we use historical transaction data to estimate their valuations.

Due to inflation, the price levels of goods and services reveal a sustained increase over a period of time. It may lead to a loss of real value if we use unit price five years ago directly. Therefore, we map historical currency to present value to eliminate the effect of inflation. Assuming the average inflation rate is r, n is the number of year gap between the original year and the target, the present value PV of historical price can be calculated using (3).

$$\mathrm{PV} = \mathrm{p} \times (1 + r)^n \qquad (3)$$

If we are going to estimate consumers' reservation price and generate profitable bundles in the month m, only the months that belong to the same cluster G_m will be considered in following steps. For a consumer $c \in C$ and an item $i \in I$, we extract his purchase records $T_{c,i}$ from the transaction set, pick up the records that happened in the month in G_m along with their timestamp and price mapped to present value. We assumed his valuation of a given product equals to its price when he made the first purchase. The relationship between the consumer's reservation price R and the number of purchases np forms the following function $R = (1 + \theta)^{np} \times PV$. Each successful transaction makes his valuation increased by θ ($\theta > 0$). For example, if the unit price mapped to present value for an item is $PV = \$2$ and $\theta = 0.1$, a consumer's reservation price when he made the first purchase was *\$2*, which increased to *\$2.2* at the second purchase and *\$2.42* at the third time. But for the month with no purchase, we assumed their valuation were less than the posted price, and dropped exponentially by θ. We order all records according to the year and month sequence and assign each year a weight. For the year y_j, the weight is $w_{y_j} = \beta^{j-1}$. If $\beta > 1$, earlier months are assigned smaller weights and later months have larger ones, representing the latest purchases have more impact on their future behaviors. Whereas the former purchases influent their future decisions more if $\beta < 1$. All months play the same role in estimation when $\beta = 1$. Table II shows the purchase records for a consumer $c \in C$ with an item $i \in I$. A consumer's approximate reservation is estimated using (4).

$$R_{c,i} = \frac{\sum_{j=1}^{S} \sum_{m_k \in G_m} w_{y_j,m_k} \times v_{y_j,m_k}}{\sum_{j=1}^{S} \sum_{m_k \in G_m} w_{y_j,m_k}} \qquad (4)$$

Considering that the reservation price is an extremely subjective factor, and some unpredictable factors may cause bias during estimation, we use an interval to represent a consumer's reservation price instead of a single value.

TABLE II. PURCAHSE RECORDS FOR CONSUMER *C* WITH PRODUCT *I*

Year	Month	Purchase or not	Price (Present Value)	Valuation	Weight
y_1	m_1	Y	PV_{i,y_1,m_1}	$v_{y_1,m_1} = PV_{i,y_1,m_1}$	$w_{y_1} = \beta^0$
y_1	m_2	Y	PV_{i,y_1,m_2}	$v_{y_1,m_2} = (1+\theta) \times PV_{i,y_1,m_2}$	$w_{y_1} = \beta^0$
y_1	m_3	N	PV_{i,y_1,m_3}	$v_{y_1,m_3} = (1-\theta) \times PV_{i,y_1,m_3}$	$w_{y_1} = \beta^0$
⋮	⋮	⋮	⋮	⋮	⋮
y_j	m_k	Y	PV_{i,y_j,m_k}	$v_{y_j,m_k} = (1+\theta)^{np} \times PV_{i,y_j,m_k}$	$w_{y_j} = \beta^{j-1}$
y_j	m_{k+1}	N	$PV_{i,y_j,m_{k+1}}$	$v_{y_j,m_{k+1}} = (1-\theta)^{nnp} \times PV_{i,y_j,m_{k+1}}$	$w_{y_j} = \beta^{j-1}$
⋮	⋮	⋮	⋮	⋮	⋮

Assuming the unit price for the item i is p_i, we create several intervals with each covers $0.05 \times p_i$. Examples of intervals are $[0.9 \times p_i, 0.95 \times p_i)$, $[0.95 \times p_i, p_i)$, and $[p_i, 1.05 \times p_i)$. The interval of estimated value of (4) is treated as the consumer's reservation price interval. The results for all consumers and items form an $M \times N$ valuation matrix RI, in which the value $RI_{c,i}$ represents the reservation price interval of the consumerc for the item i. We set the value to 0 for a consumer with the item he has never purchased.

However, since the valuation matrix only contains reservation price for individual items, we still need to predict their willingness to pay for a bundle b, which consists of more than one products. A recognized function deriving a consumer'svaluation for a bundle $R_{c,b}$ from its components $R_{c,i}$ proposed by Venkatesh and Kamakura is shown in (5) [20].

$$R_{c,b} = (1+\lambda) \times \sum_{i \in b} R_{c,i} \quad (5)$$

The $R_{c,i}$ here is the median of the interval that a consumer's reservation price belongs to. The coefficient λ indicating the bundle's type among complementary, substitutes, and independent. If the bundle is complementary, such as PC and printer, a consumer's willingness to pay for this bundle is higher than the sum of each composition, then $\lambda > 0$. However, for substitutes like seasonal sports tickets, $\lambda < 0$ indicating buyers do not want to pay as much as the total price when purchasing separately. λ equals to 0 when there is no relationship among the components in a bundle.

4) Bundle design

a) Association mining

Since the number of products available in a market is large, which creates numerous possible combinations, considering all potential bundles will cost too much computation. Some combinations may be profitable to business but meaningless to consumers. Through basket analysis, we can find the relationship between some merchandises really exists since they always appeared in a single transaction simultaneously, but they are independent seemingly. However, for the items that consumers never or seldom purchased together, this kind of bundles is pointless. Therefore, we only consider the itemsets that often being purchased together obtained through *Apriori* algorithm with the minimum support *min_sup*.

b) Bundle design and pricing

Bundling configuration including determination of the bundling strategy and price is done based on the potential bundle set B (frequent itemsets in the *Apriori* algorithm) and consumers' valuation matrix RI. Unlike previous researches, which set the bundling strategy and its constraints as prerequisites, we calculate the revenue under each of pure component, pure bundling and mixed bundling, and choose the one with the highest revenue gain instead of restricting a bundle to a specific strategy ahead. Price for a bundle under each promotion is set as the one that can maximize the seller's revenue.

We made several assumptions, which were also used in the previous studies [7].

- **Single Unit.** Each consumer purchases up to one unit for each item or bundle.
- **Single price.** Each item or bundle has exact one sales price.
- **No budget constraint.** Consumers do not have budget constraint while shopping.
- **No supply constraint.** The market can provide as much as consumers need. The occasion of "Out of Stock" will not be considered in this paper.

In practice, the consumer's rationality will make them purchase the products with price lower than their valuations. We use the variable $h_{c,i}$ to denote the purchase behavior of the consumer c with the item i. $h_{c,i} = 1$ when c takes i, and $h_{c,i} = 0$ if the purchase does not happen. $h_{c,b}$ achieves the similar purpose but shows the relationship between the consumer c and the bundle b instead of an individual item. Following the probabilistic variable used in [7], $P(h_{c,i} | p_i, R_{c,i})$ represents the probability of the occurrence of c purchases i ($h_{c,i} = 1$) with the price p_i and his reservation price$R_{c,i}$. However, we develop it to P_{pc}, P_{pb} and P_{mb} under different promotion strategies.

For each possible combination in B, we calculate the maximum revenue it can create under each bundling strategy.

Pure Component. This is an unbundling strategy, which is adopted in conventional market. Price for each commodity P_i is provided by sellers. The corresponding revenue r_{pc} is obtained by(6).

$$r_{pc} = \sum_{i \in b} \sum_{c \in C} p_i \times P_{pc}(h_{c,i} | p_i, R_{c,i}) \quad (6)$$

where

$$P_{pc}(h_{c,i} | p_i, R_{c,i}) = \begin{cases} 1, & if\ p_i \leq R_{c,i} \\ 0, & otherwise \end{cases}$$

Pure Bundling. Comparing with the pure component, this is a similar situation with bundles replacing individual items. The most significant difference is that the price for a bundle p_b is a variable, which need to be determined. Given all consumers' reservation prices for a bundle, we set cut-points p_b to calculate the number of consumers who will make a purchase and the corresponding revenue using (7). The one that makes r_{pb} maximized is chosen as the unit price for the bundle b.

$$r_{pb} = \sum_{c \in C} p_b \times P_{pb}(h_{c,b} | p_b, R_{c,b}) \quad (7)$$

where

$$P_{pb}(h_{c,b} | p_b, R_{c,b}) = \begin{cases} 1, & if\ p_b \leq R_{c,b} \\ 0, & otherwise \end{cases}$$

Mixed Bundling. This is a more complicated situation since both individual items and bundles are offered. Prediction of a consumer's choice among a bundle and its components is essential to estimating revenue. Taking the scenario containing two products X and Y as an example. A consumer's valuation $R_X = \$10$ and $R_Y = \$5$. We set λ in (5) to -0.1 so that his reservation price for the bundle of X and Y is $R_{XY} = \$13.5$. If both of them are sold as $p_X = p_Y = \$7$ and $p_{XY} = \$13$, we predict that he tends to choose X rather than the bundle since the posted prices imply $p_{XY} - p_X = \$6$, which is beyond his valuation of Y. Therefore, we set selection conditions shown below.

$$r_{mb} = \sum_{c \in C}[p_b \times P_{mb}(h_{c,b} | p_b, R_{c,b}) + \sum_{i \in b} p_i \times P'_{mb}(h_{c,i} | p_i, R_{c,i}, P_{mb})] \quad (8)$$

where

$$P_{mb}(h_{c,b} | p_b, R_{c,b}) = \begin{cases} 1, if\ p_b \leq R_{c,b}\ and\ for\ \forall s: p_b - p_s \leq R_{c,(b-s)}, \\ \quad s\ is\ a\ subset\ of\ b \\ 0, \quad otherwise \end{cases}$$

and

$$P'_{mb}(h_{c,i} | p_i, R_{c,i}, P_{mb}) = \begin{cases} 1, & if\ p_i \leq R_{c,i}\ and\ P_{mb}(h_{c,b} | p_b, R_{c,b}) = 0 \\ 0, & otherwise \end{cases}$$

With all calculations finished, next step is the simple comparison of the results of (6) – (8) and choose the strategy with the highest one for promotion.

c) Bundle selection

Bundle selection is necessary for eliminating redundant bundles and ensuring maximum revenue to sellers. We adopt this step for the following objectives:

- Avoid confliction. Promotion strategy for each bundle is selected according to their potential gain in revenue. If a combination A is assigned to pure bundling but one of its subsets is assigned to the mixed bundling, confliction will exist since components of A are also provided individually.
- Revenue maximization. With the prerequisite $\cup B = \mathrm{I}$, various configurations can be issued, but we aim to find the one with the highest revenue gain.

We use a greedy approach for bundle selection to find the eligible bundle configuration. We select bundles from all frequent itemsets based on their absolute revenue gain. The itemset that provides the highest absolute gain will be chosen for promotion, and then removed from the pickup pool along with the bundles that have items overlapped with it. Having the new set of candidate bundles, we still choose the one with the most absolute gain and repeat the process above until there is no bundle left. This method has no effect on bundling strategies so that all selected bundles are enrolled in the one where they are optimized. It can prevent confliction among bundling strategies since all bundles are non-overlapped.

Figure 3 summarizes the aforementioned features for bundle design and bundle pricing.

IV. Experiment And Evaluation

This section describes the simulation and experiments we did to test the effectiveness of our framework.

A. *Simulating Transaction Data*

Based on our proposed framework, a consumer's reservation price is estimated based on the consumer's historical purchasing behaviors. However, there is no publically available transaction datasets covering multiple years. We used simulation data set to demonstrate the efficiency of our framework.

1) Candidate transactions.

Given the number of consumers M and products N, we first generate the consumer set C and product set I, and randomly pick up a base price p_{base} for each product. Then, we generate 12 monthly candidate transaction datasets in a year with each one consists of the Cartesian product of C and I, along with a price for each combination. Considering some dynamic factors like seasonality and holidays, the price for a product in a certain month is produced by multiplying its base price and a seasonal coefficient, which is randomly generated in the range of -α to α. That is, the sale price for a product$p_i \in [(1-\alpha) \times p_{base}, (1+\alpha) \times p_{base}]$. Since the seasonal coefficient is randomly picked up for each product in each month, different seasonal patterns can be found in the candidate transaction dataset for different products. Candidate transaction dataset for the following years is obtained based on the one generated in the last step by taking the inflation rate into consideration.

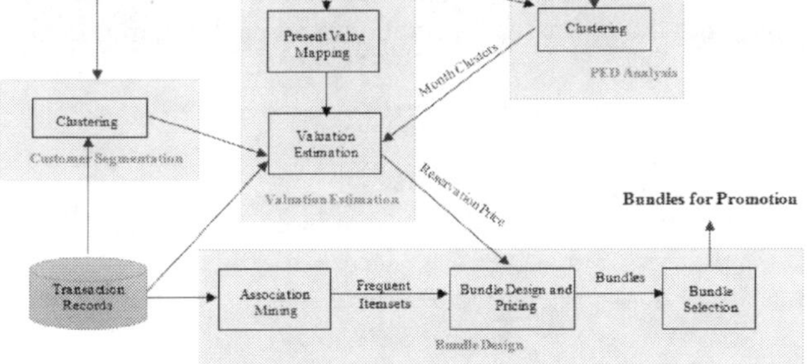

Figure 3. The system architecture of the features of the proposed framework

1) Reservation prices

We also generate a consumer's reservation price matrix with size $M \times N$. Each row represents a consumer and each column represents a product. For a product i, consumer's reservation price is given by a normal distribution with mean of p_{base} and standard deviation of $\sigma \times p_{base}$, or a uniform distribution between $(1-3\sigma) \times p_{base}$ and $(1+3\sigma) \times p_{base}$.

The reason for choosing $1 \pm 3\sigma$ as boundaries of uniform distribution is that we want to generate consumers' reservation price with same range using different distributions. The reservation price matrices are used to filter candidate transactions and evaluate our algorithm as a benchmark.

We set the number of consumers and products as 100 in the simulation. Therefore, candidate transaction dataset has 10,000 records for each month and 120,000 records for each year. To achieve PED analysis, we generate transactions covering ten years so that the sales can reveal a relatively stable pattern. Seasonal coefficient is set to 0.2, representing the unit price for a single item can fluctuate within the range of 20 percent in different months. Standard deviation of normally distributed reservation price is set to $0.1 \times p_{base}$. This setting can ensure most consumers have chances to make a purchase because 97.5% of consumers have a reservation price greater than the possible lowest unit price. Accordingly, uniformly distributed reservation price follows $U(0.7 \times p_{base}, 1.3 \times p_{base})$. The parameter settings in our simulation are listed in Table III.

2) Transaction filtering

According to the consumer rationality assumption, consumers will only purchase the products with price not exceeding their reservation prices. That makes some transactions in our candidate datasets unreasonable. Therefore, we remove the transactions in which the sales price is greater than the corresponding consumer's reservation price. The remaining transactions, along with a transaction ID for each record, form our simulated transaction set. Table IV shows the number of transactions in each year filtered by normally and uniformly distributed reservation price matrix respectively.

B. Training and Evaluation

Several experiments were implemented to test each part of our framework. We used our model to estimate the consumer's reservation price using simulated transaction data. The results were used for exploring the best bundling configuration.

1) Reservation price estimation

In order to evaluate the accuracy of the proposed model, we compare the estimated reservation price with the matrix we generated.

TABLE III. PARAMETER SETTINGS

Parameters	Meaning	Value
M	The number of consumers	100
N	The number of products	100
S	Transaction length (years)	10
α	Seasonal coefficient	0.2
σ	Standard deviation of normal distribution	0.1

TABLE IV. NUMBER OF TRANSACTIONS FILTERED BY RESERVATION PRICE MATRIX

	Normal Distribution	Uniform Distribution
year 1	59,529	59,055
year 2	59,356	59,050
year 3	59,556	59,056
year 4	59,057	58,681
year 5	59,194	58,887
year 6	59,580	59,094
year 7	59,227	59,113
year 8	59,270	58,820
year 9	59,320	59,024
year 10	59,720	59,398
Total	593,809	590,178

Our model is also compared with other two methods. The all-month estimation model does not consider the time dimension so that it uses historical transactions in all months for prediction. On contrary, the same-month estimation model uses only the transactions in the same month with the one being predicted. For example, if we are going to estimate consumer's reservation price in January, the all-month estimation model uses the whole year transactions in each year, while the same-month estimation model uses only historical transactions generated in January for estimation. However, our model analyzes previous sales records, discovers the months that have similar situation with January, and uses them in prediction.

We use the estimation result for a single item instead of the whole dataset to reveal the comparison of different models more clearly. We pick up transactions of the product PRO028 in all years and extract its price and sales volume in each month. Figure 4 shows the statistic under different reservation price distributions in the first three years. Fluctuations in each year form a relatively stable pattern, which keeps repeating during the period. Usually, the sales will rise up with a lower price and drop down with a higher price when the consumer's reservation price stay stable. However, by comparing the trend of unit price and sales, we find the relatively low price in January did not bring a high volume. Instead, its volume is lower than that in December, which has a higher unit price. A similar situation also occurs in April and September. These contradictions are caused by various reservation prices while making purchases in different months.

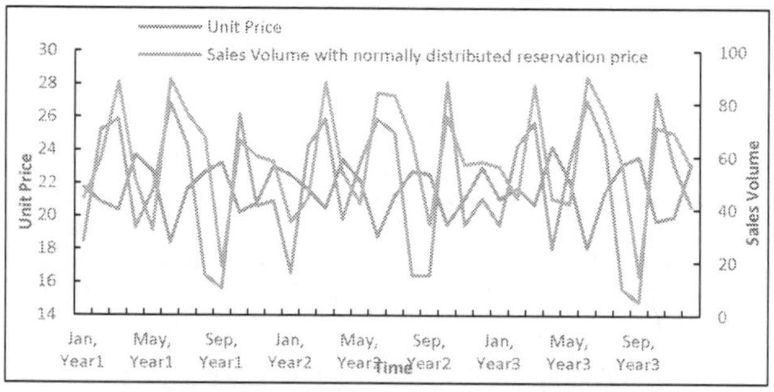

Figure 4. Unit price and sales volume for product PRO028 unider normally and uniformly distributed reservation price

To show the improvement of our model over all products, we plot the average squared loss of 100 products obtained by six models (three for each reservation distribution) in each month in Figure 5. For the product with a high price, we allow a relatively wide range of bias, while the tolerance for cheap products is much smaller.

Therefore, we use Mean Absolute Percentage Error (MAPE) defined in Equation (9) as the measurement. For both normally and uniformly distributed reservation price, our model achieves the best performance with MAPE around 3.5%. The possible bias means if a consumer's actual reservation for a single item is \$50, our estimation falls within the range of \$48 and \$52. Performance of the all-month estimation model are much better than the same-month model, ranking in the middle in comparison. The major reason for a higher bias is the failure in distinguishing potential variance of reservation price in different months. Insufficient purchase records make the same-month estimation model the worst one. MAPEs are always greater than 7%, representing the bias can be up to \$3.5 when a consumer's actual reservation equals to \$50.

$$\text{MAPE} = \frac{1}{M*N}\sum_{n=1}^{N}\sum_{m=1}^{M}\frac{|R_a - R_p|}{R_a} \qquad (9)$$

2) Moving validation

To validate the accuracy of model in prediction, we adopt the "moving" validation approach introduced in Chu and Zhang's work [5]. That is, using the monthly sales and unit price in several continuous years (in-sample) to estimate the consumer's reservation price and predict the yearly sales in the following year (out-of-sample). We adopt in-sample with both variable and fixed length to explore the effect of in-sample length on the accuracy of predicting future purchase behavior. For each in-sample, months are re-clustered using the corresponding sales and unit price so that the estimation can eliminate the effect of dynamic factors but catch the trend if it tends to stable.

Figure 6(a) shows the average MAPE for the annual sales of all products using different in-sample lengths. The annual sales in year2 is predicted using only transactions in the year1,

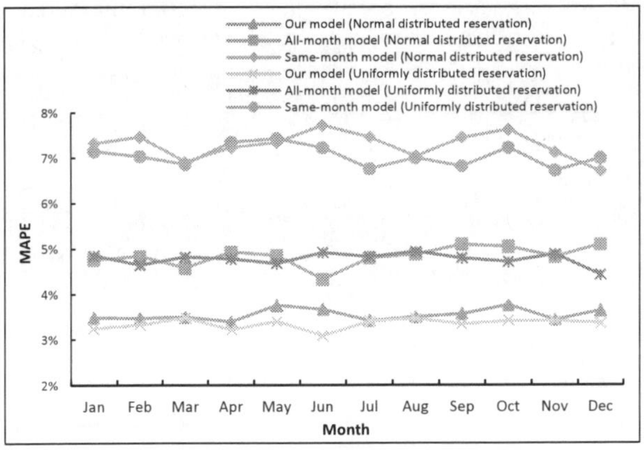

Figure 5. Average Mean Absolute Percentage Error (MAPE) of 100 products in each month using different models

and the sales in year3 is predicted using transactions in both year1 and year2, and so on. As shown in Figure 6(a), MAPE decreases with the length of in-sample growing until it reaches the lowest in year5, which means it is optimal to use transactions in previous four years to predict consumers' behaviors in the next year. MAPE with in-sample length longer than four rises again. The increase is more obvious in normally distributed reservation. A longer in-sample period can eliminate the effect of dynamic factors like climate change and special events. However, regarding the product lifecycle, an overlong in-sample may result in higher bias causing by product replacement and upgrading. Considering these factors and average MAPE shown in Figure 6(a), we fixed the length of in-sample to 4 years and the out-of-sample covers year5 to year10. MAPEs of prediction for sales in these six years are plotted in Figure 6(b). Prediction error fluctuates in a small range, representing our model can produced a stable result with the moving in-sample. This "moving" validation schema can evaluate the stability and reliability of the proposed model.

3) Bundle design

Our bundle design algorithm is based on frequent itemsets obtained by association mining. The choice of three bundling strategies is made by comparing the absolute revenue gain created by each strategy. The one that creates the most revenue gain is selected as the bundling strategy for promotion. Table V shows the number of bundles before and after bundle selection with different *min_sup* values when the bundling coefficient is set to 0 by default. We only consider the itemsets with more than one item, because a bundle with only one item is equivalent to selling it individually. With *min_sup* increasing by 0.005 each round, the number of frequent itemsets decreases exponentially, as well as the number of bundles in each strategy.

In order to avoid overlapping and confliction among bundles, we adopt bundle selection based on the absolute revenue gain they provide. Only a small part of frequent itemsets are selected as eligible bundles. When the *min_sup* is relatively small, most frequent itemsets are more profitable in mixed bundling than in pure bundling. With the *min_sup* growing, the itemsets that create more revenue in pure bundling occupy a larger proportion.

To evaluation the effect of this algorithm regarding the revenue maximization objective, we use the following measurements.

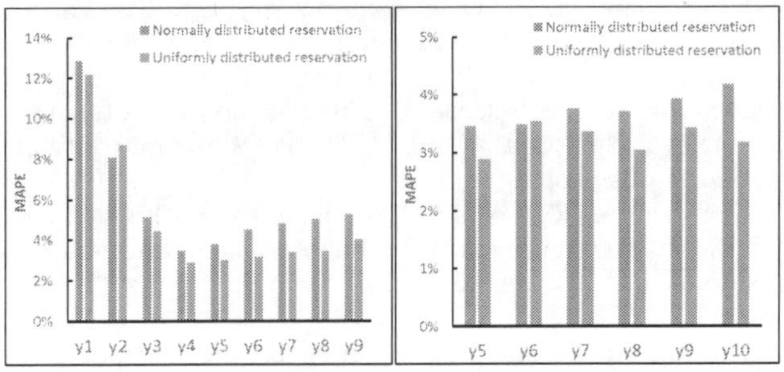

a. In-sample with variable length b. In-sample with fixed length

Figure 6. Average Mean Absolute Percentage Error (MAPE) of annual sales prediction uding different in-samples

TABLE V. THE NUMBER OF BUNDLES WITH DIFFERENT *MIN_SUP* VALUES

min_sup	Before bundle selection				After bundle selection			
	Total	*Pure components*	*Pure bundling*	*Mixed bundling*	*Total*	*Pure components*	*Pure bundling*	*Mixed bundling*
0.025	3429	28	862	2539	48	0	9	39
0.03	2352	20	672	1660	47	0	7	40
0.035	1400	9	457	934	39	0	9	30
0.04	696	3	243	450	28	0	6	22
0.045	284	0	117	167	18	0	5	13
0.05	93	0	48	45	8	0	5	3
0.055	23	0	13	10	4	0	2	2

Revenue Gain. One is to measure how much the sellers can benefit from bundling. We compare the revenue created by bundling against the baseline, which is the revenue created by selling products individually. Revenue gain is the percentage of growth over the revenue of pure components.

Surplus Gain. Another is to evaluate how much consumers can benefit from bundling. A consumer's surplus is the difference between his reservation price and the product's posted price [7]. A higher surplus gain shows the improvement in consumer's willingness to pay and satisfaction. Similar to revenue gain, surplus gain is represented by the percentage of growth in surplus of bundling over pure components.

Figure 7 shows the revenue and surplus gain with different *min_sup* values. We also calculate the bundling efficiency, which is the average gain generated by each bundle. Revenue can be increased by more than 10% by only four bundles with two products in each one when *min_sup* is set to 0.055. As *min_sup* decreases by 0.005 each round, revenue gain rises up with a decreasing rate. Although the revenue gain with a smaller *min_sup* is higher than that with a larger *min_sup*, bundling efficiency drops down a lot, indicating the higher revenue gain is the result of the growing amount of eligible bundles rather than efficiency. Bundling efficiency reached the peak when min_sup is set to 0.05, where each bundle can generate around 4% revenue gain on average. This also happens to surplus gain. Regarding the revenue gain and bundling efficiency, bundling itemsets that are frequently purchased together but separately may be more profitable. Therefore, we choose $min\_sup = 0.04$ as the default setting in the rest of this paper.

Experiment result shows suitable itemsets can be sold as bundles. Revenue gain created by bundling is around 46.8% and surplus gain is around 71.7% comparing with selling products individually.

Bundling coefficient. The bundling coefficient λ in our research can reveal the type of effect of λ on revenue and surplus gain respectively. The line of hybrid bundling is the experiment result using our model. The other two lines show the revenue/surplus gain created by pure bundling and mixed bundling among qualified bundles.

A negative λ means the consumer's reservation price for a bundle is lower than the sum of reservation for each component (subadditivity), which happens to substitutes. When λ is smaller than -0.15, mixed bundling is the only source of revenue gain. The advantage of mixed bundling becomes outstanding because it can offer bundles to the consumers with higher reservationprice while offering components to others. However, the revenue gain may be at the expense of consumer surplus since there is no surplus gain revealed. Such bundles are not desired regarding consumer satisfaction for a long term. Revenue and surplus gain comes from pure bundling increase gradually, but they are still much lower than that provided by mixed bundling. Therefore, mixed bundling is more profitable for substitutes.

A positive λ applies when items in a bundle are complementary, where consumers have super additive reservations. Overall revenue and surplus gain augment with higher λ. From Figure 8, we can also find, pure bundling is very sensitive to the increase of λ. Revenue and surplus gain created by pure bundling climb dramatically until pure bundling becomes the most profitable strategy for all qualified bundles. Mixed bundling becomes less desirable since consumers tend to purchase bundles instead of components. Our result agrees with Do, Lauw and Wang's research [7].

V. CONCLUSIONS

In this paper, we have proposed a data mining framework for bundle design and pricing. In this framework, we incorporate the time value of money for data mining tasks, and estimate the consumers' reservation prices based on historical purchasing data. All previous studies either make strong assumptions on the consumers' reservation prices or estimate the consumers' reservation prices based on a small amount of marketing surveys. The main contribution of this research is to integrate various existing techniques into a single framework. Through simulations and experiments, we have demonstrated this framework is capable of solving the bundle design problem, as well as the bundle pricing problem. As this framework does not limit to specific data mining algorithms for its various sub-tasks, we plan to compare different algorithms within this framework in future. Furthermore, we will incorporate various objective and subjective measures to evaluate the effectiveness and performance of different algorithms.

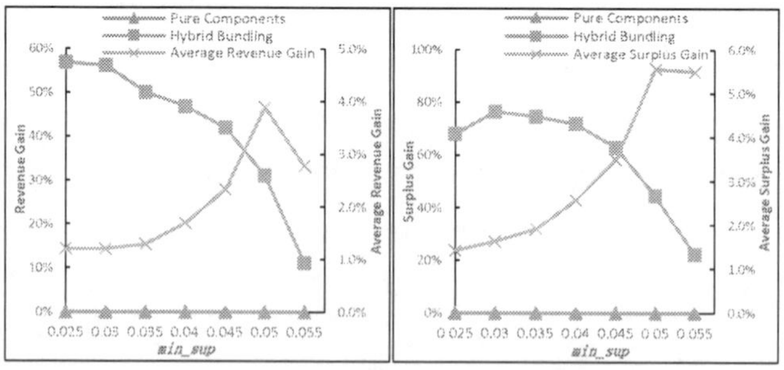

Figure 7. Experiments with different min_sup values

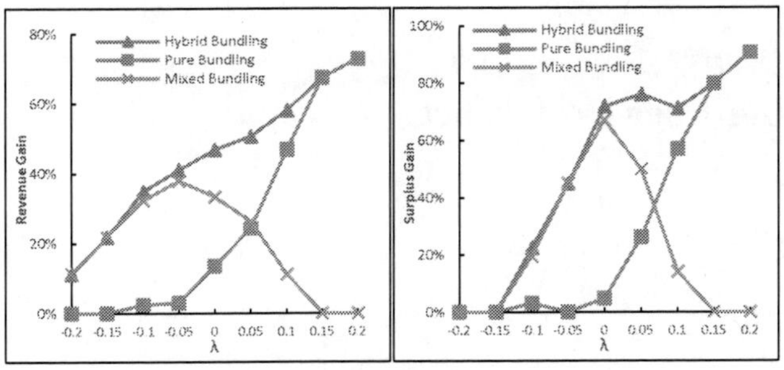

Figure 8. Experiments with different λ

REFERENCES

[1] G. Adomavicius, J. Bockstedt, and S. P. Curley, "Bundling effects on variety seeking for digital information goods," Journal of Management Information Systems, 31(4), 2015, pp. 182-212.

[2] M. Benisch and T. Sandholm, "A framework for automated bundling and pricing using purchase data," Auctions, Market Mechanisms, and their ApplicationsAnonymous, 2012.

[3] W. Chang and S. Yuan, "A markov-based collaborative pricing system for information goods bundling," Expert Systems with Applications, 36(2), 2009, pp. 1660-1674.

[4] P. Chiambaretto and H. Dumez. "The role of bundling in firms' marketing strategies: A synthesis," Recherche Et Applications En Marketing (English Edition), 27(2), 2012, pp. 91-105.

[5] C. W. Chu and G. P. Zhang, "A comparative study of linear and nonlinear models for aggregate retail sales forecasting," International Journal of production economics, 86(3), 2003, 217-231.

[6] G. S. Crawford and A. Yurukoglu, "The welfare effects of bundling in multichannel television markets." The American Economic Review, 102(2), 2012, pp. 643-685.

[7] L. Do, H. W. Lauw, and K. Wang. "Mining revenue-maximizing bundling configuration," Proceedings of the VLDB Endowment, 8(5), 2015, pp. 593-604.

[8] H. Estelami, "Consumer savings in complementary product bundles." Journal of Marketing Theory and Practice, 7(3), 1999, 107-114.

[9] K. D. Ferreira and D. D. Wu, "An integrated product planning model for pricing and bundle selection using markov decision processes and data envelope analysis," International Journal of Production Economics, 134(1),2011, pp. 95-107.

[10] S. M. Goldberg, P. E. Green, and Y. Wind, "Conjoint analysis of price premiums for hotel amenities," Journal of Business, 1984, pp. S111-S132.

[11] J. Han and M. Kamber, Data Mining: Concepts and Techniques, 2006, pp. 402.

[12] W. Hanson and R. K. Martin, "Optimal bundle pricing," Management Science, 36(2), 1990, pp. 155-174.

[13] D. Honhon and X. Pan, "Improving retail profitability by bundling vertically differentiated products," Working paper, University of Florida, Gainesville, FL, 2015.

[14] Y. Jiang, J. Shang, C. F. Kemerer, and Y. Liu, "Optimizing e-tailer profits and customer savings: Pricing multistage customized online bundles," Marketing Science, 30(4), 2011, pp. 737-752.

[15] B. Letham, W. Sun, and A. Sheopuri, "Latent variable copula inference for bundle pricing from retail transaction data," Proceedings of the 31st International Conference on Machine Learning, 2014, pp. 217-225.

[16] G. R. Liu and X. Z. Zhang, "Collaborative filtering based recommendation system for product bundling," Proceedings of the 2006 International Conference on Management Science and Engineering, 2006, pp. 251-254.

[17] K. Mikkonen, H. Niskanen, M. Pynnönen, and J. Hallikas, "The presence of emotional factors: An empirical exploration of bundle purchasing process," Telecommunication Policy, 39(8), 2015, pp. 642-657.

[18] I. S. Razo-Zapata, J. Gordijn, andP. D. Leenheer, and H. Akkermans, "Dynamic cluster-based service bundling: A value-oriented framework," Proceedings of the 2011 IEEE 13th Conference on Commerce and Enterprise Computing, 2011, pp. 96-103.

[19] D. Somefun and J. La Poutré, "Bundling and pricing for information brokerage: Customer satisfaction as a means to profit optimization," Proceedings of IEEE/WIC International Conference, 2003, pp. 182-189.

[20] R. Venkatesh and W. Kamakura, "Optimal Bundling and Pricing under a Monopoly: Contrasting Complements and Substitutes from Independently Valued Products," Journal of Business, 76(2), 2003, pp. 211-232.

[21] M. S. Yadav and K. B. Monroe, "How buyers perceive savings in a bundle price: An examination of a bundle's transaction value," Journal of Marketing Research, 1993, pp. 350-358.

[22] E. Yakıcı, O. Ö. Özener, and S. Duran, "Selection of event tickets for bundling in sports and entertainment industry," Computers & Industrial Engineering, 74, 2014, 257-269.

[23] B. Yang and C. Ng, "Pricing problem in wireless telecommunication product and service bundling," European Journal of Operational Research. 207(1), 2010, pp. 473-480.

Preference Miner: A Database Tool for Mining User Preferences

Markus Endres

University of Augsburg
Universitätsstr. 6a
86159 Augsburg, Germany
Email: endres@informatik.uni-augsburg.de

***Abstract*—Advanced personalized e-applications require comprehensive preference knowledge about their users' likes and dislikes in order to provide individual product recommendations, personal customer advice, and custom-tailored product offers. Modeling preferences as strict partial orders with *"A is better than B"* semantics has proven to be very suitable in various e-applications. In this demo, we present the *Preference Miner*, a database tool for detection of strict partial order preferences hidden in the users' log data. With preference mining personalized applications can gain valuable knowledge about their customers' preferences, which can be applied for personalized product recommendations, individual customer service, or one-to-one marketing.**

Keywords–Preference; Personalization; Data Mining; Database.

I. Motivation

In recent years, several techniques have been developed to build user adaptive web sites and personalized web applications [1]. For example, e-commerce applications use link personalization to recommend items based on the customer's buying behavior or some categorization of customers based on ratings and opinions. Research on preference handling systems makes use of quite a variety of different tools, cp. [2]. Some preference elicitation approaches have been proposed in a different manner, e.g., [3], which proposes algorithms for automatic contextual preference elicitation. However, current techniques of automatic personalization lack preference models with limited expressiveness. State-of-the-art approaches either use scores to describe preferences or just distinguish between liked and disliked values. Thus, complex *"I like A more than B"*-relationships, as well as preferences for numeric attributes cannot be expressed in a natural way. Furthermore, these approaches are not able to handle dependencies among preferences, e.g., two preferences are equally important or one preference is preferred to another.

In this demo paper, we present the *Preference Miner*, a database tool for mining user preferences. Preference Mining is a technology for the detection of preferences in the user's previous shopping or browsing behavior recorded in his log data, e.g., click data, browsing data, or explicit feedback. Important applications for preference mining are Internet shops, financial e-services or personal recommender systems where individual customer care plays a significant role [4][5].

The rest of the paper is organized as follows: In Section II we introduce the preference background. Section III describes our demo architecture and Section IV contains our conclusion.

II. Preference Background

A database preference $P = (A, <_P)$ is a strict partial order, where $A = \{A_1, \ldots, A_d\}$ denotes a set of attributes with corresponding domains $\mathrm{dom}(A_i)$. The domain of A is defined as Cartesian product of $\mathrm{dom}(A_i)$, $<_P \subseteq \mathrm{dom}(A) \times \mathrm{dom}(A)$ and $x <_P y$ is interpreted as "y is better than x".

A set of intuitive preference constructors for base and complex preferences is defined in [6]. These definitions of preference constructors have been proven to be appropriate to describe user wishes. On categorical data there are POS(A, POS-set), NEG(A, NEG-set), POS/POS(A, POS1-set, POS2-set), and POS/NEG(A, POS-set, NEG-set). The POS-set $\subseteq \mathrm{dom}(A)$ of a POS preference defines a set of values that are better than all other values of $\mathrm{dom}(A)$. Analogously, the NEG set describes disliked values. In the POS/POS preference the POS1-set defines the most preferred values, whereas the POS2-set defines the second-preferred values when nothing better is available. The POS/NEG preference defines preferred and non-preferred values. In E-graph of an EXPLICIT(A, E-graph) preference, a user can specify any better-than relationships. Numerical preference constructors are AROUND(A, z), BETWEEN($A, [low, up]$), LOWEST(A), and HIGHEST(A). In AROUND the desired value is z, but if this is not feasible values with the nearest distance from z are best alternatives. BETWEEN prefers values within a $[low, up]$ interval and LOWEST resp. HIGHEST prefer lower and higher values. A Pareto preference $P := P_1 \otimes \ldots \otimes P_m$ treats the underlying preferences as equally important whereas a Prioritization $P := P_1 \& \ldots \& P_m$ treats P_1 more important than P_2, and so on. A more detailed description of the preference model is given in [7].

Example 1. *Assume a dataset called "Notebooks", which contains information about notebooks bought by customers. The data contains different attributes like the size of the hard disk (HDD), the make (Acer, Lenovo, ...), or the amount of RAM. The wish for a notebook having a HDD around 1TB and made by Acer (equally important preferences) can be expressed as*

$$\mathit{AROUND}(\text{HDD, 1TB}) \otimes \mathit{POS}(\text{Make, \{Acer\}})$$

We developed a miner for preferences which detects all kinds of base preferences as well as complex preferences like Pareto and Prioritization within log data. For the detection of preferences, our algorithms apply well-established data mining techniques like clustering and density estimation [8]. The preference mining algorithms together with proofs of correctness can be found in [9].

III. Preference Miner Implementation

Figure 1 represents the overall architecture of our Preference Miner implemented in Java 1.8[1]. As input the user or an application program tells the Preference Miner which log-relation to analyze and on which attributes preferences should be detected. Thereby, the log-relations come from a database or any text based file (.txt, .csv, .tsv, etc.).

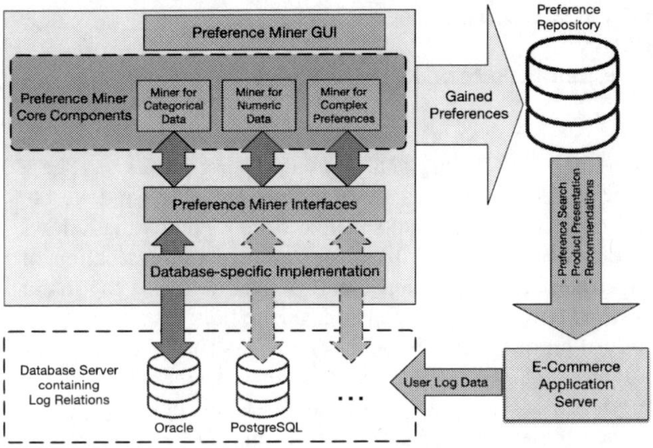

Figure 1. Preference Miner architecture.

The Preference Miner implements preference mining algorithms ("Preference Miner Core Components"), where all data intensive operations, such as clustering or density estimation are executed on the database layer for high performance. The core components contain algorithms for mining preferences on categorical and numerical data as well as a miner for complex preferences. To be independent from a specific database system, all database independent operations are implemented as part of the Preference Miner, whereas database specific operations are only specified ("Preference Miner Interfaces").

The graphical user interface (Figure 2) of the Preference Miner allows the comfortable invocation of the preference mining algorithms on the specified attributes and afterwards presents the results. Here, the Preference Miner detected three preferences on the log-relation "Notebooks" mentioned in Example 1. All detected preferences are managed intelligently in an appropriate preference database, the *Preference Repository*, cp. Figure 1. We developed such a Preference Repository [10], which is a storage structure for preferences. A set of access functions allows easy inserts, updates, deletions and selects on the repository. With it the application server can perform dynamic query personalization [1] for preference-based product-search, individualized product presentation, or personalized recommendations.

Since our implementation executes all data-intensive operations on the database layer we can achieve a very good performance behavior. Our tests on a commercial database server has shown that mining numerical preferences is the fastest task. Mining Pareto preferences or Prioritization needs less than a second in the average for 50,000 tuples on a standard computer. Detailed performance measurements for each algorithm can be found in [9]. The good efficiency of our preference mining algorithms allows their usage for *online preference mining*: while interacting with a customer the e-application can check online his preferences and therefore can react flexibly to his wishes during the sales process.

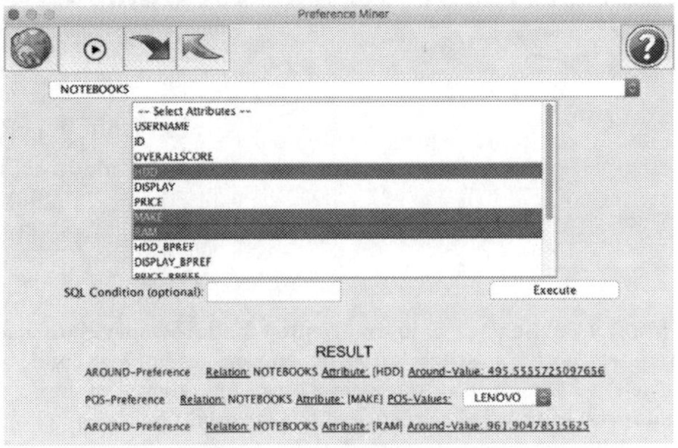

Figure 2. Preference Miner GUI.

IV. Conclusion

The goal of this work is to provide a tool for mining user preferences form log data. Such preference knowledge can be very useful for personalized applications. Sales advice can be adapted to the customer's individual preferences, e.g., if he likes low prices or a special make. Furthermore, preferences gained with Preference Mining are useful for personalized product recommendations and for the composition of individual product bundles.

Acknowledgements

This work has been partially funded by the German Federal Ministry for Economic Affairs and Energy according to a decision by the German Bundestag, grant no. ZF4034402LF5. We want to thank Stefan Holland for support and providing us with the basic source code of the preference miner algorithms.

References

[1] K. Stefanidis, G. Koutrika, and E. Pitoura, "A Survey on Representation, Composition and Application of Preferences in Database Systems," ACM TODS, vol. 36, no. 3, 2011, pp. 19:1–19:45.

[2] S. Kaci, Working with Preferences: Less Is More, 1st ed. Springer Publishing Company, Incorporated, 2011.

[3] S. de Amo, M. S. Diallo, C. T. Diop, A. Giacometti, D. Li, and A. Soulet, "Contextual Preference Mining for User Profile Construction," Inf. Syst., vol. 49, no. C, 2015, pp. 182–199.

[4] Y. Ioannidis and G. Koutrika, "Personalized Systems: Models and Methods from an IR and DB Perspective," in Proceedings of VLDB '05. ACM, 2005, p. 1365.

[5] B. Satzger, M. Endres, and W. Kießling, "A Preference-Based Recommender System," in Proceedings of EC-Web '06, ser. LNCS, vol. 4082, 2006, pp. 31 – 40.

[6] W. Kießling, "Foundations of Preferences in Database Systems," in Proceedings of VLDB '02, Hong Kong, China, 2002, pp. 311–322.

[7] W. Kießling, M. Endres, and F. Wenzel, "The Preference SQL System - An Overview," Bulletin of the Technical Commitee on Data Engineering, IEEE Computer Society, vol. 34, no. 2, 2011, pp. 11–18.

[8] M. J. A. Berry and G. Linoff, Data Mining Techniques. Wiley, New York, 1997.

[9] S. Holland, M. Ester, and W. Kießling, "Preference Mining: A Novel Approach on Mining User Preferences for Personalized Applications," in Proceedings of PKDD '03, ser. LNCS, vol. 2838. Springer, 2003, conf, pp. 204–216.

[10] S. Holland and W. Kießling, "Situated Preferences and Preference Repositories for Personalized Database Applications," in Proceedings of ER '04, ser. LNCS, vol. 3288. Springer, 2004, conf, pp. 511–523.

[1]The tool is available at https://github.com/endresma/PreferenceMiner.git

A Column-Oriented Text Database API Implemented on Top of Wavelet Tries

Stefan Böttcher, Rita Hartel, Jonas Manuel
University of Paderborn, Department of Computer Science
Paderborn, Germany
email: {stb@, rst@, jmanuel@live.}uni-paderborn.de

***Abstract*—Whenever column-oriented main-memory databases require both, a space efficient storage of strings and an efficient evaluation of operations on these strings, a compressed indexed sequence of strings might be a good choice to fulfill these requirements. A data structure that compresses the string sequence and at the same time supports efficient evaluation of basic read and write operations is the Wavelet Trie. In this paper, we extend the Wavelet Trie by different set-oriented read operations relevant for column-oriented databases like union, intersection and range-queries, and describe how they can be implemented on top of the Wavelet Trie. Furthermore, in our evaluations, we show that performing typical operations on string sequences like searching for exact matches or prefixes, range queries, insert, or delete operations, and operations on two string sequences like merge or intersection, can be performed faster directly on the Wavelet Trie than simulating these operations on bzip2- or gzip-compressed data.**

Keywords- Column-oriented database management systems; compression; compressed indexed sequences of strings.

I. INTRODUCTION

Column-oriented DataBase Management Systems (DBMS) organize their data tables within column stores, each containing an ordered sequence of entries. This data organization technique is preferable especially when used for read-intensive applications like data warehouses, where in order to analyze the data, queries and aggregates have to be evaluated on sequences of similar data contained in a single column [1]. A second advantage of column-oriented data stores is that they can be compressed stronger than row oriented data stores, as each column and therefore each contiguous sequence of data contains data from the same domain and thus contains less entropy.

As long as main-memory availability is a run-time bottleneck, data compression is beneficial to virtually "enhance" the capacity of the main-memory, i.e., column-oriented data stores can benefit from storing their string columns in form of *compressed indexed sequences of strings*. A major challenge when using a compressed data structure for a string column is to support typical database operations in efficient time without full decompression of the compressed data structure.

Column stores like, for instance, C-STORE [1], Vertica [2] or SAP HANA [3] typically rely on combinations of compression techniques like Run-Length Encoding, Delta Encoding, or dictionary-based approaches. These compression techniques do not contain a self-index, but have to occupy additional space to store an index that allows for efficient operations like, for instance the evaluation of range queries. When main-memory availability is the major run-time bottleneck, we consider this to be a disadvantage.

In contrast, the Wavelet Tree is a self-index data structure and can be regarded as an enhancement of variable length encodings (e.g. Huffman [4], Hu-Tucker [5]) that rearranges the encoded string S in form of a tree and thereby allows for random access to S. Variations of the Wavelet Tree use the tree topology to enhance Fibonacci encoded data [6] or Elias and Rice variable length encoded data [7]. In [8] an n-ary Wavelet Tree is used instead of a binary Wavelet Tree (e.g., a 128-ary Wavelet Tree by using bytes instead of bits in each node of the Wavelet Tree). A pruned form of the Wavelet Tree is the Skeleton Huffman tree [9] leading to a more compressed representation. Although avoiding the need for an additional index, Wavelet Trees have the disadvantage that common prefixes in multiple strings are stored multiple times.

This disadvantage is avoided by the Wavelet Trie [10][11], which is a self-index, i.e., avoids the storage of extra index structures, and can be regarded as a generalization of the Wavelet Tree [12] for string sequences S and the Patricia Trie [13]. That is why in this paper, we use a Wavelet Trie to store compressed indexed sequences of strings.

Wavelet Tries support the following basic operations that are used within column-oriented DBMS: the operations *access(n)* that returns the n-th string of this column and that is used for example when finding values of the same database tuples contained in other columns, or *search(s)/searchPrefix(s)* that searches for all positions within the current column that contains the value s (or that have the prefix s). Beside these elementary search operations, Wavelet Tries support elementary data manipulation operations on the compressed data format as, e.g., to insert a string at a given position, to append a string, or to delete a string from the sequence.

[10] and [11] introduce the concept of the Wavelet Trie and discuss the complexity of the following operations:

- Access(pos) returns the pos-th string of the sequence

- Rank(s, pos)/RankPrefix(s, pos) return the number of occurrences of string s (or strings starting with prefix s) up to position pos
- Select(s, i)/SelectPrefix(s, i) returns the position of the i-th string s (or string starting with prefix s) of the sequence
- Insert(s, pos) inserts the string s before position pos
- Append(s) appends s to the end of the sequence
- Delete(pos) deletes the string at position pos

which is sufficient to support the most elementary database operations in column stores.

However, in order to support more enhanced data analysis, efficient query processing should go beyond these elementary operations. Here, the main remaining challenge is to support efficient complex read operations like range queries, union, and intersection on column stores without decompression of large parts of the compressed data.

Our goal is that these operations on compressed data are executed not only with a smaller main-memory footprint, but also faster on compressed data compared to a decompress-read approach that first decompresses the data before a read operation (or write operation) is done.

Our first contribution is to extend the Wavelet Trie [10][11] published in 2012 by Grossi and Gupta by concepts and efficient implementations of enhanced database operations (intersection, union, and range queries).

Our second contribution is an evaluation, comparing the performance of the Wavelet Trie with bzip2 and gzip. We show that performing typical operations on string sequences like searching for exact matches or prefixes, range queries, or update operations like insertion or deletion, or operations on two string sequences like merge or intersection, directly on the Wavelet Trie is faster than simulating these operations on bzip2- and gzip-compressed data.

In Section 2, we introduce the basic concepts used in the following sections. In Section 3, we explain different operations on the Wavelet Trie and discuss how to implement them. In Section 4, we show an extensive performance evaluation in which we compare the performance of these operations on the Wavelet Trie with the performance of the gzip and bzip2 compression.

II. BASIC CONCEPTS

Similarly to [10][11], we define the Wavelet Trie as follows:

Definition (Wavelet Trie): Let S be a non-empty, prefix free sequence of binary strings, $S=(s_0,\ldots, s_n)$, $s_i \in \{0,1\}^*$, whose underlying string set $S_{set}=\{s_0,\ldots,s_n\}$ is prefix-free. The Wavelet Trie of S, denoted WT(S), is built recursively as follows:

(i) If the sequence consists of a single element only, i.e., $s_0 = \ldots = s_n$, the Wavelet Trie is a node labeled with $\alpha = s_0 = \ldots = s_n$.

(ii) Otherwise, let α be the longest common prefix of S. For any $0 \leq i < n$, we can write $s_i = \alpha b_i \gamma_i$, where b_i is a single bit. For $b \in \{0,1\}$, we can then define two sequences $S_{\alpha 0} = (\gamma_i \mid b_i=0)$ and $S_{\alpha 1} = (\gamma_i \mid b_i=1)$, depending on whether the string s_i begins with α0 or α1, and the bitvector $\beta = (b_i)$. The bitvector β discriminates whether the suffix γ_i is in $S_{\alpha 0}$ or $S_{\alpha 1}$.Then, the Wavelet Trie of S is the tree whose root is labeled with α and β, and whose children (respectively labeled with 0 and 1) are the Wavelet Tries of the sequences $S_{\alpha 0}$ and $S_{\alpha 1}$.

Remarks:

The requirement that S has to be a prefix free sequence, i.e., no string s_i is allowed to be a prefix of a string s_j, is not a critical restriction, as a prefix free set of strings can be easily constructed for any set S, by adding a terminal symbol not occurring in S to each string $s \in S$.

If the sequence consists of a single element only, we know by the number of corresponding bits within the β of the parent node the size n of the sequence. If the node does not have a parent node, we cannot derive the size of the sequence. In that case, we could either store the size externally or add a binary string s_{new}, $s_{new} \neq s_i$, $i \in \{0,\ldots,n\}$ to the end of the sequence S.

In order to apply the Wavelet Trie to a sequence of words $W=(w_0,\ldots,w_n)$, we compute the sequence of binary strings $SW=(ht(w_0),\ldots,ht(w_n))$, where ht(w) applies the Hu-Tucker algorithm [5] to the word w, yielding a lexicographic Huffman code for w, i.e., $ht(w_i) <_{lexi} ht(w_j) \Leftrightarrow w_i <_{lexi} w_j$, where $<_{lexi}$ denotes "less than in lexicographical order".

Whenever we describe operations that work on two Wavelet Tries, we assume that both Wavelet Tries are based on the same Hu-Tucker-Encoding.

III. DATABASE OPERATIONS ON TOP OF THE WAVELET TRIE

In the following sections, we denote the left child of a Wavelet Trie node as its 0-child, and the right child of a Wavelet Trie node as its 1-child.

A. *Search/Query Operations*

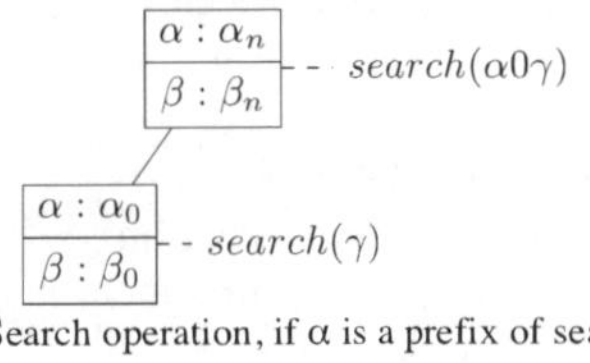

Figure 1. Search operation, if α is a prefix of search string s.

This operation searches for the positions of all binary strings equal to or starting with the given binary string s.

As an auxiliary method, we use the generalization of the select operation to a list of positions: $B.select(b, (p_1,\ldots,p_n))=(B.select(b,p_1),\ldots,B.select(b,p_n))$, where $B.select(b, p_n)$ denotes the position of the p_n^{th} bit b in a binary string B.

In order to search for all positions of the string s in the Wavelet Trie's root node, we go down the tree representing the Wavelet Trie recursively, until we have found all bits of the binary string s. If we require an exact match, we have found all bits, and we have reached the end of the α of a leaf node, we "translate" the positions of the leaf node into the corresponding positions of the root node with the help of the select operation. That is, if $r=(p_1,\ldots,p_n)$ is the result computed for the n's b-child, then n.β.select(b, $(p_1,\ldots,p_n)$) is the result for node n. Similarly, if we search for all positions of binary strings starting with the given prefix s, and have found all bits of s on the current path in the Wavelet Trie, we do not care, whether or not we have reached a leaf node, and translate the current positions into positions of the Wavelet Trie's root node.

In more detail, the search works as follows: Let the current node n with label α (and β, if n is no leaf node) have a parent node pa, such that n is the b-child of pa and β of pa contains k b-bits and assume that we search for binary strings starting with a prefix s.

If $s=\alpha$, or s is a prefix of α, we return the list of positions $(1,\ldots,k)$.

Furthermore, if $s\neq\alpha$, α is a prefix of s and n is no leaf node, s is of the form $s=\alpha b\gamma$ (with a potentially empty γ; c.f. Figure 1). In this case, we perform the search operation for binary string γ on n's b-child, resulting in a list of positions $(p_1,\ldots, p_n)$. In this case, we return the list of positions n.β.select(b, $(p_1,\ldots,p_n)$).

If none of the above cases matches, the Wavelet Trie does not contain a binary string matching the search criteria, and we return an empty list of positions.

B. Between/Range Queries (less than, greater than)

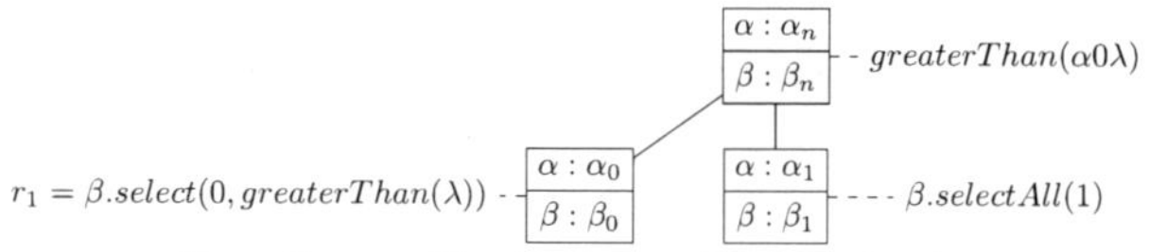

Figure 2. greaterThan if α is a prefix of search string s.

The operation between(s_1,s_2) returns a set of positions of strings r, such that $s_1\leq r\leq s_2$. Similarly, the operation lessThan(s) returns a set of positions of strings r, such that $r\leq s$, and the operation greaterThan(s) returns a set of positions of strings r, such that $r\geq s$. In this section, we explain how to implement the operation greaterThan(s). To adapt this operation in order to implement between(s_1,s_2) or lessThan(s) is quite straightforward.

Again, we use as auxiliary operations the generalization, B.select(b, $(p_1,\ldots,p_n)$) := (B.select(b, p_1),…,B.select(b, p_n)), of the select operation to a list of positions. Furthermore, we use the operation B.selectAll(b) := B.select(b,(1,…,rank(b,|B|)) which returns the positions of all bits b within the sequence B.

Let the current node n be a node with labels α and β.

If α=s or s is a prefix of α, i.e., $\alpha=sb\delta$ (with a potentially empty δ), we know that all strings represented by the Wavelet Trie rooted in n are greater than or equal to s, i.e., we return the set of positions $\{1, \ldots, |\beta|\}$.

In the other case, if α is a prefix of s, i.e., $s=\alpha b\lambda$, we have to consider the value of b. If b=1, all strings represented by the Wavelet Trie rooted in n's 0-child are less than s. Therefore, we have to apply the operation r'=greaterThan(λ) to n's 1-child n_1, and return r=β.select(1, r'). If b=0, the result set r consists of two sub-sets r_1 and r_2 with $r=r_1\cup r_2$ which are computed as follows. As all strings represented by the Wavelet Trie rooted in n's 1-child are greater than s, r_1= β.selectAll(1). Afterwards, we have to apply the operation r'=greaterThan(λ) to n's 0-child, to get r_2= β.select(0, r') (c.f. Figure). Finally, we return $r=r_1\cup r_2$.

Note that we can similarly create a Wavelet Trie that consists of strings greater than or equal to s, if we do not only return the list of results, but delete all strings not belonging to a result positions.

C. Intersection

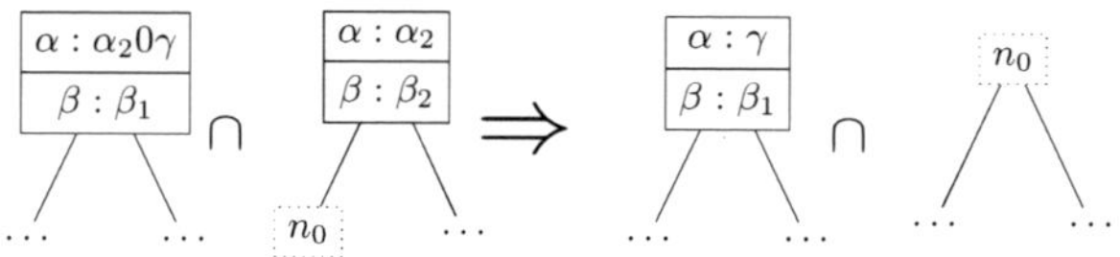

Figure 3. Intersection if α_1 is a prefix of α_2.

This operation computes the set-intersection of two Wavelet Tries t_1 and t_2, i.e., it computes a Wavelet Trie that represents a lexicographically ordered list of all strings s that occur in both, t_1 and in t_2.

Let n_1 be the current node of t_1 and n_2 be the current node of t_2, where n_1 has the labels α_1 and β_1 and n_2 has the labels α_2 and β_2.

If $\alpha_1=\alpha_2$ and n_1 and n_2 are leaf nodes, return n_1 as resulting Wavelet Trie.

If $\alpha_1=\alpha_2$ and n_1 and n_2 are inner nodes, compute the result node r_0 of the intersection of the 0-child of n_1 and of the 0-child of n_2 and the result node r_1 of the intersection of the 1-child of n_1 and of the 1-child of n_2. Then return a new node n, with $\alpha=\alpha_1$, β consists of $|r_0|$ 0 bits followed by $|r_1|$ 1 bits, and n has r_0 as 0-child and has r_1 as 1-child.

Let now either α_1 be a prefix of α_2 or vice versa. Let us assume w.l.o.g. that α_2 is a prefix of α_1, i.e., $\alpha_1=\alpha_2 b\gamma$ (c.f. Figure). In this case, we change α_1 into $\alpha_1=\gamma$ and intersect this new node with the b-child of n_2. If after the intersection, the β of the result node contains only 1 bits or only 0 bits, we collapse it with its single child node b-child n_b and thereby delete its (1-b)-child.

Let n_0 be the 0-child of n_b and n_1 be the 1-child of n_b. Let furthermore α_b and β_b be the labels of node n_b. Then the new labels of node n are $\alpha=\alpha_n b\alpha_b$ and $\beta=\beta_b$. Furthermore, n_0 becomes the new 0-child of n and n_1 becomes the new 1-

child of n. Figure shows the state before and after collapsing the node for b=0.

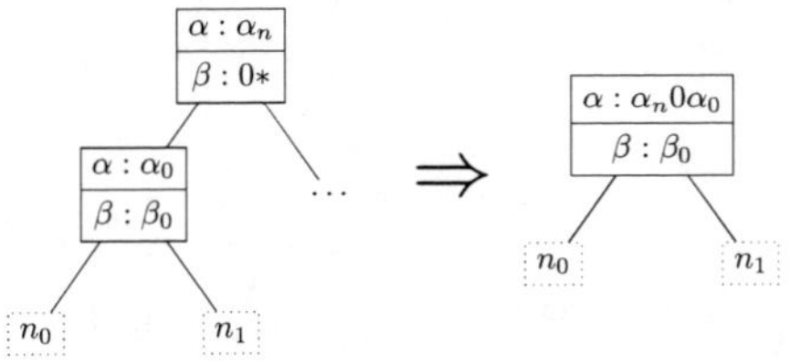

Figure 4. Before and after collapsing the node.

In all other cases, the intersection is empty. This includes the case that neither α_1 is a prefix of α_2 nor α_2 is a prefix of α_1 nor $\alpha_1=\alpha_2$ and the case that $\alpha_1=\alpha_2$ and exactly one node of n1, n2 is a leaf node and the other is an inner node.

D. Merge/Append + Union

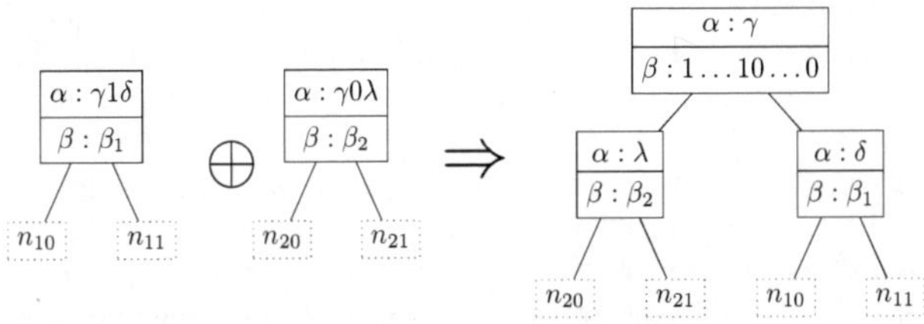

Figure 5. Appending Tries t_1 and t_2 if α_1 and α_2 share a common prefix.

This operation unites/merges two Wavelet Tries t_1 and t_2, i.e., it inserts the string sequence s_2 represented by Wavelet Trie t_2 at a given position pos into the string sequence s_1 represented by Wavelet Trie t_1. Note that this operation is only defined if the set $s_1 \cup s_2$ is prefix free.

Let n_1 be the current node of t_1 and n_2 be the current node of t_2, where n_1 has the labels α_1 and β_1 and n_2 has the labels α_2 and β_2.

If $\alpha_1=\alpha_2$ and n_1 and n_2 are leaf nodes, nothing has to be done, and the operation is finished. If $\alpha_1=\alpha_2$ and both nodes are inner nodes, we insert β_2 at position pos into β_1, merge the 0-child of n_2 at position β_1.rank(0,pos) into the 0-child of n_1 and merge the 1-child of n_2 at position β_1.rank(1,pos) into the 1-child of n_1. Note that the cases that n_1 is a leaf node, but n_2 is not a leaf node, and vice versa, cannot occur, as $s_1 \cup s_2$ is prefix free.

If α_1 is a prefix of α_2, i.e., $\alpha_2=\alpha_1 b\delta$, we insert b $|\beta_2|$ times at position pos into β_1. We change α_2 into δ and merge n_2 into the b-child of n_1 at position β_1.rank(b,pos).

If α_2 is a prefix of α_1, i.e., $\alpha_1=\alpha_2 b\lambda$, we create a new node n with labels $\alpha=\alpha_2$ and β consisting of $|\beta_1|$ bits b in which we insert β_2 at position pos. The b-child of the node n is then the result of merging the b-child of n_2 at position β_1.rank(b,pos) into a node with labels $\alpha=\gamma$ and $\beta=\beta_1$, having the children of n_1 as children. The (1-b)-child of the node n is the (1-b)-child of n_2.

Otherwise, α_1 and α_2 share a common prefix. Let γ be the common prefix of α_1 and α_2, and let us assume w.l.o.g. that $\alpha_1=\gamma 1\delta$ and $\alpha_2=\gamma 0\lambda$ (c.f. Figure). Then, we create a new node n with labels $\alpha=\gamma$ and β consisting of $|\beta_1|$ bits 1 in which we insert $|\beta_2|$ bits 0 at position pos. The 0-child of node n is then a node with $\alpha=\lambda$ and $\beta=\beta_2$ having the children of n_2 as child nodes, and the 1-child of node n is a node with $\alpha=\delta$ and $\beta=\beta_1$ having the children of n_1 as child nodes.

E. Insert/Append

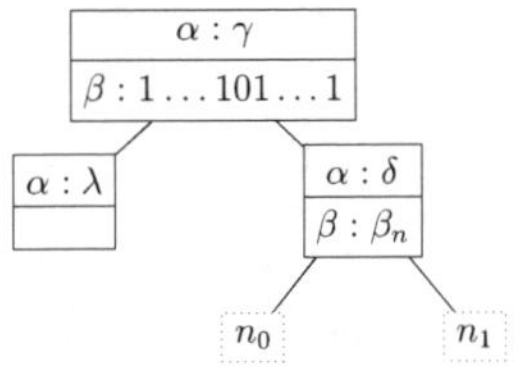

Figure 6. Result of insert operation if s and α_n have a common prefix.

This operation inserts a binary string s into the Wavelet Trie at position pos (or appends it to the end, if pos refers to a position after the number i of entries in the Wavelet Trie.

We consider the current node n of the Wavelet Trie (initially the root node) having the labels α_n and β_n and the binary string s to be inserted at position pos. As we require the Wavelet Trie before and after the insertion to be prefix free, we know that s must not be a prefix of α_n.

If α_n is a prefix of s, i.e., $s=\alpha_n b\delta$, where b is a bit, we insert bit b at position pos into β_n, and insert the binary string δ into the b-child of n at position rank(b,pos).

If n is a leaf node of the Wavelet Trie, and α_n=s, we are completed and do not need to do anything else.

Let γ be the common prefix of α_n and s and let us assume w.l.o.g. that $\alpha_n=\gamma 1\delta$ and $s=\gamma 0\lambda$. Note that γ might even be an empty binary string. Let n_0 be the 0-child of n, and let n_1 be the 1-child of the current node. In this case, we change n into a node with $\alpha=\gamma$, and β consists of $|\beta_n|$ 1-bits and one 0-bit at position pos. The new 0-child of n is a node n' with $\alpha=\lambda$. The new 1-child of n is a node n'' with $\alpha=\delta$ and $\beta=\beta_n$. n'' gets n_0 as 0-child and n_1 as 1-child. Figure shows this case after having inserted s into α_n.

F. Delete

This operation deletes the binary string s_{pos} at position pos from the Wavelet Trie.

In order to delete the binary string s_{pos} at position pos from the current node n (initially the root node), we delete the bit b at position pos from β. If β afterwards still contains 0-bits and 1-bits and n's b-child is not a leaf node, we continue to delete the bit at position rank(b,pos) from n's b-child.

If β contains either only 0-bits or only 1-bits (i.e., β=0* or β=1*, in general β=b*), we have to collapse the current node with its b-child n_b and thereby delete its (1-b)-child as described in Section 2.

IV. EVALUATION

We compared our implementation of the Wavelet Trie with the common compressors gzip and bzip2. We did not compare our implementation with delta-encoding as delta-encoding has the following disadvantage. Delta-encoding cannot support any of the range queries, i.e., our prefix search (II.A), Between, LessThan, and GreaterThan (II.B), because equal strings are encoded different, depending on the previous string. Even intersection (II.C) is not supported. Therefore, delta-encoding does not meet our requirements.

The dictionary-based approach, assigning a segregated Huffman code to each entry results in a bit sequence that supports alphabetical comparisons. Run-length encoding compressing longer bit sequences also supports alphabetical comparisons. Both approaches are orthogonal and compatible to our approach, i.e. can be combined with it. As therefore, a performance comparison with dictionary-based approaches or with RLE is not useful, we have compared our approach with the powerful and widely use compressors gzip und bzip2.

We ran our tests on Mac OS X 10.5.5, 2.9 GHz Intel Core i7 with 8 GB 1600 MHz DDR3 running Java 1.8.0_45.

To evaluate rather text-centric operations, we used 114 texts of the project Gutenberg [14] with file sizes from 78 kB up to 7.3 MB to build a heterogeneous corpus. In order to simulate database operations of a column-oriented database, we used author information extracted from DBLP [15]. Out of these informations, we generated lists consisting of 2500 up to 100000 authors.

In all time measurements, we performed 10 redundant runs and computed the average CPU time for all these runs.

A. Compression and Decompression

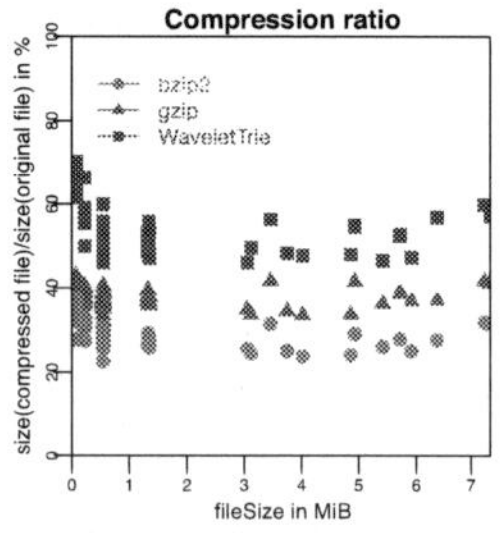

Figure 7. Compression ratio.

When evaluating the pure compression and decompression of Wavelet Trie, gzip and bzip2, we get the result that bzip compresses strongest while Wavelet Trie compresses worst (c.f. Figure), and that gzip compresses and decompresses fastest while Wavelet Trie compresses and decompresses slowest (c.f. Figure 8).

The main difference between the Wavelet Trie and the generic compressors is that the Wavelet Trie supports many operations on the compressed data, while gzip and bzip2 require to at least decompress the compressed data first, and for some operations to recompress the modified data

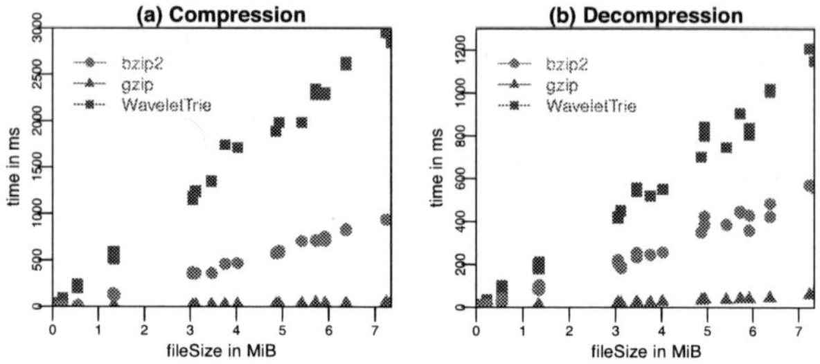

Figure 8. Compression and decompression time.

afterwards. This means, there are a lot of applications that do not require the Wavelet Trie to decompress, as the concerning operations can be evaluated on the compressed data directly. We show the benefit of using the Wavelet Trie in the following subsections, in which we evaluate the performance of the different operations.

B. Insert and Delete

As a first operation, we compared the insert and the delete operation directly on the Wavelet Trie with the pure decompression time of bzip2 and of gzip. We performed these operations on the documents of our Gutenberg corpus. Figure 9 shows the results. The insertion of the word 'database', which does not occur in any of the documents, as 50th word is faster than the pure decompression of bzip2 and as fast as the pure decompression of gzip. The same holds for the deletion of the 50th word. Please consider that the compression or decompression times for bzip2 and gzip neither contain the time needed to insert (or to delete respectively) a string nor the time needed to recompress the modified results.

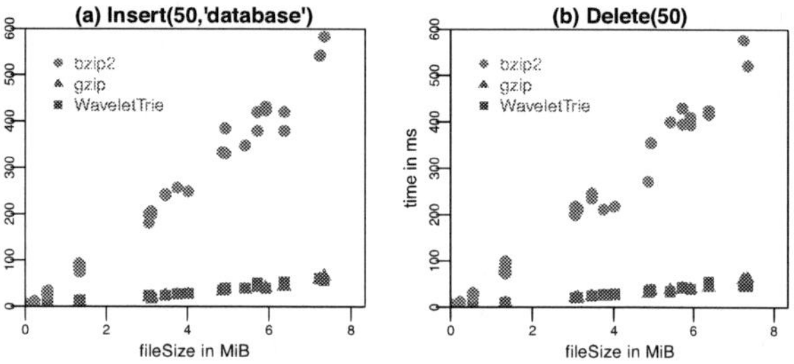

Figure 9. (a) Insertion and (b) Deletion in the Wavelet Trie compared to bzip2 and gzip decompression time.

C. Search and searchPrefix

Figure 10 shows the search times for (a) a single word and (b) all words starting with a given prefix directly in the Wavelet Trie compared to the time needed for the pure decompression of bzip2 and gzip. We searched within our Gutenberg corpus for all positions of the word 'file', which is contained in each file, and for all positions of words starting with the prefix 'e'. Although the times for bzip2 and gzip comprise the pure decompression, i.e., no search operation is performed on the decompressed bzip2 or the decompressed gzip file, the search directly on the Wavelet

Trie is faster than the pure decompression time of bzip2 and gzip.

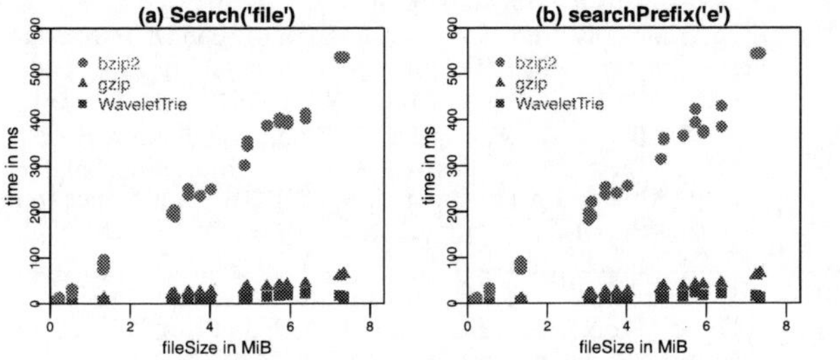

Figure 10. Search times for words in the Wavelet Trie compared to pure decompression time of bzip2 and of gzip.

D. Range queries

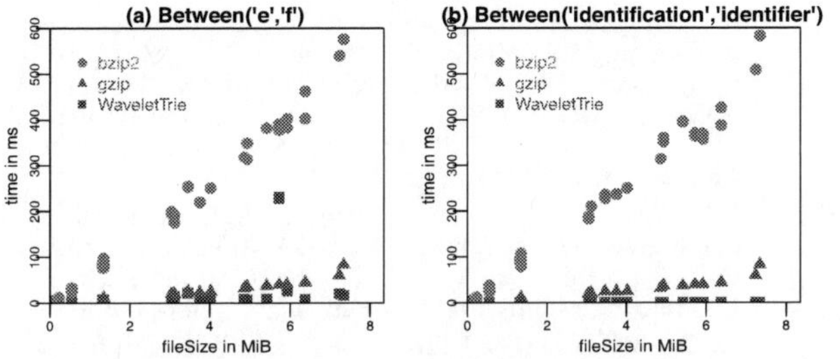

Figure 11 Range queries on the Wavelet Trie compared to pure decompression time of bzip2 and gzip.

Figure 11 shows the results of comparing the search times (a) for words greater than 'e' but less than 'f' and (b) for words greater than 'identification' and less than 'identifier' directly on the Wavelet Trie with the pure decompression time of bzip 2 and gzip. These operations were again evaluated on the Gutenberg corpus. Although the times for bzip2 and gzip comprise the pure decompression, i.e., no search operation is performed, the search directly on the Wavelet Trie is faster than the pure decompression time of bzip2 and gzip. The more specific the search query is, and thus the smaller the search result, the better is the performance benefit of the Wavelet Trie compared to bzip2 and gzip.

E. Intersection

The following tests were performed on our dblp author corpus. Figure 12 shows the results of comparing the intersection operation on two author lists with the sequence of decompression, concatenating the two lists (as we did not want to measure a maybe inefficient string intersection method), and recompressing the result list of the intersection using bzip2 and gzip. We computed the result list of the intersection prior to the test runs, i.e., the time needed to compute the intersection was not measured. We used two different sets of lists: the first is duplicate-free, whereas, in the second set, 50% of the list entries of the second list occur also in the first list. If the lists are completely disjoint, the intersection computed directly on the Wavelet Trie is faster than the simulated operation for bzip2 and as fast as this operation for gzip. If there is a large overlapping of the lists, gzip is faster than the Wavelet Trie, which still is faster than bzip2.

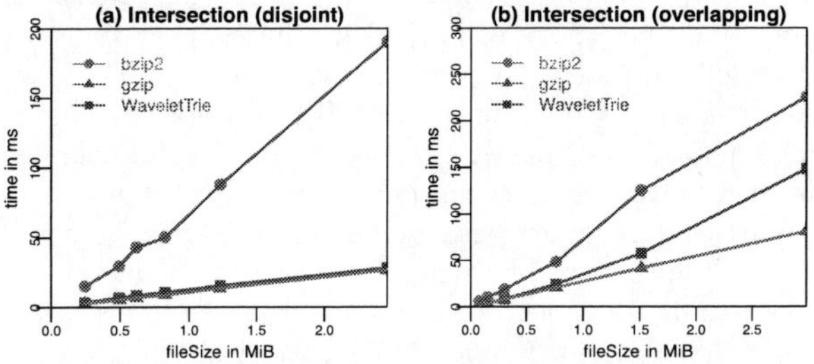

Figure 12. Computing the intersection directly on the Wavelet Trie compared to decompression, list concatenation and recompression time of bzip2 and gzip.

F. Merge/Union

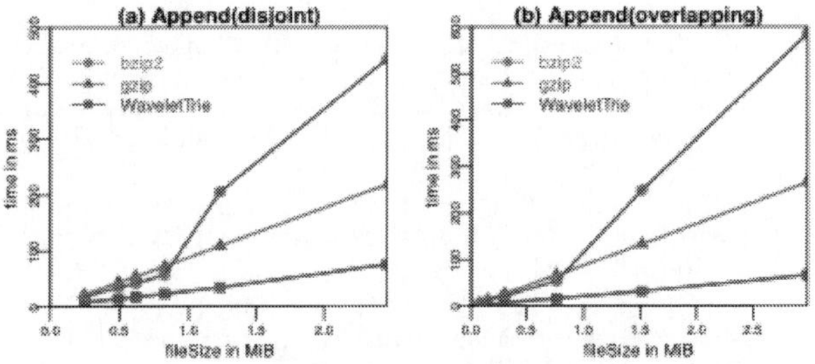

Figure 13. Comparison of the time to append two lists for Wavelet Trie, bzip2 and gzip.

Finally, we evaluated the time to append one list to another list (c.f. Figure 13) and the time to insert a list at position 50 into a second one (c.f. Figure 14).

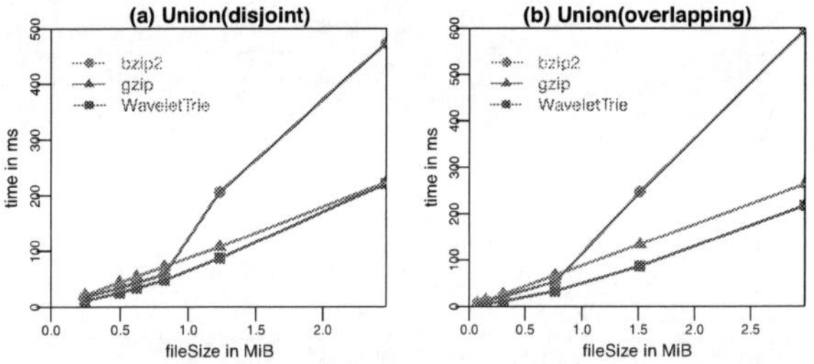

Figure 14. Comparison of the time to merge a list into another one for Wavelet Trie, bzip2 and gzip.

We performed both tests for disjoint lists as well as for lists that overlap in 50% of the entries. Again, we compared the time with the sequence of decompression, concatenating the two lists, and recompressing the concatenated list by using either bzip2 or gzip. In both cases and for both operations, this operation on the Wavelet Trie is faster than the simulation of this operation for bzip2 and for gzip. The benefit of the Wavelet Trie in comparison to bzip2 and gzip is bigger for append operations than for the merge operation that inserts one list at a given position into the second one.

V. CONCLUSION

In this paper, we presented and evaluated an extension of the Wavelet Trie [10][11] that allows to represent compressed indexed sequences of strings. As our evaluations have shown, operations like insertion, deletion, search queries, range queries, intersection and union can be performed on the compressed data as fast as or even faster than the simulation of these operations with the help of generic compressors like bzip2 or gzip. We therefore believe that the Wavelet Trie is a good approach to be used, e.g., in column-oriented main-memory databases to enhance the storage or memory capacity at the same time as the search performance.

REFERENCES

[1] M. Stonebraker et al., "C-Store: A Column-oriented DBMS," in Proceedings of the 31st International Conference on Very Large Data Bases, Trondheim, Norway, August 30 - September 2, 2005, 2005, pp. 553–564.

[2] A. Lamb et al., "The Vertica Analytic Database: C-Store 7 Years Later," Proc. VLDB Endowment, vol. 5, no. 12, pp. 1790–1801, 2012.

[3] F. Färber et al., "SAP HANA Database - Data Management for Modern Business Applications," ACM Sigmod Rec., vol. 40, no. 4, pp. 45–51, 2012.

[4] D. A. Huffman, "A Method for the Construction of Minimum-Redundancy Codes," in Proceedings of the IRE, 1952, vol. 40, no. 9, pp. 1098–1101.

[5] T. C. Hu and A. C. Tucker, "Optimal Computer Search Trees and Variable-Length Alphabetical Codes," SIAM J. Appl. Math., vol. 21, no. 4, pp. 514–532, 1971.

[6] S. T. Klein and D. Shapira, "Random Access to Fibonacci Codes," Stringology, 2014, pp. 96–109, 2014.

[7] M. Külekci, "Enhanced variable-length codes: Improved compression with efficient random access," in Proc. Data Compression Conference DCC–2014, 2014, pp. 362–371.

[8] N. R. Brisaboa, A. Fariña, S. Ladra, and G. Navarro, "Reorganizing Compressed Text," in Proceedings of the 31st Annual International ACM SIGIR Conference on Research and Development in Information Retrieval, 2008, pp. 139–146.

[9] J. Herzberg, S. T. Klein, and D. Shapira, "Enhanced Direct Access to Huffman Encoded Files," in Data Compression Conference, 2015., 2015, p. 447.

[10] R. Grossi and G. Ottaviano, "The Wavelet Trie: Maintaining an Indexed Sequence of Strings in Compressed Space," *CoRR*, 2012. [Online]. Available: http://arxiv.org/abs/1204.3581. [Accessed: Mar, 2017].

[11] R. Grossi and G. Ottaviano, "The Wavelet Trie: Maintaining an Indexed Sequence of Strings in Compressed Space," in Proceedings of the 31st ACM SIGMOD-SIGACT-SIGART Symposium on Principles of Database Systems, PODS 2012, Scottsdale, AZ, USA, May 20-24, 2012, 2012, pp. 203–214.

[12] R. Grossi, A. Gupta, and J. S. Vitter, "High-order entropy-compressed text indexes," in SODA '03 Proceedings of the fourteenth annual ACM-SIAM symposium on Discrete algorithms, 2003, vol. 39, no. 1, pp. 841–850.

[13] D. R. Morrison, "PATRICIA---Practical Algorithm To Retrieve Information Coded in Alphanumeric," J. ACM, vol. 15, no. 4, pp. 514–534, 1968.

[14] "Project Gutenberg," 2015. [Online]. Available: http://www.gutenberg.org/. [Accessed: Mar, 2017].

[15] "DBLP: computer science Bibliography." [Online]. Available: http://dblp.uni-trier.de. [Accessed: Mar, 2017].

CitySense: Retrieving, Visualizing and Combining Datasets on Urban Areas

Danae Pla Karidi, Harry Nakos, Alexandros Efentakis, Yannis Stavrakas
IMIS, Athena RC
email: {danae, xnakos, efentakis, yannis}@imis.athena-innovation.gr

***Abstract*— Social networks, available open data and massive online APIs provide huge amounts of data about our surrounding location, especially for cities and urban areas. Unfortunately, most previous applications and research usually focused on one kind of data over the other, thus presenting a biased and partial view of each location in question, hence partially negating the benefits of such approaches. To remedy this, this work presents the CitySense framework that simultaneously combines data from administrative sources (e.g., public agencies), massive Point of Interest APIs (Google Places, Foursquare) and social microblogs (Twitter) to provide a unified view of all available information about an urban area, in an intuitive and easy to use web-application platform. This work describes the engineering and design challenges of such an effort and how these different and divergent sources of information may be combined to provide an accurate and diverse visualization for our use-case, the urban area of Chicago, USA.**

Keywords- Social networks; Crowdsourcing; Open data; Geographic visualization.

I. INTRODUCTION AND MOTIVATION

The emergence of social networks, microblogging platforms, check-in applications and smartphone / Global Positioning System (GPS) devices in recent years has generated vast amounts of data regarding the location of users. To exploit this vastly growing data, recent research has focused on utilizing the geographic aspect of this information for event detection, sentiment analysis of users, place-name disambiguation [1][2], identification of popular hotspots and their temporal variation, identifying and visualizing the typical movement pattern of users throughout the day [3][4], as well as improving existing city maps [5][6]. However, volunteered geographic information (VGI) contributed by online users is imprecise and inaccurate by design and it should, thus, be used with extra caution for critical applications.

Likewise, the increasing necessity for efficient location-based services and effective online advertising drove leading web providers (e.g., Google, Here, Bing, Foursquare) to store and offer Point of Interest (PoI) information to their users, usually through the use of online Application Programming Interfaces (APIs). Such an approach has several benefits, since the users not only have access to information about their nearby PoIs but they may also provide (or view) reviews or notify their friends of their current whereabouts. The same web services also allow shop-owners and enterprises to advertise their stores and the services they offer. However, as any commercial offering there are limitations on the use of those APIs, thus providing users with a very locally-limited view of the existing city infrastructure that cannot be directly used to extract additional information for city-scale areas.

On a separate front, the open data movement argued that citizens should have access to the data collected by government agencies, since they are the ones funding data collection through their taxes. A second strong supporting argument is that public access to government data helps individuals and enterprises to create apps that boost the economy and provide better services to the citizens, at no additional cost. Some countries and cities have openly released such data, which provide another alternative view of urban areas. Although this open data is official, curated, of excellent quality and impossible to collect by individuals, it has the obvious disadvantage that it cannot be real-time, it is usually not available through APIs and most importantly it may be updated at very infrequent intervals (e.g., census data), therefore at risk of being rather outdated.

Overall, the aforementioned three sources of information, i.e., volunteered geographic information, online PoI data and official open data each have their own strengths and weaknesses, regarding accuracy, update-rate, ease of use and availability. Likewise, applications or research that utilize and rely on only one of those types of data offer a biased and imprecise view of reality that could potentially be misleading. To remedy this, this work proposes the *CitySense* framework that utilizes open data from administrative sources, online PoI APIs and social microblogs (tweets) to provide a unified view of our use-case, the urban area of Chicago. The main innovation and focus of the paper is to show how disparate datasets of various origins can be combined to provide a more complete picture of a geographical area. The corresponding web application [47] may be viewed with any modern web browser (Chrome, Firefox). Our emphasis is on how to efficiently spatially aggregate, visualize and present the end-user with an aesthetically pleasing and intuitive view of available raw data for any of these three sources, with minimum intervention, so that the end-user could freely interpret this information at his own will. As such, the CitySense application could be easily extended with additional features with minimal effort. The paper does not attempt to give a detailed description of all the algorithms used and explain in depth all the technical decisions taken; the focus is rather in providing a high-level view of the problems in order to motivate the approach, and in introducing the main elements of the solution. Overall, CitySense is a dynamic urban area viewer that integrates various datasets related to an urban area, providing a rich visualization of a city's life.

As a motivating example, consider a newcomer to the city, who has to search for a house in an unfamiliar area. She has to answer some questions, in order to narrow down and locate the neighborhoods to search. These questions may involve criteria like education facilities (''Where are the most popular residential neighborhoods having high level educational facilities?'') and security (''Where is the downtown area with the lowest criminality measures?''). As another example, consider a tour operator that needs to track the tourist activity in a city, in order to offer improved tour packages and services. However, monitoring massive tourist activity using traditional methods would require lots of efforts, examination of many updating sources, hence huge costs and time involving off-line on-the-spot observation.

The outline of this work is as follows. Section II presents related work. Section III describes the objectives, the architecture and the web-based application of CitySense. Section IV describes the CitySense technical challenges. Finally, Section V gives conclusions and directions for future work.

II. RELATED WORK

In recent years, as data from location sharing systems are constantly increasing, researchers have proposed a wide variety of "urban sensing" methods, based on location data derived from all kinds of sources: social media posts and check-ins, cellphone activity, taxicab records, demographic data, etc. Scientists combined social sciences, computer science and data mining tools, in order to derive useful knowledge regarding the life of cities. Cranshaw et al. [7] tried to reveal the dynamics of a city based on social media activity, while in [8][9], authors characterized sub-regions of cities by mining significant patterns extracted from geo-tagged tweets. Frias-Martinez et al. [10] focused on deriving land uses and points of interest in a specific urban area based on tweeting patterns and Noulas et al. [11] analyzed user check-in dynamics, to mine meaningful spatio-temporal patterns for urban spaces analysis. Much work has been done in the field of using social media textual and semantic content for urban analysis purposes. For example, Pozdnoukhov et al. [12] conducted real-time spatial analysis of the topical content of streaming tweets. Moreover, Noulas et al. [13] proposed the comparison of urban neighborhoods by using semantic information attached to places that people check in, while Kling et al. [14] applied a probabilistic topic model to obtain a decomposition of the stream of digital traces into a set of urban topics related to various activities of the citizens using Foursquare and Twitter data. Grabovitch-Zuyev et al. [15] studied the correlation between textual content and geospatial locations in tweets and Kamath et al. [16] used the spatio-temporal propagation of hashtags to characterize locations. Prediction methodologies have widely used geo-tagged social content. For example, Kinsella et al. [17] created language models of locations extracted from geotagged Twitter data, in order to predict the location of an individual tweet, in [18]-[21], the authors aimed to model friendship between users by analyzing their location trails and Cheng et al. [22] estimated a Twitter user's city-level location based purely on the content of the user's tweets. Moreover, researchers have focused on trend and event detection by detecting correlations between topics and locations [23][24]. Lately, many works have been published focusing on urban mobility patterns. For example, Veloso et al. [25] analyzed the taxicab trajectory records in Lisbon to explore the distribution relationship between pick-up locations and drop-off locations. In [26], the authors explored real-time analytical methodologies for spatio-temporal data of citizens' daily travel patterns in urban environment. The authors of [27]-[31] used the moving trajectory data of mobile phone users to study city dynamics and human mobility, while the authors of [32]-[35] analyzed the human mobility using social media data. Another field connected to urban analysis is the geodemographic classifications, which represent small area classifications that provide summary indicators of the social, economic and demographic characteristics of neighborhoods [36]. In the area of location demographics and socio-economic prediction and correlation, researchers have proposed a variety of methods based on geo-tagged social media data [37]-[39].

A wide variety of applications that describe the life of urban areas have been developed so far. For example, EvenTweet [40] is a framework to detect localized events in real-time from a Twitter stream and to track the evolution of such events over time. Moreover, the "One million Tweet Map" [41] is a web app that displays the last million tweets over the world map in real-time. Every second the map is updated, dropping twenty of the earliest tweets and plotting out the latest twenty keeping the number of tweets hovering at 1,000,000, showing clustered tweets in regions around the world, while users are able to zoom in or out on the map, and cause the re-aggregation of the clusters. Furthermore, the "tweepsmap" [42] application provides users with efficient geo-targeted twitter analytics and management and "trendsmap" [43] and "tweetmap" [44] shows the geo located latest trends from Twitter on a map. In Urban Census Demographics visualization field, the "Mapping America: Every City, Every Block" [45] enables users to browse local data from the Census Bureau's American Community Survey, based on samples from 2005 to 2009. Finally, "Social Explorer" [46] provides map based tools for visual exploration of demographic information, including the U.S. Census, American Community Survey, United Kingdom Census, Canadian Census, Eurostat, FBI Uniformed Crime Report, American election results, Religious Congregation Membership Study, World Development Indicators.

Although those works provide thorough insights in some aspects of life in an urban area, they fail to provide an integrated and global view of the city and to enable the user

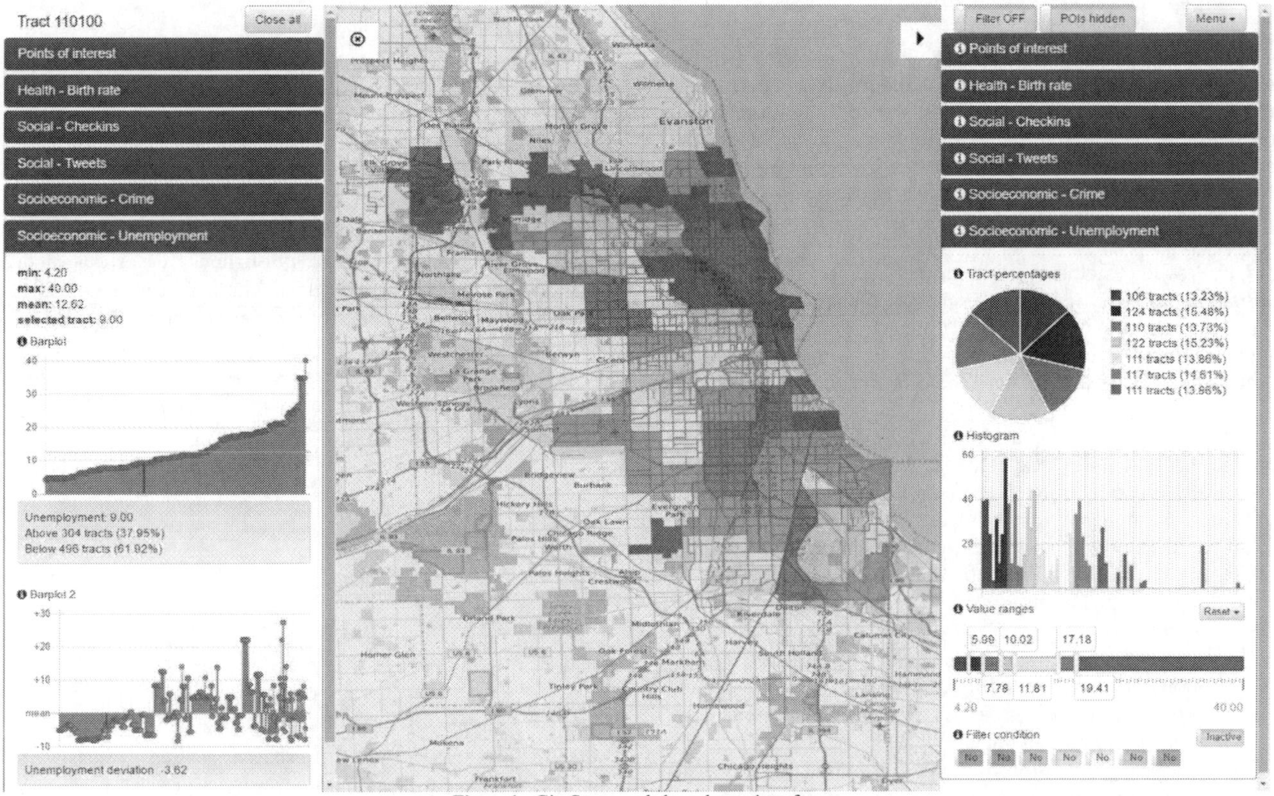

Figure 1. CitySense web-based user interface

to interactively answer questions by combining datasets. CitySense aims to fill these gaps by integrating multiple data sources and providing an interactive user interface supporting filters, multiple view options and drill down abilities.

III. BROWSING INTEGRATED CITY DATA

In this section, we present an overview of CitySense. We also discuss the objectives and present the features of the application.

A. Objectives and Architecture

CitySense is a dynamic urban area viewer, that integrates various datasets related to an urban area and provides a rich visualization of a city's life. The application can answer questions at many levels by exploiting the variety of datasets referring to a city and joining disparate data sources in an easy way. Users can view several aspects of city life statically or over time, for the whole city or for each part, mixing data sources to uncover patterns and information that would not be obvious from just observing the datasets.

The CitySense application [47] aims to provide a fast and easy way to:

- combine disparate data sources regarding various city aspects,
- filter data and drill down through a map-based visualization environment, and
- answer questions, explore and discover valuable information to convey the sense of the city.

The system architecture is presented in Figure 2 and includes the front-end Web-based Application of CitySense, the Data Infrastructure and Refresher units, the GeoServer that is discussed in Section IV-C and the CityProfiler subsystem (the dotted box in Figure 2) that was developed to collect the data related to the city from the data sources and is presented in detail in Section III-B.

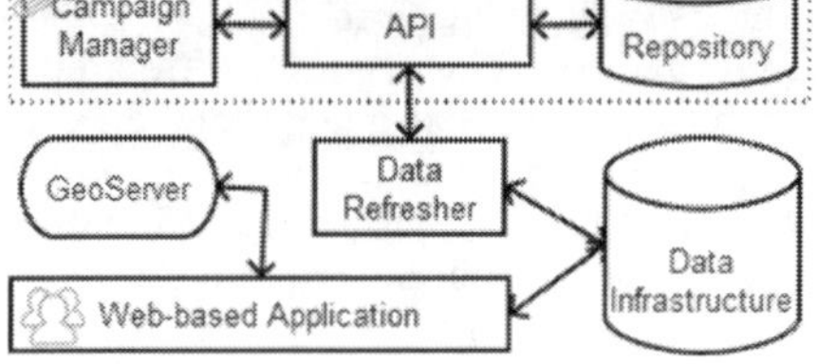

Figure 2. CitySense architecture

A screenshot of the CitySense web-based user interface is shown in Figure 1. The city of Chicago was selected for the pilot application, due to the amount and quality of official census data that are available. An additional reason is that Chicago's residents are exhibiting strong social media activity; moreover, a sufficient number of Points of Interest (PoIs) is available as well.

B. *Harvesting Data with CityProfiler*

CityProfiler (included in the dotted box in Figure 2) is a subsystem of CitySense, responsible for collecting data related to an urban area from diverse sources. Its basic functionality is to collect all available PoIs and tweets that come from the city and to store them in a repository together with relevant metadata.

CityProfiler provides an API and a GUI through which applications and users, respectively, can define and perform new collection campaigns. Each campaign, which is defined by certain parameters, results in an independent collection. These parameters control the individual crawlers that gather data through available APIs, and are the following:

- Crawling Duration: defines the duration of the campaign.
- Crawler Selection: selects which of the available crawlers (corresponding to distinct data sources like Foursquare, Google Maps, Facebook, Twitter, etc.) will participate in the campaign.
- Crawling Location: defines a crawling location by setting a point on the map and a range around it.
- Category Selection: selects target PoI categories and optionally keywords for the crawling to be based on. Keywords are used to narrow crawling, when the PoI category employed is deemed too broad (e.g., keyword "high school" is used when crawling Google Places for high schools, since "school" is the only applicable category). Category Selection can also collect all PoIs in a location, regardless of their category.
- Crawling Frequency Selection: some of the collected data need a systematic update, because of the changes that might occur to PoIs (e.g., a coffee shop might become a bar or new PoIs might show up). CityProfiler can perform repetitive campaigns with large duration in which multiple collections can be performed using the same parameters. Frequency Selection defines, therefore, how often the campaign should automatically restart.

CityProfiler is able to perform multiple campaigns in parallel, therefore there is a need of a Coordinator (see Figure 2) to control the crawlers and manage the campaigns. Moreover, CityProfiler manages resources in an intelligent way ensuring that all the restrictions imposed by the sources are met (e.g., maximum number of requests per time period), and that overlapping requests are avoided. Retrieved data are cleaned to exclude duplicates, and are temporarily stored in a repository.

C. *Data Preprocessing and Integration*

CitySense aims to shed light on the life of a city by exploiting three types of data: Points of Interest, Social Media and Open Census Data. PoI and Social Media Data are generated constantly by users and services. Therefore, we collect and update them in a regular and automatic way using CityProfiler, as discussed in Section III-B. Unlike these types of data, Open Census Data are generated by diverse sources (local authorities) at unpredictable time intervals. Moreover, they are published in various data formats (CSV, tab delimited, etc.). Therefore, Open Census Data require a case-dependent preprocessing and integration procedure keeping pace with their publication and taking into account the variety of data sources and formats. Finally, the diverse nature of these datasets requires a special integration regarding the aspect of time as well.

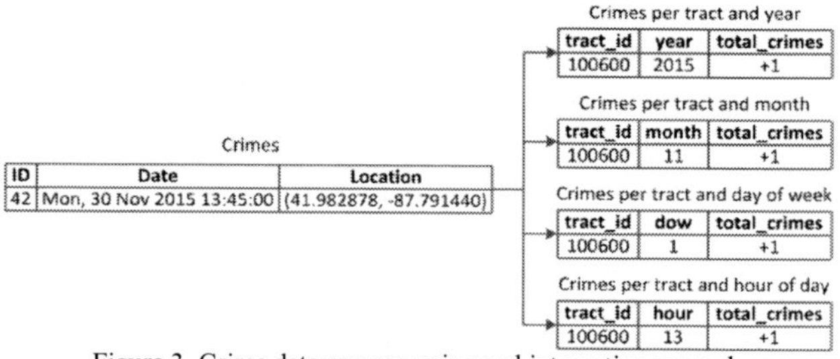

Figure 3. Crime data preprocessing and integration example

An example of the preprocessing and integration transformation regarding Crime data is presented in Figure 3. On the left side of the figure, we observe a single row of crime data that was downloaded in CSV format. This row represents a crime incident and contains its time and location. On the right side of the figure, we observe how this crime is represented in our database. Specifically, it is assigned to a tract (a specific geographical partition of the city) based on its location. The specific crime instance is represented by increasing the counter (total_crimes) in four tables, each representing a different time granularity: per year, month, day of week and hour of day.

D. *CitySense Features and Design*

Figure 1 shows CitySense web-based user interface. The central element of the visualization is the map of Chicago, which is divided in smaller sections, called tracts. Tracts are existing administrative divisions already used by the Chicago city government departments. Chicago contains 801 tracts and each of them describes a small area that is considered to be relatively uniform and corresponds ideally to about 1200 households (2000-4000 residents). Tract boundaries are always visible (blue line) on the map and when an individual tract is chosen its boundaries are highlighted with a red border line.

On the two sides of the map, CitySense provides two complementary views of Chicago. The first view appears on the right side and provides functions regarding the city as a whole. Hence, users can define visualization and filter options and observe the results both on the coloring of the city map and on distribution charts. The second view, is on the left side, and provides charts concerning only the selected tract, dark-highlighted on the map. This view, which appears when a tract is selected, helps users drill down to observe the special characteristics of each tract and to compare it with the city's overview. These views can be active concurrently, enabling users to observe different datasets in a general level and in tract level at the same time.

Both views provide visualizations and charts tailored to the corresponding dataset. For example, as shown in Figure 1, map coloring and charts visualize the Unemployment dataset. To select a dataset, the user has to select a *data drawer*. Data drawers (dark rectangles) can be accessed concurrently in both views and represent the available datasets, e.g., "Points of Interest", "Health - Birth rate", "Social – Tweets", etc. According to the type of the particular dataset (see Section IV-A) each data drawer can contain different UI elements like pie charts, histograms, color range sliders and implement suitable functionality like value-based map coloring, temporal and combined filtering and superimposed PoI information.

The map coloring is based on user adjustable color range sliders that are available in each data drawer. Such a slider is presented in Figure 4 (top). After the color ranges are adjusted, users can define one or more colors as filtering parameters for combining various datasets. In other words, CitySense combines datasets (data drawers) by filtering the tracts based on their color. A color filtering slider, where only the violet color (leftmost) is defined as filtering condition, is shown in Figure 4 (bottom).

The tracts that satisfy the conditions set in all data drawers are colored grey on the map. Figure 5 shows the filter output for Social-Tweets and Socioeconomic-Crime datasets.

Certain datasets are visualized based on temporal aspects (per month/day/hour). The temporal functions described here are shown in Figure 6. Thus, users can select the time granularity, e.g., month of year, day of week, hour of day to adjust the charts and map coloring accordingly. Additionally, users can color the map or view the tract charts based on a specific month, day, or two-hour interval.

Finally, the CitySense application enables the user to see superimposed PoI information on the map at any moment. The user can select one or more categories (Food, Residence, Outdoors & Recreation, etc.) and the corresponding PoIs appear on the map as shown in Figure 7.

IV. TECHNICAL CHALLENGES

In this section, we present in detail the technical challenges of the CitySense application.

A. Organizing Disparate Datasets

In order to convey the sense of a city CitySense must integrate and visualize a variety of datasets. The data sources that are integrated consist of demographic, social media and PoI data. The diverse nature of these datasets requires a different integration manipulation regarding the aspect of time. As we show in Table 1:

- Open Census Data can be visualized both in a static (overtime) or in a temporal way (per month/ day/hour). For instance, Health and Unemployment

Figure 4. Coloring and filtering color slider

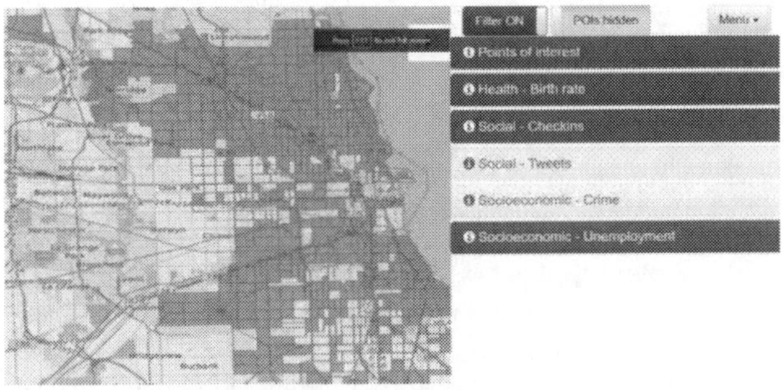

Figure 5. Filtered map

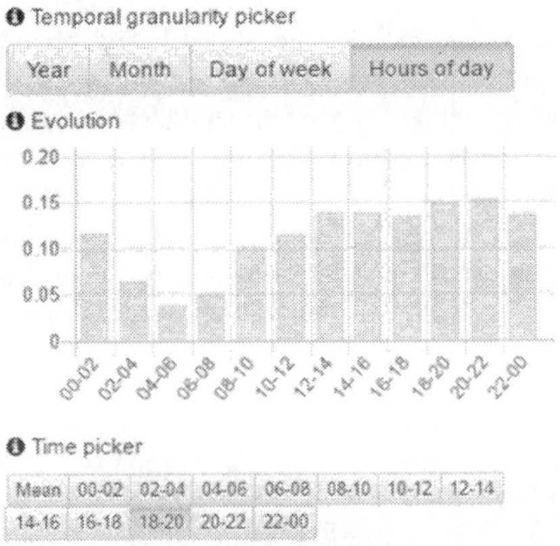

Figure 6. Temporal pickers

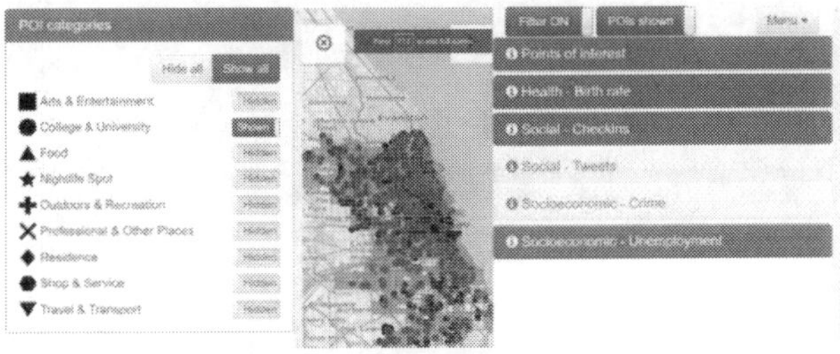

Figure 7. Filtered map with PoIs

data are visualized statically and Crime data temporally.

- Social Media Data can be visualized in a static, temporal or dynamic way, although they are produced and gathered dynamically (real time). The feature of real time dynamic visualization of social media data is currently being developed.
- Point of Interest Data are visualized in a static way.

TABLE I. DIVERSITY OF DATASET VISUALIZATION REGARDING TIME

	static	temporal	dynamic
Open Census Data	✓	✓	
Social Media Data	✓	✓	✓ ongoing development
Point of Interest Data	✓		

The above organization of data helped to overcome their diversity and provide coherent visualization and treatment within the application.

A related problem is that of the initialization of the user-adjustable color range sliders. Our goal was to provide a reasonable use of map coloring to help users draw conclusions about the city. Therefore, we provided two options for initialization. The first, the value-based initialization option, breaks the slider based on equidistant values. However, this approach is sensitive to data with extreme outlier values or extreme concentration in certain ranges. The second option provides a percentage-based initialization, hence breaks the slider based on equal distribution percentages. However, this approach is sensitive to having many tracts with almost equal values. As an example, Figure 8 shows the value-based initialization for crime data.

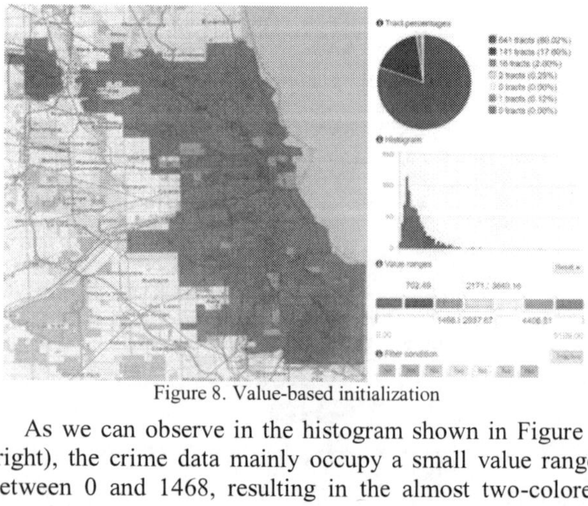

Figure 8. Value-based initialization

As we can observe in the histogram shown in Figure 8 (right), the crime data mainly occupy a small value range, between 0 and 1468, resulting in the almost two-colored map (violet and indigo – colors may not be visible on printed document) of Figure 8 (left). To address this issue we use the percentage-based initialization, which is presented in Figure 9.

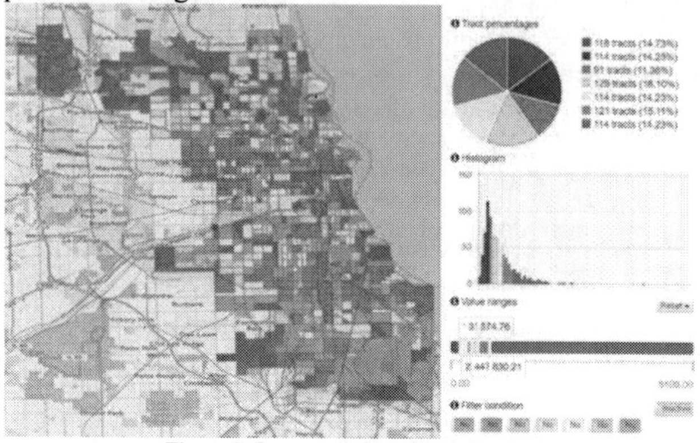

Figure 9. Percentage-based initialization

The resulting map coloring shown in Figure 9 (left) is obviously improved. However, as we can observe in the tract percentages shown in Figure 9 (right), the crime data distributions are not equally divided, because some tracts have almost equal values with respect to the range step and, therefore, cannot be equally classified.

B. Acquiring Data of an Area

CityProfiler gathers PoI data from an urban area by performing calls to API services like Google Places and Foursquare, which set restrictions and constraints. A naïve crawling of PoIs, in terms of a whole city, would not be able to collect the entire amount of PoIs, but only a small portion of it as dictated by the rules imposed by the source. CitySense deals with this issue by breaking the area to smaller parts in advance. Specifically, the city is divided in squares of longitude and latitude of 0.03 degrees before the PoI crawling. In case this method doesn't gather all the PoIs, then recursion is used.

Additionally, CityProfiler collects real-time social data from the city. In order to achieve this, CityProfiler performs a real-time crawling of tweets with Twitter Streaming API, using a location box which encompasses the city as filter parameter. Only the geo-located tweets (that are posted along with their latitude and longitude) are collected. In order to collect social check-ins and the PoIs that they were posted at, CityProfiler performs a call to Foursquare API every time a tweet contains a Swarm (mobile app that allows users to share their location within their social network) link. This way, the application collects temporal information concerning geo-located tweets, including their hashtags and check-ins posted at city PoIs.

C. Implementation and Efficiency Issues

Several implementation decisions had to be made, so that the application would run efficiently. The application needed to be lightweight with respect to memory and processing power consumption, as well as responsive with respect to the end-user experience.

At certain parts of the application a large number of geometries, namely tens of thousands of PoIs, needs to appear on the screen simultaneously. The option of handling each geometry as a separate entity and drawing it on the map separately would require much memory and processing power especially when zooming in and out the map. The approach employed is based on drawing relevant geometries as one image layer containing all geometries. GeoServer (shown in Figure 2) is leveraged for generating and serving image layers. For additional efficiency, the built-in caching functionality of image layers by GeoServer is utilized. This way subsequent requests may use already generated image layers.

The application's requirements involve aggregate queries on data, spanning the geospatial and temporal dimensions. Such queries take much time, if performed on raw data, resulting in degradation of responsiveness for the end-user. In order to avoid costly operations during runtime, a preprocessing stage is employed. The database design for preprocessed data was driven by the critical use cases available to the end-user via the UI. As an example, the user is able to query for check-in data, aggregated per tract, pertaining to a specific PoI category and a specific day of week. Raw check-in data contain the geographic coordinates of the PoI, the category of the PoI, as well as the date and time of the check-in, across two tables. Tract geometries are stored in a separate table as well. Such a query cannot be executed instantaneously. During the preprocessing stage, the coordinates of the PoIs are mapped to the intersecting tracts, the days of week are extracted from date and time, and aggregation per tract and day of week is performed. The preprocessing results are stored in database tables. This way efficient querying for check-ins, in a specific PoI category, on a specific day of week, is achieved. Separate tables are employed to deal with different time granularity aspects of the temporal dimension, i.e., there exist separate tables for years, months, days of week, hours of day. Another optimization measure in the same direction is the delegation of heavy computations to the initialization stage of application services. This has an effect on the start-up time of the application, but speeds up requests during runtime.

The application currently encompasses a relatively small number of datasets, so data handling is manageable using PostgreSQL database system. If the datasets grow in number, a data warehouse can be used to facilitate data management and efficient processing of aggregate queries.

D. Adapting to Other Cities

One of our primary concerns during the development of the CitySense framework was adaptability of the framework to other cities. Adaptation of CitySense to another city is comprised of three major tasks, partitioning of the city area, integration of Open Census Data and implementation of the relevant access methods, and specialization of the front-end according to the available city data.

1) City Area Partitioning

CitySense is essentially parametric with respect to the attributes that define the city of interest, namely a bounding rectangle that encloses the city and a partitioning scheme for the city. The partitioning scheme may in theory consist of an arbitrary set of polygons that collectively cover the whole city. Choosing a partitioning scheme is, nevertheless, not that straightforward. In order to effectively choose a partitioning scheme, official administrative partitioning schemes should be looked into (e.g., community areas, ZIP codes, census tracts), focusing on partitioning schemes used in Open Census Data of interest. Disregarding such partitioning schemes and employing an arbitrary one could result in Open Census Data of interest rendered either useless or hard to map to the employed partitioning scheme. Should the official partitioning scheme be considered too fine-grained, grouping could be applied to the small partitions, in order to acquire a more coarse-grained partitioning scheme to use. Should the official partitioning scheme be too coarse-grained, segmentation of the large partitions into smaller ones would result in a more fine-grained partitioning scheme to use.

2) Open Census Data Integration and Access

Open Census Data is the most cumbersome type of data to integrate into CitySense. While CityProfiler data are the same, irrespective of the city of interest, Open Census Data could be vastly different, even among different types of Open Census Data for the same city. Open Census Data could be stored in database tables or files. As long as data transfer from the back-end to the front-end is of the same form, regardless of the type of data, all underlying implementation details have no other constraints. Open Census Data will often make use of a specific partitioning scheme that will generally diverge from the partitioning scheme applied to the city. Such data will need to be mapped to the employed partitioning scheme. There is no recipe for universally handling this issue, hence the aforementioned suggestion to let Open Census Data drive the choice of a partitioning scheme for the city. Open Census Data with temporal and/or categorical dimensions should be stored in a way that will facilitate efficient data retrieval based on corresponding parameters. The methods that implement data access should also support temporal and/or categorical parameters, if should such dimensions exist for a specific type of Open Census Data. While parameters are specific to each type of Open Census Data, the response from the back-end should always be of the same form, so that all response data can be treated uniformly by the front-end.

3) Front-end Specialization

Specialization of the front-end in order to support the city data available by the back-end is the final task in the process of CitySense adaptation. Each dataset is represented by a data drawer both in the left and the right sidebar. All datasets follow the same protocol with respect to the data sent by the back-end. The only thing that needs to be specialized per dataset is the data picker, in case that one exists for a specific dataset. The data picker is used to navigate categorically and/or temporally within the dataset. The data picker parameters will be transformed to request parameters that are received by the back-end. The back-end response will follow the data transfer protocol. The data drawer, therefore, needs no other specialization before it can display the received data.

E. *Linear Prediction Model*

Very often the datasets are not independent of each other. For example, infant mortality is very likely to be income-related, and is increased in areas with low income. One way to predict values of a variable (response) based on the corresponding values of other variables (predictors) is to find a suitable linear model based on the method of least squares. There are two reasons for constructing such models:

- They can provide an "exploratory analysis" of data. Through comparing the predicted values with the actual it is possible that correlations between variables can be explored, e.g., crimes are associated with income and unemployment.
- They can provide an estimation of a missing value for a tract, since this value can be inferred based on the values of predictors for this tract.

The CitySense application supports the construction of linear models for any of the available datasets. As an example, we consider crime data. From the application menu, we can create linear models (select "New model fit"), regarding crime as response and any combination of predictors. As an example, consider Crime as response, with predictors the Income, the Unemployment, the Checkins and the Points of Interest. The result of the model (the prediction for the crime values), which are shown in Figure 10, when compared with the actual data for crime, confirms the association of crime with the specific predictors.

Figure 10. Linear model visualization

Moreover, before the model construction, there was no crime value for the upper left tract in the dataset. As we observe in Figure 10, the same tract has a value and appears in red color. Since this tract is selected (red outline), the data for that tract as derived from the linear model are shown in the left tray.

V. CONCLUSION AND FUTURE WORK

In this work we presented CitySense, a dynamic urban area viewer that provides a rich visualization of city's life, by integrating disparate datasets. The application helps answer questions and reveals several aspects of city life that would not be obvious from just observing the datasets. In order to accomplish that, we developed special data collection and managing tools, rich visualization and filtering functions and dealt with several technical challenges. Currently, we are developing the feature of dynamic visualization of social media data (tweet posts, check-ins and hashtags). The support for dynamic datasets could be used to cover city power consumption and traffic data in the future. Another future target concerns the incorporation of road network information into our system. Users could calculate the actual distance between PoIs, by exploiting special road network based functions provided by CitySense. Finally, as more and more data is integrated through CitySense, the problem of scalability will arise. Therefore, a cloud data infrastructure is considered to fit CitySense's future data storing and managing needs.

ACKNOWLEDGMENT

This work was partially supported by the "Research Programs for Excellence 2014-2016 – CitySense".

REFERENCES

[1] Crooks, A., et al. "Crowdsourcing urban form and function." International Journal of Geographical Information Science 29.5 (2015), (pp. 720-741).

[2] Drymonas, E., Efentakis, A., Pfoser, D. (2011, September). "Opinion mapping travelblogs." In Proceedings of Terra Cognita workshop (in conjunction with the 10th international semantic web conference) (pp. 23-36).

[3] Efentakis, A., Brakatsoulas, S., Grivas, N., Lamprianidis, G., Patroumpas, K., Pfoser, D. (2013, November). "Towards a flexible and scalable fleet management service." In Proceedings of the Sixth ACM SIGSPATIAL International Workshop on Computational Transportation Science (p. 79).

[4] Efentakis, A., Grivas, N., Lamprianidis, G., Magenschab, G., Pfoser, D. (2013, November). "Isochrones, traffic and DEMOgraphics." In Proceedings of the 21st ACM SIGSPATIAL International Conference on Advances in Geographic Information Systems (pp. 548-551).

[5] Efentakis, A., Brakatsoulas, S., Grivas, N., Pfoser, D. (2014, March). "Crowdsourcing turning restrictions for OpenStreetMap." In EDBT/ICDT Workshops (pp. 355-362).

[6] Efentakis, A., Grivas, N., Pfoser, D., Vassiliou, Y. (2017). "Crowdsourcing turning-restrictions from map-matched trajectories." Information Systems, 64, (pp. 221-236).

[7] Cranshaw, J., Schwartz, R., Hong, J. I., Sadeh, N. (2012). "The livehoods project: Utilizing social media to understand the dynamics of a city." Association for the Advancement of Artificial Intelligence.

[8] Wakamiya, S., Lee, R., Sumiya, K. (2012, February). "Crowd-sourced urban life monitoring: urban area characterization based crowd behavioral patterns from twitter." In Proceedings of the 6th International Conference on Ubiquitous Information Management and Communication (p. 26).

[9] Lee, R., Wakamiya, S., Sumiya, K. (2013). "Urban area characterization based on crowd behavioral lifelogs over Twitter." Personal and ubiquitous computing, 17(4), (pp. 605-620).

[10] Frias-Martinez, V., Soto, V., Hohwald, H., Frias-Martinez, E. (2012, September). "Characterizing urban landscapes using geolocated tweets." International Confernece on Social Computing (SocialCom) (pp. 239-248).

[11] Noulas, A., Scellato, S., Mascolo, C., Pontil, M. (2011). "An Empirical Study of Geographic User Activity Patterns in Foursquare." International Conference on Web And Social Media (ICWSM) (pp. 70-573).

[12] Pozdnoukhov, A., & Kaiser, C. (2011, November). "Space-time dynamics of topics in streaming text." In Proceedings of the 3rd ACM SIGSPATIAL International Workshop on Location-Based Social Networks (pp. 1-8).

[13] Noulas, A., Scellato, S., Mascolo, C., Pontil, M. (2011). "Exploiting Semantic Annotations for Clustering Geographic Areas and Users in Location-based Social Networks." The Social Mobile Web, 11(2).

[14] Kling, F., & Pozdnoukhov, A. (2012, November). "When a city tells a story: urban topic analysis." In Proceedings of the 20th International Conference On Advances in Geographic Information Systems (pp. 482-485).

[15] Grabovitch-Zuyev, I., Kanza, Y., Kravi, E., Pat, B. (2014, June). "On the correlation between textual content and geospatial locations in microblogs." In Proceedings of Workshop on Managing and Mining Enriched Geo-Spatial Data (p. 3).

[16] Kamath, K. Y., Caverlee, J., Lee, K., Cheng, Z. (2013, May). "Spatio-temporal dynamics of online memes: a study of geo-tagged tweets." In Proceedings of the 22nd International Conference on World Wide Web (pp. 667-678).

[17] Kinsella, S., Murdock, V., O'Hare, N. (2011, October). "I'm eating a sandwich in Glasgow: modeling locations with tweets." In Proceedings of the 3rd international workshop on Search and mining user-generated contents (pp. 61-68).

[18] Cranshaw, J., Toch, E., Hong, J., Kittur, A., Sadeh, N. (2010, September). "Bridging the gap between physical location and online social networks." In Proceedings of the 12th ACM International Conference On Ubiquitous Computing (pp. 119-128).

[19] Crandall, D. J., Backstrom, L., Cosley, D., Suri, S., Huttenlocher, D., Kleinberg, J. (2010). "Inferring social ties from geographic coincidences." Proceedings of the National Academy of Sciences, 107(52).

[20] Cho, E., Myers, S. A., Leskovec, J. (2011, August). "Friendship and mobility: user movement in location-based social networks." In Proceedings of the 17th ACM SIGKDD International Conference on Knowledge Discovery and Data Mining (pp. 1082-1090).

[21] Backstrom, L., Sun, E., Marlow, C. (2010, April). "Find me if you can: improving geographical prediction with social and spatial proximity." In Proceedings of the 19th International Conference on World Wide Web (pp. 61-70).

[22] Cheng, Z., Caverlee, J., Lee, K. (2010, October). "You are where you tweet: a content-based approach to geo-locating twitter users." In Proceedings of the 19th ACM International Conference on Information and Knowledge Management (pp. 759-768).

[23] Budak, C., Georgiou, T., Agrawal, D., El Abbadi, A. (2013). "Geoscope: Online detection of geo-correlated information trends in social networks." Proceedings of the VLDB Endowment, 7(4), (pp. 229-240).

[24] Lee, R., and Sumiya, K. (2010, November). "Measuring geographical regularities of crowd behaviors for Twitter-based geo-social event detection." In Proceedings of the 2nd ACM SIGSPATIAL International Workshop on Location Based Social Networks (pp. 1-10).

[25] Veloso, M., Phithakkitnukoon, S., Bento, C. (2011, November). "Sensing urban mobility with taxi flow." In Proceedings of the 3rd ACM SIGSPATIAL International Workshop on Location-Based Social Networks (pp. 41-44).

[26]] Liu, L., Biderman, A., Ratti, C. (2009, June). "Urban mobility landscape: Real time monitoring of urban mobility patterns." In Proceedings of the 11th International Conference on Computers in Urban Planning and Urban Management (pp. 1-16).

[27] Ratti, C., Frenchman, D., Pulselli, R. M., Williams, S. (2006). "Mobile landscapes: using location data from cell phones for urban analysis." Environment and Planning B: Planning and Design, 33(5), (pp. 727-748).

[28] Reades, J., Calabrese, F., Sevtsuk, A., Ratti, C. (2007). "Cellular census: Explorations in urban data collection." IEEE Pervasive Computing, 6(3).

[29] Gonzalez, M. C., Hidalgo, C. A., Barabasi, A. L. (2008). "Understanding individual human mobility patterns." Nature, 453(7196), (pp. 779-782).

[30] Calabrese, F., Diao, M., Di Lorenzo, G., Ferreira, J., Ratti, C. (2013). "Understanding individual mobility patterns from urban sensing data: A mobile phone trace example." Transportation research part C: Emerging Technologies, 26, (pp. 301-313).

[31] Taniar, D., Goh, J. (2007). "On mining movement pattern from mobile users." International Journal of Distributed Sensor Networks, 3(1), (pp. 69-86).

[32] Chua, A., Marcheggiani, E., Servillo, L., Moere, A. V. (2014, November). "Flowsampler: Visual analysis of urban flows in geolocated social media data." In International Conference on Social Informatics (pp. 5-17).

[33] Toole, J. L., Herrera-Yaqüe, C., Schneider, C. M., González, M. C. (2015). "Coupling human mobility and social ties." Journal of The Royal Society Interface, 12(105).

[34] Hawelka, B., Sitko, I., Beinat, E., Sobolevsky, S., Kazakopoulos, P., Ratti, C. (2014). "Geo-located Twitter as proxy for global mobility patterns." Cartography and Geographic Information Science, 41(3), (pp. 260-271).

[35] Cheng, Z., Caverlee, J., Lee, K., Sui, D. Z. (2011). "Exploring millions of footprints in location sharing services." International Conference on Web And Social Media (ICWSM), (pp. 81-88).

[36] Harris, R., Sleight, P., Webber, R. (2007). "Geodemographics, GIS and Neighbourhood Targeting." Journal of Direct, Data and Digital Marketing Practice, 8, (pp. 364-368).

[37] Longley, P. A., Adnan, M. (2016). "Geo-temporal Twitter demographics." International Journal of Geographical Information Science, 30(2), (pp. 369-389).

[38] Hristova, D., Williams, M. J., Musolesi, M., Panzarasa, P., Mascolo, C. (2016, April). "Measuring urban social diversity using interconnected geo-social networks." In Proceedings of the 25th International Conference on World Wide Web (pp. 21-30).

[39] Llorente, A., Garcia-Herranz, M., Cebrian, M., Moro, E. (2015). "Social media fingerprints of unemployment." PloS one 10(5).

[40] Abdelhaq, H., Sengstock, C., Gertz, M. (2013). "Eventweet: Online localized event detection from twitter." Proceedings of the VLDB Endowment, 6(12), (pp. 1326-1329).

[41] The one million tweet map. (2017, April 8). Retrieved from http://onemilliontweetmap.com

[42] Tweepsmap. (2017, April 8). Retrieved from https://tweepsmap.com

[43] Trendsmap Realtime Local Twitter Trends. (2017, April 8). Retrieved from http://trendsmap.com

[44] MapD Tweetmap. (2017, April 8). Retrieved from https://www.mapd.com/demos/tweetmap

[45] Mapping America: Every City, Every Block. (2017, April 8). Retrieved from http://www.nytimes.com/projects/census/2010/explorer.html

[46] Social Explorer. (2017, April 8). Retrieved from https://www.socialexplorer.com/explore/maps

[47] CitySense. (2017, April 8). Retrieved from http://citysense.imis.athena-innovation.gr:8080/citysense/

Statistical Implicative Analysis Approximation to KDD and Data Mining:

A Systematic and Mapping Review in **K**nowledge **D**iscovery **D**atabase Framework

Rubén A. Pazmiño-Maji
Escuela Superior Politécnica de Chimborazo
Riobamba, Ecuador
Email: rpazmino@espoch.edu.ec

Francisco J. García-Peñalvo
Department of Computer Science
University of Salamanca
Salamanca, Spain
Email fgarcia@usal.es

Miguel A. Conde-González
Department of Computer Science
University of León
León, Spain
Email: miguel.conde@unileon.es

***Abstract*— According to Scopus, only in the year 2016, there were 15747 scientific papers about data mining and KDD. These have been and remain useful technologies. In this paper, we determine the approximation level of SIA to KDD and Data Mining. To this end, we have created an approximation framework based on definition and step process proposed by Fayyad. We use mapping review and systematic review from literature published in the last 5 years in bibliographic databases ACM, EBSCO, Google Scholar, IEEE, ProQuest, Scopus and WOS. We started with 200 papers and finally, 35 had all quality criteria. This paper also describes the SIA papers and identifies a series of future research in SIA, KDD and Data Mining.**

Keywords-Statistical Implicative Analysis; Knowledge Discovery Database; data mining, systematic review, mapping review.

I. Introduction

In recent years, our capacity to generate, transform, store, analyze and visualize data has increased, basically due to the high processing power and the low cost of the machines. However, within these huge and different types of data there is a lot of unknown information. The discovery of this information is possible thanks to Data Mining (DM), which among other sophisticated techniques applies artificial intelligence to find patterns and relationships within the data allowing the creation of models, that are abstract representations of reality. Common tasks in Knowledge Discovery in Databases (KDD) are rule induction, classification and clustering problems, recognition pattern, predictive modeling, dependency detection, and so on [1].

A. The KDD process for extracting knowledge

The first KDD workshop was in August 20, 1989, Detroit MI, USA, enabling researchers and practitioners to gather around KDD. We define the KDD process as [2]: "The non-trivial process of identifying valid, novel, potentially useful, and ultimately understandable patterns in data".

Data mining (DM) is a step in the general process to constituting the KDD process (see Figure 1). Data mining allows us to use specific algorithms for extracting patterns (including classification rules or trees, regression, clustering, sequence modeling, dependency, and line analysis) from data. Table I shows steps and subprocess in the KDD process [3]:

TABLE I: Steps and Subprocess in KDD

Step	Subprocess	Name
1		Learning the application domain
	A	Selection
2		Creating a target dataset
	B	Preprocessing
3		Data cleaning and preprocessing
	C	Transformation
4		Data reduction and projection
	D	Data Mining
5		Choosing the function of data mining
6		Choosing the data mining algorithm(s)
7		Data mining
	E	Interpretation/Evaluation
8		Interpretation
9		Using discovered knowledge

B. Statistical Implicative Analysis and the Knowledge discovery

Statistical Implicative Analysis (SIA) was created by Regis Gras [4], thirty eight years ago and has a set of data analysis tools that that allows us to approach knowledge on the basis of the information contained in the database (individuals and variables). The approach is performed starting from the generation of asymmetric rules [5] between variables and variables classes, represented by tables (clusters non-hierarchical) [6], graphs (association rules) [7] and dendrograms (hierarchical clusters, hierarchical oriented clusters) [8]. The statistical theory [9] and application of SIA are in continuous expansion and development. The SIA software tool is called CHIC [10] [11], the last Windows version is 7.0 and the CHIC free multiplatform version is called RCHIC [12]. SIA has an international group of active researchers since 2000 [13]. Usual CHIC functions are: Similarity Tree, Implicative Graph, Cohesion Tree and Reduction. Some of the complementary options implemented in CHIC are: the entropy is used when analyzing a large data sample; the supplementary variables are qualitative variables such as gender, education level or economic category; the contribution is used to know what are the subjects or classes of subjects more responsible for computed implications and the typicality indicates the typical subjects of the population for computed implications.

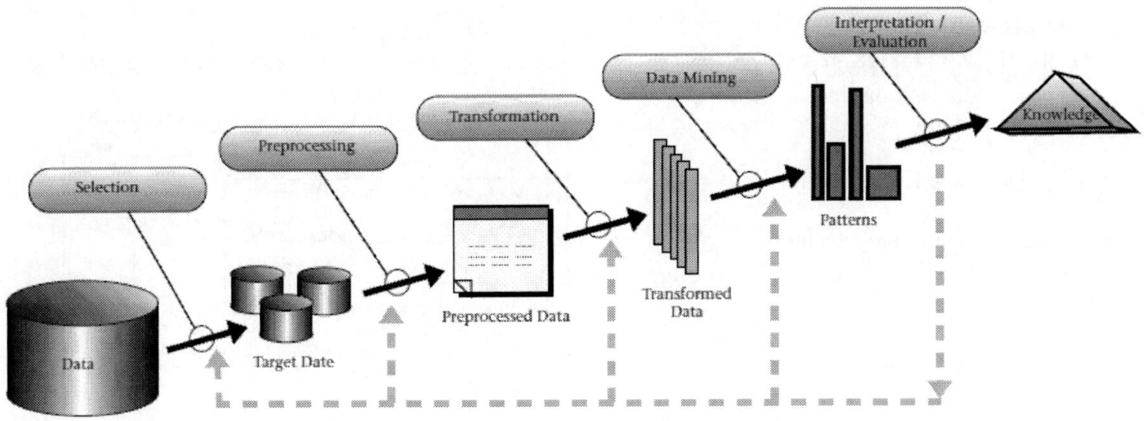

Figure 1. Overview of the steps constituting the KDD process [3].

The aim of this paper is to describe SIA papers in the last 5 years, to determine the position of SIA in KDD and DM, and identify a series of future research.

C. *Paper framework*

The approximation framework of Statistical Implicative Analysis to Knowledge Discovery and Data Mining are the KDD definition and the KDD steps proposed by Usama Fayyad [3]. This approximation allowed us to propose a new definition of SIA and to determine the steps that constitute the SIA process. We emphasize that this paper is a first approximation of SIA to Data Mining.

Section II describes the systematic and mapping review of literature and the steps in the research realized. Section III describes the results and their discussion. Finally, Section IV describes the conclusions.

II. METHOD

In this section we show in detail the steps of the methodology used.

A. *Systematic and mapping review of literature*

In the planning of systematic and mapping review the objectives were identified and the protocol was defined [14] [15]. The Protocol shows the method used in the systematic review and mapping to minimize the bias of researchers and that the methodology can be reproduced. Below we summarize the protocol used:

B. *Research questions*

The systematic mapping aims to answer these questions:
MQ1: What are the SIA papers by countries?
MQ2: Which are the SIA papers types?
MQ3: Which are the SIA papers Areas?
MQ4: What are the SIA papers tendency?

The systematic review aims to answer the question below:
RQ1: Which KDD step is the closest to SIA papers?
RQ2: Which KDD step is the furthest from SIA papers?
RQ3: How close are the SIA papers to KDD steps?
RQ4: How close are the SIA papers to KDD subprocess?
RQ5: How close are the SIA papers to Data Mining steps?
RQ6: Can you define the SIA based KDD definition?
RQ7: Can you define the process for SIA based KDD?

C. *PICOC method*

The paper of Petticrew and Roberts [16], proposed the PICOC method to define our scope:

- Population (**P**): Statistical implicative analysis papers in last five years (2012-2016).
- Intervention (**I**): SIA papers with explicit analysis process, in last five years (2012-2016).
- Comparison (**C**): No comparison intervention.
- Outcomes (**O**): SIA approximation percentages to KDD stages
- Context(**C**): SIA computational solutions.

D. *Time period*

The last 5 years (2012 to 2016)

E. *Sources*

The search was done in the following bibliographic databases [17]:

- EBSCO [18],
- Google Scholar [19],
- IEEExplore [20],
- ProQuest [21],
- Scopus [22],
- WOS [23],
- Web of Science [24],
- ACM [25].

To answer the research questions raised, the inclusion and exclusion criteria were defined. They also allowed us to select the source SIA papers.

F. *Inclusion and exclusion criteria*

The inclusion criteria (IC) [26] are presented below:

IC1: The papers used a SIA methods real application

IC2: The proposed solution is applied on specialized software (Chic, Rchic, etc.)

IC3: The SIA process application is possible to make explicit

IC4: The papers are written in English language

IC5: The papers are reported in peer reviewed Workshop or Conference or Journal or Technical Reports

The exclusion criteria are presented below:

EC1: The paper is essentially theoretical, historical or a literature review

EC2: The SIA process application is not possible to make explicit

EC3: The SIA papers analysis methods do not use computer programs

EC4: The papers are written in Spanish, Italian, Portuguese or French language.

G. *Search string*

The group of primary studies were defined [27]. The final search string was described as follows: ("statistical implicative analysis" OR SIA) AND (LIMIT-TO (PUBYEAR, 2016) OR (LIMIT-TO (PUBYEAR, 2015) OR (LIMIT-TO (PUBYEAR, 2014) OR (LIMIT-TO (PUBYEAR, 2013) OR (LIMIT-TO (PUBYEAR, 2012)) [28, 29] showed studies on control, if the search chain found relevant studies.

H. *Review and mapping steps*

The review and mapping were carried out and the details for this step are presented in the following subsection.

Figure 2 shows the steps of systematic and mapping review with SIA papers.

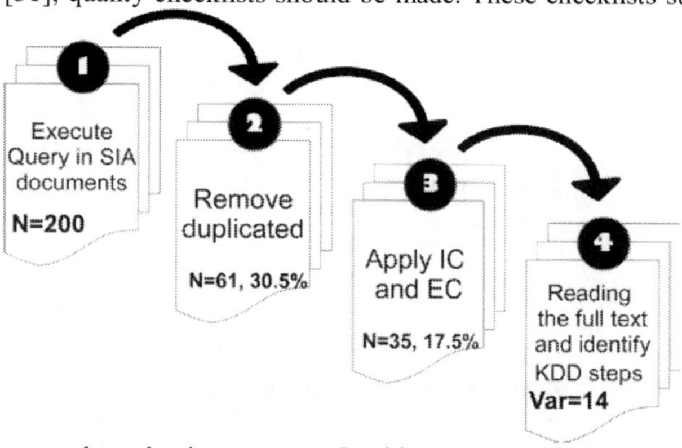

Figure 2. SIA papers mapping and review process

According to Kitchenham [30] and literature mapping [31], quality checklists should be made. These checklists support the selection process. In this way, we produced the following checklist of quality.

I. *Quality assessment*

The quality assessment questions are presented below in Table II:

TABLE II: QUALITY ASSESSMENT QUESTIONS

Questions	Answers		
	Yes=1	*No=0*	*Half=0.5*
1. Are the SIA research goals clearly specified?			
2. Are the research aims achieves?			
3. Are the used data clearly described and their selection justified?			
4. Are the pre-processed data in SIA papers clearly described?			
5. Are the transformed data in SIA papers clearly described?			
6. Are the SIA's papers algorithms clearly described and their selection justified?			
7. Are the SIA's papers methods clearly described and their selection justified?			
8. Is the data analysis process done by the computer?			
9. How clear are the links between data, transformed data, analysis, interpretation and conclusions?			

III. RESULT AND DISCUSSION

In this section we show the results obtained in the mapping and systematic review process.

A. *Mapping literature review*

In this section we describe the results and their discussion about mapping and systematic literature review.

1) *What are the SIA papers by countries?*

Figure 3. Percentage of SIA papers by countries [22]

Figure 3 shows that the most frequent countries in the selected literature are from France (40.0%) and Poland (16.7%). France is the most frequent country because SIA theory was originated with Regis Gras born in France.

2) Which are the SIA papers types?

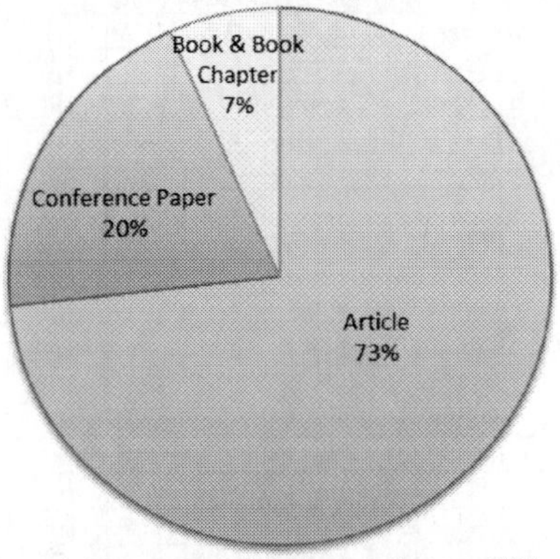

Figure 4. Percentage of SIA papers by type [22]

Figure 4 illustrates that studies from the chosen literature are 73% Articles, 20% Conference Papers, and 7% Book Chapter Books. This is because SIA international congress is producing new papers every two years.

3) Which are the SIA papers areas?

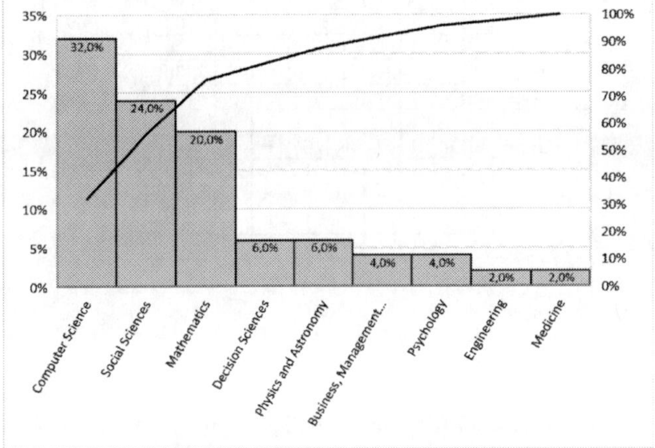

Figure 5. Percentage of SIA papers by Area [22]

Figure 5 illustrates that most of the studies have targeted

Computer Science (32.0%), Social Sciences (24.0%), Mathematics (23.6%) and Decision Sciences (6%). The four areas added are approximately 80%, this is because SIA theory was originated on didactic, mathematics and his methods are used in computer science.

4) What are the SIA papers tendency?

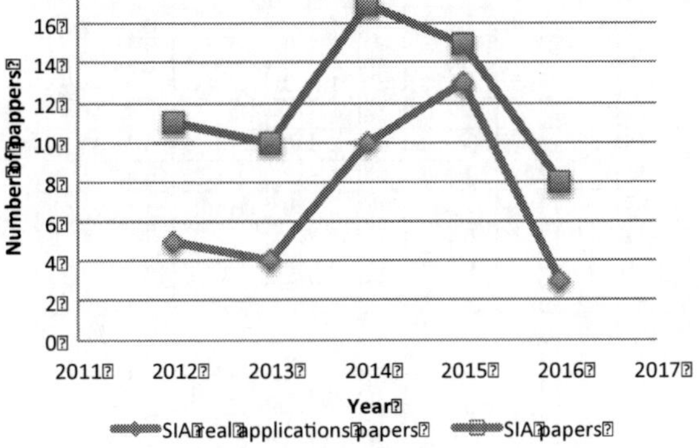

Figure 6. SIA papers by year

Figure 6 shows the tendency of SIA papers in general (in red) and SIA real applications papers (in blue), in the last five years. SIA real applications papers tend to increase because there are fewer the theoretical, historical or a literature review papers than real applications papers.

B. Systematic literarture review

In this section we describe the results and their discussion about systematic review.

1) Which KDD step is the closest to SIA papers.

Steps 1 (Learning the application domain) and steps 2 (Creating a target dataset) with 100 % both, are the steps closest to KDD steps. This is because, all SIA real applications papers need a goal and a target dataset.

2) Which KDD step is the furthest from SIA papers?

Step 7 (Data mining) with 31 %, is the step furthest to KDD steps. This is because, most papers showed not a Data Mining pattern clearly, had descriptive analysis, histograms, bar diagrams, box plots and SIA graphics like a similarity tree, cohesion tree, implicative graph or reduction.

3) How close are the SIA papers to KDD steps?

Table III shows the reference of 35 SIA papers, the compliance or not of KDD steps process 1 to 9 (see introduction, quality assessment and [18]). Also, Table III shows in the last two columns the numbers of positive compliance and the respective percentage. The final percentage is the 74,6 %, which is medium high close to KDD steps process. This means that KDD steps process and SIA steps process are the same in a 74,6 %.

TABLE III: SIA PAPERS & KDD STEPS RELATED TO TABLE I

SIA	KDD steps										
papers	*1*	*2*	*3*	*4*	*5*	*6*	*7*	*8*	*9*	*N*	*%*
[32]	1	1	0	0	1	1	0	1	1	6	66,7
[33]	1	1	1	1	1	1	0	1	1	8	88,9
[34]	1	1	0	0	1	1	1	1	1	7	77,8
[35]	1	1	0	0	1	0	0	0	0	3	33,3
[36]	1	1	0	0	1	1	0	1	1	6	66,7
[37]	1	1	0	0	1	0	0	1	1	5	55,6
[38]	1	1	1	1	1	1	1	1	1	9	100,0
[39]	1	1	1	0	1	0	0	1	0	5	55,6
[40]	1	1	0	1	1	1	1	1	1	8	88,9
[41]	1	1	1	0	1	0	0	1	1	6	66,7
[42]	1	1	1	1	1	1	0	1	1	8	88,9
[43]	1	1	0	1	1	1	1	1	0	7	77,8
[44]	1	1	1	0	1	1	1	1	1	8	88,9
[45]	1	1	1	0	1	1	0	1	1	7	77,8
[46]	1	1	1	1	1	0	1	1	1	8	88,9
[47]	1	1	1	1	1	1	1	1	1	9	100,0
[48]	1	1	0	0	1	1	0	1	1	6	66,7
[49]	1	1	1	1	1	0	1	1	1	8	88,9
[50]	1	1	1	0	1	0	0	0	0	4	44,4
[51]	1	1	1	0	1	1	0	0	0	5	55,6
[52]	1	1	1	1	1	1	0	1	1	8	88,9
[53]	1	1	1	0	1	0	0	1	1	6	66,7
[54]	1	1	1	1	0	0	0	1	1	6	66,7
[55]	1	1	0	1	1	1	0	1	0	6	66,7
[56]	1	1	1	1	1	1	0	1	1	8	88,9
[57]	1	1	1	1	1	0	0	1	1	7	77,8
[58]	1	1	1	0	1	0	0	1	1	6	66,7
[59]	1	1	1	1	1	1	1	1	1	9	100,0
[60]	1	1	1	1	1	0	1	1	1	8	88,9
[61]	1	1	1	1	1	1	1	1	1	9	100,0
[62]	1	1	1	1	0	0	0	0	0	4	44,4
[63]	1	1	1	1	1	0	0	1	1	7	77,8
[64]	1	1	0	0	1	1	0	1	1	6	66,7
[65]	1	1	1	0	1	0	0	1	1	6	66,7
[66]	1	1	1	0	1	0	0	1	1	6	66,7

4) How close are the SIA papers to KDD subprocess?

Table III shows the reference of 35 SIA papers, the compliance or not of KDD subprocess A to E (see introduction, quality assessment and [18]). Table IV shows in the last two columns the numbers of positive compliance and the respective percentage. The final percentage 94,2 %, means that KDD and SIA subprocess are very similar.

5) How close are the SIA papers to the Data Mining steps?

Observing step 5 (Choosing the function of data mining, 94%), step 6 (Choosing the data mining algorithm, 54%), step 7 (Data mining, 31%) and subprocess (Data mining, 86%) we have 66.4% of approach to Data Mining process. It is a medium high percentage. This is because the SIA methods can be similar to the Data Mining methods.

TABLE IV: SIA PAPERS & KDD SUBPROCESS RELATED TO TABLE I

SIA	KDD subprosses						
papers	*A*	*B*	*C*	*D*	*E*	*N*	*%*
[32]	1	1	1	1	1	5	100
[33]	1	1	1	1	1	5	100
[34]	0	1	1	1	1	4	80
[35]	1	1	1	0	1	4	80
[36]	1	1	1	1	1	5	100
[37]	1	1	1	1	1	5	100
[38]	1	1	1	1	1	5	100
[39]	1	1	1	1	1	5	100
[40]	1	1	1	1	1	5	100
[41]	1	1	1	1	1	5	100
[42]	1	1	1	1	1	5	100
[43]	1	1	1	0	1	4	80
[44]	1	1	1	1	1	5	100
[45]	1	1	1	1	1	5	100
[46]	1	1	1	1	1	5	100
[47]	1	1	1	1	1	5	100
[48]	1	1	1	1	1	5	100
[49]	1	1	1	1	1	5	100
[50]	1	1	1	0	1	4	80
[51]	1	1	1	0	1	4	80
[52]	1	1	1	1	1	5	100
[53]	1	1	1	1	1	5	100
[54]	1	1	0	1	1	4	80
[55]	1	1	1	1	1	5	100
[56]	1	1	1	1	1	5	100
[57]	1	1	1	1	1	5	100
[58]	1	1	1	1	1	5	100
[59]	1	1	1	1	1	5	100
[60]	1	1	1	1	1	5	100
[61]	1	0	1	1	1	4	80
[62]	1	1	0	0	1	3	60
[63]	1	1	1	1	1	5	100
[64]	1	0	1	1	1	4	80
[65]	1	1	1	1	1	5	100
[66]	1	1	1	1	1	5	100

6) Can you define the SIA process based in KDD process?

The SIA definition based on the KDD process could be:

Statistical Implicative Analysis is the process of identifying valid, useful, and understandable, r-rules in data.

In the previous SIA definition, the words valid, useful, and understandable depend on the researcher interpretation of the SIA methods used and the results obtained. The novel word is not in a SIA definition because the use of SIA methods is novel in Data Mining.

7) Can you define the process for SIA based KDD?

Figure 7 shows the steps graphic constituting the SIA process (based in KDD).

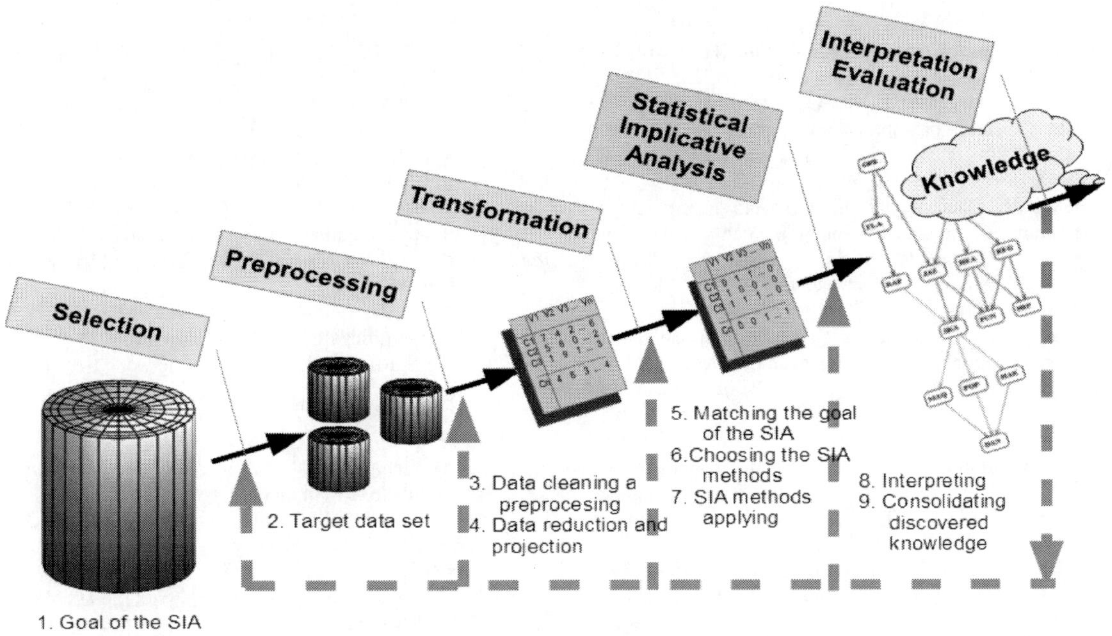

Figure 7. Proposal based in KDD, of the steps constituting the SIA process

IV. CONCLUSIONS

The aim of this paper is to describe SIA papers in last 5 years (2012-2016), to determine the approximation of SIA to KDD and DM, and identify a series of future research. To describe SIA papers, we use the mapping and systematic literature review methods. The most frequent country in the selected literature is France (40%); also 73% of the chosen literature are Articles. The studies were targeted in Computer Science (32.0%), Social Sciences (24.0%), Mathematics (23.6%), and Decision Sciences (6%). The four areas are approximately 80% of SIA papers total areas.

It is important to note that the results obtained depend closely on the approximation framework used, in this case the steps of the Faday process. It was determined that SIA and KDD are strongly related, with a contention relationship of SIA to KDD. In the first approximation, considering all steps without subprocesses, a contention of 74.6% corresponding to medium high approximation was obtained. In the second approach, considering all the subprocesses a contention of SIA to KDD of 94.2% was obtained that is high approximation to KDD process. This is summarized by indicating that the overall approximation rate considering the complete Faday process is 84.4% which is medium high approximation. The approximation achieved allowed to propose the steps that constitute the SIA process analysis, besides a new definition. The process D and steps 5 and 6 allowed us to give a first approximation of the SIA to data mining, obtaining 66.4% of contention between SIA and Data Mining corresponding to medium high percentage.

The future research in SIA, KDD and Data Mining can be to answer the following questions: Do SIA methods work with big data? Can we use similarity tree and cohesion tree like a data mining hierarchical cluster method? Can we use implicative graph like a data mining rule induction method? and Can we use reduction like a data mining cluster method?. For example we have the questions: Do SIA methods work with big data? Can we use similarity tree and cohesion tree like a data mining hierarchical cluster method? Can we use reduction SIA method like a data mining cluster method? and Can we use implicative graph like a data mining rule induction method?. The answer to the abode questions is future research in SIA, KDD and Data Mining.

ACKNOWLEDGMENT

We would like to thank the University of Salamanca PhD programme on Education in the Knowledge Society scope. Similarly, we want to thank Escuela Superior Politécnica de Chimborazo for funding to perform this research.

REFERENCES

[1] V. V. Asencios, "Data Mining y el descubrimiento del conocimiento," *Industrial Data,* vol. 7, pp. 083-086, 2014.

[2] U. Fayyad, G. Piatetsky-Shapiro, and P. Smyth, "From data mining to knowledge discovery in databases," *AI magazine,* vol. 17, p. 37, 1996.

[3] U. Fayyad, G. Piatetsky-Shapiro, and P. Smyth, "The KDD process for extracting useful knowledge from

volumes of data," *Communications of the ACM,* vol. 39, pp. 27-34, 1996.

[4] T. Yorozu, M. Hirano, K. Oka, and Y. Tagawa, "Electron spectroscopy studies on magneto-optical media and plastic substrate interface," *IEEE translation journal on magnetics in Japan,* vol. 2, pp. 740-741, 1987.

[5] R. Gras, R. Couturier, F. Guillet, and F. Spagnolo, "Extraction de règles en incertain par la méthode statistique implicative," *Comptes rendus des 12èmes Rencontres de la Société Francophone de Classification,* pp. 148-151, 2005.

[6] R. Gras and S. A. Almouloud, "A implicação estatística usada como ferramenta em um exemplo de análise de dados multidimensionais," *Educ Mat Pesqui,* vol. 4, pp. 75-88, 2002.

[7] R. Gras, J.-C. Régnier, and F. Guillet, "Analyse Statistique Implicative. Une méthode d'analyse de données pour la recherche de causalités," *Toulouse (França): Cepadues,* 2009.

[8] G. Ritschard, "De l'usage de la statistique implicative dans les arbres de classification," *Troisieme Rencontre Internationale-Analyse Statistique Implicative,* pp. 305-316, 2005.

[9] M. Bailleul, "Des réseaux implicatifs pour mettre en évidence des représentations," *Mathématiques et sciences humaines. Mathematics and social sciences,* 2001.

[10] R. Couturier and S. A. Almouloud, "Historique et fonctionnalités de CHIC," ed, 2009.

[11] R. Couturier and R. Gras, "CHIC: traitement de données avec l'analyse implicative," in *EGC*, 2005, pp. 679-684.

[12] Fento-St. (2017, 2017/04/29/10:52:33). *Rchic - | Raphael Couturier*. Available: http://members.femto-st.fr/raphael-couturier/en/rchic

[13] J.-C. REGNIER. (2017, 2017-04-29 05:39:21). *A.S.I. 9 - 9th International Meeting Statistical Implicative Analysis*. Available: http://sites.univ-lyon2.fr/asi9/?page=1&lang=en

[14] F. W. Neiva, J. M. N. David, R. Braga, and F. Campos, "Towards pragmatic interoperability to support collaboration: A systematic review and mapping of the literature," *Information and Software Technology,* vol. 72, pp. 137-150, 2016.

[15] C. Okoli and K. Schabram, "A guide to conducting a systematic literature review of information systems research," *Sprouts Work. Pap. Inf. Syst,* vol. 10, p. 26, 2010.

[16] M. Petticrew and H. Roberts, *Systematic reviews in the social sciences: A practical guide*: John Wiley & Sons, 2008.

[17] C. Costa and L. Murta, "Version control in distributed software development: A systematic mapping study," in *Global Software Engineering (ICGSE), 2013 IEEE 8th International Conference on*, 2013, pp. 90-99.

[18] (2017/04/29/11:17:05). *EBSCOhost Login*. Available: http://search.ebscohost.com/

[19] (2017/04/29/11:22:57). *Google Académico*. Available: https://scholar.google.es/

[20] (2017/04/29/11:35:51). *IEEE Xplore Digital Library*. Available: http://ieeexplore.ieee.org/Xplore/home.jsp

[21] ProQuest. (2017, 2017/04/29/15:31:05). *ProQuest - Connect*. Available: http://search.proquest.com/

[22] (2017/04/29/11:41:48). *Scopus - Welcome to Scopus*. Available: https://www.scopus.com/home.uri

[23] (2017/04/29/11:45:14). *ScienceDirect.com | Science, health and medical journals, full text articles and books*. Available: http://www.sciencedirect.com/

[24] T. REUTERS. (2017, 2017/04/29/15:25:40). *Web of Science [v.5.24] - Colección principal de Web of Science*. Available: apps.webofknowledge.com

[25] A. f. C. Machinery. (2017, 2017/04/29/15:11:19). *ACM Digital Library*. Available: http://dl.acm.org/

[26] R. A. Pazmiño-Maji, F. J. García-Peñalvo, and M. A. Conde-González, "Approximation of statistical implicative analysis to learning analytics: a systematic review," in *Proceedings of the Fourth International Conference on Technological Ecosystems for Enhancing Multiculturality*, 2016, pp. 355-376.

[27] H. Zhang and M. Ali Babar, "On searching relevant studies in software engineering," 2010.

[28] A. Tolk, C. D. Turnitsa, and S. Y. Diallo, "Ontological implications of the levels of conceptual interoperability model," in *Proc. 10th World Multi-conf. on Systemics, Cybernetics and Informatics*, 2006, pp. 105-111.

[29] L. Kutvonen, "Tools and infrastructure facilities for controlling non-functional properties in inter-enterprise in collaborations," in *Enterprise Distributed Object Computing Conference Workshops, 2008 12th*, 2008, pp. 423-432.

[30] B. Kitchenham, R. Pretorius, D. Budgen, O. P. Brereton, M. Turner, M. Niazi, and S. Linkman, "Systematic literature reviews in software engineering–a tertiary study," *Information and Software Technology,* vol. 52, pp. 792-805, 2010.

[31] C. A. Ellis, S. J. Gibbs, and G. Rein, "Groupware: some issues and experiences," *Communications of the ACM,* vol. 34, pp. 39-58, 1991.

[32] S. D. Anastasiadou, V. Batiou, and E. Valkanos, "Occupational Mobility Dimensions in Greece," *Procedia Economics and Finance,* vol. 19, pp. 325-331, 2015 2015.

[33] S. Anastasiadou and E. A. Panitsides, "AND NOW WHITHER..? EUROPEAN UNION LIFELONG LEARNING POLICY: A TWO LEVEL ANALYSIS," *The Economies of Balkan and Eastern Europe Countries in the changed World,* p. 41, 2014 2014.

[34] R. Belohlavek, D. Grissa, S. Guillaume, E. M. Nguifo, and J. Outrata, "Boolean factors as a means of clustering of interestingness measures of association rules," *Annals of Mathematics and Artificial Intelligence,* vol. 70, pp. 151-184, 2014 2014.

[35] N. Bonneton-Botte, H. Hili, F. De La Haye, and Y. Noel, "Drawings of the hand and numerical skills in children of preschool age," *Canadian Journal of Behavioural Science-Revue Canadienne Des Sciences Du Comportement,* vol. 47, pp. 207-215, Jul 2015.

[36] R. Coutrier, R. A. Pazmiño Maji, M. Á. Conde González, and F. J. García-Peñalvo, "Statistical implicative analysis for educational data sets: 2 analysis with RCHIC," 2015 2015.

[37] R. Couturier and R. Pazmiño, "Use of Statistical Implicative Analysis in Complement of Item Analysis," *International Journal of Information and Education Technology,* vol. 6, p. 39, 2016.

[38] T. Delacroix and A. Boubekki, "An application of multiple behavior SIA for analyzing data from student examsApplications multiples de l´ASI pour l´analyse des données des examens d´étudiants," *Educação Matemática Pesquisa,* vol. 16, 2014 2014.

[39] B. Di Paola, O. R. Battaglia, and C. Fazio, "Non-Hierarchical Clustering as a method to analyse an open-ended questionnaire on algebraic thinking," *South African Journal of Education,* vol. 36, pp. 1-13, 2016 2016.

[40] T.-N. Do, "Using Local Rules in Random Forests of Decision Trees," 2015, pp. 32-45.

[41] I. Elia, S. Özel, A. Gagatsis, A. Panaoura, and Z. E. Y. Özel, "Students' mathematical work on absolute value: focusing on conceptions, errors and obstacles," *ZDM - Mathematics Education,* vol. 48, pp. 895-907, 2016.

[42] C. Fazio, O. R. Battaglia, and B. Di Paola, "Investigating the quality of mental models deployed by undergraduate engineering students in creating explanations: The case of thermally activated phenomena," *Physical Review Special Topics-Physics Education Research,* vol. 9, p. 020101, 2013 2013.

[43] C. Fazio, O. R. Battaglia, and R. M. Sperandeo-Mineo, "Quantitative and qualitative analysis of the mental models deployed by undergraduate students in explaining thermally activated phenomena," *2013 ICPE-EPEC,* pp. 354-364, 2014 2014.

[44] C. Fazio, B. Di Paola, and I. Guastella, "Prospective elementary teachers' perceptions of the processes of modeling: A case study," *Physical review special topics-physics education research,* vol. 8, p. 010110, 2012 2012.

[45] C. Fernández and S. Llinares, "Implicative relations between strategies used in solving proportional and non-proportional problems," *Revista Latinoamericana de Investigacion en Matematica Educativa,* vol. 15, pp. 9-33, 2012.

[46] I. M. Gómez-Chacón, "Meta-emotion and mathematical modeling processes in computerized environments," in *From beliefs to dynamic affect systems in mathematics education*, ed: Springer, 2015, pp. 201-226.

[47] S. Guillaume, D. Grissa, and E. M. Nguifo, "Categorization of interestingness measures for knowledge extraction," *arXiv preprint arXiv:1206.6741,* 2012 2012.

[48] H. Khaled, S. Ghanem, and R. Couturier, "Analysis of Bejaia University Computer Science students' marks through the CHIC software and Statistical Implicative Analysis," in *2014 4th International Symposium ISKO-Maghreb: Concepts and Tools for knowledge Management (ISKO-Maghreb)*, 2014, pp. 1-8, 10.1109/ISKO-Maghreb.2014.7033473.

[49] I. Kohanova, "Analysis of University Entrance Test from mathematics," *Acta Didactica Universitatis Comenianae Mathematics,* vol. 12, pp. 31-46, 2012 2012.

[50] U. Kortenkamp and S. Ladel, "Flexible use and understanding of place value via traditional and digital tools," *RESEARCH REPORTS KNO-PI,* vol. 33, 2014 2014.

[51] I. C. Lerman and S. Guillaume, "Comparing two discriminant probabilistic interestingness measures for association rules," in *Studies in Computational Intelligence* vol. 471, F. Guillet, B. Pinaud, G. Venturini, and D. A. Zighed, Eds., ed, 2013, pp. 59-83.

[52] J. Melusova and K. Vidermanova, "Upper-secondary students' strategies for solving combinatorial problems," *Procedia-Social and Behavioral Sciences,* vol. 197, pp. 1703-1709, 2015 2015.

[53] K. Nikolantonakis and L. Vivier, "Positions numeration in any base for future elementary school teachers in France and Greece: one discussion via registers and praxis," *Menon, Florina,* vol. 2, pp. 99-114, 2013 2013.

[54] E. A. Panitsides and S. Anastasiadou, "Lifelong Learning Policy Agenda in the European Union: A bi-level analysis," *Open Review of Educational Research,* vol. 2, pp. 128-142, 2015 2015.

[55] D. Pasquier and R. Gras, "In the interest of the statistical analysis implicative (ASI) for exploratory research in psychology," *Psychologie Francaise,* vol. 57, pp. 161-173, 2012.

[56] D. Pasquier and L. Rioux, "Satisfaction et confort au travail. L'apport de la démarche implicative," *Psychologie du Travail et des Organisations,* vol. 20, pp. 275-293, 2014 2014.

[57] G. Pavlovicova and J. Zahorska, "The Attitudes of Students to the Geometry and Their Concepts about Square," *Procedia-Social and Behavioral Sciences,* vol. 197, pp. 1907-1912, 2015 2015.

[58] N. Q. Phan, H. X. Huynh, F. Guillet, and R. Gras, "Classifying objective interestingness measures based on the tendency of value variation," 2015, pp. 143-172.

[59] N. Pizzolato, C. Fazio, R. M. S. Mineo, and D. P. Adorno, "Open-inquiry driven overcoming of epistemological difficulties in engineering undergraduates: A case study in the context of thermal science," *Physical Review Special Topics-Physics Education Research,* vol. 10, p. 010107, 2014 2014.

[60] L. Rioux and D. Pasquier, "A longitudinal study of the impact of an environmental action," *Environmental Education Research,* vol. 19, pp. 694-707, 2013 2013.

[61] G. G. Stella and A. D. Sofia, "HUMAN RESOURCES DIMENSIONS: AN APPROACH OF GREEK MANAGERS," *The Economies of Balkan and Eastern Europe Countries in the changed World,* p. 59, 2014 2014.

[62] K. Ţilková, "Testing Pre-service Primary Education Teachers in Quadrilaterals," 2014.

[63] M. van den Heuvel-Panhuizen, I. Elia, and A. Robitzsch, "Kindergartners' performance in two types of imaginary perspective-taking," *ZDM Mathematics Education,* vol. 47, pp. 345-362, 2015.

[64] L. Zamora-Matamoros, D.-S. Jorge Rey, and L. Portuondo-Mallet, "Fundamental Concepts on Classification and Statistical Implicative Analysis for Modal Variables," *Revista Colombiana de Estadistica,* vol. 38, pp. 335-n/a, 2015 2015.

[65] K. Žilková, "Misconceptions in Pre-service Primary Education Teachers about Quadrilaterals," *Journal of Education, Psychology and Social Sciences,* vol. 1, 2015 2015.

[66] K. Zilková, J. Guncaga, and J. Kopácová, "(MIS) CONCEPTIONS ABOUT GEOMETRIC SHAPES IN PRE-SERVICE PRIMARY TEACHERS," *Acta Didactica Napocensia,* vol. 8, p. 27, 2015 2015.

A Knowledge Graph for Travel Mode Recommendation and Critiquing

Bill Karakostas
VLTN GCV
Antwerp, Belgium
Bill.karakostas@vltn.be

Dimitris K. Kardaras
Athens University of Economics and Business
Athens, Greece
kardaras@aueb.gr

***Abstract*— The paper presents a knowledge based system for travel mode recommendation and critiquing. The system recommends the best travel mode for travelling between locations, based on user recommendations. The system's knowledge is stored in a graph database where the nodes represent locations and the edges the travel modes available for travelling between locations. Weights attached to each edge represent the degree of popularity of different modes for travelling on that route. The system is capable of recommending itineraries containing the highest recommended travel modes. The system also can critique a user proposed itinerary based on the travel modes it contains. We have evaluated the approach comparing system generated recommendations with user recommendations in online travel forums.**

Keywords- travel recommender system, graph database, multi mode travel, intelligent route planner, intelligent critiquing

I. INTRODUCTION

Research from the World Travel and Tourism Council (WTTC) indicates that the contribution of travel and tourism to world GDP grew for the sixth consecutive year in 2015, rising to a total of 9.8% of world GDP (US$7.2 trillion). According to WTTC, the tourism sector employs 284 million people, which globally represents 1 in 11 jobs. Stimulating demand and improving the traveler experience has been the endeavour of travel related commercial enterprises who are employing IT for that purpose. IT systems in various shapes (i.e., as static online information and advice, or through intelligent travel assistants) have been used to assist the travellers through the different stages of their trip, i.e., in planning, consuming, and also for post-travel feedback and ratings.

A particular class of intelligent information assistants known as *recommender systems* [1] has been used in the travel domain, to provide travellers with relevant recommendations regarding their trips. Some of the travel recommenders draw their knowledge from sources that describe travel and tourist locations, travel modes and other related aspects (called the *content based recommendation* approach), while others employ the experience of fellow travelers in order to provide relevant recommendations (an approach known as *collaborative filtering*). It has been suggested however, that most of the existing recommender systems only provide location-centric recommendations to travellers about 'things to do', once they get to their destination.

Some advanced recommenders, like SAMAP [2] and PaTac [3], are even capable of analysing the connection possibilities between the activities using different means of transport i.e., on foot, by bike, by car, or by public transport. This category of recommenders has similarities to automated travel planners. However, travel planners mainly rely on domain knowledge about routes and their properties, such as available travel modes, online timetables, knowledge of the average travel times and so on. Such knowledge is hard to acquire, integrate and maintain. On the other hand, travel knowledge elicited directly from the travel users themselves, maybe easier to acquire, due to the proliferation of travel related web sites such as forums. This knowledge may be less accurate and more subjective than the knowledge employed by travel planners, but that is compensated by the large volumes of available data.

Finally, another feature that travel planners are lacking is critiquing user proposed routes. Often users have a particular route in mind that they want to follow, but they want other user's opinion as to whether their route represents a good choice. A recommender system augmented with critiquing capabilities can comment on user proposals by comparing the users' routes (or the routes' legs, modes of transport etc), with what other users have recommended.

The paper therefore presents a travel route recommender and critique that does not rely on objective travel knowledge such as travel timetables, travel times and distances but on user recommendations. The system is capable of recommending the most popular means of transport between two locations. This differs from the typical travel planner's ability to find the best route between two places based on criteria such as travel time or cost. As argued above the route that optimises one or more of such parameters is not always the most popular with the users.

The structure of the paper is as follows. Section II surveys research approaches for travel and route recommendation. Section III presents the core of the approach including the architecture of the system, the organization of the knowledge base, the knowledge elicitation method and the implementation approach. Section IV describes the recommendation and critiquing algorithms, while Section V presents the testing and evaluation approach followed.

Finally, Section VI provides an appraisal of the significance of the work and its findings, as well as areas for future research.

II. Intelligent Systems for Travel and Route Planning and Recommendation

Current literature shows that recommendation is a common service in the tourism subdomains of travel and travel services such as accommodation (i.e., hotel recommendations), used to make the site more appealing to users. Such recommender systems try to mimic the interactivity that occurs in traditional interactions with travel agents, for example when a user seeks advice on a possible holiday destination [4].

Some recommender systems recommend not only lists of places that match the user's preferences but also help to create a route through several attractions [5]. For example, CT-Planner [6] and [7] offers tour plans that can be refined gradually as the users express their preferences and characteristics (e.g., willingness to walk, walking speed, etc.). The recommender system described in [8] integrates automated selection of locations with finding the shortest path. Other recommender system takes into account factors such as the expected duration of the visit, the opening and closing times of the attractions and the distance between them. Examples of such systems include City Trip Planner [9], CRUZAR [10], Smart City [11], Otium [12] and e-Tourism [13]. Some advanced recommenders, are capable of analysing the connection possibilities between locations by different means of transport (walking, bike, car, public transport, etc.).

A related category of intelligent systems are Computer *Aided Critiquing systems*. The concept of a critique has been applied in diverse domains, including: medical, programming/software engineering and architectural design [14]. Critiquing system have been used by designers to improve their design artifacts by providing feedback. [15] analyse existing critiquing systems in terms of critiquing process, critiquing rules, and intervention techniques.

Travel planning however is a complex and dynamic process because there are multiple factors that influence the destination choice. Destination choice is determined by the availability of travel facilities and by the user's preferences such as length of travel, mode of transportation, accommodation type, and activity theme. Our approach exploits the benefits of itinerary planning using established graph search techniques to reduce the planning effort and the cost of information search for travellers.

III. System Architecture

Because planning is an inherently hard problem where optimal solutions often can only be approximated. Some planning systems for tourists reported are therefore not based on recommendations but instead use classic planning approaches like Operations Research techniques [8]. Our approach uses recommendations as heuristic planning rules that enable users to travel between the locations they want to visit in the most recommended way. Such recommendations act as shortcuts that reduce the space search effort in finding suitable routes between locations. Our approach therefore, combines the benefits of collaborative filtering with those of knowledge based approaches.

As shown in Figure 1, the knowledge of the travel mode recommender is captured in a knowledge graph linking locations with the most recommended modes of travel. The following section discusses the structure and content of the travel knowledge graph, while section IV presents the recommendation and critiquing processes.

The KB contains knowledge about tourist locations as well as of the recommended ways for travelling between locations, weighted by the degree of their recommendation. The knowledge is represented as a directed cyclic graph; we call the *travel knowledge graph*. Thus locations are represented as graph nodes and travel modes as graph vertices (edges). For example, for travelling between locations (nodes) A and B there can be *n possible travel modes* $m_1, m_2, \ldots, m_n$ where each mode m_k has a weight w_k (a real number greater than zero) that represents the degree of recommendation of that travel mode.

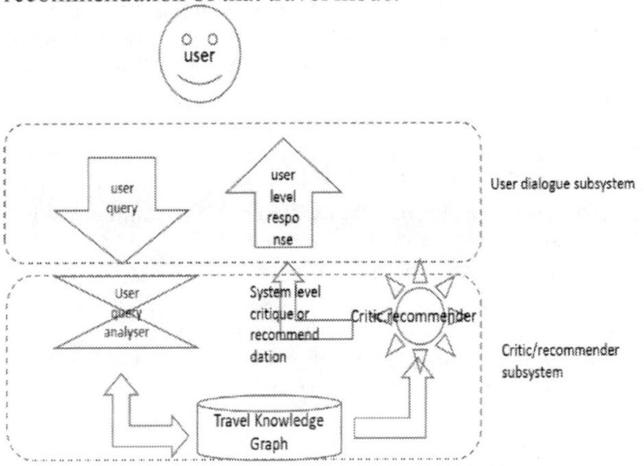

Figure. 1 Architecture of the recommender/critique system

When it is not possible to travel directly between two nodes A and B, a path P (called an itinerary in our approach) consists of intermediate nodes I1, I2,..., Ik connected by edges that form a path between A and B. Itineraries do not have to be acyclical graphs, i.e., a node can appear multiple times in an itinerary. Itineraries have to be finite however.

An optimal itinerary for travelling from A to B consists of a path I1, I2,..., Ik where every edge connecting two nodes In-1 and In corresponds to the highest recommended travel mode between the two locations.

In our knowledge graph model nodes represent cities, towns and other geographical areas of visiting interest or acting as hubs, i.e., facilitating the travel to other locations. Every node is connected to at least one other node via at least one edge that corresponds to a particular travel mode (road, rail, car, ferry, etc). Two nodes can be connected by multiple edges, representing the fact that locations are usually connected with multiple modes of transport. This approach represents an abstraction of a physical transportation network. For example, in a physical transportation network there may be a road linking A to B. In our approach however the links represent modes of transport, not physical connections, thus there will be two or more separate edges connecting A and B, representing private/hired car and (public) bus, running over the same (physical) road.

If a particular transport mode is not available between two locations, then it is simply not represented in the graph, while if it is available but there are no recommendations for it, (or against it) is assigned a recommendation weight of zero. In our approach, the direction of the travel is important, therefore all links are directed. For example, when travelling from A to B, bus might be the recommended travel mode, while in the reverse order it may not be recommended, due for example to the overcrowding of the returning bus. The directionality of the links is taken into account by the travel planner module in our approach.

The recommendation weight of each transport mode (edge) between two locations has a weight that represents its degree of recommendation. Recommendations are calculated according to the frequency with which a particular mode of transport is commented (in a positive or negative manner) in the travel forums. All recommendations are normalised within a scale 1 to 5 (i.e., from 'not recommended' to 'highly recommended').

For experimentation purposes we decided to populate the knowledge base will cover the geographical region of Italy known as Amalfi coast. This is a very popular touristic area of Italy attracting millions of tourists each year and attracts large online discussions on forums such as TripAdvisor. For example, the Italy forum of Trip Advisor contained more than 362,000 topics and 2million posts, as of 2016. Nodes for the transport network were selected by identifying the most frequently mentioned locations around Amalfi coast and by consulting constructed using online GIS sources such as OpenStreet Map and Google Maps. Recommendation weights for travel modes between Amalfi cost locations were elicited from general and specific travel advice of expert users who have travelled the route more than two times, as per the example below.

Recommendation Advice:

High speed trains between major cities run faster than any car: Venice, Bologna, Florence, Rome, Naples and Salerno are all linked by bullet trains. .... The big sights of Italy (Rome, Florence, Venice, Sorrento/Naples/Capri/Amalfi, and Cinque Terre) are inconvenient by car and easy by public transportation.

The recommendation weights are calculated as follows:

Assume as set of locations $L = \{l_i\}$ where i=1,…,n indicate locations, i.e. nodes on the travel graph that customers could potentially visit. Expert users' reviews are collected regarding the travel modes and their quality. Consider the set of travel modes $M = \{m_k\}$, where k=1,…,m the various available travel modes, such as private car, hired car, bus, train, plane, etc., for travelling between two locations. Let $E = \{E^q_{m_k,i,j}\}$ be the set of expert users' comments regarding the quality of m_k travel mode, of between two locations. Text mining tools such as the Knime can be used for analysing reviews and calculating the frequencies of terms related to travel modes and commented levels of travel quality. The E assumes five levels of travel quality (q) and uses linguistic variables and their corresponding fuzzy sets are shown below:

$$E = \begin{cases} verylow(0,0.10,0.25) \\ low(0.15,0.30,0.45) \\ medium(0.35,0.50,0.65) \\ high(0.55,0.70,0.85) \\ veryhigh(0.75,0.90,1) \end{cases}$$

Expert users comment on the suitability of a travel mode by using one of the above linguistic variables. Assume that $f^q_{m_k,i,j}$ indicates the frequency of using a linguistic variable $e^q_{m_k}$ to show the quality of travel by m_k travel mode, between two locations. By using the modal values of $e^q_{m_k}$ linguistic variables, the frequency of using a quality level is used to calculate the suitability of each travel mode as follows:

$s^{m_k}_{i,j} = \sum_{k,q} (f^{e^q}_{m_k,i.j} * e^q_{m_k,i,j})$, $\forall (i,j)$ location. Thus, $s^{m_k}_{i,j}$ shows the recommendation degree for travelling between locations by (i,j) by each m_k travel mode, i.c $s^{bus}_{i,j}$, $s^{privatecar}_{i,j}$, $s^{train}_{i,j}$, etc. The recommendation weight $r^{m_k}_{i,j}$ then for travelling between locations (i,j) is $r^{m_k}_{i,j} = \max\{s^{m_k}_{i,j}\}$, with m_k indicating the most suitable thus, most recommended travel mode.

For an itinerary (I), all possible paths (P) on the travel graph that connect the departing (S) location and the destination (D) of a trip are considered. Thus, drawing on the cognitive maps theory, the recommendation weight for travelling between S and D is:

$R^{m_k}_{S,D} = \max\{\prod_{i,j} (r^{m_k}_{i,j})\}$, where S and D indicate the departing and destination locations respectively, the $r^{m_k}_{i,j}$ the recommendation degrees of each edge (i,j) along all possible paths, and the m_k shows the recommended travel mode.

Figure 2 shows a visual representation of the travel recommendation graph as implemented in the Neo4J graph database [16]. For visual clarity nodes of different type (e.g., city, town, village, see-sight area) are represented with different colour codes. Upon clicking on a node or edge the user can obtain information about the node attributes and their values. Neo4J has its own graph query language called

Cypher that was used to construct and run queries against the knowledge base.

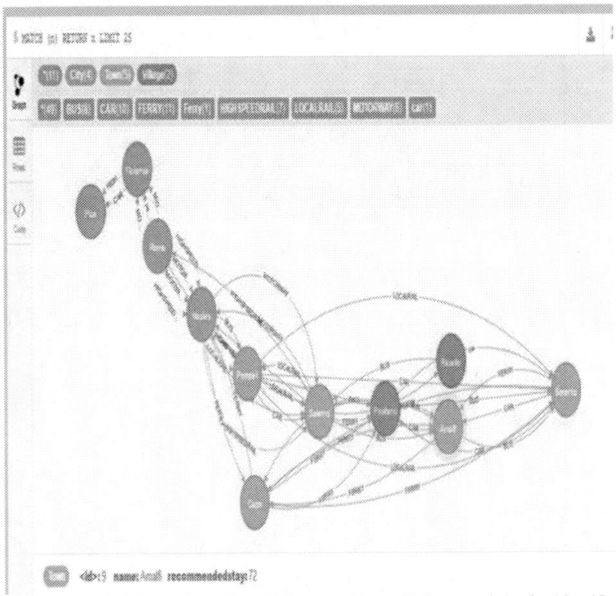

Figure. 2 Representation of the travel knowledge graph in the Neo4J graph database system

Figure 3 shows an example of such a query for constructing an itinerary for travelling between Rome and the town of Amalfi using only the highest recommended travel modes. Such plans are not optimal from a conventional planning perspective as they do not optimise travel time or distance, they represent however, the most popular ways that other travellers have used to travel between locations.

IV. THE RECOMMENDATION AND CRITIQUING ALGORITHMS

The recommendation algorithm can be formalised as follows: Given a user proposed tour consisting of locations l_1, l_2,..., l_k to be visited, recommend an itinerary that visits the required locations using the most recommended travel. The recommendation will consist of an itinerary l'_1 - m'_1 -> l'_2 m-'2 ->... , where l'_1, l'_2,... are locations from the user proposal with possible additional locations (hubs) added by the recommender system and each m'_k is the recommender way of travelling between locations l_k and l_{k+1}.

The following is a real user request from the TripAdvisor Italy Forum:

"What's the best itinerary for a 2 days trip to see Pompeii and the Amalfi coast from Rome..."

Producing a recommendation for the above requires the following steps:

Query analysis and constraint setting: Travel itinerary must include Pompeii. Paths between Rome and Amalfi will need to be produced. The query assumes returning back to Rome.

Query formulation in Cypher: This essentially involves formulating a query for finding all paths from Rome to Amalfi (that include Pompeii) and back, that use the highest recommended travel modes. The code snipper below shows the relevant query for finding all paths using Neo4J Cypher query language.

Cypher query: MATCH p=(a)-[*]->(b) WHERE (a.name = 'Rome') AND (b.name='Amalfi')RETURN DISTINCT nodes(p);

The above query returned 306 unique plans in the current version of the KB. Some of the itineraries are shown in figure 4. Heuristics can be used to prune the number of results by retaining paths that do not include too many revisits to the same locations and can fit within the time constraints set by the user (2 day).

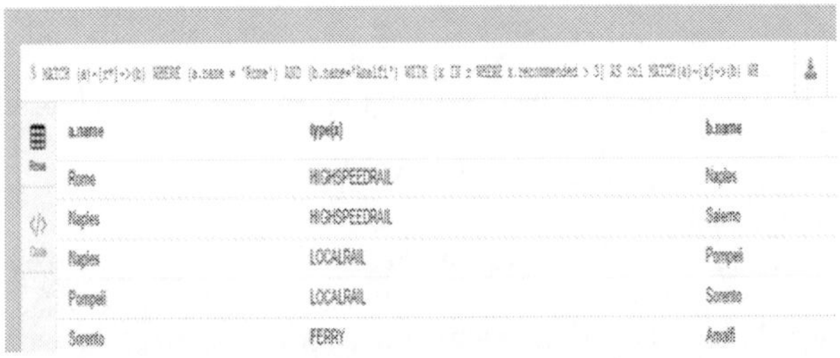

a.name	type(x)	b.name
Rome	HIGHSPEEDRAIL	Naples
Naples	HIGHSPEEDRAIL	Salerno
Naples	LOCALRAIL	Pompei
Pompei	LOCALRAIL	Sorento
Sorento	FERRY	Amalfi

Figure. 3 Recommended travel modes between locations

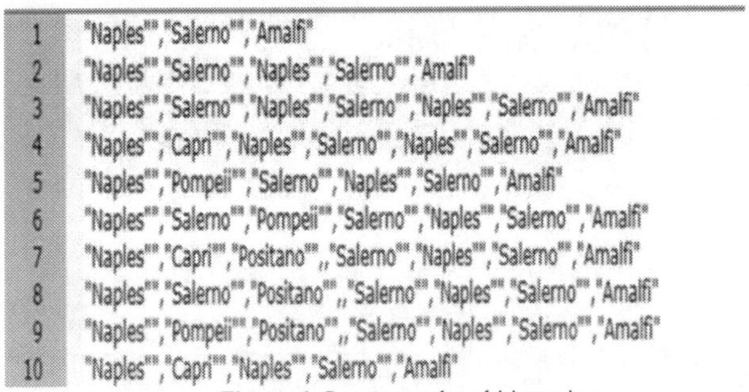

1	"Naples"","Salerno"","Amalfi"
2	"Naples"","Salerno"","Naples"","Salerno"","Amalfi"
3	"Naples"","Salerno"","Naples"","Salerno"","Naples"","Salerno"","Amalfi"
4	"Naples"","Capri"","Naples"","Salerno"","Naples"","Salerno"","Amalfi"
5	"Naples"","Pompeii"","Salerno"","Naples"","Salerno"","Amalfi"
6	"Naples"","Salerno"","Pompeii"","Salerno"","Naples"","Salerno"","Amalfi"
7	"Naples"","Capri"","Positano",,"Salerno"","Naples"","Salerno"","Amalfi"
8	"Naples"","Salerno"","Positano",,"Salerno"","Naples"","Salerno"","Amalfi"
9	"Naples"","Pompeii"","Positano",,"Salerno"","Naples"","Salerno"","Amalfi"
10	"Naples"","Capri"","Naples"","Salerno"","Amalfi"

Figure. 4. System produced itineraries

The critiquing algorithm can be formulated as follows. Given a user proposed route l1-m1->l2-m2>... compare the mode of each route leg with that which is highest recommended in the KB. Calculate an overall 'recommendability score' for the itinerary, for both cases, i.e. the one proposed by the user and the ones recommended by the system, by using algorithm and the formulas discussed in section III. The difference between critiquing and recommendation is that in critiquing the user itinerary is more detailed. The system does not propose a new itinerary but compares against the highest recommended one. This process can be iterative, i.e., the user can adopt her original plan, based on the received critique.

V. SYSTEM EVALUATION

Shani et al. [17] propose three different approaches for recommender system validation: offline validation, user studies and online experiments. In our approach because of resource constraints we opted for an offline experiment which however used real data both in terms in case of requests for recommendations and of actual recommendations taken from an online travel forum. While this approach is not as insightful as an online experiment, it can provide evidence of the performance of the recommender compared to actual users, without incurring the cost of user studies or online experiments. The objective of the evaluation was to test whether the recommender is exhibiting a behaviour that is close to that of the human recommender. Thus we had to find user recommendations for the same itinerary and compare the system produced recommendations to that of the average or typical user. We first however had to find a way to measure the similarity of recommendations. In our approach we opted for the overlap coefficient [18] (or, Szymkiewicz-Simpson coefficient) which is a similarity metric that measures the overlap between two sets, and is defined as the size of the intersection divided by the smaller of the size of the two sets, as shown in the following formula.

$$overlap(X,Y)=|X \cap Y|/\min(|X|,|Y|)$$

We employ the overlap coefficient to two requests for recommendation cases described below. For each request we elicited user recommendations from the TripAdvisor Italy forum. These recommendations were not taken into account when populating the travel knowledge graph, hence they do not constitute 'training data' for the recommender. We construct the system recommendation using the approach described in Section IV and we compare it to each user recommendation to calculate an average overlap score between the system and the user recommendations. We also calculate the mean, variance and standard deviation of user recommendations overlappings to determine how much user recommendations overlap with each other.

TABLE I. CALCULATION OF OVERLAPPINGS FOR ROME TO POZITANO RECOMMENDATIONS.

Rec #id	User recom. avg. overlap	User recommendation	User-system Overlap score
1	0.5	Rome -high speed train -> Salerno- ferry-> Positano	1
2	0.5	Rome -high speed train -> Salerno- ferry-> Positano	1
3	0	Rome -high speed train -> Naples -car -> Sorrento -car-> Pompeii -car -> Sorrento -ferry -> Capri -ferry -> Sorrento -car -> Positano	0.43
4	0.375	Rome -high speed train-> Salerno -bus -> Amalfi -bus -> Positano	0.33
5	0.375	Rome -high speed train -> Salerno -taxi -> Positano	0.5
		Mean overlap of user recommendations: 0.35 Variance 0.0421 SD: 0.205	Average system-user overlap score:0.65

Table I shows what users actually recommended as itineraries for the Rome to Positano trip, how these recommendations overlap with each other on average and with the system recommendation. For this query, the system created the recommendation (Rome -high speed train -> Salerno- ferry->Positano) thus totally agreeing with the first two recommendations of Table I. Assuming a normal distribution in the overlapping values of user recommendations, we can observe that the system recommendation overlappings falls within two standard deviations of the mean, i.e., it has a typical overlapping (or similarity) to the user recommendations.

VI. CONCLUSIONS

Our approach integrates the formal/GIS view of travel planning (e.g., by following the shortest or the fastest route) with heuristic knowledge such as fellow user itinerary heuristics and recommendations that serve as shortcuts and help to reduce the cost of information search for the traveller. The attributes attached to nodes and edges can be extended with different features, reflecting other important travel considerations such as cost daily and seasonal variations. For example, roads that are very busy during the Summer period and thus get low recommendation might be more quiet in other seasons. Also, some modes along routes might be seasonal, for example some ferry lines might operate only in the Summer period.

The system could be extended with further reasoning capabilities, for example case based reasoning. Case based reasoning (CBR) has been already utilised in several recommender systems [19]. Previous travel experiences can be stored as cases in the knowledge base and new recommendations would entail recalling similar experiences from the knowledge base and reuse them partially, completely or modified.

Profiling could also be introduced to support more personalised recommendations. It has been argued however, [4] that in the case of travel this is very hard because each traveller's decision making profile is unique.

User proposed itineraries could be compared to existing recommended itineraries stored in the graph knowledge base. There is a lot of mathematical background in measuring graph similarity, for example by using distance measures like the Hamming distance, the simple matching coefficient, the Euclidean distance, and other metrics, and these could be utilised. However, such measures consider only little domain knowledge during the similarity assessment, while more sophisticated methods consider the different importance of individual attributes [20]. For example, two trips might visit the same locations [21] in the same order but the time spent on each location and the activities of the traveller could be very different.

ACKNOWLEDGMENT

Work described in this paper was partially funded by Horizon 2020 Research and Innovation Programme under Project 'Eutravel' (grant agreement No 636148).

REFERENCES

[1] J. Schafer, J. Konstan, and J. Riedl, "Recommender systems in e-commerce," In EC '99 Proceedings of the 1st ACM conference on Electronic Commerce, 1999.

[2] L. Castillo, et al., "Samap: An user-oriented adaptive system for planning tourist visits," Expert Systems with Applications, 34, 1318–1332, (2008).

[3] L. Ceccaroni, V., Codina, M., Palau, and M. Pous, "PaTac: Urban, ubiquitous, personalized services for citizens and tourists," In Third international conference on the digital society (ICDS 2009), February 1–7, 2009.

[4] F. Ricci, "Travel recommender systems," IEEE Intelligent Systems, 17(11/12), 55–5, 2002.

[5] P. Vansteemwegen, and W., Souffriau, "Trip planning functionalities:State-of-the-art and future," Information Technology and Tourism 12(4), 305-315, 2011.

[6] Y., Kurata, "CT-planner2: More flexible and interactive assistance for day tour planning. ENTER 2011. In Information and communication technologies in tourism (pp. 25–37), Innsbruck, Austria, 2011.

[7] Y., Kurata, and T., Hara. "CT-planner4: Toward a more user-friendly interactiveday-tour planner," In Information and communication technologies in tourism 2014 (pp. 73–86). Springer International Publishing, 2013.

[8] W., Souffriau and P., Vansteenwegen, "Tourist Trip Planning Functionalities: State–of–the–Art and Future Current Trends in Web Engineering," vol. 6385 of the series Lecture Notes in Computer Science pp 474-485, Springer 2010.

[9] P., Vansteenwegen, W., Souffriau, B., Vanden and D., Van Oudheusden, "The city trip planner: An expert system for tourists," Expert Systems with Applications, 38(6), 6540–6546, 2010.

[10] I., Mínguez, D., Berrueta, and L., Polo, "CRUZAR: An application of semantic matchmaking to e-tourism. In Y. Kalfoglou (Ed.), Cases on semantic interoperability for information systems integration: Practices and applications" (pp. 255–271). Hershey, PA: Information Science Reference, 2010.

[11] A., Luberg, T., Tammet, and P., Järv, "Smart city: A rule-based tourist recommendation system," In R. Law, M. Fuchs, & F. Ricci (Eds.), Information and communication technologies in tourism 2011. ENTER 11, January 26th–28th 2011, Innsbruck, Austria. Springer-Verlag, 2011.

[12] A., Montejo-Ráez, J., Perea-Ortega, M., García-Cumbreras, and F., Martínez-Santiago, "Otium: A web based planner for tourism and leisure," Expert Systems with Applications, 38, 10085–10093, 2011.

[13] L., Sebastià, I., Garcia, E., Onaindia, and C., Guzman, "E-tourism: A tourist recommendation and planning application," International Journal on Artificial Intelligence Tools, 18(5), 717–738, 2009.

[14] A., Mohd , J., Hosking, and J., Grundy, "A taxonomy of computer-supported critics," Information Technology (ITSim), International Symposium in, Volume: 3, 2010.

[15] O., Yeonjoo, M., Gross, and E., Yi-Luen Do, "Computer-aided critiquing systems. Lessons learned and new research directions. computer-aided critiquing systems," Lessons learned and new research directions, 2008.

[16] I., Robinson, J., Webber and E., Eifrem, "Graph Databases. New Opportunities for Connected Data," Second Edition O Reilly, 2015.

[17] G., Shani and Gunawardana, A. "Evaluating Recommendation Systems," Microsoft Technical Report 2009.

[18] D., Szymkiewicz and G., Simpson in http://paleo.cortland.edu/class/stats/documents/11_Similarity, last viewed December 2016.

[19] F., Ricci, D., Fesenmaier, N., Mirzadeh, H., Rumetshofer, E., Schaumlechner, A., Venturini, K., Wöber and A.H., Zins "Dietorecs: a case-based Travel advisory system. In Destination Recommendation Systems: Behavioural Foundations and Applications," (eds D.R. Fesenmaier, H. Werthner and K.W. Wöber) ©CAB International, 2006.

[20] A., Stahl, "Learning of knowledge-intensive similarity measures in case-based reasoning," PhD Thesis University of Kaiserslautern, 2004.

[21] A., Umanets, A., Ferreira, and N., Leite, "GuideMe – A Tourist Guide with a Recommender System and Social Interaction," Procedia Technology, Volume 17, pp. 407-414, 2014.

BayesNet and Artificial Neural Network for Nowcasting Rare Fog Events

Two different Models for 1-Hour Fog Prediction at Linate Airport

Gaetano Zazzaro, Gianpaolo Romano, Paola Mercogliano
Italian Aerospace Research Centre, CIRA
Capua (CE), Italy
email: {g.zazzaro, g.romano, p.mercogliano}@cira.it

Paola Mercogliano
Euro-Mediterranean Center on Climate Change, CMCC
Capua (CE), Italy
email: paola.mercogliano@cmcc.it

***Abstract*— Fog represent high impact atmospherical phenomena especially for aviation. In particular, in 2001 the Linate Airport in Milan was interested by a disaster, the deadliest air disaster to ever occur in Italian aviation history, due to un-forecasted thick fog. For this reason, improvement of fog monitoring and forecast tool is a challenge topic for the aviation community. Moreover, forecasting fog is an important issue for air traffic safety because adverse visibility conditions represent one of the major causes of traffic delay and of the economic loss associated with such phenomena. In such context, the present work illustrates a Data Mining application for the fog forecast on a short time range (1 hour) on Linate airport. Indeed two predictive models have been trained using an historical dataset of 18 years of fog observations and other relevant meteorological parameters collected in the Synop message by applying BayesNet and Neural Network algorithms. The performances evaluation shows the complete model for fog events forecasting presents 90% of instances correctly predicted. The work has been carried on according to the standard process (CRISP-DM) for Knowledge Discovery in Database Process.**

Keywords-Data Mining; Forecast Fog; Bayesian Networks, Artificial Neural Networks; Knowledge Discovery in Meteorological Database Process; Weka; CRISP-DM.

I. INTRODUCTION

Forecasting of adverse weather condition, having high impact on the different phases of the flight (e.g., taxing, landing, take off), is an important issue for air traffic safety. For this reason, many efforts are spent by aviation research for improving the capability to forecast them on different time range. For example, adverse visibility conditions severely affect air traffic operations especially during the landing and take-off phases and thereby reduce the capacity of an airport. This leads to the built-up of a wave of delayed flights in case demand exceeds the reduced capacity, which is especially critical at major hubs, such as, for Italy, Linate during peak times. Since these hubs are central nodes in the air traffic network, the effect also spreads causing the event to be of much more than just local importance. Indeed the occurrence of low ceilings and/or poor visibility conditions restricting the flow of air traffic into major airport terminals is one of the major causes of traffic delay and of the economic loss associated with such phenomena [1]. For these reasons, a fast forecasting is crucial to manage the occurrence of these events and to mitigate their impact over the whole airport system. Consequently, it is important to deeply understand the process leading to the formation of fog and justifies the efforts made by meteorologists to forecast such events.

In this paper, we introduce a method for fog nowcasting (short-range forecasting of 1 hour) on Linate Airport in Milan using Data Mining techniques. Indeed Data Mining (DM) [2] – also called "Knowledge Discovery in Databases" – refers to the process of extraction or "mining" useful knowledge from large amounts of data. DM draws upon ideas, such as sampling, estimation, and hypothesis testing from statistics and search algorithms, modeling techniques, and learning theories from artificial intelligence, pattern recognition, and machine learning.

DM can represent a useful analysis method for this complex meteorological phenomenon because it has the ability to work with many data described by a high number of variables.

In order to obtain DM models for fog prediction, we used an historical dataset consisting of 164.352 meteorological SYNOP observations collected at Milan's Linate airport station from January 1996 until September 2014.

Knowledge Discovery in Database Process, that we carried on in order to predict fog events, is been conducted according to the standard process conceived from the Cross-Industry Standard Process for DM (CRISP-DM) [3]. Every step of the process has been supported by the validation of domain experts. In this work we used the Weka tool (Version 3.6.14) (Waikato Environment for Knowledge Analysis) [4] to carry on DM analysis. In particular, we used the Weka Explorer interface to mine data by applying Bayesian and Artificial Neural Networks algorithms.

A. Structure of the paper

The paper is organized by describing all the CRISP phases one by one. In Section II, the Business Understanding is carried on in order to understand the fog phenomenon and its development, to explore the state of the art from meteorological and DM points of view, and to fix DM goals. In Section III, we illustrate the data collection, the data sources, the variables and statistics of the attributes. In Section IV, we explain all the activities of the Data Preparation phase aimed at constructing the final datasets to be mined; in particular, the preprocessing phase and the hold-out method. In Section V, we provide details about the Modeling phase: from the identification of target functions to model testing. Finally, in Section VI, we present the Evaluation phase and, in Section VII, we show our considerations.

II. BUSINESS UNDERSTANDING

This first step of the CRISP-DM process includes fixing of the business objectives, Data Mining goals and assess situation.

A. Fog Formation and State of the Art of Fog Nowcasting

Fog is basically a cloud of small water droplets near ground level and sufficiently dense to reduce horizontal visibility to less than 1 km (3281 feet). The word fog also may refer to clouds of smoke particles, ice particles, or mixtures of these components. Under similar conditions, but with visibility greater than 1000 m, the phenomenon is termed a mist or haze, depending on whether the obscurity is caused by water drops or solid particles. The formation of fog is due to the condensation of water vapor on condensation nuclei (non-gaseous solid particles) to form water droplets, near the ground. Fog usually develops when relative humidity is near 100% and when the air temperature and dew point temperature are close to each other or less than 4°F (2.5°C). When air reaches 100% of relative humidity, its dew point is said to be saturated and can thus hold no more water vapor. As a result, the water vapor condenses to form water droplets and fog. The formation of fog is a complex process involving highly non-linear interactions between surface and sub-surface processes, atmospheric radiation, turbulence and flows. Such interactions are not adequately described by the current operational Numerical Weather Prediction (NWP) [5], because the vertical and horizontal resolutions are larger than the corresponding fog scales [6] that are of the order of 1 km on the horizontal scale and up to few ten meters on the vertical scale. For these reasons these models [1] [7] [8] are unable to treat complex three-dimensional flows due to their poor representation of horizontal heterogeneities [6].

In order to overcome such limitations, dedicated NWP models have been implemented [9] in order to predict the formation of fog in regions of complex terrain and reach horizontal grid resolution of 1km or better. The disadvantage of such models lies on the computational costs required to run them [5]. For this reason, they can be applied only on small domains and on high speed computer [5].

Finally, the statistical methods [10] can overcome the above-mentioned problems but they require long time series of homogeneous data and they can be used only for specific locations for which the fog events can be correlated to the local conditions. In fact fog events can be triggered by different physical causes and their characteristic strongly depends on the specific geographical location [11].

Traditional data analysis techniques (including statistical and physical driven techniques) have been often faced with practical difficulties in meeting the challenges posed by new datasets including meteorological datasets (with a high number of records, variables, sources, etc.). DM techniques can represent useful analysis methods because they are able to investigate different meteorological variables coming from numerous datasets. DM techniques provide a high level of prediction in terms of consistency and frequency of correct predictions.

Prediction is the most used DM task in meteorology domain. DM has been applied successfully to predict different weather elements like wind speed [12] [13], rainfall [14] [15], cloud [16] and temperature [17] [18].

DM description task is carried on in [19] and [20] by using Decision Trees and Bayesian Networks in order to create some fog local indices, based on the post-processing of meteorological variables. The same methods were used in [21] for creation of some basic neural network structures that were further adapted to local prediction models. This approach was implemented and tested in various conditions of major Australian airports. The fog formation and its important parameters were identified based on collected historical dataset from the International Airport of Rio de Janeiro [22]. In [23] the authors describe three short-range fog-forecasting models by applying Bayesian Networks in order to predict fog events between 0-3 hours on Paris Charles De Gaulle airport.

The availability of a long time series data set (SYNOP data) together with the necessity to describe such phenomenon in a specific site (Milan's Linate airport), make the DM approach one of the best solutions in describing and short range forecasting fog phenomena.

B. Business Objectives and Data Mining Goals

The Business objective is to develop an algorithm, which is able to describe, and nowcast fog phenomenon over Milan's Linate Airport, using DM techniques and Synop data. In particular, the objective is to forecast a fog event on the time range of 1 hour, associating a prediction probability. Classification models will be trained in order to forecast fog events. Of course, probabilities can be transferred into crisp event forecasts, but since developments in air traffic management systems point towards more and more automation and decision support, direct use of probabilities will be favored because it enables detailed cost benefit analysis for triggering decisions

III. DATA UNDERSTANDING

This step of the CRISP-DM includes the initial data collection, data description, data exploration, and the verification of data quality.

A. Data Collection

In order to build a predictive model using DM techniques for fog forecast, a historical dataset made up of fog observations and relevant meteorological parameters needs to be built. Data have been collected from ECMWF MARS Archive [24] containing the surface Synoptic observations (SYNOP) provided by Linate meteorological station.

TABLE I. LIST OF METEOROLOGICAL VARIABLES

#	Name	Description	Units
1	Date	Date of the observation	Date
2	Pressure	Force per unit area exerted against a surface by the weight of the air above that surface	Pa

3	three hour pressure change	Change of the pressure with respect to three hours ago	Pa
4	char pressure tendency	Coded values indicating how the pressure has changed during one hour	-
5	wind direction	Wind direction at 10 m	Deg
6	wind speed	Wind speed at 10 m	kn
7	Visibility	It represents the greatest distance at which a black object of suitable dimensions can be seen. Visibility values below 1 km indicate the presence of fog	m
8	present weather	Coded values describing the weather phenomena present at the time of the observation. Values between 40-49 indicate the presence of fog	-
9	past weather1	Coded values describing weather phenomena occurring during the preceding hour	-
10	past weather2	Coded values describing weather phenomena occurring during the two preceding hours	-
11	cloud cover	Values between 0 and 8 indicating the fraction of the celestial dome covered by all clouds visible. It is estimated in eighths (okta) of sky covered by clouds. Clear sky is indicated with 0 okta, overcast with 8	okta
12	height of base of cloud	Height of bases of clouds above ground level	m
13	cloud type	Coded values reporting the type of cloud and the state of sky	-
14	Dewpoint	Temperature at which moist air saturated with respect to water at a given pressure has a saturation mixing ratio equal to the given mixing ratio (ratio between the mass of water vapour and the mass of dry air)	°C
15	Drybulb	Temperature of the air measured with a thermometer shielded to radiation and humidity	°C

SYNOP observations are recorded every hour. A list of the meteorological variables used for DM and selected from the SYNOP message is reported in the TABLE I.

B. Fog Event Description

Each fog event can be defined as a sequence of SYNOP records with a visibility attribute value less or equal than 1000 meters. Each record describes the weather conditions observed. Fog events are characterized by an initial and final SYNOP message: the first recording is the head of the event; the last one is the end of fog event; one or more persistences of YES are between the head and ending in the single fog event.

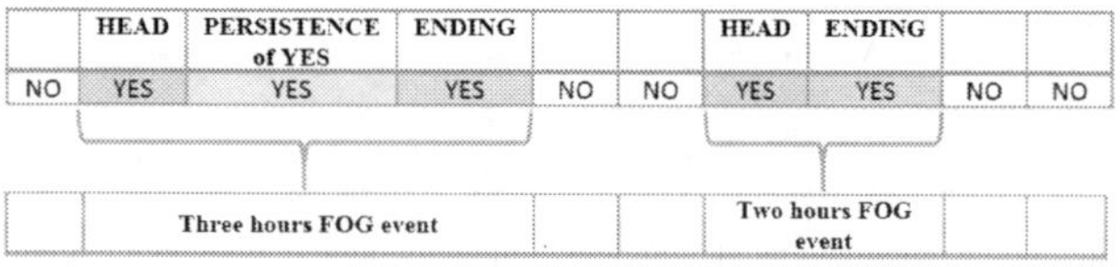

Figure 1. Sequences of recordings.

In Figure 1, two examples of fog events are reported: the first event lasts three hours and the second one lasts two hours (the second event has no persistence of YES because it lasts only two hours and the first hour is the head while the last one is the end).

C. Data Exploration

The collected dataset contains 164.352 instances belonging to the period from 1st January 1996 until 30th September 2014. Using the WEKA's explorer interface [4] [28] we are easily able to view histograms for each attribute in TABLE I and plot matrices of different attribute combinations. WEKA also displays basic statistics for each numeric attribute. In the following, some histograms are reported in order to investigate data and variables. For example, Figure 2 reports the number of instances of Dewpoint variable in the dataset considered. Dewpoint histogram presents a distribution similar to a Gaussian one.

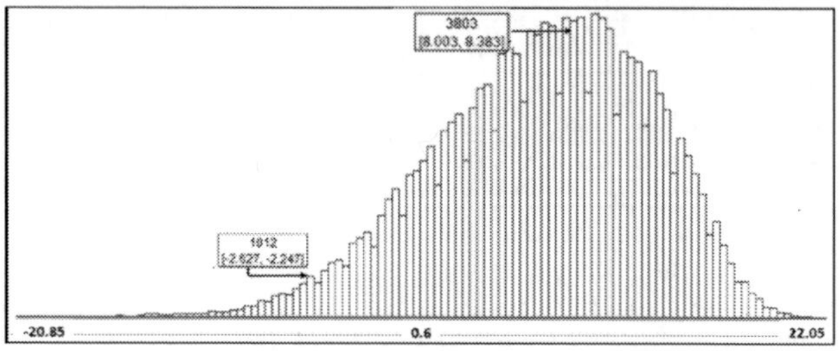

Figure 2. Histogram of instances by Dewpint attribute.

In TABLE II some basic statistics are reported.

TABLE II. STATISTICS OF DEWPOINT ATTRIBUTE

Statistic	Value
Minimum	-20.85
Maximum	22.05
Mean	8.001
StdDev	5.636
Missing	10741 (6.53%)
Distinct	375

The dewpoint temperature has a very low minimum value. This indicates that there are some outliers in the data set, which are removed in the next CRISP step.

IV. DATA PREPARATION

In order to obtain the final dataset that can be used in the modeling phase, data have been preprocessed to report them in a format usable by DM algorithms. In the original dataset there are 10676 missing records corresponding to the same number of missing hours. For these recordings, we have only date and time variables. The other attributes are all null. These missing records are removed from the original dataset, obtaining a new dataset with 153.676 instances.

A. Variables Transformation and Target Class Creation

The meteorological parameters coded according to the World Meteorological Organization (WMO) code tables [25] have been converted from numeric to nominal type in order to report them in a format usable by DM algorithm. Such conversion is also required for a clearer reading of data and results. After the conversion, the target attribute has been identified according to the domain expert indications. Indeed the presence of fog is detected if visibility is less than or equal to 1 km [26].

The histogram of target class of Figure 3 shows how fog is a quite rare meteorological event on Linate airport: fog occurs about once every 53 events. Target class is unbalanced.

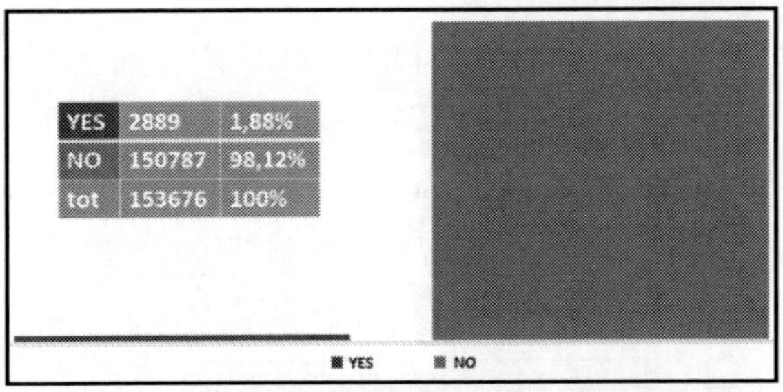

Figure 3. Histogram of instances by class target attribute

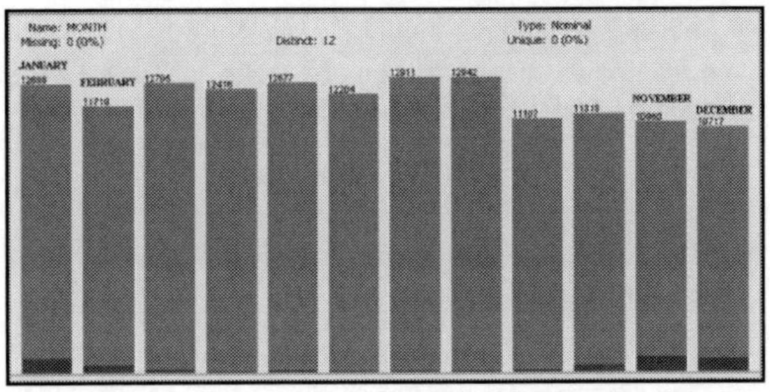

Figure 4. Histogram of instances by Month attribute, from Jan. to Dec.

In order to visualize the distribution of FOG according to the variation of variables, the graph of Figure 4 shows that fog events, which are represented in blue color, occur mostly from October to March. In addition, from the histogram of instances by Hour attribute (not reported), fog events occur in the early hours of the morning and in the late evening.

B. Model Design

The one-hour prediction model has to be able to recognize both the beginning and the end of a fog event. Therefore, two models have been trained, *A-model* and *B-model*:

1. *A-model* is used in order to predict the persistence of NO and the discontinuities from NO to YES (heads of new fog events).
2. *B-model* is used in order to predict the persistence of YES and the discontinuities from YES to NO (endings of fog events that are heads of NO-fog events), instead.

As a consequence, *A-model* is used when the occurring visibility (visibility at time t0) is greater than 1000 m and *B-model* in the other cases. A summary of this criterion is reported in TABLE III.

TABLE III. RULE FOR MODELS APPLICATION

if visibility at time t0 > 1000m then *A-model* else *B-model*

C. Hold-Out Method and Forecast Sets Preparation

For DM goal, we adopted the working strategy named hold-out method [27]. In this method, the original data with labeled examples is partitioned into two disjoint sets, called the training and test sets, respectively. A classification model is induced from the training set and its performances are evaluated on the test set. The accuracy of the classifier can be estimated based on the accuracy of the induced model on the test set.

As test set we choose the records belonging to the last 13 months of meteorological observations, from 1st September 2013 until 30th September 2014. This test set is called 1YEAR, it has 9314 full weather observations and it has roughly the same target class distribution of whole dataset.

The DM models should be able to predict fog after one hour from the recording of the last available SYNOP data. So, in order to easily forecast fog events, a new dataset is released starting from the dataset available after Data Preparation step. Shifting upwards of a position the time series of FOG variable, we obtain a new target attribute (FOG+1) describing the condition of fog at time $t_{0+1hour}=t_1$, while the meteorological attributes remains at time t_0. Such elaboration allows getting a new training set, called FOG+1, and a new test set, called 1YEAR+1.

In order to obtain two predicting models (*A-model* and *B-model*), each one of two datasets (FOG+1 and 1YEAR+1) has been splitted in two subsets.

*A*_FOG+1, *B*_FOG+1 aim to train *A-model* and *B-model*, respectively, *A*_1YEAR+1 is useful to evaluate the performances of *A-model*, while *B*_1YEAR+1 is useful to evaluate the performances of *B-model*.

The next schema summarizes all of the steps of the Data Preparation phase.

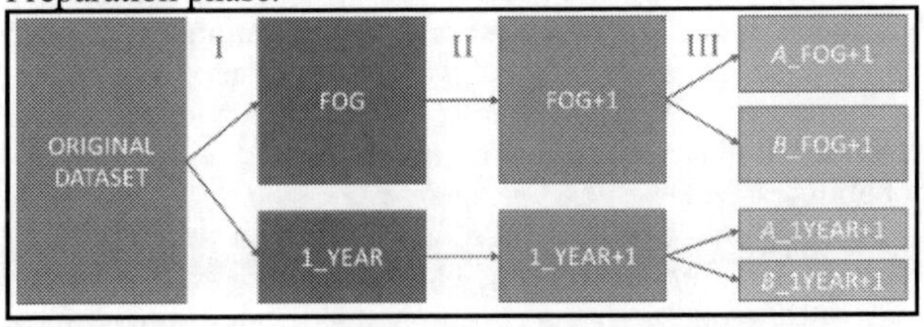

Figure 5. Forecast Sets Preparation Schema

In particular, after the step I, detailed in Figure 5, the original dataset has been cleaned and splitted in two subsets; after the step II the label class of the two datasets has been upward shifted for one hour. Finally, in order to obtain the training and the test sets for *A-model* we have selected FOG="NO", and to obtain the training and test sets for *B-model* we have selected FOG="YES". Therefore, we have applied the rules of TABLE IV and TABLE V:

TABLE IV. *RULE FOR A_FOG+1 AND A_1YEAR+1 SETS*

FOG	FOG+1	
NO	NO	← Persistence of NO
NO	YES	← Head of fog event

TABLE V. *RULE FOR B_FOG+1 AND B_1YEAR+1 SETS*

FOG	FOG+1	
YES	YES	← Persistence of YES
YES	NO	← Ending of fog event

In addition, in order to overcome the class imbalance problem (Figure 3), the class labels of training sets have been under sampled, obtaining the same numbers of records with FOG+1="NO" and FOG+1="YES". However, the two test sets retain the original class target distributions.

Finally, the Data Preparation produces the four datasets presented in TABLE VI, including their sizes.

TABLE VI. DATASETS ROLES AND DIMENSIONS

	A-model	*B-model*
Training	*A*_FOG+1 1380	*B*_FOG+1 1392
Test	*A*_1YEAR+1 9046 records	*B*_1YEAR+1 135 records

V. MODELING

After the Data Preparation follows the Modeling phase, in which the two forecast models are trained and tested.

DM models are simple predictors for time series, where the prediction of outputs for time t_1 is based on the sequence of historical data observed at time t_0.

All obtained prediction models of fog events have been compared and the achieved results have been evaluated by means of adequate performance metrics able to highlight the classifying ability with respect to the fog events and the no-fog events separately (e.g., confusion matrix, AUC). The testing of the two 1-hour classification models show good performances, as in next Sections reported.

Starting from the two new datasets *A*_FOG+1 and *B*_FOG+1, we are able to train forecast models by using DM techniques. Indeed a forecast model is a function that takes into account the meteorological variables measured at time t_0 and computes a binary variable FOG+1 that indicates the presence or absence of fog at time t_1 and the respective probabilities.

In the next Sections, the best obtained models are described but, for the sake of clarity, in our project many predictive models have been trained and only the performances of a Bayesian Net and an Artificial Neural Network are highly satisfactory for one-hour fog predictions on Linate airport database.

A. The A-model

The *A-model* is a Bayesian Network classifier. It has been trained on the *A*_FOG+1 dataset (obtained from FOG+1 set using the instances tagged by FOG="NO"). For the sake of clarity, the training set *A*_FOG+1 is obtained by balancing the target class FOG+1, using the WEKA filter SpreadSubsample that under samples the dataset in order to obtain the same number of FOG+1="YES" and FOG+1="NO" instances. This balancing technique is used in order to overcome the class imbalance problem.

In this way, A-set presents 690 records tagged by FOG+1="NO" and 690 records tagged by FOG+1="YES". The *A-model* is trained by using BayesNet WEKA algorithm, fixing P=3 and A=0.25 by applying cross-validation method with k = folds = 10. *A-model* performs on 10-fold cross-validation and it shows the performances included in TABLE VII, TABLE VII, and TABLE IX:

TABLE VII. *A-MODEL* EVALUATION

Total Number of Instances	1380	
Correctly Classified Instances	1214	(87.971 %)
Incorrectly Classified Instances	166	(12.029 %)

TABLE VIII. *A-MODEL* DETAILED ACCURACY BY CLASS

=== Detailed Accuracy By Class ===				
Class	TP Rate	FP Rate	Precision	ROC Area
YES	0.884	0.125	0.876	0.932
NO	0.875	0.116	0.883	0.932

TABLE IX. CONFUSION MATRIX OF *A-MODEL*

Forecast		← Classified as	
YES	NO		
610	80	**YES**	**Observed**
86	604	**NO**	

A-model shows the performances on *A*_1YEAR+1 Test Set included in TABLE X, TABLE XI, and TABLE XII.

TABLE X. *A-MODEL* EVALUATION ON *A_1YEAR+1*

Total Number of Instances	9046	
Correctly Classified Instances	8480	(93.7431 %)
Incorrectly Classified Instances	566	(6.2569 %)

TABLE XI. *A-MODEL* DETAILED ACCURACY BY CLASS

Class	TP Rate	FP Rate	Precision	ROC Area
YES	0.732	0.062	0.051	0.934
NO	0.938	0.268	0.999	0.934

TABLE XII. CONFUSION MATRIX OF *A-MODEL* ON *A_1YEAR+1*

Forecast		← Classified as	
YES	NO		
30	11	**YES**	**Observed**
555	8450	**NO**	

In this test, we analyze the capability of the *A-model* to predict the persistence of the condition FOG="NO" or the presence of the head of the fog events (FOG="YES").

B. The B-model

The B-classifier is an Artificial Neural Network (ANN) trained on the balanced *B*_FOG+1 dataset (obtained from FOG+1 set using the instances tagged by FOG="YES" and balancing the target class FOG+1 by using the WEKA filter SpreadSubsample). In this way, *B*_FOG+1 presents 696 records tagged by FOG+1="NO" and 696 records tagged by FOG+1="YES".

The *B-model* is trained by using the MultilayerPerceptron algorithm of WEKA, with 10 hidden layers (H=10) and N=1000 that is the number of epochs to train through. It performs on 10-fold cross-validation and it shows the performances included in TABLE XIII, TABLE XIV, and in TABLE XV:

TABLE XIII. THE B-MODEL EVALUATION

Total Number of Instances	1392	
Correctly Classified Instances	1207	(86.71 %)
Incorrectly Classified Instances	185	(13.29%)

TABLE XIV. THE *B-MODEL* DETAILED ACCURACY BY CLASS

Class	TP Rate	FP Rate	Precision	ROC Area
YES	0.888	0.154	0.852	0.891
NO	0.846	0.112	0.883	0.891

TABLE XV. CONFUSION MATRIX OF THE *B-MODEL*

Forecast		← Classified as	
YES	**NO**		
618	78	**YES**	**Observed**
107	589	**NO**	

B-model shows the performances on B_1YEAR+1 of TABLE XVI, TABLE XVII, and TABLE XVIII.

TABLE XVI. THE *B-MODEL* EVALUATION ON *B_1YEAR+1*

Total Number of Instances	135	
Correctly Classified Instances	109	(80.74%)
Incorrectly Classified Instances	26	(19.259%)

TABLE XVII. THE *B-MODEL* DETAILED ACCURACY BY CLASS

Class	TP Rate	FP Rate	Precision	ROC Area
YES	0.828	0.25	0.881	0.814
NO	0.75	0.172	0.614	0.814

TABLE XVIII. CONFUSION MATRIX OF THE *B-MODEL* ON *B_1YEAR+1*

Forecast		← Classified as	
YES	**NO**		
82	17	**YES**	**Observed**
9	27	**NO**	

In this test we analyze the capability of the *B-model*, when the instances FOG="YES" is present, to predict in the following hour the persistence of the condition FOG="YES" or the presence of the end of the fog events.

VI. MODEL EVALUATION

Evaluation of the performance of a classification model is based on the number of test records correctly and incorrectly predicted by the model. Good results correspond to large numbers along the main diagonal of the confusion matrix and small, ideally zero, off-diagonal elements.

The confusion matrix of the *A-model* on A_1YEAR+1 Test Set shows 555 records incorrectly classified as "YES" (TABLE XII), corresponding to 555 false positives instances (555 recordings without fog incorrectly predicted as heads of fog events). The TABLE XIX shows the distribution of such False Positives by Month attribute. 74% of False Positive instances occur in [September, January].

TABLE XIX. DISTRIBUTION OF FALSE POSITIVES BY MONTH

# of records	Month	Total number of hours in the month
100	September 2013	720
49	October 2013	744
102	November 2013	720
99	December 2013	744
62	January 2014	744
12	February 2014	672
73	March 2014	744
18	April 2014	720
15	May 2014	744
5	June 2014	720
15	July 2014	744
5	August 2014	744
Tot=555		

The Figure 6 shows the histogram of False Positives by Hour attribute. About 80% of False Positive instances occur in [00:00, 09:00] (range of Hour attribute).

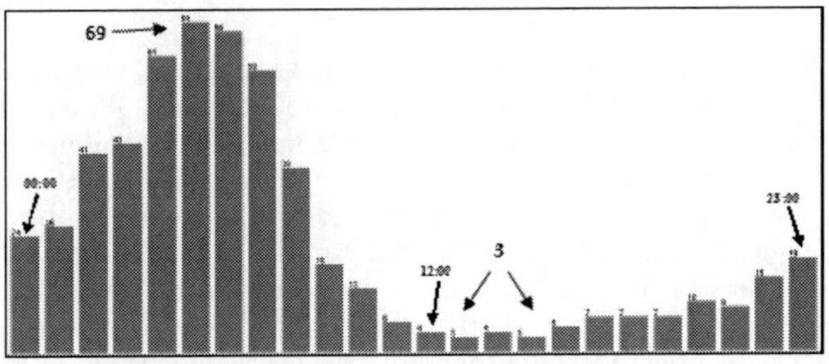

Figure 6. Histogram of false positives by Hour attribute

In addition, about 75% of False Positive instances occur when visibility ranges from [1200m, 4500m] (range of Visibility attribute). About 70% of False Positives occur when the 'Height of base of cloud' attribute is in [30m, 1000m] range and about 81% in [0kn, 7.77kn] range of 'Wind speed'. Therefore, False Positives have higher occurrence when these favorable meteorological conditions for fog presence are recorded, as low wind speed intensity and low cloud. The TABLE XX shows the distribution of False Positives by 'Present Weather' attribute.

TABLE XX. FALSE POSITIVES DISTRIBUTION BY 'PRESENT WEATHER'

# of records	Present weather
56	Drizzle
17	Rain
9	Fog
305	Mist
136	No Meteors
25	Fog or Ice Fog
7	Patches
Tot=555	

The histograms and the statistic distributions prove that most of predicted false positives occur when the observed visibility conditions are below 5 km due to the presence of meteorological conditions that can reduce visibility (mist, drizzle, rain or fog). It has been considered that the present model considers only prediction of low visibility due to fog presence, while there are also other physical sources causing the reduction of the visibility. Therefore, even if these events are classified as false positives for fog event presence (because the observed visibility is greater than 1000 m), they correctly classify the events being physically characterized by low visibility conditions.

Furthermore, most of the incorrectly predictions occur during months and hours often interested by fog events (autumn and winter seasons, night and early hours of the day), and during which a reduction of visibility conditions occur.

Finally, the *B-model* performs worse than the *A-model*. However, this evaluation does not worry us considering the significant increase of flight safety.

Anyway, considering the difficulty of the prediction of this atmospherical phenomenon results can be considered very promising for further investigation.

VII. CONCLUSIONS

This paper reports the description of a statistical tool to forecast in a very rapid time the occurrence of low visibility events over the airport area. This method is essentially based on the use of an historical time series of SYNOP data available over Linate airport and on the DM techniques. SYNOP are a meteorological data message available in many airport, therefore the method can potentially be extended easily to different other airports. Two different classifiers have been trained in order to obtain two models that together are able to predict fog events on 1 hour time range. In order to reach this aim, the Data Understanding, Data Preparation, Modeling and Evaluation phases of CRISP-DM have been carried out.

Data Understanding phase included the collection, description and exploration of data used for DM. Data Preparation phase allowed to elaborate data in order to obtain the dataset to be used for Modeling phase. In the Modeling phase, two different forecasting models (*A-model*, *B-model*) have been produced by applying BayesNet and Neural Network algorithms. Preliminary results show that the two models encourage the forecast of fog events on 1-hour time range. *A-model* presents a percentage of correct classified instances of 93.74% and a percentage of true positive rate of about 73.2% corresponding to heads of fog events correctly predicted. Additionally *B-model* presents a percentage of correct classified instances of 80.74% and a percentage of true positive rate of 75% corresponding to ends of fog events correctly predicted. Furthermore, both models have a very high percentage of correct classification of persistences of FOG="NO" and FOG="YES".

In addition, future investigations could quantify the performances for detecting sharp transients, i.e., change of status from no-fog to fog and vice versa.

ACKNOWLEDGMENT

The authors would express their gratitude for funding part of this work in equal parts to the SESAR programme (www.sesarju.eu) funded by the European Union, Eurocontrol and its industrial members and to Selex ES GmbH. This work have contributed to the design of an integrated Ground Weather Monitoring System (GWMS) in SESAR project 15.04.09.c lead by Selex ES. Moreover, the authors would also mention the project TECVOL II founded by the Italian PRORA where the upgrade of the tool has been developed.

REFERENCES

[1] T. Bergot, D. Carrer, J. Noilhan, and P. Bougeault, "Improved Site-Specific Numerical Prediction of Fog and Low Clouds: A Feasibility Study", Weather and Forecasting 20, 627–646, 2005.

[2] P. Tan, M. Steinbach, and V. Kumar, "Introduction to Data Mining", Pearson Addison Wesley, 2005.

[3] P. Chapman et al., "CRISP DM 1.0. Data mining guide", 2000.

[4] M. Hall, E. Frank, G. Holmes, B. Pfahringer, P. Reutemann, and I.H. Witten (2009), "The WEKA Data Mining Software: An Update", SIGKDD Explorations, Volume 11, Issue 1.

[5] R. Capon, Y. Tang, R. Forbes, and P. Clark, "A very high resolution model for local fog forecasting", Cost Action 722 Report, 2008.

[6] T. Bergot et al., "Intercomparison of single-column numerical models for the prediction of radiation fog", Cost Action 722 Report, 2008.

[7] B.W. Golding, "Nimrod: a system for generating automated very short range forecasts", Meteorol. Appl. 5, 1-16, 1998.

[8] I. Gultepe and J. Milbrandt, "Microphysical observations and mesoscale model simulation of a warm fog case during FRAM project", Pure Appl. Geophys. 164, 7/8, this issue, 2007.

[9] R. Capon, "Fog forecasting at very high resolution with the Met Office Unified Model", Met Office Forecasting Research Technical Report 444, JCMM Report 149 (available at http://www.metoffice.gov.uk), 2004.

[10] Pasini, V. Pelino, and S. Potestà, "A neural network model for visibility nowcasting from surface observations: results and sensitivity to physical input variables", J. Geophys. Res.106, 14951–14959, 2001.

[11] W. Jacobs and V. Nietosvaar, Foreword. Cost Action 722 Final Report, 2008.

[12] M.F. Al-Roby and A.M. El-Halees, "Data Mining Techniques for Wind Speed Analysis", Journal of Computer Eng., Vol.2, No.1, 2011.

[13] G. Li and J. Shi, "On comparing three artificial networks for wind speed forecasting", Applied Energy, vol.87, no.7, pp.2313-2320, Jul.2010.

[14] C.T. Dhanya and D.N. Kumar, "Data Mining for Evolving Fuzzy Association Rules for Predicting Monsoon Rainfall of India", Journal of Intelligent Systems, Vol. 18, No. 3, 2009.

[15] S. Dong-Jun and J.P. Breidenbach, "Real-Time correction of Spatially Nonuniform Bias in Radar Rainfall Data Using Rain Gauge Measurements", Hydrometeorology, Vol.3, no.2, pp.93-111, 2002.

[16] L. Hluchy et al, "Prediction of significant meteorological phenomena using advanced data Mining and integration methods", Fuzzy Systems and Knowledge Discovery (FSKD), vol. 6. pp. 2998-3002, 10-12 Aug. 2010.

[17] S.N. Kohail and A.M. El-Halees, "Implementation of Data Mining Techniques for Meteorological Data Analysis", Int. Journal of Information and Communication Technology Res., Vol.1, No3, 2011.

[18] S. Kotsiantis, A. Kostoulas, S. Lykoudis, A. Argiriou, and K. Menagias, "Using Data Mining Techniques for Estimating Minimum, Maximum and Average Daily Temperatures Values", International Journal of Mathematical, Physical and Engineering Sciences, pp. 16-20, 2007.

[19] G. Zazzaro, "An index for local fog forecast by applying data Mining techniques", Fog Remote Sensing and Modeling (FRAM) Workshop, Dalhousie University, Halifax, Nova Scotia, 21-22 May, 2008.

[20] G. Zazzaro, P. Mercogliano, and F.M. Pisano, "Data Mining to Classify Fog Events by applying Cost-Sensitive Classifier", CISIS 2010, The Fourth International Conference on Complex, Intelligent and SW Intensive Systems, Krakow, Poland, 15-18 February 2010.

[21] G.T. Weymouth, "Dealing with uncertainty in fog forecasting for major airports in Australia", In 4thConference on Fog, Fog Collection and Dew, La Serena, Chile, pp. 73-76, 2007.

[22] F.F. Ebecken, "Fog Formation Prediction in Coastal Regions Using Data Mining Techniques", in International Conf. On Environmental Coastal Regions, Cancun, Mexico, vol 2, pp. 165-174, 1998.

[23] G. Zazzaro, P. Mercogliano, G. Romano, V. Rillo, and S. Kauczok, "Short Range Fog Forecasting by applying Data Mining Techniques", 2nd IEEE International Workshop on Metrology for Aerospace, At Benevento, Italy, June 3-5 2015, Volume: pp 460-465.

[24] ECMWF. Mars User Guide. User Support. Operations Dep.2013.

[25] World Meteorological Organization, 2011. Manual on Codes. WMO-No. 306. Volume I.2.

[26] W.T. Roach, "Back to basics: Fog: Part 1—Definitions and basic physics", Weather 49.12 (1994): 411-415.

[27] J. Han and M. Kamber, "Data Mining: Concepts and Techniques", Morgan Kaufmann Publishers, 2001.

[28] I.H. Witten and E. Frank, "Data Mining. Practical Machine Learning Tools and Techniques", Morgan Kaufmann, 2005.

OntoEDIFACT: An Ontology for the UN/EDIFACT Standard

Boulares Ouchenne and Mhamed Itmi

Normandie Univ, INSA Rouen, LITIS, 76000 Rouen, France
Email: {boulares.ouchenne,mhamed.itmi}@insa-rouen.fr

***Abstract*—In this paper, we propose an OWL encoded ontology (OntoEDIFACT) to ontologize the United Nations/Electronic Data Interchange For Administration, Commerce and Transport (UN/EDIFACT) standard. Our ontology provides a lightweight representation that captures general concepts about basic components of the standard, and also provides extensibility for adding complex components in a hierarchical manner. Our approach separates the conceptualization from knowledge base (KB) integration. So, we start by the conception of the knowledge model and we finish by building the KB through instantiating the knowledge model from the last version of the standard. The knowledge base consists of a triple stores, publicly available through a SPARQL endpoint. We have developed some services for exploiting the KB and discussed some future applications.**

Keywords–Ontology; EDI; EDIFACT; SPARQL-Endpoint.

I. INTRODUCTION

Generally, E-commerce is associated with buying and selling operations that are carried out via the Internet. This is a very biased view because E-commerce includes any transaction in which, the parties interact electronically. Electronic Data Interchange (EDI) [1][2][3] enables the exchange of structured business documents (purchase orders, invoices, etc.) between IT systems of trading partners. The use of a structured and readable format allows transferring of documents from one application to another located in a different locations, without any human interpretation and/or intervention. The EDI was designed to replace the transmission of information through paper and to overcome inefficient manual document exchange. Basically, EDI is designed with respect to the principle that the data should be entered once into the system, then it can be transmitted electronically among interested parties. In the most common scenario, the cycle starts when a buyer sends an EDI purchase order to a seller. The latter, first sends an acknowledgement to the buyer, then at the time of shipment, he sends a shipping notice followed by an invoice. All these documents are transmitted through EDI. Finally, the buyer sends his bank account information for the payment of the invoice, and funds are electronically transferred to the seller's bank account.

The design of EDI seems to be simple, but its implementation requires a thorough consensus on data elements, codes, rules of syntax and format. The exchange of electronic information is built on a common, universal, multi-sector language allowing an open and easy communication between all economic stakeholders. In other words, we can transfer data between heterogeneous systems to the extent that we use a common format. There are various standards that constitute the basis for a specific-area data exchange. A few examples are NIEM, AINSI X12, EDIFACT and XBRL. Each standard is characterized by its scope of use (North of America for AINSI X12 and NIEM, EDIFACT for the international).

UN/EDIFACT is the international EDI standard developed by the United Nations. This standard specifies a set of international standards, directories and guidelines for the electronic interchange of structured data. UN/EDIFACT provides a set of data structures (called MESSAGES) each of which, serves to transmit a particular message (Purchase order, Invoice, etc.). Each of these structures is an aggregate of content items (SEGMENTS and ELEMENTS). UN/EDIFACT does not define the medium by which the message is sent, or the protocols used in any particular form of communication. The standard is completely neutral in this aspect. It focuses only on the content of messages.

The UN/EDIFACT is a standard for EDI trading widely recognized by both commercial and non-commercial sectors. Recently, organizations have a tendency to adopt UN/EDIFACT to the long term for a structured governance with an international visibility. An example (taken from Wikipedia [4]) of an EDIFACT message used to answer to a flight ticket (FRA-JFK-MIA) availability request is presented below:

```
UNA:+.? '
UNB+IATB:1+6XPPC+LHPPC+940101:0950+1'
UNH+1+PAORES:93:1:IA'
MSG+1:45'
IFT+3+XYZCOMPANY AVAILABILITY'
ERC+A7V:1:AMD'
IFT+3+NO MORE FLIGHTS'
ODI'
TVL+240493:1000::1220+FRA+JFK+DL+400+C'
PDI++C:3+Y::3+F::1'
APD+74C:0:::6++++++6X'
TVL+240493:1740::2030+JFK+MIA+DL+081+C'
PDI++C:4'
APD+EM2:0:1630::6+++++++DA'
UNT+13+1'
UNZ+1+1'
```

Beside the widespread adoption of the UN/EDIFACT, the standard suffers from its poor design, confusing or a lack of semantics and its complicated formatted text which is non-understandable for a non-specialist. Those difficulties pushed us to propose an ontology to unambiguously specify the meaning of components of the UN/EDIFACT standard and relationships among them.

This paper is organized as follows. Section 2 provides a detailed description of the OntoEDIFACT ontology. Section 3 presents the software architecture of our prototype, freely

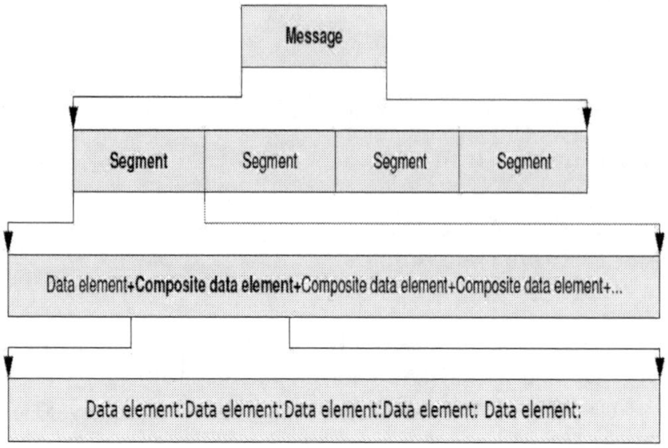

Figure 1. EDIFACT messages structure.

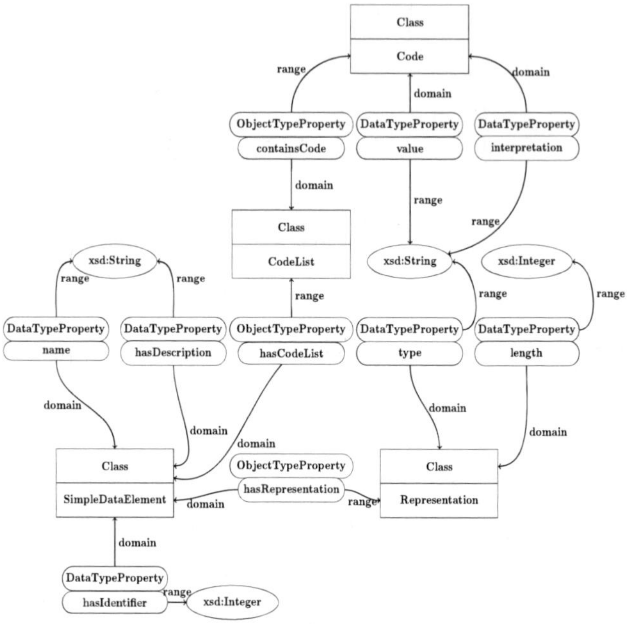

Figure 2. Simple Element Modeling.

accessible via the Web. Section 4 briefly discusses some related works. Finally, we give our conclusions and outline future works in Section 5.

II. Designing the OntoEDIFACT Ontology

This section describes the approach used to design the OntoEDIFACT ontology, as well as the four main components of OntoEDIFACT, namely simple elements, composite elements, segments and messages. We have defined several requirements to which our ontology must answer. First, we want to develop a general ontology in order to (i) be apprehended by the EDI community without the need to be an expert of UN/EDIFACT standard, (ii) to be independent of the version of the UN/EDIFACT standard and (iii) the structure of our ontology must also facilitate its settlement and its evolution by using possibilities of expression offered by the description languages (in terms of knowledge representation and reasoning). During the design of our ontology, we have endeavored to apply the commonly recommended techniques of the community [5][6]. Finally, since the OntoEDIFACT is described in OWL2 [7], we have taken advantage of possibilities offered by this language in terms of expressiveness.

A. The structure of EDIFACT Messages

A in EDIFACT format is structured as depicted in Figure 1. A message is composed of an ordered set of segments. Segments can be grouped in groups which comprises an ordered set of segments. Furthermore, the message structure defines whether data segments and segment groups are mandatory or optional, and indicates how many times a particular segment or a group can be repeated. A segment comprises an ordered list of stand-alone data elements and/or composite data elements. The segment definition indicates the data elements to be included in the segment, the sequence of the data elements and whether each data element is mandatory or optional. A composite data element comprises an ordered list of two or more component data elements. The composite data element definition specifies the component data elements to be included in the composite data element, the sequence of the component data elements and whether each component data element is mandatory or optional.

B. Modeling of Simple Data Elements

Simple Data Elements are the primary unit which, correspond to the lowest level of data in EDIFACT standard. They represent data types and contain single data element value. A simple data element is defined by:

- Its EDIFACT identification code number.
- Its name and its description.
- Its structure that defines its type and length.
- Eventually a predefined code list that it can take.

Figure 2 shows the OWL serialization of simple data elements. The model is structured around a set of abstract entities, each describing a conceptual object (Code, Representation, etc.). Each entity is associated with its attributes (represented by `owl:DatatypeProperty`) and relations with other entities (represented by `owl:ObjectProperty`).
A simple data element is modeled by an OWL class `SimpleDataElement`. A set of data properties have been introduced to express the relationship between objects and their data values, such as numerical values (i.e., `hasIdentifier` to represent the identification) and textual values (i.e., `hasDescription` for the description and `name` for the name of the simple data element). We have also introduced two data object properties (`hasRepresentation` and `hasCodeList`) to express respectively, the relationship between a simple data element and its representation or its code list. There are two kinds of simple data elements:

1) Simple data elements with free values (e.g., the simple data element account name[1]): in order to model valid formats of data elements values, an OWL class `Representation` and two data properties

[1]http://www.unece.org/fileadmin/DAM/trade/untdid/d16b/tred/tred1146.htm

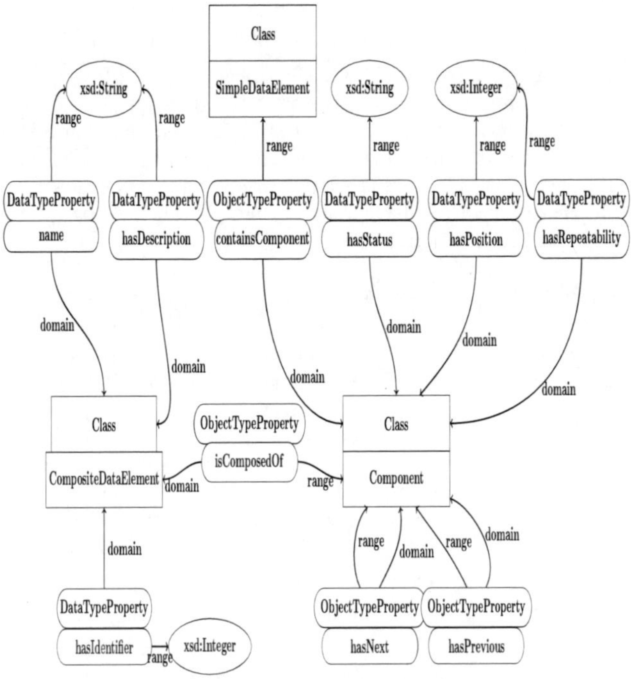

Figure 3. Composite Element Modeling.

are introduced. The first one (`type`), is used to define whether the characters used for representing the simple data element are numeric, alphabetic or alphanumeric. The second one (`length`) is used to represent the maximum number of characters allowed to represent the simple data element.

2) Simple data elements with predefined values (e.g., the simple data element geographic area code[2]): the particularity of this kind is that, values have to be taken from an agreed list of code values. To model the list of predefined codes, we used an OWL class `CodeList` and an object property (`containsCode`) to specify codes belonging to the codes list. Furthermore, an OWL class `Code` and two data properties (`value` and `interpretation`) are used to specify respectively the value that can take and the interpretation of each value.

C. Modeling of Composite Data Elements

Composite data elements are concatenations of two or more simple data elements. A composite data element is defined by:

- Its EDIFACT identification code.
- Its name and its description.
- Its composition.

Figure 3 shows the OWL serialization of composite data elements. A composite data element is modeled by an OWL class `CompositeDataElement`. We reused data properties which have been introduced previously (i.e., `hasIdentifier`,`hasDescription` and `name`), and we have introduced one object property (`isComposedOf`) to express the relationship between a composite data element and its components (simple data elements). An OWL class `Component` is introduced to specify the component data elements to be included in the composite data element. Furthermore, some properties are also introduced:

1) `containsComponent`: an object property that specifies the simple data element to be included into the composite data element.
2) `hasStatus`: a data property to specify whether the simple data element is mandatory or optional.
3) `hasPosition`: a data property to specify the sequence of components (simple data elements) in the composite data element.
4) `hasRepeatability`: a data property specifying the repeatability of the component (the maximum number of occurrence).
5) `hasPrevious` and `hasnext`: object properties that specifies respectively, the previous and the next component.

D. Modeling of Segments

A segment is an ordered list of related data components (simple and/or composite) usually associated in a functional way and thus manipulated as such by the partners of the exchange (the sender and the receiver). For instance, consider the segment address [3] which contains, information about the road, postal code, town, country, etc. Each segment is standardized and is reproduced identically in all messages which use it. A segment is defined by:

- Its EDIFACT code (a three capital letters abbreviation of its name).
- Its name and its function.
- Its composition.

Figure 4 shows the OWL serialization of a segment. A segment is modeled by an OWL class `Segment`. We reused data properties which have been introduced previously (i.e., `hasIdentifier` and `name`), and we have introduced a data property (`hasFunction`) to express the function for which it was defined. We also reused concepts (`Component`), object and data properties defined in the previous subsection to indicate the data element (simple and/or composite) to be included in the segment, the sequence of the components, to indicate whether they are mandatory or optional, and to indicate how many times a particular simple or composite element can be repeated.

E. Modeling of Messages

Messages are the main structure of the EDIFACT exchange standard. They correspond to specific business messages and cover the needs of different sectors of economic activity (order, invoice, payment order, etc.). A message is defined by:

- Its EDIFACT code (a six capital letters abbreviation of its name).
- Its name and its composition.

Figure 5 shows the OWL serialization of a message. A message is modeled by an OWL class `Message`. We reused

[2]http://www.unece.org/fileadmin/DAM/trade/untdid/d16b/tred/tred3279.htm

[3]http://www.unece.org/fileadmin/DAM/trade/untdid/d16b/trsd/trsdadr.htm

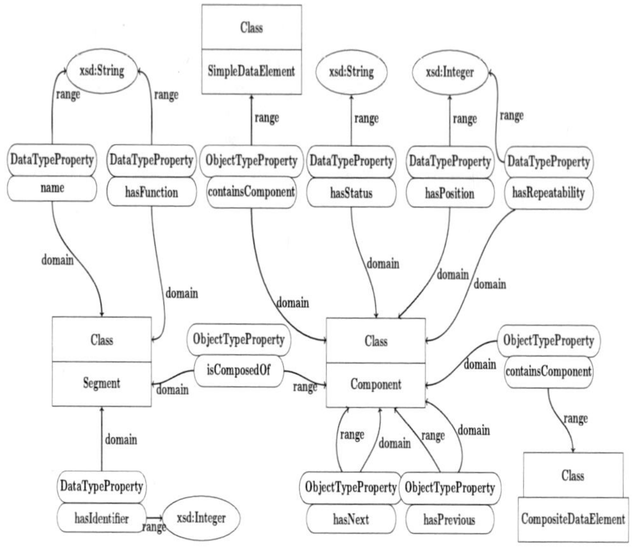

Figure 4. Segment Modeling.

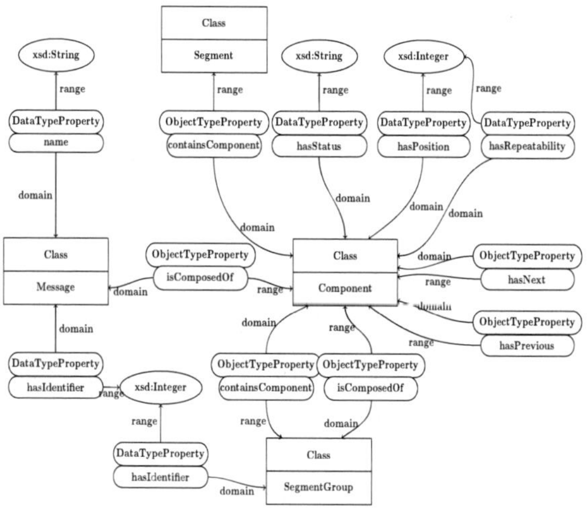

Figure 5. Message Modeling.

data properties which have been introduced previously (i.e., `hasIdentifier` and `name`), and we also introduced an OWL class `SegmentGroup` to represent group of segments. The possibility of grouping segments comes from the need to gather logical sets of information, or to repeat these logics of sets (simple or grouped). Thus, we can constitute groups of hierarchically dependent segments with the possibility that a segment group may contain other groups. We also reused concepts (`Component`), object and data properties defined previously to indicate the segments and/or groups of segments to be included into the message or into the group of segments, the sequence of the components, whether they are mandatory or optional, and to indicate how many times a particular segment or a group can or have to be repeated.

III. Implementation and Application

Figure 6 shows the high-level architecture of our prototype. Two main steps have oriented our software development process: the conversion of UN/EDIFACT Messages into RDF triplets format and the development of tools to interrogate and visualize the results. The results are represented as a knowledge base (an RDF dataset) which can then be queried using SPARQL queries.

A. Populating the Ontology

Ontology population is the task of creating individuals (instances) in each class in the OntoEDIFACT ontology, adding data properties between the instances and their literal values, as well as establishing object properties between instances in different classes. The objective of this step is to convert the entire content, syntax and data structures of the EDIFACT standard in order to produce RDF triplets format. To carry out this step, we have developed parsers that apply the strategy defined below and we have used the following frameworks:

- The Jena API [8], which is a free and open source Java framework for building Semantic web applications.
- The Jena TDB triplestore [9], which provides several methods for large scale storage and queries of RDF datasets.
- The JSoup [10] parser, which provides a very convenient Java library for extracting and manipulating data from HTML documents.

All the specifications of the UN/EDIFACT standard are available on the official website [11] of the UNECE. From this website our parsers have extracted the necessary information to populate our ontology. Each year, the UN/EDIFACT standard is reviewed and updated twice. In our prototype, we used the last version (D.16B), which is the second update of the year 2016. Each version of UN/EDIFACT is grouped in four directories:

1) The directory of simple data element[4]: This directory contains 646 HTML pages. Our program start by populating the ontology with simple data elements. For each HTML page specifying a simple data element, an individual 'SE' of class `SimpleDataElement` is created. Afterward, the HTML content is parsed to extract the identifier, the name and the description. These values are associated to the individual 'SE' through data properties (`hasIdentifier`, `name` and `hasDescription`).
   If the simple data element has a list of predefined codes, an individual 'CL' of class `CodeList` is also created and linked to the individual 'SE' through the object property `hasCodeList`. For each code that the simple element can take, an individual 'C' of class `Code` is created and linked to the individual 'CL' through the object property `containsCode`. Finally, the value and the interpretation of the corresponding code are extracted and associated to the individual 'C' through the data properties (`value` and `interpretation`).
   For simple data elements with free values, an individual 'R' of class `Representation` is created

[4] http://www.unece.org/fileadmin/DAM/trade/untdid/d16b/tred/tredi2.htm

and linked to the individual 'SE' through the object property `hasRepresentation`. The type and the maximum length are then extracted and associated to the individual 'R' through data properties (`type` and `length`).

2) The directory of composite data element[5]: This directory contains 198 HTML pages. For each HTML page specifying a composite data element, an individual 'CE' of class `CompositeDataElement` is created. Then, the HTML content is parsed to extract the identifier, the name and the description. These values are associated to the individual 'CE' through data type properties (`hasIdentifier`, `name` and `hasDescription`). For each component of the composite elements, an individual 'C' of class `Component` is also created and linked to the individual 'CE' through object type property (`isComposedOf`. The repeatability, the position and the status are extracted and associated to the individual 'C' through data properties (`hasStatus`, `hasPosition` and `hasRepeatability`). At last, an object property (`containsComponent`) is used to link the individual 'C' to the simple data element composing the individual 'CE'.
3) The directory of segments[6]: This directory contains 156 HTML pages. For each HTML page specifying a segment, an individual 'S' of class `Segment` is created. Then, the HTML content is parsed to extract the identifier, the name and the function. These values are associated to the individual 'S' through data type properties (`hasIdentifier`, `name` and `hasFunction`). For each component of the segment, an individual 'C' of class `Component` is created and linked to the individual 'S' through object type property (`isComposedOf`). The repeatability, the position and the status are extracted and associated to the individual 'C' through data properties (`hasStatus`, `hasPosition` and `hasRepeatability`). At last, an object property (`containsComponent`) is used to link the individual 'C' to the simple or the composite element composing the individual 'S'.
4) The directory of messages[7]: This directory contains 195 HTML pages. For each HTML page specifying a message, an individual 'M' of class `Message` is created. Then, the HTML content is parsed to extract the name and the identifier. These values are associated to the individual 'M' through data type properties (`hasIdentifier` and `name`). For each component of the message, an individual 'C' of class `Component` is created and linked to the individual 'M' through the object property (`isComposedOf`. The repeatability, the position and the status are extracted and associated to the individual 'C' through data properties (`hasStatus`, `hasPosition` and `hasRepeatability`). At last, an object property (`containsComponent`) is used to link the individual 'C' to the segment or the group of segments composing the individual 'M'. We notice that an individual of class `SegmentGroup` is created for each new group segment encountered, and handled as a component of the message as the same way of segments.

[5]http://www.unece.org/fileadmin/DAM/trade/untdid/d16b/trcd/trcdi2.htm
[6]http://www.unece.org/fileadmin/DAM/trade/untdid/d16b/trsd/trsdi2.htm
[7]http://www.unece.org/fileadmin/DAM/trade/untdid/d16b/trmd/trmdi2.htm

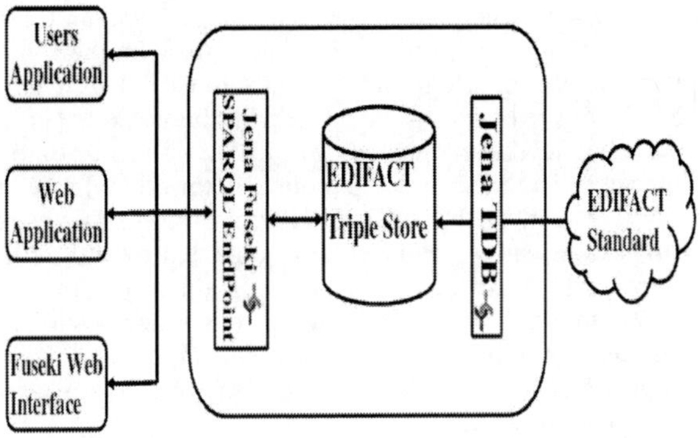

Figure 6. Architecture.

B. *Querying and visualization of the data-set*

Once the data set is populated automatically, we have exposed it through three intuitive ways.
The first one is simple Java Web-based [8] application deployed on a WildFly[9] application server (a set of Servlets and JSP pages). It provides a user-friendly interface that helps users to view all the necessary information for designing and creating EDIFACT components by selecting the suitable classes, objects and properties.
The second one is through the Fuseki web user interface[10]. It offers an easy-to-use querying interface that incorporates a lot of functionality. A user can specify SPARQL SELECT queries to directly manipulate the designated components and to view or to download sets of results in several formats (JSON, XML, CSV, etc.).
Finally, for external users applications using traditional framework for querying and analyzing RDF data(Jena [8], Mulgara [11] and Sesame [12] for Java developers or CubicWeb [13] for Python developers).

IV. Related Work

Despite the exhaustive list of tools proposed by several companies to create XML schema and to convert between EDI standards or formats ([12][13][14]), very few works deal with the issues of ontologization of EDI standard, as illustrated by the research works in [15][16][17]. The authors of [16] propose an ontology for specifying ANSI X12 format. Using this ontology, they encoded the entire version of January 2005 (Data Elements, Composite Data Elements, Segments, and most used Transaction). In order to build this ontology, authors start by specifying the format of X12 components as a classes (Transactions, Segment Groups, etc.), data and

[8]http://realgrain.litislab.fr/EDIFACT-PROJECT/ServletMainEDIFACT
[9]http://wildfly.org/
[10]http://realgrain.litislab.fr:3030/sparql.tpl
[11]http://mulgara.org/
[12]http://rdf4j.org/
[13]https://www.cubicweb.org/

object properties. The process of creation of individuals for each class from HTML files of the X12 specification, is done semi-automatically. In [15], authors propose an ontology codified in OWL to conceptualize the EDIFACT standard. First, authors start by creating classes for each of EDIFACT standard component. Then, they introduce data and object properties to link objects belonging to classes with their values. To populate the ontology, authors developed custom parsers for the (D.97A) version. Comparing with the work of [15], our approach has several advantages. Particularly, that our ontology is generic and can be used to populate the knowledge base with any version of the standard. Parsers for the last version (D.16B) are developed and can be customized for any anterior or future version. Also, in [15] all individual are grouped in one OWL file and this fact can weigh down applications that use this ontology. In our approach, users can choose (through SPARQL requests) only EDIFACT messages that they need in their applications.

V. Conclusion and Future Works

In this paper, we have presented an ontology OntoEDIFACT (publicly available online [18]) which, has given a semantic representation to the UN/EDIFACT standard. This Ontology has been designed following best practices in ontology engineering. Then, we briefly discuss the functionalities of tools that automatically populate the ontology with instances from the last version of the standard (D.16B). These tools are able to parse HTML web pages containing specifications of UN/EDIFACT components to RDF triples. Finally, a SPARQL endpoint has been implemented and some services have been designed to consume these triples. Of course some improvements can be made to our ontology. For instance, an enrichment phase with external ontologies is underway development. So far, we are aware of the following practical applications that can make use of OntoEDIFACT:

- Indexing UN/EDIFACT documents [19][20] to search efficiently for specific contents inside a large document base.
- Interoperability between the several EDI standards using techniques of ontologies alignment [21]. An investigation work to interoperate the ANSI X12 ontology [16] with the OntoEDIFACT is ongoing.
- Generating XML schema for UN/EDIFACT messages from the OWL representation of each message using straightforward transformation techniques [22].

Acknowledgment

This research is supported by the ≪CLASSE2≫ project: co-financed by the European Union with the European regional development fund (ERDF) and Normandy Region.

References

[1] N. C. Hill and D. M. Ferguson, "Electronic data interchange: A definition and perspective," 1989.

[2] S. Sawabini, "Introduction to edi," Conference Proceedings EDI 2000: EDI, EC, and You, pp. 1–36.

[3] F. Bergeron and L. Raymond, "The advantages of electronic data interchange," SIGMIS Database, vol. 23, no. 4, Oct. 1992, pp. 19–31. [Online]. Available: http://doi.acm.org/10.1145/146553.146556

[4] Wikipedia. Edifact-wikipedia. [Online]. Available: https://en.wikipedia.org/wiki/EDIFACT [retrieved: 03, 2017]

[5] A. Gangemi and V. Presutti, "Ontology design patterns," in Handbook on Ontologies, 2009, pp. 221–243. [Online]. Available: http://dx.doi.org/10.1007/978-3-540-92673-3_10

[6] T. R. Gruber, "Toward principles for the design of ontologies used for knowledge sharing," Int. J. Hum.-Comput. Stud., vol. 43, no. 5-6, Dec. 1995, pp. 907–928. [Online]. Available: http://dx.doi.org/10.1006/ijhc.1995.1081

[7] M. Horridge and P. Patel-Schneider. OWL 2 web ontology language. manchester syntax (second edition). [Online]. Available: http://www.w3.org/TR/owl2-manchester-syntax/ [retrieved: Dec., 2012]

[8] J. J. Carroll, I. Dickinson, C. Dollin, D. Reynolds, A. Seaborne, and K. Wilkinson, "Jena: Implementing the semantic web recommendations," in Proceedings of the 13th International World Wide Web Conference on Alternate Track Papers &Amp; Posters, ser. WWW Alt. '04. New York, NY, USA: ACM, 2004, pp. 74–83. [Online]. Available: http://doi.acm.org/10.1145/1013367.1013381

[9] JenaTDB. Apache jena - tdb. [Online]. Available: https://jena.apache.org/documentation/tdb/ [retrieved: 03, 2017]

[10] Jsoup. jsoup: a java html parser library. [Online]. Available: https://jsoup.org/ [retrieved: 03, 2017]

[11] EDIFACT. Edifact directories. [Online]. Available: https://www.unece.org/tradewelcome/un-centre-for-trade-facilitation-and-e-business-uncefact/outputs/standards/unedifact/directories/2011-present.html [retrieved: 03, 2017]

[12] Altova. Xml global and altova reduce data integration costs with the launch of the enterprise-ready xml integration workbench. [Online]. Available: https://www.altova.com/ [retrieved: 03, 2017]

[13] Smooks. The smooks framework. [Online]. Available: http://www.smooks.org/ [retrieved: 03, 2017]

[14] S. Studio. The stylus studio edi to xml. [Online]. Available: http://www.stylusstudio.com/edi/ [retrieved: 03, 2017]

[15] R. Engel, C. Pichler, M. Zapletal, W. Krathu, and H. Werthner, "From encoded edifact messages to business concepts using semantic annotations," in Proceedings of the 2012 IEEE 14th International Conference on Commerce and Enterprise Computing, ser. CEC '12. Washington, DC, USA: IEEE Computer Society, 2012, pp. 17–25. [Online]. Available: http://dx.doi.org/10.1109/CEC.2012.13

[16] D. Foxvog and C. Bussler, "Ontologizing edi: First steps and initial experience," in Proceedings of the International Workshop on Data Engineering Issues in E-Commerce, ser. DEEC '05. Washington, DC, USA: IEEE Computer Society, 2005, pp. 49–58. [Online]. Available: http://dx.doi.org/10.1109/DEEC.2005.13

[17] D. B. Foxvog and Christoph, "Ontologizing edi semantics," in Proceedings of the 2006 International Conference on Advances in Conceptual Modeling: Theory and Practice, ser. CoMoGIS'06. Berlin, Heidelberg: Springer-Verlag, 2006, pp. 301–311. [Online]. Available: http://dx.doi.org/10.1007/11908883_36

[18] T. E. Ontology. The edifact ontology. [Online]. Available: http://realgrain.litislab.fr/OntoEDIFACT.owl [retrieved: 03, 2017]

[19] E. Desmontils and C. Jacquin, "Indexing a web site with a terminology oriented ontology," in Proceedings of the First International Conference on Semantic Web Working, ser. SWWS'01. Aachen, Germany, Germany: CEUR-WS.org, 2001, pp. 549–565. [Online]. Available: http://dl.acm.org/citation.cfm?id=2956602.2956638

[20] F. Fürst and F. Trichet, "Integrating domain ontologies into knowledge-based systems," in Proceedings of the Eighteenth International Florida Artificial Intelligence Research Society Conference, Clearwater Beach, Florida, USA, 2005, pp. 826–827. [Online]. Available: http://www.aaai.org/Library/FLAIRS/2005/flairs05-142.php

[21] S. Pavel and J. Euzenat, "Ontology matching: State of the art and future challenges," IEEE Trans. on Knowl. and Data Eng., vol. 25, no. 1, Jan. 2013, pp. 158–176. [Online]. Available: http://dx.doi.org/10.1109/TKDE.2011.253

[22] I. Bedini, C. Matheus, P. F. Patel-Schneider, A. Boran, and B. Nguyen, "Transforming XML schema to OWL using patterns," in ICSC 2011 - 5th IEEE International Conference on Semantic Computing, Palo Alto, United States, 2011, pp. 1–8. [Online]. Available: https://hal.archives-ouvertes.fr/hal-00624055

A Causality-Based Feature Selection Approach For Multivariate Time Series Forecasting

Youssef Hmamouche*, Alain Casali* and Lotfi Lakhal*
*LIF - CNRS UMR 6166, Aix Marseille Université, Marseille, France
Email: firstname.lastname@lif.univ-mrs.fr

***Abstract*—The study of time series forecasting has progressed significantly in recent decades. The progress is partially driven by growing demand from different industry branches. Despite recent advancements, there still exist several issues that need to be addressed in order to improve the accuracy of the forecasts. One of them is how to improve forecasts by utilizing potentially extra information carried by other observed time series. This is a known problem, where we have to deal with high dimensional data and we do not necessarily know the relationship between variables. To deal with this situation, the challenge is to extract the most relevant predictors that will contribute to forecast each target time series. In this paper, we propose a feature selection algorithm specific to forecasting multivariate time series, based on (i) the notion of the Granger causality, and on (ii) a clustering strategy. Lastly, we carry out experiments on several real data sets and compare our proposed method to some of the most widely used dimension reduction and feature selection methods. Experiments illustrate that our method results in improved accuracy of forecasts compared to the evaluated methods.**

Keywords*–*Multivariate Time Series Forecasting; Granger Causality; Feature selection.

I. INTRODUCTION

Time series analysis incorporates a set of tools, methods, and models in order to describe the evolution of data over time. It has been developed primarily for the purposes of forecasting and business analysis. Time series analysis is an important component of any business intelligence system insofar as it generates new, valuable data by combining trends, forecasts, correlations, causalities *etc.* in intelligent ways. Consequently, time series analysis produces original, exploitable information that can then be used as a critical input to the decision-making process and, ergo, can contribute to more intelligent and effective decisions.

The first time series forecast models were introduced in the 1920s. These were followed shortly by the first application of the univariate Auto-Regressive model [1]. Advanced versions of these models are still in use today. Based on the Auto-Regressive principle, those models take into account data history in order to make forecasts. Nevertheless, despite their innovativeness, these first models only consider a single time series in their predictions and, thus, fail to utilize a significant amount of potentially-exploitable data. With this in mind, in the latter half of the last century, researchers began to lend greater attention to refining forecast models that exploit multiple time series [2]. Most of the algorithms used today for multivariate time series forecasting, which includes the algorithms most commonly used for economic forecasting, are based on concepts developed during this period.

Multivariate analysis is increasingly preferred by data scientists over univariate analysis. The latter is simpler than the former as it only takes into account the previous values of a respective time series. Multivariate models, on the other hand, seek to understand the behavior and characteristics of the time series in question by explaining each series based (i) on its previously observed values, Iin addition to (ii) the previously observed values of other series in the data set. This approach is particularly important when handling financial data because, indeed, the value of one variable often does not only depend on its previous values, but also on the past values of other variables in the same dataset. As such, in order to obtain the most accurate outputs, it is necessary to factor in as inputs all the relevant information from other variables when making forecasts [3]. Unfortunately, utilizing all the existing variables in a multivariate model in a way that achieves optimal results has yet to be perfected: (i) in some cases, existing models are simply not able to incorporate all variables; (ii) in other cases, models may not, for reasons that we will discuss, produce more accurate forecasts. For instance, the authors of [4], working with real data from Australia and the United States, were not able to improve accuracy of their forecasts when using more than $30\% - 60\%$ of the existing predictors.

In this paper, we propose a feature selection method specific to time series forecasting. We argue that our approach handle relatively the problem of dependencies between variables, which is a major drawback of many exisiting methods. Specifically, we are able to do so by explaining causalities between variables (i) using the Granger causality graph [5], and (ii) then clustering them. The proposed approach is currently being used in two industrial prototypes, which are to be used for different purposes: (i) the first one is designed to provide a tool for buyers, informing them when to purchase a product for their company; (ii) and the second prototype is used for detecting fraud in public markets. The objective of our work on both prototypes is the same: to forecast prices based on raw materials and/or finished products.

This paper is organized as follows: the first three sections are dedicated to related work: Section II is dedicated to prediction models, Section III is related to feature selection and dimension reduction methods and Section IV is devoted to the Granger causality. In Section V, we detail our approach. In Sections VI and VII, we perform experiments and comparison study on real data sets. And in Section VIII, we summarize our contributions and put forth possible future research.

II. PREDICTION MODELS

Many prediction models which are currently being developed are based on the idea of Auto-Regressive model $\text{AR}(p)$ [6]. This model expresses a univariate time series as a linear function of its p precedent values:

$$y_t = \alpha_0 + \alpha_1 y_{t-1} + \cdots + \alpha_p y_{t-p} + \epsilon_t$$

Where p is the order of the model, $\alpha_0 \dots \alpha_p$ are the parameters of the model, and ϵ_t is a white noise error term. The Moving Average model (MA) has the same expression, but for the error terms. The ARMA(p, q) model [6] combines these two models by considering both past error terms and values. For non-stationary time series, the ARIMA(p, d, q) model [6] is more preferable, it applies the ARMA(p, q) model after a differencing step, in order to obtain stationary time series, where d is the order of differenting (computing d times the differences between consecutive observations). In [7], the Vector Auto-Regressive VAR model is introduced as an extension of the AR model. Consider a k-dimensional time series Y_t, the VAR(p) system expresses each univariate variable of the multivariate time series Y_t as a linear function of the p previous values of itself and the p previous values of the other variables:

$$Y_t \quad = \alpha_0 + \textstyle\sum_{i=1}^{p} A_i Y_{t-i} + \epsilon_t,$$

where ϵ_t is a white noise with a mean of zero, and $A_1, \dots, A_p$ are $(k \times k)$ matrix parameters of the model. In [8], the Vector Error Correction (VECM) is introduced. This model transforms the VAR model by taking into account non-stationarity of the time series and by including cointegration equations. To simplify matters, let us consider two univariate time series (x_t, y_t) integrated of orger one, which means non stationary, but the first difference $(\Delta x_t = x_t - x_{t-1})$ is stationary. The VECM Model can be written as follows:

$$\Delta y_t = \alpha_{0y} - \gamma_y(\beta_0 y_{t-1} - \beta_1 x_{t-1}) + \sum_{i=1}^{p} v_{iy} \Delta y_{t-i} + \sum_{i=1}^{p} w_{iy} \Delta x_{t-i} + \epsilon_t$$

$$\Delta x_t = \alpha_{0x} - \gamma_x(\beta_0 y_{t-1} - \beta_1 x_{t-1}) + \sum_{i=1}^{p} v_{ix} \Delta y_{t-i} + \sum_{i=1}^{p} w_{ix} \Delta x_{t-i} + \epsilon_t$$

Where $\beta_0 y_{t-1} - \beta_1 x_{t-1}$ is stationary, the coefficients (β_0, β_1) are the cointegrating parameters, and (γ_y, γ_x) are the error correction parameters. If there exist no coefficients (β_0, β_1) such that $\beta_0 y_{t-1} - \beta_1 x_{t-1}$ is stationary, then x_t and y_t are not cointegrated and the VECM model is reduced to the VAR form.

III. Feature Selection and Dimension Reduction Methods

Feature selection refers to the act of extracting subset of the most relevant variables (features) of size k from a set of variables of size $n >> k$. While, dimension reduction methods consist in generating an artificial features with smallest dimension from the originals by combining them. Therefore, from a descriptive analysis point of view, feature selection is more interesting. However, both of them can be used to optimise the inputs of prediction models. Using all the existing variables in a multivariate model has two principal drawbacks. First, it can affect the rightness of the predictions computations. For example, in Auto-Regressive based models, if the number of regressors is proportional to the sample size, the ordinary least squares (OLS) forecasts are not efficient, and the challenge with these situtations is to reduce dimensionality of predictors [9]. Second, it prevents from detecting the most relevant variables, which can degrade forecasts accuracy [4].

The Principal Component Analysis (PCA) is one of the most common dimension reduction methods used [10]. Based on a set of variables, this method takes advantage of the inter-correlation between them. The idea is to generate the principal variables that describe as much as possible the original variables using a linear transformation. The Kernel PCA method is a non-linear principal component analysis proposed as an extension of PCA, by considering non-linear correlation between variables [11]. The Recursive Feature Elimination (RFE) technique works by recursively removing variables and building a model on those variables that remain [12]. These methods are widely used in forecasting time series, for example PCA and Kernel PCA have been adopted in two-step approach which reduces first the number of predictors, and then a applies a forecasting model [13]–[15]. Univariate appoaches are based on the principle of selecting variables by ranking them according to a statistical test or a similarity measure. For instance, in [16], a method based on causality is proposed. The algorithm selects variables that cause the target, and it shows good results compared with some dimension reduction methods.

IV. Granger Causality

The purpose of this section is to redefine the Granger causality [5], and to detail the statistical test used to estimate the bivariate causality between two time series. Let us consider two univariate time series x_t, y_t. The Granger definition of causality acknowledges the fact that x_t causes y_t if it contains information helpful to predict y_t. In other words, if by removing x_t from the available information used to predict y_t at the current time, the prediction results for y will be affected.

We detail here the standard Granger causality test [17], which uses the VAR model with a trend term. The test compares two models, (i) the first one only takes into account the precedents values of y_t and (ii) the second uses both x_t and y_t in order to predict y_t. If there is a significant difference between the two models, then it can be ascertained that the added variable, *i.e.*, x_t causes y_t:

$$\text{Model}_1: \quad y_t = \alpha_0 + \alpha t + \sum_{i=1}^{p} \alpha_i y_{t-i} + \epsilon_t$$

$$\text{Model}_2: \quad y_t = \alpha_0 + \alpha t + \sum_{i=1}^{p} \alpha_i y_{t-i} + \sum_{i=1}^{p} \beta_i x_{t-i} + \epsilon_t$$

The next step of the test is to compare the residual sum of squares (RSS) of these models using the Fisher test. The statistic of the test is expressed as follow:

$$F = \frac{(\text{RSS}_1 - \text{RSS}_2)/p)}{(\text{RSS}_2/n - 2p - 1)}$$

Where RSS_1 and RSS_2 are the residual sum of squares related to Model_1 and Model_2 respectively, n is the size of the predicted vector. Two hypotheses are tested, the null hypothesis H_0: $\forall i \in \{1, \dots, p\}, \beta_i = 0$ (which means x does not cause y) and H_1: $\exists i \in \{1, \dots, p\}$, $\beta_i \neq 0$. Under the null hypothesis H_0, F follows the Fisher distribution with $(p, n - 2p - 1)$ degrees of freedom, then the test is carried out at a level α in order to examine the null hypothesis of non causality.

V. OUR PROPOSAL

We focus here on the selection of the top predictor variables based on the Granger causality as a relationship between variables. Let us consider $Y = \{y_1, y_2, \dots, y_n\}$ a multivariate time series and a target variable y. The idea is to choose a subset of Y, for which we have the more accurate forecasts. Let us underline that from a theoretical point of view, there are $\sum_{i=1}^{k} \binom{n}{i}$ possible partitions of size less than or equal to k. And in general, there are 2^n possible partitions, which means 2^n possible models [9]. In addition, the Granger causality is not a monotone function, as a consequence, finding the best subset of variables that maximizes the causality is a NP-hard problem. One solution is to choose a set of variables having strong causality regarding to the target y as investigated in [16]. However, this approach does not take into account hidden relationship between variables, which means that we could use the same information even when using many variables.

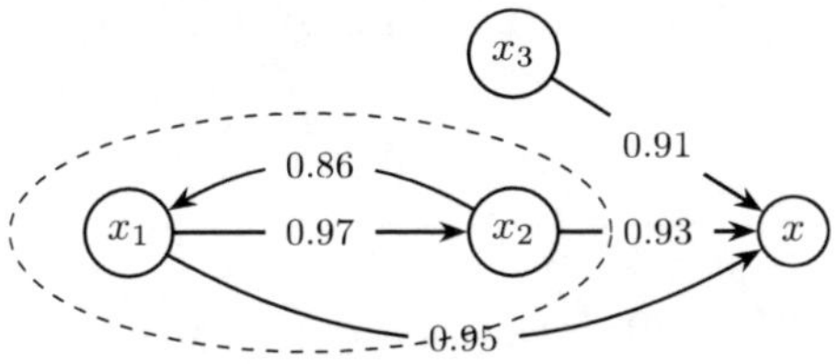

Figure 1. Illustration of dependencies between time series using Granger causality graph

In Figure 1, we show a small Granger causality graph describing dependencies between 4 variables. Let us try to select two variables as predictors for the target variable, *i.e.,* x. Selecting variables by ranking them according to causality leads to getting x_1 and x_2. However, x_1 and x_2 might provide the same information because x_1 causes x_2.

We propose a new method to deal with this problem based on clustering the Granger causality graph or the adjacency matrix using Partitioning Around Medoids (PAM) algorithm [18]. The p-value of the test is the probability to observe the given result under the assumption that H_0 is true, which means the probability of non causality. We consider so the causality as one minus p-value in order to express values of causalities in the range $[0, 1]$.

A. Algorithm of the proposed method

The algorithm of the proposed method can be divided into three steps:

- Building the adjacency matrix of causalities between variables.
- Clustering the set of all the possible predictors variables, by minimizing the causalities between clusters, and maximizing the causality within clusters, using the PAM method.
- Choosing one element from each cluster, the one that maximizes the causality on the target variable.

In Figure 2, the GSM (Granger Selection method) algorithm summarizes our approach. It generates for each target variable y, k variables that contributes to the prediction of y.

Input: Set of predictors time series $Y = \{y_1, y_2, \dots, y_n\}$, y the target variable, MINCAUS Min-Causality threshold, k the selection size
Output: GSM-CL the selected variables associated to y

```
for i = 1 to n do
    if Y.size() ⩽ k then
        Y = Y \ {y_i}
    end if
    if Y.size() ⩽ k then
        return GSM-CL = Y
    end if
end for
/* The clustering step. */
Let Mc be the dissimilarity matrix of predictors
for each x_i, x_j in Y such that i ≠ j do
    Mc[i,j] = Mc[j,i] = 1 − max(causality(x_i → x_j), causality(x_j → x_i))
end for
Clusters = pam(Mc, k)
/* The selection step. */
for each Cluster cl in Clusters do
    GSM-CL = GSM-CL ∪ arg max_{cl_j ∈ cl} (causality(cl_j → y))
end for
return GSM-CL
```

Figure 2. The GSM Algorithm.

B. Example

Consider $Y = \{y_1, \dots, y_8\}$ a set of predictors and a target variable y_9. Let's apply the GSM algorithm in order to select 4 predictor variables from Y that will contribute to forecast y.

1) The matrix of causalities: First, the algorithm computes the Granger causalities between variables in pairs. In this example, we take the matrix of causalities of our data sets corresponding to the dataset ts_1 described in Section VI-A:

$$MC = \begin{bmatrix} 1.00 & 0.935 & 0.999 & 0.999 & 0.832 & 0.998 & 0.998 & 0.933 & 0.998 \\ 0.28 & 1.00 & 0.877 & 0.87 & 0.224 & 0.785 & 0.801 & 0.999 & 0.868 \\ 0.033 & 0.656 & 1.00 & 0.106 & 0.479 & 0.944 & 0.775 & 0.082 & 0.905 \\ 0.028 & 0.647 & 0.239 & 1.00 & 0.483 & 0.944 & 0.776 & 0.096 & 0.905 \\ 0.7 & 0.457 & 0.977 & 0.978 & 1.00 & 0.343 & 0.031 & 0.398 & 0.901 \\ 0.808 & 0.417 & 0.818 & 0.817 & 0.906 & 1.00 & 0.997 & 0.431 & 0.722 \\ 0.274 & 0.742 & 0.992 & 0.992 & 0.942 & 0.959 & 1.00 & 0.906 & 0.788 \\ 0.327 & 0.999 & 0.998 & 0.998 & 0.427 & 0.895 & 0.996 & 1.00 & 0.900 \\ 0.304 & 0.071 & 0.581 & 0.584 & 0.205 & 0.448 & 0.999 & 0.754 & 1.00 \end{bmatrix}$$

2) Clustering and selecting the final variables: The algorithm partitions the variables based on the symmetrical matrix (as mentioned in the algorithm 2) using the PAM method. The idea behind symmetrizing the matrix of causalities is to build clusters where there is at least one causality between each pairs of variables, so it is logical to use the maximum. Let us underline also that the classical PAM algorithm partitions elements from a symmetric dissimilarity matrix, by minimizing dissimilarities within clusters. In our case, the algorithm maximizes causalities within clusters. That is why we use 1 minus the causality matrix as an input of the PAM method. Then, from each cluster, the algorithm chooses the element that has maximal causality on the target. The clustering vector associated to $\{y_1, \dots, y_8\}$ obtained is $(1, 2, 1, 1, 3, 1, 4, 2)$. And based on the causalities to the target (last column of the adjacency matrix), the selected variables are $\{y_1, y_5, y_7, y_8\}$.

3) Evaluation of the clusters: The quality of the causalities founded depends on, first the type of the data. And second, on the evaluation of the clustering task. In our case, we evaluate the quality of the clusters using the following objective function:

$$\text{minimize } G(x) \quad = \textstyle\sum_i^n \sum_j^n (1 - max(c_{ij}, c_{ji})) \times z_{ij},$$

where,

1) $z_{ij} = \begin{cases} 1 & \text{if } y_i, y_j \text{ belong to the same cluster} \\ 0 & \text{otherwise.} \end{cases}$
2) c_{ij} = causality($y_i \rightarrow y_j$).

This evaluation can be used in general as measure of causal relationships in multivariate time series. In the example, the value of G is 0.000168.

VI. EXPERIMENTS

We present in this part the methodologies adopted to carry out the experiments. We compare our method with four existing methods, selectKf: univariate feature selection method using the F-test statistical test, selectKc: univariate feature selection method using the Granger causality test [16], PCA: Principal Component Analysis [19], KERNEL PCA: Kernel Principal Component Analysis [11], and our proposal.

Vector Error Correction (VECM) [8] model is adopted to forecast the multivariate time series generated by the feature selection and dimension reduction methods. The univariate ARIMA model (see II) is also evaluated to show the forecasting results with no predictors variables. For our proposal, we use a p_value threeshold of the Granger causality test at 10%, and the lag parameters of the VECM and ARIMA models are determined according to the Akaike's Information Criterion (AIC) [20]. Experiments are made on an single computer with processor 2,2 GHz Intel Core i7 and 16Gb of RAM.

A. The used Data Sets

The first data set used comes from our current project. The second data set are taken from the Machine Learning Repository website [21], and the third one represents macroeconomic time series of United Sates [22]. A brief description of these data sets including the number of variables and observations and the target variables is presented in Table I.

B. Measuring forecast accuracy

The training step is carried out on the first 90% of the input series, and an evaluation on the last 10% real values is performed by one step ahead forecasts using rolling window VECM and ARIMA models. The measure of prediction accuracy used is the normalized root mean square error (NRMSE):

$$\text{NRMSE} = \frac{1}{\bar{y}} \sqrt{\frac{\sum_{i=1}^{h} (y_i - \hat{y_i})^2}{h}} \tag{1}$$

Where $(\hat{y_1}, \dots, \hat{y_h})$ are the forecasts, $(y_1, \dots, y_h)$ are the real values and $\bar{y}$ is the average value of y_t.

The comparison between methods will be the same if we use the mean squared error MSE or the root-mean-square RMSE. We use the NRMSE in order to have normalized and relative evaluations.

TABLE I. DESCRIPTION OF THE USED DATA SETS.

Data sets	Number of series	Number of observations	Description
ts_1	9	1090	Our Dataset, expressing the prices of International Index containing Oil, Propane, Gold, euros/dollars, Butane, Cac40, and others, between 2013/03/12 and 2016/03/01, aiming to forecast the Cac40.
ts_2	8	563	Data sets includes returns of Istanbul Stock Exchange (ISE) with seven other international index; SP, DAX, FTSE, NIKKEI, BOVESPA, MSCE_EU, MSCI_EM from Jun 5, 2009 to Feb 22, 2011.
ts_3	36	360	Monthly coincident and leading economic indexes of economic activity in the United States, for forecasting four series: industrial production IP, real personal income less transfer payments GMYXP8, real manufacturing and trade sales MT82, and employee-hours in nonagricultural establishments LPMHU.

VII. COMPARATIVE STUDY

In a first time, we measure forecast accuracy using the univariate ARIMA model. The results obtained are shown in Table II. This will allow us to compare how much the reduced model; VECM with dimension reduction of the predictors will perform compared with the univariate model.

TABLE II. EVALUATING FORECAST ACCURACY OF THE ARIMA MODEL.

Data sets	Target series	NRMSE
ts1	CAC40	0.0136
ts2	ISE	0.1004
ts3	IP	0.0094
	GMXY	0.0094
	LPMHU	0.0103
	MT82	0.0175

We show in Table III the forecast evaluations of each data set, by considering different numbers of predictors variables for each experiment. Let us underline that for the dataset ts_3, which contains 36 variables, the performance accuracy decreased when we use more than 11 predictors. This is why the results in the Table III are shown for a number of predictors, *i.e.*, k, less or equal than 11.

For dimension reduction methods PCA and Kernel PCA, it is possible to have both automatic number of features k or a specific number given in the input, which is not the case for the univariate selection method using the Granger causality test [16] which selects features naturally. The number of features generated using this method can be seen in Figure 3c.

Our proposal can be extended to provide an automatic number of features by using some methods of selection for the optimal number of clusters of the PAM method. However, the number of variables computed in advance is generally not optimal in term of forecasting, since the optimal value must be determined according to the forecast accuracy. For this reason we evaluate different values of the number of predictors, *i.e.*, k.

TABLE III. EVALUATING FORECASTS ACCURACY WITH DIFFERENT REDUCTION SIZES k.
* INDICATES THAT THE REDUCTION SIZE K IS GREATER THAN THE NUMBER OF VARIABLES,
- IF AN ERROR OF RESOLUTION OCCURS.

Data sets	Targets series	Methods	Normalized root mean squared error (NRMSE)										
			Number of features k										
			1	**2**	**3**	**4**	**5**	**6**	**7**	**8**	**9**	**10**	**11**
ts1	**CAC40**	**kpca**	0.0136	0.0136	0.0137	0.0136	0.0136	0.0136	0.0136	0.0136	*	*	*
		pca	0.0137	0.0137	0.0135	0.0135	0.0135	0.0135	0.0135	0.0135	*	*	*
		selectKc	0.0134	0.0134	0.0134	0.0134	0.0134	0.0134	0.0134	0.0134	*	*	*
		gsm	0.0134	0.0134	0.0134	0.0135	0.0134	0.0134	**0.0133**	0.0134	*	*	*
		selectKf	0.0136	0.0136	0.0136	0.0136	0.0135	0.0134	0.0134	0.0134	*	*	*
ts2	**ISE**	**kpca**	0.0991	0.1093	0.1100	0.1145	0.1141	0.1109	0.1210	*	*	*	*
		pca	0.0991	0.1093	0.1101	0.1145	0.1141	0.1109	0.1210	*	*	*	*
		selectKc	0.1239	0.1239	0.1239	0.1239	0.1239	0.1239	0.1239	*	*	*	*
		gsm	**0.0983**	0.1128	0.1174	0.1127	0.1129	0.1208	0.1210	*	*	*	*
		selectKf	0.1020	0.1206	0.1247	0.1203	0.1298	0.1208	0.1210	*	*	*	*
ts3	**IP**	**kpca**	0.0090	0.0092	-	-	-	-	-	-	-	-	-
		pca	0.0102	0.0095	0.0111	0.0111	0.0102	0.0108	0.0104	0.0105	0.0178	0.0195	0.0215
		selectKc	0.0161	0.0161	0.0161	0.0161	0.0161	0.0161	0.0161	0.0161	0.0161	0.0161	0.0161
		gsm	0.0091	**0.0084**	0.0086	0.0090	0.0094	0.0095	0.0115	0.0169	0.0186	0.0223	0.0232
		selectKf	0.0093	0.0092	0.0093	0.0095	0.0123	0.0122	0.0103	0.0132	0.0141	0.0142	0.0164
	GMXY8	**kpca**	0.0189	0.0202	0.0228	-	-	-	-	-	-	-	-
		pca	0.0084	**0.0082**	0.0091	0.0100	0.0101	0.0102	0.0103	0.0109	0.0148	0.0162	0.0177
		selectKc	0.0082	0.0082	0.0082	0.0082	0.0082	0.0082	0.0082	0.0082	0.0082	0.0082	0.0082
		gsm	0.0089	0.0093	0.0098	0.0096	0.0094	0.0098	0.0122	0.0121	0.0135	0.0139	0.0146
		selectKf	0.0087	0.0099	0.0099	0.0100	0.0099	0.0098	0.0103	0.0107	0.0108	0.0162	0.0177
	LPMHU	**kpca**	0.0079	0.0127	-	-	-	-	-	-	-	-	-
		pca	0.0075	0.0073	0.0074	0.0080	0.0080	0.0082	0.0080	0.0082	0.0084	0.0100	0.0111
		selectKc	0.0104	0.0104	0.0104	0.0104	0.0104	0.0104	0.0104	0.0104	0.0104	0.0104	0.0104
		gsm	0.0076	0.0074	0.0073	**0.0071**	0.0078	0.0074	0.0078	0.0097	0.0096	0.0090	0.0085
		selectKf	0.0077	0.0078	0.0080	0.0082	0.0080	0.0087	0.0080	0.0094	0.0096	0.0103	0.0113
	MT82	**kpca**	0.0171	0.0171	-	-	-	-	-	-	-	-	-
		pca	0.0168	0.0178	0.0179	0.0169	0.0170	0.0166	0.0168	0.0173	0.0275	0.0277	0.0294
		selectKc	0.0206	0.0206	0.0206	0.0206	0.0206	0.0206	0.0206	0.0206	0.0206	0.0206	0.0206
		gsm	0.0162	0.0165	0.0154	0.0158	0.0154	**0.0154**	0.0161	0.0248	0.0234	0.0263	0.0240
		selectKf	0.0170	0.0170	0.0169	0.0171	0.0183	0.0188	0.0197	0.0203	0.0208	0.0205	0.0231

Evaluations in Table III show that overall, the GSM currently outperforms most of the target time series compared with the ARIMA model and the methods previously evoked. We can not show the statistical significance of forecast in all cases, since the differences between the obtained results are relatively small according to the NRMSE, but practically, by making more predictions, it is important to take into account any improvement. As a side note, it is worth to mention that some authors, such as [23], have argued that statistical significance testing of forecast accuracy should be avoided, as test results may be misleading and that practice may actually harm the progress of forecasting field. However, in Figure 3 we compare the number of features that provides the best accuracy for each method with the minimal number giving better or the same forecast accuracy by our proposal. We remark that the performance of those methods can be reached by our proposal using smallest number of features in most cases.

VIII. CONCLUSIONS

In the context of forecasting with many variables, the goal is to develop optimized models, performing both descriptive and predictive tasks [24]. That can be achieved, in (i) by optimizing the structure of the multivariate models, *i.e.*, reducing the number of predictors, while improving the forecast accuracy, and (ii) by providing an explanation of the dependencies between all variables. The application of feature selection and dimension reduction methods as a preprocessing step before the prediction is a reasonable solution to this issue, except that the former are slightly advantageous since they extract a subset of variables from the originals, while the latter reduce dimensionality by generating artificial variables. In the litterature, a considerable interest has been paid to correlation-based methods. That can be coherent regarding to regression or classification. But in forecasting, and especially with lags, the predictive aspect of the selected features is not negligible. In comparison, a little attention has been paid to the role of causality in feature selection. In the current reseach, we investigated its role in the context of time series forecasting and propose the Granger Selection Method.

Experiments on real data sets and a comparative study with others methods show an improvement of the forecast accuracy and a reduction of the number of input predictors. The measure adopted is the Granger causality, but the proposed algorithm is applicable for other measures of dissimilarity between time series. In the future, we aim to adopt a more deeper analysis on the graph of causalties than the clustering approach, in order to tackle dependencies between time series. We aim also to apply our approach on other prediction models, as well as study the applicability of feature selection methods according to the types of models (prediction, classification, regression, *etc.*).

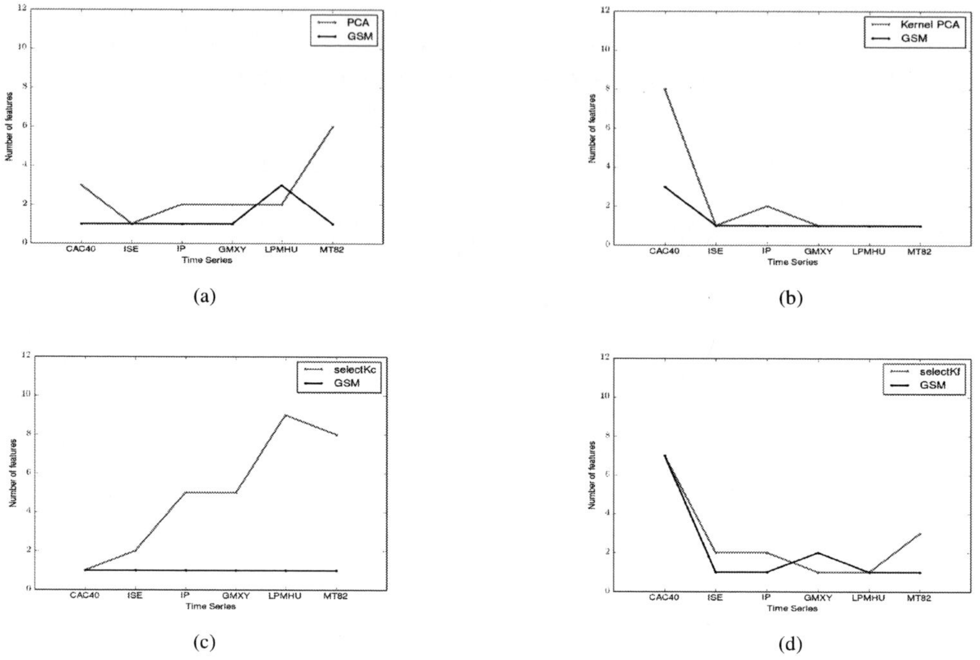

Figure 3. Comparison On The Number Of Predictors Providing The Same Or Better Forecast Accuracy By Our Proposal With The Methods Used.

REFERENCES

[1] G. Walker, "On periodicity in series of related terms," Proceedings of the Royal Society of London. Series A, Containing Papers of a Mathematical and Physical Character, vol. 131, no. 818, 1931, pp. 518–532.

[2] P. Whittle, "The analysis of multiple stationary time series," Journal of the Royal Statistical Society. Series B (Methodological), 1953, pp. 125–139.

[3] H. Lütkepohl, New introduction to multiple time series analysis. Springer Science & Business Media, 2005.

[4] B. Jiang, G. Athanasopoulos, R. J. Hyndman, A. Panagiotelis, F. Vahid et al., "Macroeconomic forecasting for Australia using a large number of predictors," Monash University, Department of Econometrics and Business Statistics, Tech. Rep., 2017.

[5] C. W. Granger, "Testing for causality: a personal viewpoint," Journal of Economic Dynamics and control, vol. 2, 1980, pp. 329–352.

[6] G. E. Box, G. M. Jenkins, and G. C. Reinsel, "Time series analysis: Forecastingand control," San Francisco: Holdenday, 1976.

[7] M. Quenouille, The analysis of multiple time-series, ser. Griffin's statistical monographs & courses. Griffin, 1957.

[8] S. Johansen, "Estimation and hypothesis testing of cointegration vectors in gaussian vector autoregressive models," Econometrica: Journal of the Econometric Society, 1991, pp. 1551–1580.

[9] J. H. Stock and M. W. Watson, "Forecasting with many predictors," Handbook of economic forecasting, vol. 1, 2006, pp. 515–554.

[10] H. Abdi and L. J. Williams, "Principal component analysis," Wiley Interdisciplinary Reviews: Computational Statistics, vol. 2, no. 4, 2010, pp. 433–459.

[11] B. Schölkopf, A. Smola, and K.-R. Müller, "Nonlinear component analysis as a kernel eigenvalue problem," Neural computation, vol. 10, no. 5, 1998, pp. 1299–1319.

[12] X.-w. Chen and J. C. Jeong, "Enhanced recursive feature elimination," in Machine Learning and Applications, 2007. ICMLA 2007. Sixth International Conference on. IEEE, 2007, pp. 429–435.

[13] X. Zhong and D. Enke, "Forecasting daily stock market return using dimensionality reduction," Expert Systems with Applications, vol. 67, 2017, pp. 126–139.

[14] P. C. Molenaar, "A dynamic factor model for the analysis of multivariate time series," Psychometrika, vol. 50, no. 2, 1985, pp. 181–202.

[15] B. Abraham and G. Merola, "Dimensionality reduction approach to multivariate prediction," Computational statistics & data analysis, vol. 48, no. 1, 2005, pp. 5–16.

[16] Y. Sun, J. Li, J. Liu, C. Chow, B. Sun, and R. Wang, "Using causal discovery for feature selection in multivariate numerical time series," Machine Learning, vol. 101, no. 1-3, 2015, pp. 377–395.

[17] C. W. Granger, B.-N. Huangb, and C.-W. Yang, "A bivariate causality between stock prices and exchange rates: evidence from recent asian-flu?" The Quarterly Review of Economics and Finance, vol. 40, no. 3, 2000, pp. 337–354.

[18] L. Kaufman and P. J. Rousseeuw, "Partitioning around medoids (program pam)," Finding groups in data: an introduction to cluster analysis, 1990, pp. 68–125.

[19] W. N. Venables and B. D. Ripley, Modern applied statistics with S-PLUS. Springer Science & Business Media, 2013.

[20] H. Akaike, "A new look at the statistical model identification," IEEE transactions on automatic control, vol. 19, no. 6, 1974, pp. 716–723.

[21] M. Lichman, "UCI machine learning repository," 2013, URL: http://archive.ics.uci.edu/ml [accessed: 2017-02-16].

[22] J. H. Stock and M. W. Watson, "New indexes of coincident and leading economic indicators," NBER macroeconomics annual, vol. 4, 1989, pp. 351–394.

[23] J. S. Armstrong, "Significance tests harm progress in forecasting," International Journal of Forecasting, vol. 23, no. 2, 2007, pp. 321–327.

[24] G. Shmueli et al., "To explain or to predict?" Statistical science, vol. 25, no. 3, 2010, pp. 289–310.

The Absolute Consistency Problem of Graph Schema Mappings with Uniqueness Constraints

Takashi Hayata*, Yasunori Ishihara* and Toru Fujiwara*
*Graduate School of Information Science and Technology
Osaka University, Suita, Japan
Email: {t-hayata, ishihara, fujiwara}@ist.osaka-u.ac.jp

***Abstract*—A schema mapping is a formal representation of the correspondence between source and target data in a data exchange setting. Schema mappings have been extensively studied so far in relational and XML databases. However, in graph databases, they have not received much attention yet. A given schema mapping is said to be absolutely consistent if every source data instance has a corresponding target data instance. Absolute consistency is an important property because it guarantees that data exchange never fails for any source data instance. In this paper, we define schema mappings for graph databases with uniqueness constraints. Our graph databases consist of nodes, edges, and properties, where a property is a key-value pair and gives detailed information to nodes. A uniqueness constraint guarantees the uniqueness of specified properties in the whole graph database, and therefore, is useful for realizing the functionality of primary keys in graph databases. Then, in this paper, we propose five classes of graph schema mappings for which absolute consistency is decidable in polynomial time.**

Keywords–graph database; property; uniqueness constraint; schema mapping; absolute consistency.

I. INTRODUCTION

In recent years, graph-structured data has become pervasive. For example, route information of transportation and communication network, connection of people on social networking services and so on are often cited. These data originally have a graph structure, and it is natural to store and manipulate them on a database while keeping the graph structure. Because of these backgrounds, graph databases have attracted attention in recent years. Graph-structured data has a feature of being flexible. This means that we can flexibly change the graph structure. Figure 1 illustrates flight route map between airports, where airports are represented by nodes. Each node has a unique *node id* (1–6) and a *property* (a key-value pair such as $Airport : ORY$). Figure 2 is a graph which represents direct flight information between countries. We can obtain this graph by integrating nodes whose countries are the same. In this way, you may want to obtain abstract data rather than concrete data. Also, considering big data analysis, it may be possible to discover new features by extracting only data having certain characteristics. Schema mappings are the foundation of such data exchange.

A schema mapping represents the correspondence between source databases and target databases. It is useful for formalizing data exchange between systems with different schemas and schema evolution caused by system change. Schema mappings have been extensively studied in relational databases [1]–[3] and XML databases [3]–[5]. On the other hand, schema mappings for graph databases have not been actively studied yet. Schema mappings of graph databases without properties is discussed in [6]. A study of schema mappings from a relational schema to a graph schema is reported in [7].

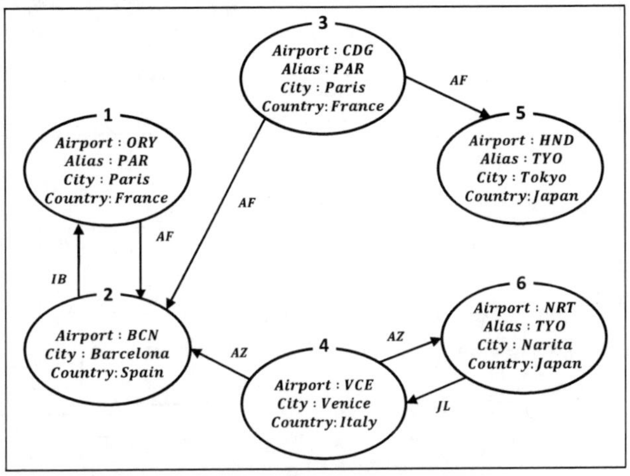

Figure 1. Flight route map between airports.

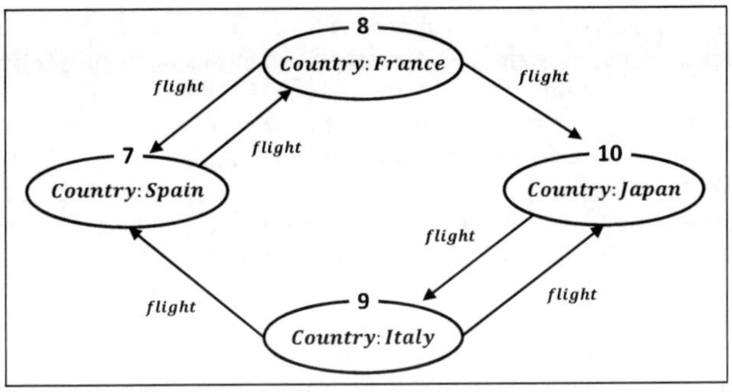

Figure 2. Flight information between countries.

In considering schema mappings, it is important to check the absolute consistency [4] of schema mappings. In XML databases, complexity of the absolute consistency problem has been studied [4], [8]. A schema mapping is absolutely consistent if any source database has a corresponding target database. Absolute consistency guarantees that data exchange based on the schema mapping never fails. Figure 3 illustrates flight information between IATA codes. We can compute this figure by applying a specific schema mapping to Figure 1 (see Example 5 for details). However, if there is a constraint that IATA codes are unique, this mapping does not satisfy the absolute consistency because a source graph in Figure 1 has

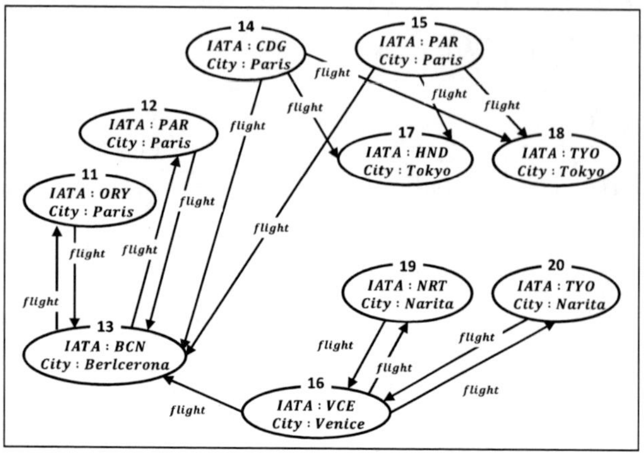

Figure 3. Flight information between IATA codes.

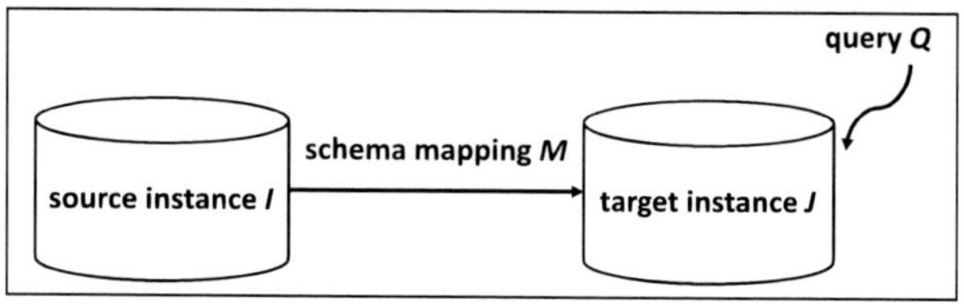

Figure 4. The the general setting of data exchange [3].

not a corresponding target graph.

The purpose of this paper is twofold. The first purpose is to define schema mappings for graph databases with properties. As stated above, the existing study [6] focuses on graph schema mappings without properties. However, properties enrich the expressive power of graph databases. In our study, we target graph databases such that nodes have properties. In addition, we introduce constraints on properties called *uniqueness constraints*, which are adopted by Neo4j [9]. A uniqueness constraint guarantees the uniqueness of a node with the specified property in the whole graph database. Then we define schema mappings for graph databases with properties and uniqueness constraints. The other purpose is to investigate classes of schema mappings for which absolute consistency is tractable. In this paper, we propose three classes whose member is always absolutely consistent. Then we propose two more classes for which absolute consistency is decidable in polynomial time.

II. RELATED WORK

Data exchange is a problem of finding an instance of a target schema, given an instance of a source schema and a specification of the relationship between the source and the target. Such a target instance should correctly represent information from the source instance under the constraints imposed by the target schema, and it should allow one to evaluate queries on the target instance in a way that is semantically consistent with the source data. Figure 4 shows the image of the general setting of data exchange. In this figure, we have fixed source and target schemas, an instance I of the source schema, and a schema mapping M that specifies the relationship between the source and the target schemas. The goal is to construct an instance J of the target schema, based on I and M, and answer queries against the target data in a way consistent with the source data. Such a target instance is called a solution for the given source instance. As can be seen from Figure 4, a schema mapping is an important concept underlying data exchange.

In the relational scenario, schema mappings and data exchange have been studied in much literature (e.g., [1]–[3]). They define schema mappings and address the problem of materializing target instances and the problem of query answering.

In the XML scenario, schema mappings and data exchange have been studied in much literature (e.g., [3]–[5], [8]). Compared to the relational model, the tree model gives more opportunities for expressing structural properties of data even with simple queries based on patterns. On the other hand, schemas impose strong conditions on the structure of source and target instances, entering into complex interactions with source-to-target dependencies. These strong conditions cause consistency problem which is one of the central issues in XML data exchange. In [4], [8], they address the consistency and absolute consistency problems of XML schema mappings. A schema mapping is consistent if some source instance has a corresponding target instance. Also, a schema mapping is absolutely consistent if any source instance has a corresponding target instance. In XML schema mappings, it has been proved that the consistency problem is undecidable if we consider the comparison of data values [3]. Without considering the comparison of data values, it has been proved that the consistency problem is solvable in exponential time [3]. It has been proved that the absolute consistency problem for schema mappings based on downward navigation is decidable in EXPSPACE and NEXPTIME-hard [3], [4]. Some tractability results on consistency and absolute consistency problems between restricted schemas are reported in [8], [10].

In the graph scenario, schema mappings and data exchange have not been actively studied yet. In [6], they define schema mappings for graph data and address some problems of data exchange. Like relational and XML databases, they address the problem of materializing solutions and the problem of query answering. But they focus on graph schema mappings without properties and constraints such as uniqueness constraints, and hence schema mappings are always absolutely consistent in their setting.

Bidirectional transformations refer to a mechanism that maintains consistency through conversion between two sources of information. As one approach to bidirectional transformations, Triple Graph Grammars (TGGs) are well known, which define the correspondence between two different types of models in a declarative way [11]–[13]. A rule in a TGG is a triple of a source graph, a correspondence graph, and a target graph, and by applying rules to an axiom, both models are generated simultaneously. In TGGs, it is easy to define the correspondence between two different types of models, but it is not trivial to find the corresponding target instance when a source instance is given, as considered in data exchange. That is because TGGs grow a source graph, a correspondence graph, and a target graph in parallel, so it is first necessary to find how to apply rules to an axiom to obtain the source instance.

III. Definitions

A. Graph Databases

A *graph schema* S is a tuple (Σ, K), where

- Σ is a finite set of *edge labels*, and
- K is a finite set of *keys*.

Let fix a countable set $\mathcal{O}$ of *values*. A *property* (of a node) is a pair of a key in K and a value in $\mathcal{O}$. A *graph database* G over a graph schema $S = (\Sigma, K)$ is a tuple (N, E, f), where

- N is a finite set of *node ids*,
- $E \subseteq N \times \Sigma \times N$ is a finite set of *labeled edges*, and
- $f : N \times K \to \mathcal{O}$ is a partial function which binds node ids and properties.

When $f(n, k)$ is undefined, it is interpreted that node n does not have a property with key k, and we write $f(n, k) = \perp$. In this paper, it is assumed that edges have no properties.

Example 1: Let fix $\mathcal{O}$ as $\{ORY, BCN, CDG, VCE, HND, NRT, PAR, TYO, Paris, Barcelona, Venice, Tokyo, Narita, France, Spain, Italy, Japan\}$. Consider a graph schema $S = (\Sigma, K)$, where $\Sigma = \{IB, AF, AZ, JL\}$ and $K = \{Airport, Alias, City, Country\}$. Figure 1 illustrates a graph database $G = (N, E, f)$ over S, where

- $N = \{1, 2, 3, 4, 5, 6\}$,
- $E = \{(1, AF, 2), (2, IB, 1), (3, AF, 2), (3, AF, 5), (4, AZ, 2), (4, AZ, 6), (6, JL, 4)\}$, and
- $f(1, Airport) = ORY$, $f(1, Alias) = PAR$, $f(1, City) = Paris$, $f(1, Country) = France$, $f(2, Airport) = BCN$, $f(2, City) = Barcelona$, $f(2, Country) = Spain$, $f(3, Airport) = CDG$, $f(3, Alias) = PAR$, $f(3, City) = Paris$, $f(3, Country) = France$, and so on.

B. Uniqueness Constraitnts

A uniqueness constraint is specified as a set of keys and ensures that properties of the specified keys are unique in a graph database. In other words, there should not be different nodes with the same value for the specified keys.

Definition 1 (Uniqueness Constraints): A *uniqueness constraint* U over a graph schema $S = (\Sigma, K)$ is a subset of K. A graph database $G = (N, E, f)$ *satisfies* U if the following condition holds:

$$\forall n, n' \in N, \forall k \in U,$$
$$(f(n,k) \neq \perp) \wedge (f(n',k) \neq \perp) \wedge (f(n,k) = f(n',k))$$
$$\Rightarrow n = n'.$$

Example 2: The graph database shown in Figure 3 does not satisfy $U = \{IATA\}$ because $f(12, IATA) = f(15, IATA)$ and $f(18, IATA) = f(20, IATA)$. On the other hand, the graph database shown in Figure 2 satisfies $U = \{Country\}$ because for each value $o \in \mathcal{O}$, there is at most one node n such that $f(n, Country) = o$.

C. Graph Patterns

Graph patterns represent a part of a graph database and can be used as queries for a given graph database. We also use graph patterns for describing mapping rules in schema mappings for graph databases.

Let fix a countable set $\mathcal{X}$ of variables representing values. A *graph pattern* π over a graph schema $S = (\Sigma, K)$ is a tuple (θ, μ, λ), where

- θ is a finite set of *node variables*,
- $\mu \subseteq \theta \times \text{REG}(\Sigma) \times \theta$ is a finite set of *path patterns*, where REG(Σ) is the set of regular expressions over Σ, and
- $\lambda \subseteq \{v.k == x \mid v \in \theta, k \in K, x \in \mathcal{X}\}$ is a finite set of *equalities* such that if two equalities $(v.k == x)$ and $(v.k == y)$ are in λ, then x and y are the same variable.

We assume that no node variables are shared by different graph patterns, although variables in $\mathcal{X}$ are shared in general, as in mapping rules defined later.

We define the semantics of a graph pattern π in terms of homomorphisms. Let $g : \mathcal{X} \to \mathcal{O}$ be a mapping that assigns a value to each variable. Let $G = (N, E, f)$ be a graph database. A graph pattern $\pi = (\theta, \mu, \lambda)$ is *modeled* by (G, h, g) if homomorphism $h : \pi \to G$ satisfies the following conditions:

1) for each node variable $v \in \theta$, $h(v) \in N$,
2) for each path pattern $(v, L, u) \in \mu$, there is a path from $h(v)$ to $h(u)$ in G such that the edge label sequence along the path matches the regular expression L, and
3) for each equality $(v.k == x) \in \lambda$, $f(h(v), k) = g(x)$.

We write $(G, h, g) \models \pi$ if π is modeled by (G, h, g). The semantics of π under S and g is defined as follows:

$$[[\pi]]_{S,g} = \{G \text{ over } S \mid (G, h, g) \models \pi \text{ for some } h\}.$$

Example 3: Let fix $\mathcal{X}$ as $\{x\}$ and $\mathcal{O}$ as $\{A, B\}$. Let $V = \{s, t, u, v\}$ be a finite set of node variables. Consider a graph schema $S = (\Sigma, K)$, where $\Sigma = \{a, b\}$ and $K = \{k\}$. Figure 5 illustrates a graph pattern $\pi = (\theta, \mu, \lambda)$ over S, where

- $\theta = \{s, t, u, v\}$,
- $\mu = \{(s, a, t), (u, b, v)\}$, and
- $\lambda = \{(s.k == x), (t.k == x)\}$.

Figure 6 illustrates a graph database $G = (N, E, f)$ over S, where

- $N = \{1, 2, 3, 4\}$,
- $E = \{(1, a, 2), (3, a, 4), (3, b, 1), (2, c, 4)\}$, and
- $f(1, k) = A$, $f(2, k) = A$, $f(3, k) = A$, and $f(4, k) = B$.

As shown in Figure 7, a homomorphism h such that $(G, h, g) \models \pi$ maps s into 1, t into 2, u into 3, and v into 1. We can confirm that the graph pattern π represents a part of the graph database G.

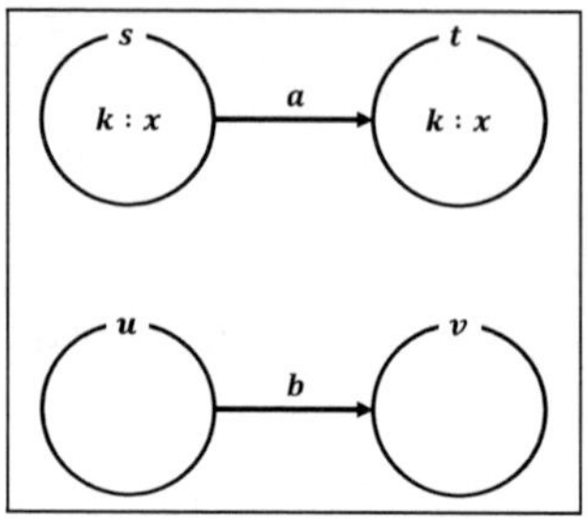

Figure 5. A graph pattern π.

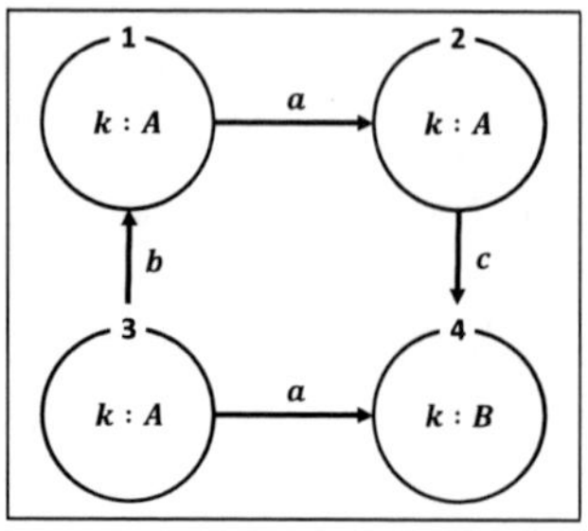

Figure 6. A graph database G.

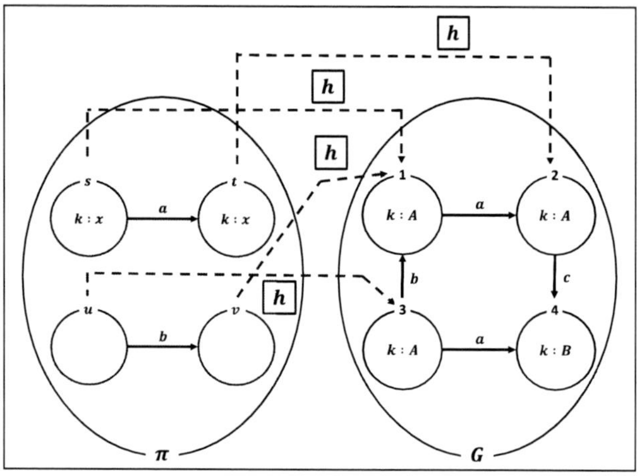

Figure 7. A homomorphism $h : \pi \to G$.

D. Schema Mappings

Schema mappings represent the correspondence between source databases and target databases. We define schema mappings for graph databases with properties from now.

Let S_S be a source graph schema and S_T a target graph schema. Let U_S and U_T be uniqueness constraints over S_S and S_T, respectively. A schema mapping M from S_S to S_T is a tuple $((S_S, U_S), (S_T, U_T), \Delta)$, where Δ is a finite set of *mapping rules* of the form $\pi_S \to \pi_T$. Here, $\pi_S = (\theta_S, \mu_S, \lambda_S)$ and $\pi_T = (\theta_T, \mu_T, \lambda_T)$ are graph patterns over S_S and S_T, respectively. Each λ_S must be *linear* with respect to variables in $\mathcal{X}$, that is, each variable in $\mathcal{X}$ appears at most once in λ_S.

Definition 2 (Solutions): Let $M = ((S_S, U_S), (S_T, U_T), \Delta)$ be a schema mapping. Let G_S be a graph database over S_S satisfying U_S, and G_T a graph database over S_T satisfying U_T. A pair (G_S, G_T) *satisfies* M if the following condition holds: For each $(\pi_S \to \pi_T) \in \Delta$ and for any $g_S : \mathcal{X} \to \mathcal{O}$, there exists $g_T : \mathcal{X} \to \mathcal{O}$ such that

1) $g_S(x) = g_T(x)$ for each variable $x \in \mathcal{X}$ appearing in both π_S and π_T; and
2) if $G_S \in [[\pi_S]]_{S_S, g_S}$, then $G_T \in [[\pi_T]]_{S_T, g_T}$.

If a pair (G_S, G_T) satisfies M, we write $(G_S, G_T) \models M$, and G_T is called a *solution* for G_S under M. Let $\mathrm{Sol}_M(G_S)$ denote the set of solutions for G_S under M.

Without loss of generality, we assume that no variables in $\mathcal{X}$ are shared by different mapping rules.

Example 4: Let $S_S = (\Sigma_S, K_S)$ and $S_T = (\Sigma_T, K_T)$ be graph schemas such that

- $\Sigma_S = \{IB, AF, AZ, JL\}$,
- $K_S = \{Airport, Alias, City, Country\}$,
- $\Sigma_T = \{flight\}$, and
- $K_T = \{Country\}$.

Also, let

- $U_S = \{Airport\}$,
- $U_T = \{Country\}$, and
- $\Delta = \{\pi_S \to \pi_T\}$,

where $\pi_S = (\theta_S, \mu_S, \lambda_S)$ and $\pi_T = (\theta_T, \mu_T, \lambda_T)$ are graph patterns such that

- $\theta_S = \{v_1, v_2\}$,
- $\mu_S = \{(v_1, (IB|AF|AZ|JL), v_2)\}$,
- $\lambda_S = \{(v_1.Country == x), (v_2.Country == y)\}$,
- $\theta_T = \{u_1, u_2\}$,
- $\mu_T = \{(u_1, flight, u_2)\}$, and
- $\lambda_T = \{(u_1.Country == x), (u_2.Country == y)\}$.

Then, the graph database in Figure 2 is a solution for that in Figure 1 under $M = ((S_S, U_S), (S_T, U_T), \Delta)$.

Definition 3 (Absolute Consistency): A schema mapping $M = ((S_S, U_S), (S_T, U_T), \Delta)$ is *absolutely consistent* if $\mathrm{Sol}_M(G_S) \neq \emptyset$ for every graph database G_S over S_S satisfying U_S.

Example 5: Let $M = ((S_S, U_S), (S_T, U_T), \Delta)$ be a schema mapping, where $S_S = (\Sigma_S, K_S)$ and $S_T = (\Sigma_T, K_T)$ be graph schemas such that

- $\Sigma_S = \{IB, AF, AL, JL\}$,
- $K_S = \{Airport, Alias, City, Country\}$,
- $\Sigma_T = \{flight\}$, and
- $K_T = \{IATA, City\}$.

Also, let

- $U_S = \{Airport\}$,
- $U_T = \{IATA\}$, and
- $\Delta = \{\pi_{S_1} \to \pi_{T_1}, \pi_{S_2} \to \pi_{T_2}, \pi_{S_3} \to \pi_{T_3}, \pi_{S_4} \to \pi_{T_4}\}$,

where $\pi_{S_1} = (\theta_{S_1}, \mu_{S_1}, \lambda_{S_1})$, $\pi_{T_1} = (\theta_{T_1}, \mu_{T_1}, \lambda_{T_1})$, $\pi_{S_2} = (\theta_{S_2}, \mu_{S_2}, \lambda_{S_2})$, $\pi_{T_2} = (\theta_{T_2}, \mu_{T_2}, \lambda_{T_2})$, $\pi_{S_3} = (\theta_{S_3}, \mu_{S_3}, \lambda_{S_3})$, $\pi_{T_3} = (\theta_{T_3}, \mu_{T_3}, \lambda_{T_3})$, $\pi_{S_4} = (\theta_{S_4}, \mu_{S_4}, \lambda_{S_4})$, and $\pi_{T_4} = (\theta_{T_4}, \mu_{T_4}, \lambda_{T_4})$ are graph patterns such that

- $\theta_{S_1} = \{u_1, u_2\}$,
- $\mu_{S_1} = \{(u_1, (IB|AF|AZ|JL), u_2)\}$,
- $\lambda_{S_1} = \{(u_1.City == x_1), (u_1.Airport == y_1), (u_2.City == z_1), (u_2.Airport == w_1)\}$,
- $\theta_{T_1} = \{v_1, v_2\}$,
- $\mu_{T_1} = \{(v_1, flight, v_2)\}$,
- $\lambda_{T_1} = \{(v_1.City == x_1), (v_1.IATA == y_1), (v_2.City == z_1), (v_2.IATA == w_1)\}$,
- $\theta_{S_2} = \{u_3, u_4\}$,
- $\mu_{S_2} = \{(u_3, (IB|AF|AZ|JL), u_4)\}$,

- $\lambda_{S_2} = \{(u_3.City == x_2), (u_3.Airport == y_2), (u_4.City == z_2), (u_4.Alias == w_2)\}$,
- $\theta_{T_2} = \{v_3, v_4\}$,
- $\mu_{T_2} = \{(v_3, flight, v_4)\}$,
- $\lambda_{T_2} = \{(v_3.City == x_2), (v_3.IATA == y_2), (v_4.City == z_2), (v_4.IATA == w_2)\}$,
- $\theta_{S_3} = \{u_5, u_6\}$,
- $\mu_{S_3} = \{(u_5, (IB|AF|AZ|JL), u_6)\}$,
- $\lambda_{S_3} = \{(u_5.City == x_3), (u_5.Alias == y_3), (u_6.City == z_3), (u_6.Airport == w_3)\}$,
- $\theta_{T_3} = \{v_5, v_6\}$,
- $\mu_{T_3} = \{(v_5, flight, v_6)\}$,
- $\lambda_{T_3} = \{(v_5.City == x_3), (v_5.IATA == y_3), (v_6.City == z_3), (v_6.IATA == w_3)\}$,
- $\theta_{S_4} = \{u_7, u_8\}$,
- $\mu_{S_4} = \{(u_7, (IB|AF|AZ|JL), u_8)\}$,
- $\lambda_{S_4} = \{(u_7.City == x_4), (u_7.Alias == y_4), (u_8.City == z_4), (u_8.Alias == w_4)\}$,
- $\theta_{T_4} = \{v_7, v_8\}$,
- $\mu_{T_4} = \{(v_7, flight, v_8)\}$, and
- $\lambda_{T_4} = \{(v_7.City == x_4), (v_7.IATA == y_4), (v_8.City == z_4), (v_8.IATA == w_4)\}$.

Given a graph in Figure 1 as a source instance and this schema mapping, we can compute a graph in Figure 3, if we do not consider U_T. However, taking into account U_T, the graph in Figure 3 does not satisfy U_T because $f(18, IATA) = f(20, IATA)$. That is, this schema mapping M is not absolutely consistent.

The size $|M|$ of a schema mapping $M = ((S_S, U_S), (S_T, U_T), \Delta)$ is the sum of the sizes of S_S, U_S, S_T, U_T, and Δ. The size of a schema $S = (\Sigma, K)$ is the sum of the numbers of elements in Σ and K. The size of a uniqueness constraint U is the number of elements in U. The size of Δ is the sum of the sizes of graph patterns appearing in Δ. The size of a graph pattern $\pi = (\theta, \mu, \lambda)$ is the sum of the numbers of elements in θ, μ, and λ.

IV. Tractable Classes of Schema Mappings for Absolute Consistency

Let $M = ((S_S, U_S), (S_T, U_T), \Delta)$ be a schema mapping, where $S_S = (\Sigma_S, K_S)$ and $S_T = (\Sigma_T, K_T)$. In this section, we show that the absolute consistency of M is decidable in polynomial time if M belongs to one of the following five classes:

1) K_S is empty;
2) U_T is empty;
3) K_T is a singleton;
4) U_S is empty; and
5) Δ is a singleton and the mapping rule is projecting, where $\pi_S \to \pi_T$ is *projecting* if the set of variables for values appearing in π_T is a subset of those appearing in π_S.

For example, the schema mapping shown in Example 4 belongs to not only the third class but also the fifth class because Δ is a singleton and the set $\{x, y\}$ of variables appearing in π_T is the same as that in π_S.

A. Three Easy Classes

In this section, we show that M is always absolutely consistent if M belongs to one of the first three classes. First, we show the following lemma, which states the existence of a graph database G_0 that matches any graph pattern.

Lemma 1: Let $S = (\Sigma, K)$ be a graph schema and U be a uniqueness constraint over S. There is a graph database G_0 over S satisfying U such that for any graph pattern π over S, there is $g : \mathcal{X} \to \mathcal{O}$ such that $G_0 \in [[\pi]]_{S,g}$.

Proof: Define $G_0 = (N_0, E_0, f_0)$ as follows:

- $N_0 = \{n\}$,
- $E_0 = \{(n, a, n) \mid a \in \Sigma\}$, and
- $f_0(n, k)$ is the same value for all $k \in K$.

It is easy to see that G_0 satisfies the lemma. ■

Theorem 1: M is absolutely consistent if K_S is empty.

Proof: We show that G_0 introduced in the proof of Lemma 1 is a solution for any G_S over S. Suppose that $G_S \in [[\pi_S]]_{S_S,g_S}$ for some $(\pi_S \to \pi_T) \in \Delta$ and $g_S : \mathcal{X} \to \mathcal{O}$. Since K_S is empty, λ_S is also empty, and hence π_S has no variable in $\mathcal{X}$. Therefore, the first condition of Definition 2 holds for any $g_T : \mathcal{X} \to \mathcal{O}$. By Lemma 1, we have $G_0 \in [[\pi_T]]_{S_T,g}$ for some g. ■

The next lemma says that each graph pattern is matched by a graph database with the "same shape."

Lemma 2: Let $S = (\Sigma, K)$ be a graph schema and $\pi = (\theta, \mu, \lambda)$ be a graph pattern over S. For any $g : \mathcal{X} \to \mathcal{O}$, $[[\pi]]_{S,g}$ is not empty.

Proof: Consider the following graph database $G_\pi = (N_\pi, E_\pi, f_\pi)$:

- N_π contains θ, where node variables are regarded as node ids,
- for each $(v_0, L, v_n) \in \mu$, E_π contains $(v_0, a_1, v_1), \ldots, (v_{n-1}, a_n, v_n)$ such that $a_1 \cdots a_n$ matches L and $v_1, \ldots, v_{n-1}$ are not in θ, and
- $f_\pi(v, k) = x$ for each $(v.k == x) \in \lambda$, where variable x is regarded as a value.

It is easy to see that such G_π is well defined and $G_\pi \in [[\pi]]_{S,id}$, where $id(x) = x$ for every variable x.

Now, consider a graph database $G_{\pi,g}$ obtained by replacing each value x in G_π with $g(x)$. Then, $G_{\pi,g} \in [[\pi]]_{S,g}$. ■

Theorem 2: M is absolutely consistent if U_T is empty.

Proof: Let G_S be a source graph database over S_S satisfying U_S. Consider a target graph database G_T over S_T that contains G_{π_T,g_S} as its subgraph for all $g_S : \mathcal{X} \to \mathcal{O}$ such that $G_S \in [[\pi_S]]_{S_S,g_S}$ for some $(\pi_S \to \pi_T) \in \Delta$, where G_{π_T,g_S} is the same graph database as in the proof of Lemma 2. Such G_T always exists since U_T is empty. Also, G_T is a solution for G_S because $G_{\pi_T,g_S} \in [[\pi_T]]_{S_T,g_S}$. ■

Theorem 3: M is absolutely consistent if K_T is a singleton.

Proof: Consider again the target graph database G_T in the proof of Theorem 2. Since $U_T \subseteq K_T$, we have $U_T = \emptyset$ or $U_T = K_T$. In either case, G_T satisfies U_T. Actually, if U_T and K_T are the same singleton sets, each node of G_T has at most one property, and the nodes with the same property can be an identical node. ■

B. No Uniqueness Constraints for Source Databases

Now, we consider the case where $U_S = \emptyset$. In this case, the variables appearing in the graph patterns for source databases can have independent, arbitrary values. Hence, we can statically analyze M based on abstract interpretation, where the variable names represent abstract values.

Let X_S and X_T be the sets of variables for values appearing in π_S and π_T, respectively, for some mapping rule $(\pi_S \to \pi_T) \in \Delta$. Let $X = X_S \cup X_T$. Define

$$\Lambda_T = \bigcup_{(\pi_S \to (\theta_T, \mu_T, \lambda_T)) \in \Delta} \lambda_T.$$

Define $\sim$ as the least equivalence relation on X satisfying the following condition: $x \sim y$ if $v.k == x$ and $v.k' == y$ are in Λ_T for some $k \in U_T$, $k' \in K_T$, and $z \in X_S$ such that $x \sim z$.

Roughly speaking, the condition in the following theorem says that if a target node has a key k in U_T and the value of k is dependent on a value in the source database, then all the other keys of the node must be dependent on the same value.

Theorem 4: $M = ((S_S, \emptyset), (S_T, U_T), \Delta)$ is absolutely consistent if and only if there are no distinct variables x, $y \in X_S$ such that $x \sim y$.

Proof: (Only if part.) Suppose that $x \sim y$ for some distinct variables x, $y \in X_S$. It can be shown that $(v.k == z)$ and $(v.k' == y)$ in Λ_T such that $x \sim z$ and $k \in U_T$.

For the simplest case, let us consider the case where $(v.k == x)$ and $(v.k' == y)$ in Λ_T for some $k \in U_T$. Consider two mappings g_1 and g_2 such that $g_1(x) = g_2(x)$ but $g_1(y) \neq g_2(y)$. There is a source database G_S such that $G_S \in [[\pi_S]]_{S_S, g_1}$ and $G_S \in [[\pi_S]]_{S_S, g_2}$ because the uniqueness constraints for source databases is empty. Now, a solution $G_T = (N_T, E_T, f_T)$ for G_S must satisfy the following conditions:

- G_T has a node n_1 such that $f_T(n_1, k) = g_1(x)$ and $f_T(n_1, k') = g_1(y)$; and
- G_T has a node n_2 such that $f_T(n_2, k) = g_2(x)$ and $f_T(n_2, k') = g_2(y)$.

Since $k \in U_T$, n_1 and n_2 must be the same node, but that contradicts the assumption that $g_1(y) \neq g_2(y)$.

The general cases can be shown in a similar way.

(If part.) Let G_S be a source graph database over S_S. Let $G_T = (N_T, E_T, f_T)$ be a target graph database containing all $G_{\pi_T, g_{\pi_S, g_S}}$ defined below, such that $G_S \in [[\pi_S]]_{S_S, g_S}$ for some $(\pi_S \to \pi_T) \in \Delta$ and $g_S : X_S \to \mathcal{O}$. We will show that G_T is a solution for G_S and U_T can be satisfied by G_T.

First, we define $G_{\pi_T, g_{\pi_S, g_S}}$. Suppose that $G_S \in [[\pi_S]]_{S_S, g_S}$ for some $(\pi_S \to \pi_T) \in \Delta$ and $g_S : X_S \to \mathcal{O}$. For each of such pairs of π_S and g_S, we choose $g_{\pi_S, g_S} : X_T \to \mathcal{O}$ so that

$$g_{\pi_S, g_S}(x) = \begin{cases} g_S(y) & \text{if } x \sim y \text{ for some } y \in X_S, \\ o_{\pi_S, g_S, x} & \text{otherwise,} \end{cases}$$

where $o_{\pi_S, g_S, x}$ is a unique, distinct value in $\mathcal{O}$ determined by π_S, g_S, and x. g_{π_S, g_S} is well defined because each equivalence class derived by $\sim$ has at most one variable in X_S. Now, $G_{\pi_T, g_{\pi_S, g_S}} \in [[\pi_T]]_{S_T, g_{\pi_S, g_S}}$ is the graph database introduced in the proof of Lemma 2.

It is obvious that G_T is a solution for G_S because G_T contains all $G_{\pi_T, g_{\pi_S, g_S}} \in [[\pi_T]]_{S_T, g_{\pi_S, g_S}}$. Let $n \in N_T$ be a node id of some $G_{\pi_T, g_{\pi_S, g_S}}$. Suppose that $f_T(n, k) = o$ for some key $k \in U_T$ and value $o \in \mathcal{O}$. There must be an equality $v.k == x$ in π_T. We consider the following two cases:

1) If $x \sim y$ for some $y \in X_S$, then by the definitions of $\sim$ and g_{π_S, g_S}, we have $f_T(n, k') = o$ for any $k' \in K_T$ such that $f_T(n, k')$ is defined. Therefore, all such nodes $n \in N_T$ with $f_T(n, k) = o$ can be an identical node.
2) If there is no $y \in X_S$ such that $x \sim y$, then o must be a unique value in G_T, hence the existence of n does not violate U_T.

In summary, U_T can be satisfied by G_T. ■

The equivalence relation $\sim$ can be computed in $O(|M|^3)$ time. Hence we have the following theorem:

Theorem 5: The absolute consistency of M is decidable in polynomial time if U_S is empty.

C. A Single Projecting Rule

Now, we consider the case where $\Delta = \{\pi_S \to \pi_T\}$ and $\pi_S \to \pi_T$ is projecting. Let X be the set of variables for values appearing in π_S. Since U_S is not empty, the values of the variables in X are not independent. For example, suppose that π_S has the following equalities: $v.k == x$, $u.k == y$, $v.k' == z$, and $u.k' == w$. If $k \in U_S$, equality between x and y causes equality between z and w. To capture this phenomenon, below we introduce a function $\mathcal{E}_{\pi_S, U_S}(EQ)$ which returns, for a given set of equalities on X, all the resultant equalities caused by π and U.

Formally, let $\pi = (\theta, \mu, \lambda)$ be a graph pattern with variables in X, and $U \subseteq K$ be a uniqueness constraint. For $EQ \subseteq X \times X$, define $\mathcal{E}_{\pi,U}(EQ) \subseteq X \times X$ as the least equivalence relation such that

1) $EQ \subseteq \mathcal{E}_{\pi,U}(EQ)$, and
2) for any pair $(x, y) \in \mathcal{E}_{\pi,U}(EQ)$ and any node variables v, $u \in \theta$, if $(v.k == x), (u.k == y) \in \lambda$ for some key $k \in U$, then $(z, w) \in \mathcal{E}_{\pi,U}(EQ)$ for every $z, w \in X$ such that $(v.k' == z), (u.k' == w) \in \lambda$ for some $k' \in K$.

Let EQ_g denote the equivalence relation on variables induced by $g : X \to \mathcal{O}$, i.e., $(x, y) \in EQ_g$ if and only if $g(x) = g(y)$. The following two lemmas say that EQ_g is a fixpoint of $\mathcal{E}_{\pi,U}$ if and only if there are G, h, and g such that $(G, h, g) \models \pi$ and G satisfies U.

Lemma 3: Suppose that $(G, h, g) \models \pi$ and G satisfies a uniqueness constraint U. Then, $EQ_g = \mathcal{E}_{\pi,U}(EQ_g)$.

Proof: Since $EQ_g \subseteq \mathcal{E}_{\pi,U}(EQ_g)$ by definition, it suffices to show that $g(z) = g(w)$ for any pair $(z, w) \in \mathcal{E}_{\pi,U}(EQ_g)$. Consider the shortest proof $P_{(z,w)}$ of the membership of an arbitrary $(z, w) \in \mathcal{E}_{\pi,U}(EQ_g)$, i.e., an application sequence of reflexivity, symmetry, transitivity, and the two rules of the definition of $\mathcal{E}_{\pi,U}$. We show $g(z) = g(w)$ by the induction on the length of $P_{(z,w)}$.

For the basis, there are two cases. If (z, w) is in $\mathcal{E}_{\pi,U}(EQ_g)$ by reflexivity, then z and w are the same variable. If (z, w) is in $\mathcal{E}_{\pi,U}(EQ_g)$ by the first rule of the definition of $\mathcal{E}_{\pi,U}$, then (z, w) must be in EQ_g. In both cases, we have $g(z) = g(w)$.

For the induction step, there are three cases. If (z, w) is in $\mathcal{E}_{\pi,U}(EQ_g)$ by symmetry, we must already have $(w, z) \in$

$\mathcal{E}_{\pi,U}(EQ_g)$. Then, we have $g(z) = g(w)$ by the inductive hypothesis. If (z, w) is in $\mathcal{E}_{\pi,U}(EQ_g)$ by transitivity, we can show that $g(z) = g(w)$ in a similar way to the symmetry case. Now, suppose that (z, w) is in $\mathcal{E}_{\pi,U}(EQ_g)$ by the second rule of the definition of $\mathcal{E}_{\pi,U}$. Then, there are some pair $(x, y) \in \mathcal{E}_{\pi,U}(EQ_g)$, node variables $v, u \in \theta$, and keys $k \in U$ and $k' \in K$ such that $(v.k == x)$, $(u.k == y)$, $(v.k' == z)$, $(u.k' == w) \in \lambda$. Since $(G, h, g) \models \pi$, we have $f(h(v), k) = g(x)$, $f(h(u), k) = g(y)$, $f(h(v), k') = g(z)$, and $f(h(u), k') = g(w)$, where $G = (N, E, f)$. It holds that $g(x) = g(y)$ by the inductive hypothesis. Since G satisfies uniqueness constraint U and U contains k, we have $h(v) = h(u)$. Hence, $g(z) = f(h(v), k') = f(h(u), k') = g(w)$. ■

Lemma 4: Suppose that $EQ = \mathcal{E}_{\pi,U}(EQ)$. Then, there are G, h, and g such that G satisfies the uniqueness constraint U, $(G, h, g) \models \pi$, and $EQ = EQ_g$.

Proof: Suppose that $EQ = \mathcal{E}_{\pi,U}(EQ)$, where $\pi = (\theta, \mu, \lambda)$. Choose an arbitrary $g : X \to \mathcal{O}$ such that $EQ_g = EQ$.

Let θ/EQ be the finest equivalence classes of node variables such that if there are $(x, y) \in EQ$ and $k \in U$ such that $(v.k == x), (u.k == y) \in \lambda$, then v and u are in the same equivalence class in θ/EQ. Let $[v]$ denote the equivalence class which v belongs to.

Similarly to G_π in the proof of Lemma 2, consider a graph database $G = (N, E, f)$ such that

- N contains θ/EQ, where the equivalence classes are regarded as node ids,
- for each $(v_0, L, v_k) \in \mu$, E contains (n_0, a_1, n_1),..., (n_{k-1}, a_k, n_k) such that $a_1 \cdots a_k$ matches L, $n_0 = [v_0]$, $n_k = [v_k]$, and v_1,..., v_{k-1} are not in θ/EQ, and
- $f([v], k') = g(x)$ for each $(v.k' == x) \in \lambda$.

To see that G is well defined, consider the shortest proof $P_{(v,u)}$ of that $[v] = [u]$, i.e., an application sequence of reflexivity, symmetry, transitivity, and the definition of θ/EQ. We show $f([v], k') = f([u], k')$ for all $k' \in K$ by the induction on the length of $P_{(v,u)}$.

For the basis, there are two cases. If $[v] = [u]$ by reflexivity, then $v = u$, and hence $f([v], k') = f([u], k')$. If $[v] = [u]$ by the definition of θ/EQ, there are $(x, y) \in EQ$ and $k \in U$ such that $(v.k == x), (u.k == y) \in \lambda$. Since EQ is a fixpoint of $\mathcal{E}_{\pi,U}$, we have $(z, w) \in EQ$ for every $z, w \in X$ such that $(v.k' == z), (u.k' == w) \in \lambda$, by the second rule of the definition of $\mathcal{E}_{\pi,U}$. Hence, $f([v], k') = g(z) = g(w) = f([u], k')$.

The induction step is trivial. If $[v] = [u]$ by symmetry, then we have $[u] = [v]$, and by the inductive hypothesis, $f([u], k') = f([v], k')$ for all $k' \in K$. The case of transitivity can be shown in a similar way.

Now, we have to show that G satisfies U. Assume contrarily that G does not satisfy U. There would be $v, u \in \theta$ and $k \in U$ such that $[v] \neq [u]$ and $f([v], k) = f([u], k)$. Hence, there would be $v' \in [v]$, $u' \in [u]$, x, $y \in X$ such that $(v'.k == x), (u'.k == y) \in \lambda$ and $(x, y) \in EQ$. However, by the definition of θ/EQ, we must have $[v'] = [u']$. This is a contradiction. ■

Theorem 6: Let $M = ((S_S, U_S), (S_T, U_T), \{\pi_S \to \pi_T\})$ be a schema mapping such that $\pi_S \to \pi_T$ is projecting. M is absolutely consistent if and only if every fixpoint of $\mathcal{E}_{\pi_S,U_S}$ is also a fixpoint of $\mathcal{E}_{\pi_T,U_T}$.

Proof: Immediate from Lemmas 3 and 4 since $\pi_S \to \pi_T$ is projecting. ■

In what follows, we show that the condition in Theorem 6 can be checked in polynomial time. The condition seems to require the computation of $\mathcal{E}_{\pi_S,U_S}$ and $\mathcal{E}_{\pi_T,U_T}$ for exponentially many EQs. Surprisingly, by the following two lemmas, such computation can be reduced to the computation for only EQs that are singletons.

Lemma 5: The followings are equivalent:

1) Every fixpoint of $\mathcal{E}_{\pi_S,U_S}$ is also a fixpoint of $\mathcal{E}_{\pi_T,U_T}$.
2) $\mathcal{E}_{\pi_T,U_T}(EQ) \subseteq \mathcal{E}_{\pi_S,U_S}(EQ)$ for each subset $EQ \subseteq X \times X$.

Proof: (1 $\Rightarrow$ 2) Let $EQ \subseteq X \times X$. Let $EQ_S = \mathcal{E}_{\pi_S,U_S}(EQ)$ and $EQ_T = \mathcal{E}_{\pi_T,U_T}(EQ)$. Since EQ_S is a fixpoint of $\mathcal{E}_{\pi_S,U_S}$, it is also a fixpoint of $\mathcal{E}_{\pi_T,U_T}$, i.e., $EQ_S = \mathcal{E}_{\pi_T,U_T}(EQ_S)$. Since EQ is a subset of EQ_S, we have $EQ_T = \mathcal{E}_{\pi_T,U_T}(EQ) \subseteq \mathcal{E}_{\pi_T,U_T}(EQ_S) = EQ_S$.

(2 $\Rightarrow$ 1) Let EQ be a fixpoint of $\mathcal{E}_{\pi_S,U_S}$. Then, $\mathcal{E}_{\pi_T,U_T}(EQ) \subseteq \mathcal{E}_{\pi_S,U_S}(EQ) = EQ$. On the other hand, by the definition of $\mathcal{E}_{\pi_T,U_T}(EQ)$, we have $EQ \subseteq \mathcal{E}_{\pi_T,U_T}(EQ)$. Hence $EQ = \mathcal{E}_{\pi_T,U_T}(EQ)$. ■

Lemma 6: The followings are equivalent:

1) $\mathcal{E}_{\pi_T,U_T}(EQ) \subseteq \mathcal{E}_{\pi_S,U_S}(EQ)$ for each subset $EQ \subseteq X \times X$.
2) $\mathcal{E}_{\pi_T,U_T}(\{(x, y)\}) \subseteq \mathcal{E}_{\pi_S,U_S}(\{(x, y)\})$ for each pair $(x, y) \in X \times X$.

Proof: Let $EQ_S = \mathcal{E}_{\pi_S,U_S}(EQ)$ and $EQ_T = \mathcal{E}_{\pi_T,U_T}(EQ)$. The part (1 $\Rightarrow$ 2) is obvious. To show the part (2 $\Rightarrow$ 1), consider the shortest proof $P_{(z,w)}$ of the membership of an arbitrary (z, w) in EQ_T, i.e., an application sequence of reflexivity, symmetry, transitivity, and the two rules of the definition of $\mathcal{E}_{\pi,U}$. We show $(z, w) \in EQ_S$ by the induction on the length of $P_{(z,w)}$.

For the basis, there are two cases. If (z, w) is in EQ_T by reflexivity, then it is also in EQ_S by reflexivity. If (z, w) is in EQ_T by the first rule of the definition of $\mathcal{E}_{\pi,U}$, then (z, w) must be in EQ and hence it is also in EQ_S by the same rule.

For the induction step, there are three cases. If (z, w) is in EQ_T by symmetry, we must already have $(w, z) \in EQ_T$. Then, we have $(w, z) \in EQ_S$ by the inductive hypothesis, and hence, $(z, w) \in EQ_S$. If (z, w) is in EQ_T by transitivity, we can show that $(z, w) \in EQ_S$ in a similar way to the symmetry case. Now, suppose that (z, w) is in EQ_T by the second rule of the definition of $\mathcal{E}_{\pi,U}$. Then, we have $(z, w) \in \mathcal{E}_{\pi_T,U_T}(\{(x, y)\})$. By the assumption that $\mathcal{E}_{\pi_T,U_T}(\{(x, y)\}) \subseteq \mathcal{E}_{\pi_S,U_S}(\{(x, y)\})$, (z, w) is also in $\mathcal{E}_{\pi_S,U_S}(\{(x, y)\})$. Hence, $(z, w) \in EQ_S$ since $(x, y) \in EQ_S$ by the inductive hypothesis. ■

$\mathcal{E}_{\pi,U}(\{(x, y)\})$ can be computed in $O(|M|^6)$ time (by a very naive algorithm). So, the second condition of Lemma 6 can be checked in $O(|M|^8)$ time.

Theorem 7: The absolute consistency of M is decidable in polynomial time if $\Delta = \{\pi_S \to \pi_T\}$ is a singleton and $\pi_S \to \pi_T$ is projecting.

V. Conclusion

In this paper, we have defined schema mappings for graph databases with properties. In considering graph databases with properties, we have introduced uniqueness constraints, which are constraints on properties. Then, we have proposed five classes of schema mappings for which absolute consistency is decidable in polynomial time.

There still are remaining tasks. We are going to examine the complexity of the absolute consistency problem for schema mappings not belonging to the five classes because these classes seem restrictive from the practical point of view. Also, we plan to implement a program to check the absolute consistency problem for these five classes. It is also necessary to consider schema mappings for graph databases whose edges have properties as well as nodes.

Acknowledgment

We thank Professor Soichiro Hidaka at Hosei University for his kind introduction to bidirectional transformations and TGGs. We would like to thank all the reviewers for their valuable comments on our paper.

References

[1] P. Barceló, "Logical foundations of relational data exchange," SIGMOD Record, vol. 38, no. 1, 2009, pp. 49–58.

[2] R. Fagin, P. G. Kolaitis, R. J. Miller, and L. Popa, "Data exchange: semantics and query answering," Theor. Comput. Sci., vol. 336, no. 1, 2005, pp. 89–124.

[3] M. Arenas, P. Barceló, L. Libkin, and F. Murlak, Relational and XML Data Exchange, ser. Synthesis Lectures on Data Management. Morgan & Claypool Publishers, 2010.

[4] S. Amano, L. Libkin, and F. Murlak, "XML schema mappings," in Proceedings of the Twenty-Eigth ACM SIGMOD-SIGACT-SIGART Symposium on Principles of Database Systems, 2009, pp. 33–42.

[5] M. Arenas and L. Libkin, "XML data exchange: Consistency and query answering," J. ACM, vol. 55, no. 2, 2008, pp. 7:1–7:72.

[6] P. Barceló, J. Pérez, and J. L. Reutter, "Schema mappings and data exchange for graph databases," in Joint 2013 EDBT/ICDT Conferences, ICDT '13 Proceedings, 2013, pp. 189–200.

[7] I. Boneva, A. Bonifati, and R. Ciucanu, "Graph data exchange with target constraints," in Proceedings of the Workshops of the EDBT/ICDT 2015 Joint Conference (EDBT/ICDT), 2015, pp. 171–176.

[8] H. Kuwada, K. Hashimoto, Y. Ishihara, and T. Fujiwara, "The consistency and absolute consistency problems of XML schema mappings between restricted DTDs," World Wide Web, vol. 18, no. 5, 2015, pp. 1443–1461.

[9] J. J. Miller, "Graph database applications and concepts with Neo4j," in Proceedings of the Southern Association for Information System Conference, Atlanta, GA, USA, March 23-24th, 2013, 2013.

[10] Y. Ishihara, H. Kuwada, and T. Fujiwara, "The absolute consistency problem of XML schema mappings with data values between restricted dtds," in Database and Expert Systems Applications - 25th International Conference, DEXA 2014, Munich, Germany, September 1-4, 2014. Proceedings, Part I, 2014, pp. 317–327.

[11] A. Schürr, "Specification of graph translators with triple graph grammars," in Graph-Theoretic Concepts in Computer Science, 20th International Workshop, WG '94, Herrsching, Germany, June 16-18, 1994, Proceedings, 1994, pp. 151–163.

[12] F. Hermann, H. Ehrig, F. Orejas, and U. Golas, "Formal analysis of functional behaviour for model transformations based on triple graph grammars," in Graph Transformations - 5th International Conference, ICGT 2010, Enschede, The Netherlands, September 27 - - October 2, 2010. Proceedings, 2010, pp. 155–170.

[13] E. Kindler and R. Wagner, "Triple graph grammars: Concepts, extensions, implementations, and application scenarios," Department of Computer Science, University of Paderborn, Technical Report tr-ri-07-284, 2007.

A Network-based Approach to Evolution of MEDLINE

Andrej Kastrin*, Thomas C. Rindflesch† and Dimitar Hristovski‡
*Institute of Biostatistics and Medical Informatics, Faculty of Medicine, University of Ljubljana, Slovenia
Email: andrej.kastrin@mf.uni-lj.si
†Lister Hill National Center for Biomedical Communications, National Library of Medicine, Bethesda, USA
Email: trindflesch@mail.nih.gov
‡Institute of Biostatistics and Medical Informatics, Faculty of Medicine, University of Ljubljana, Slovenia
Email: dimitar.hristovski@mf.uni-lj.si

***Abstract*—MEDLINE bibliographic database can be represented as a network of nodes and edges, where the former represent biomedical concepts and the latter represent relationships among them. Nodes and edges are not uniformly distributed but rather appear in locally dense communities. We investigate the dynamics and evolution of MEDLINE using network analysis based on community modeling. This study identifies the major research focuses and the current status and trends in the life sciences. To the best of our knowledge, this is the first analysis conducted on such a large portion of the MEDLINE database.**

Keywords–Complex networks; Network analysis; Network evolution; MEDLINE.

I. Introduction

The growth of science is increasingly dynamic and interdisciplinary. Barriers (silos), both physical and conceptual, that once effectively isolated researchers are breaking down. One consequence of this is that the biomedical literature is large and complex, and the number of published papers is growing at a considerable rate. It is therefore becoming ever more important to identify and describe developing research trends and to follow their evolution over time.

The premier repository of research in the life sciences is the MEDLINE bibliographic database. It contains over 24 million citations, with around 4000 citations added daily. MEDLINE can be represented as a network of nodes and edges, where the former represent biomedical concepts and the latter represent relationships among them, as we have shown in previous research [1]. Such a network can represent the structure and dynamics of a complex system; topological properties of the network can both elucidate static patterns and predict the future by computing changes over time. Co-occurrence in the network between concepts such as genes, diseases, biological processes, or chemical compounds represents biomedical knowledge.

When a network represents the real world, its nodes and edges are not uniformly distributed but rather appear in locally dense clusters, or communities, embedded within the larger structure [2]. Community structures are often of particular interest as forming the basis of network analysis aimed at elucidating knowledge represented by the network. A community is defined as a subset of nodes sharing similar properties and recognizable as being distinct from the larger network. A complex network representing the real world (such as that representing MEDLINE) is an evolving structure that change over time either by adding new nodes or by forming new relations between existing nodes [3]. This expansion can proceed over time with considerable speed in terms of size and space over time.

Science as a complex system has been studied from the point of view of network analysis, for example through co-authorship network analysis [4] or single-word analysis [5]. In a related approach, network analysis of the development of scientific knowledge may be valuable in building theoretical models of the collective dynamics of science. Here, we investigate the dynamics and evolution of MEDLINE using network analysis based on topic modeling. Our hypothesis is that the history of the biomedical domain can be summarized in a series of co-occurrences of keywords (i.e., Medical Subject Headings (MeSH) terms) that are associated with each MEDLINE citation and that identify its important topics. MeSH is a controlled vocabulary made up of biomedical terms at several levels of specificity. We model scientific topics as evolving communities of MeSH terms over time and explore how the temporal characteristics of the MeSH network can be used to provide insight into the historical evolution of scientific thought in biomedicine. As a proof of concept, we implemented a computational experiment based on over 20 million documents in MEDLINE, from 1966 through the end of 2014. To the best of our knowledge, this is the first analysis conducted on such a large portion of the MEDLINE database. In particular, this analysis is of special interest to researchers who seek to acquaint themselves about scientific topics, trends, and collaboration opportunities.

The abstract is structured as follows. Section II describes methodology of this study and Section III provides some empirical evidence. Conclusions and the scope for future research are presented in Section IV.

II. Methods

We processed MEDLINE from 1966 up to the end of 2014, only including citations tagged with major MeSH descriptors. In the constructed network, nodes represent major MeSH descriptors, and edges between two descriptors represent co-occurrence of those descriptors in the same MEDLINE citation. Recognizing the critical events that describe changes in network structure over time constitutes one way of tracking the development of communities. To capture critical events, we converted the entire network into static subnetworks at yearly snapshots, from 1966 through 2014. These subnetworks embed the communities (groups of nodes) of MeSH terms through which their development over time can be observed. We used the Louvain community detection algorithm to identify communities of nodes in each subnetwork [6]. After discovering communities, we computed relationships between them, in order to track their evolution over time. The Jaccard coefficient was first used to determine whether two communities match [7]. Next, we characterized the content of each community by computing its density and centrality. Density measures both the strength of the edges that tie the cluster of MeSH terms together, as well as the clusters capacity to develop ever time. Centrality measures the degree of interaction of a cluster with other parts of the network. Finally, we created a strategic diagram for each time slot, which is a graphical representation of the structure of the particular scientific field. We can identify four types of clusters according to the quadrant in which they appear in the diagram: (i) motor themes, which are both well developed and important for a research field; (ii) specialized and peripheral themes; (iii) themes, which are either emerging or disappearing; and (iv) themes, which are important for a research field but are not developed.

III. Results

This study identifies the major research focuses and the current status and trends in the life sciences. Overall, we extracted about 1700 different evolving communities. Figure 1 depicts heat map of evolving communities for various timeslots. As the shade of cell darkens, the size of the community increases. We could observe interesting pattern from the plot; it seems that each community build its existence on the basis of previous communities, therefore the trend line is diagonal with rare exceptions that extends over large periods of years.

Next, in this study we provide a description of the intellectual structure and dynamics of the entire field of biomedicine from the perspective of frequently appearing MeSH descriptors. The results of this study show that (i) using MeSH terms is plausible for tracking historical events in the biomedical domain; (ii) the evolution of MEDLINE occurs in an incremental fashion; (iii) over the years increasingly diverse research disciplines are involved in the complex process of scientific evolution, and links among them become stronger; and (iv) different research areas have different dynamic evolution patterns.

IV. Conclusion

When compared to existing research, this work is innovative in three respects: (i) the experimental design incorporates the longitudinal framework based on dynamic communities, (ii) we provide visualization of the evolution of research topics, and (iii) we propose a simple community labeling approach based on MeSH terms. There are also many opportunities for future work. First, we should address the problem of filtering co-occurrences. Second, we should address automatic cluster labeling, while manual labeling is tedious, time-consuming, and expensive task. Our long-term interest is also to include temporal frequent pattern mining into the analysis.

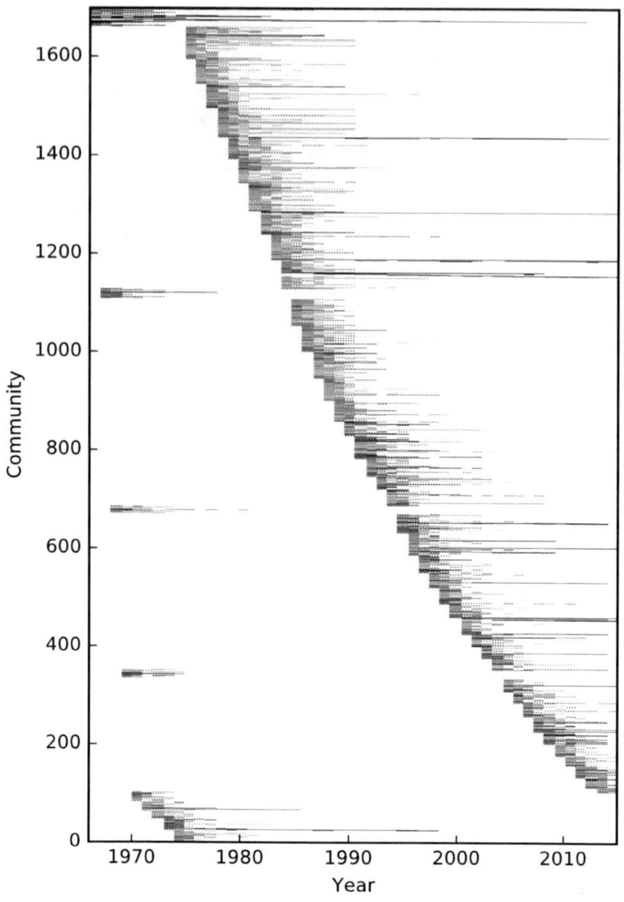

Figure 1. Heatmap of evolving communities for each timeslot

References

[1] A. Kastrin, T. C. Rindflesch, and D. Hristovski, "Large-scale structure of a network of co-occurring MeSH terms: Statistical analysis of macroscopic properties," PloS One, vol. 9, 2014, p. e102188.

[2] M. E. J. Newman and J. Park, "Why social networks are different from other types of networks," Phys Rev E, vol. 68, 2003, p. 36122.

[3] P. Holme and J. Saramki, "Temporal networks," Phys Rep, vol. 519, 2012, pp. 97–125.

[4] M. E. J. Newman, "The structure of scientific collaboration networks," Proc Natl Acad Sci USA, vol. 98, 2001, pp. 404–409.

[5] T. Kuhn, M. Perc, and D. Helbing, "Inheritance patterns in citation networks reveal scientific memes," Phys Rev X, vol. 4, 2014, p. 41036.

[6] V. D. Blondel, J.-L. Guillaume, R. Lambiotte, and E. Lefebvre, "Fast unfolding of communities in large networks," J Stat Mech Theory Exp, vol. 2008, 2008, p. P10008.

[7] P. Jaccard, "The distribution of the flora in the alpin zone," New Phytol, vol. 11, 2012, pp. 37–50.

AUTHOR INDEX

Aktas, M. 10, 16
Albayrak, S. 26
Baeth, M. 16
Begg, C. 30
Bohm, C. 37
Bottcher, S. 54
Casali, A. 97
Conde-Gonzalez, M. 70
Crowe, M. 30
Efentakis, A. 61
Endres, M. 52
Fujiwara, T. 103
Gao, Q. 43
Garcia-Penalvo, F. 70
Gokturk, M. 10
Hartel, R. 54
Hayata, T. 103
Hmamouche, Y. 97
Hristovski, D. 111
Ishihara, Y. 103
Itmi, M. 91
Karakostas, B. 78
Kardaras, D. 78
Karidi, D. 61
Kastrin, A. 111
Laiho, M. 30
Lakhal, L. 97
Laux, F. 30
Li, Y. 43
Manuel, J. 54
Mercogliano, P. 84
Nakos, H. 61
Ohnishi, S. 23
Ouchenne, B. 91
Pazmino-Maji, R. 70
Plant, C. 37
Reuben, J. 1
Rindflesch, T. 111
Romano, G. 84
Stavrakas, Y. 61
Wackersreuther, B. 37
Wang, H. 43
Yamanoi, T. 23
Yazici, I. 10
Ye, W. 37
Yildiz, M. 26
Zazzaro, G. 84
Zhou, L. 37